Complete
PHYSICS

Stephen Pople

OXFORD
UNIVERSITY PRESS

OXFORD
UNIVERSITY PRESS

Great Clarendon Street, Oxford OX2 6DP

Oxford University Press is a department of the University of Oxford.
It furthers the University's objective of excellence in research, scholarship,
and education by publishing worldwide in

Oxford New York

Athens Auckland Bangkok Bogotá Buenos Aires Calcutta
Cape Town Chennai Dar es Salaam Delhi Florence Hong Kong Istanbul
Karachi Kuala Lumpur Madrid Melbourne Mexico City Mumbai
Nairobi Paris São Paulo Shanghai Singapore Taipei Tokyo Toronto
Warsaw

with associated companies in Berlin Ibadan

Oxford is a registered trade mark of Oxford University Press
in the UK and in certain other countries

British Library Cataloguing in Publication Data
Data available

ISBN 019 914734 5

Printed in Italy G. Canale & C. S.p.A. - Borago T.se - Torino

Acknowledgements

The publisher would like to thank the following for their kind permission to reproduce the following photographs:

p 7 Tony Stone/J Strachan, **p 12** Science Photo Library/J Thomas, **p 15** SPL/European Space Agency (left), SPL/NASA (right), **p 17** PA News, **p 18** SPL/K Kent, **p 24** Tony Stone/A Husmo, **p 26** Robert Harding Picture Library, **p 31** J Allan Cash, **p 32** Telegraph Colour Library, **p 40** TCL/Colorific, **p 44** Allsport, **p 49** Planet Earth/F Jackson, **p 53** Allsport, **p 55** J Allan Cash, **p 58** SPL/R Church, **p 61** SPL/Dr J Burgess, **p 62** SPL/NASA, **p 65** SPL/A Hart-Davis, **p 66** SPL/A & H Frieder, **p 67** Robert Harding, **p 71** Tony Stone/C Condina, **p 72** Allsport, **p 78** SPL/T Takahara, **p 79** Volvo, **p 82** SPL/S Fraser (top), Tony Stone/A Levenson (bottom), **p 84** SPL/G Parker, **p 87** Still Pictures, **p 93** TCL, **p 97** Tony Stone/M Wagner, **p 98** TCL, **p 103** Oxford Scientific Films/M Birjhead, **p 107** J Allan Cash, **p 109** J Allan Cash (left), Robert Harding (centre), **p 110** SPL/P Plailley, **p 123** OSF/J Brown, **p 124** OSF/J Watts, **p 128** Corbis UK, **p 130** J Allan Cash, **p 134** OSF/T Tilford, **p 135** SPL/H Schneebeli, **p 137** SPL/D Parker, **p 141** J Allan Cash (left), Robert Harding (right), **p 142** TCL, **p 143** Spectrum, **p 147** Tony Stone/B Filet, **p 148** J Allan Cash, **p 149** SPL/P Menzel, **p 150** TCL, **p 155** SPL/D Parker, SPL/Dr K Schiller, **pp 158, 159** Science & Society Picture Library, **p 163** SPL, **p 164** SPL/D Parker, **p 165** SPL/A Tsiaras, **p 168** J Allan Cash, **p 169** J Allan Cash (top), SPL (bottom), **p 171** SPL/NASA, **p 173** SPL/A Pasieka, **p 177** Tony Stone/C Shinn, **p 178** SPL/P Menzel, **p 180** J Allan Cash, **p 186** SPL/M Dohrn, **p 190** J Allan Cash, **p 194** SPL/V de Schawnberg, **p 195** Robert Harding, **p 211** SPL/Los Alamos National Laboratory, **p 215** B & C Alexander, **p 225** Robert Harding, **p 227** J Allan Cash, **p 228** SPL/Salisbury Hospital, **p 233** Robert Harding, **p 235** J Allan Cash, **p 239** SPL/Biophoto Associates, **p 253** SPL/P Hayson (top), SPL/Dr J Burgess (left & right), **p 263** Tony Stone, **p 268** SPL/D Parker, **p 269** SPL, **p 275** SPL/M Bond, **p 276** SPL/L Mulvehill, **p 277** SPL/Silkeborg Museum, **p 279** SPL/Imperial College, **p 280** SPL/Fermilab, **p 285** SPL/NASA, **p 287** SPL/ J Sanford, **p 287** SPL/Rev R Royer, **p 290** SPL/NASA (left), SPL/L Pesek (right), **p 291** SPL/J Lodriguss (left), SPL/D Parker (right), **p 293** SPL(top), SPL/D Parker, **p 294** SPL/T Hallas, **p 295** SPL/Celestial Image Co, **p 296** SPL/US Dept of Energy, **p 297** Hale Observatories, **p 298** SPL/D Nunuk, **p 300** SPL/L Dodd, **p 305** Tony Stone/ W Krecichwast, **pp 306, 307** J Allan Cash, **p 308** SPL, **p 309** Science & Society Picture Library (top), SPL (bottom), **p 310** SPL, **p 311** Science & Society Picture Library, **p 311** SPL/NASA, **p 313** SPL/P Menzel.

Additional photography by Peter Gould

Cover photo by A & J Verkaik/The Stock Market

Illustrations by Jeff Bowles, Roger Courthold, Mike Ogden, Jeff Edwards, Russell Walker, Clive Goodyer, Jamie Sneddon, and Tech Graphics

We are grateful to the following Examination Boards for permission to use GCSE examinations questions and specimen questions (Sp = specimen).

Questions (including all multiple choice questions attributed to L. EXAM.) have been provided by London Examinations, a division of Edexcel Foundation. Edexcel Foundation, **London Examinations** accepts no responsibility whatsoever for the accuracy or method of working in the answers given.
MEG: questions from MEG reproduced by kind permission of the Midland Examining Group. The Midland Examining Group bears no responsibility for the example answers to questions taken from its past question papers which are contained in this publication.
UCLES: questions from UCLES reproduced by kind permission of the University of Cambridge Local Examinations Syndicate. The University of Cambridge Local Examinations Syndicate bears no responsibility for the example answers to questions taken from its past question papers which are contained in this publication.
SEG: questions from SEG are reproduced with the kind permission of the Southern Examining Group. The Southern Examining Group bears no responsibility for the example answers to questions taken from its past question papers which are contained in this publication.
WJEC: questions from WJEC are reproduced with the kind permission of the Welsh Joint Education Committee. The Welsh Joint Education Committee bears no responsibility for the example answers to questions taken from its past question papers which are contained in this publication.
NEAB: questions from NEAB are reproduced with the kind permission of Northern Examination and Assessment Board. The Northern Examination and Assessment Board bears no responsibility for the example answers to questions taken from its past question papers which are contained in this publication.

All answers are the responsibility of the author.

The author would like to thank Susan Pople for her help in preparing the manuscript and Dr Darren Lewis for providing answers to the questions.

Introduction

If you are studying physics at GCSE, IGCSE, CXC, or O level, then this book is designed for you. It explains the concepts that you will meet, and should help you with your experimental enquiries. Mostly, it is written in double-page units which we have called **spreads**.

Contents Here, you can see how the spreads are arranged. The spreads are grouped into sections, each dealing with a different aspect of physics.

Sections 1 to 12 The main areas of physics are covered here. Most of the spreads are about **core** topics – those found on nearly all of the examination syllabuses. But there are specially-marked spreads on **further topics** – those only found on a few syllabuses, often as options. Check with your teacher to find out which ones you need to study.

Section 13 This deals with the history of key ideas. It tells you how scientists have developed their understanding of physics over the years.

Section 14 This tells you how to plan an experimental enquiry, carry out your experiments safely, and interpret your results. It also includes suggestions for enquiries and an experimental skills checklist.

Examination questions Near the end of each section (1 to 12), there are some practice examination questions, taken from papers supplied by the examination boards. Near the back of the book, there are some multichoice questions covering all topics.

Revision checklists At the end of each section (1 to 12), there is a revision checklist giving the main topics covered in each spread.

Near the back of the book, you will also find the following:

Electrical symbols and codes This page shows you the main symbols used in circuit diagrams, and how to interpret the markings on resistors.

Answers Check your numerical (and short) answers here.

Units and elements This page includes a summary of the main units of measurement, their abbreviations, and the prefixes (such as 'kilo' and 'milli') used to form larger or smaller units. If you want to find out more about units, read spreads 1.01 and 1.02.

Index Use this if you need to look up a particular word or term.

I hope that you will find the book useful as you develop your understanding of physics and prepare for your examinations.

Stephen Pople

Contents

Note: the Further Topics *highlighted are not common to all syllabuses. Use the tick boxes* ❏ *to mark all material appropriate to the syllabus you are following.*

1 Measurements and Units 7

2 Forces and Motion 17

3 Forces and Pressure 49

4 Forces and Energy 71

Measurements and Units

- PHYSICAL QUANTITIES
- UNITS AND PREFIXES
- SCIENTIFIC NOTATION
- SI UNITS
- MASS
- TIME
- LENGTH
- VOLUME
- DENSITY

Astronomical clock in Prague, in the Czech Republic. As well as giving the time, the clock also shows the positions of the Sun and Moon relative to the constellations of the zodiac. Until about fifty years ago, scientists had to rely on mechanical clocks, such as the one above, to measure time. Today, they have access to atomic clocks whose timekeeping varies by less than a second in a million years.

1.01 Numbers and units

10 m

number   unit   (m is the symbol for metre)

When you make a measurement, you might get a result like the one above: a distance of 10 m. The complete measurement is called a **physical quantity**. It is made up of two parts: a number and a unit.

10 m really means $10 \times$ m (ten times metre), just as in algebra, $10x$ means $10 \times x$. (ten times x). You can treat the m just like a symbol in an algebraic equation. This is important when combining units.

Combining units

In the diagram above, the girl cycles 10 metres in 2 s. So she travels 5 metres every second. Her *speed* is 5 metres per second. To work out the speed, you divide the distance travelled by the time taken, like this:

$$\text{speed} = \frac{10\,\text{m}}{2\,\text{s}} \qquad \text{(s is the symbol for second)}$$

As m and s can be treated as algebraic symbols:

$$\text{speed} = \frac{10}{2} \cdot \frac{\text{m}}{\text{s}} = 5\,\frac{\text{m}}{\text{s}}$$

To save space, $5\,\dfrac{\text{m}}{\text{s}}$ is usually written as 5 m/s.

So m/s is the unit of speed.

Rights and wrongs

This equation is correct: $\text{speed} = \dfrac{10\,\text{m}}{2\,\text{s}} = 5\,\text{m/s}$

This equation is incorrect: $\text{speed} = \dfrac{10}{2} = 5\,\text{m/s}$

It is incorrect because the m and s have been left out. 10 divided by 2 equals 5, and not 5 m/s.

Strictly speaking, units should be included at *all* stages of a calculation, not just at the end. However, in this book, the 'incorrect' type of equation will sometimes be used so that you can follow the arithmetic without units which make the calculation look more complicated.

Advanced units

5 m/s is a space-saving way of writing $5\,\dfrac{\text{m}}{\text{s}}$.

But $5\,\dfrac{\text{m}}{\text{s}}$ equals $5\,\text{m}\,\dfrac{1}{\text{s}}$.

Also, $\dfrac{1}{\text{s}}$ can be written as s^{-1}.

So the speed can be written as $5\,\text{m}\,\text{s}^{-1}$.

This method of showing units is more common in advanced work.

Bigger and smaller

You can make a unit bigger or smaller by putting an extra symbol, called a prefix, in front. (Below, W stands for watt, a unit of power.)

prefix	meaning		example
G (giga)	1 000 000 000	(10^9)	GW (gigawatt)
M (mega)	1 000 000	(10^6)	MW (megawatt)
k (kilo)	1000	(10^3)	km (kilometre)
d (deci)	$\frac{1}{10}$	(10^{-1})	dm (decimetre)
c (centi)	$\frac{1}{100}$	(10^{-2})	cm (centimetre)
m (milli)	$\frac{1}{1000}$	(10^{-3})	mm (millimetre)
μ (micro)	$\frac{1}{1\,000\,000}$	(10^{-6})	μW (microwatt)
n (nano)	$\frac{1}{1\,000\,000\,000}$	(10^{-9})	nm (nanometre)

Powers of 10

$$1000 = 10 \times 10 \times 10 = 10^3$$
$$100 = 10 \times 10 = 10^2$$
$$0.1 = \frac{1}{10} = 10^{-1}$$
$$0.01 = \frac{1}{100} = \frac{1}{10^2} = 10^{-2}$$
$$0.001 = \frac{1}{1000} = \frac{1}{10^3} = 10^{-3}$$

'milli' means 'thousandth', *not* 'millionth'

Scientific notation

An atlas says that the population of Iceland is this:

270 000

There are two problems with giving the number in this form. Writing lots of zeros isn't very convenient. Also, you don't know which zeros are accurate. Most are only there to show you that it is a six-figure number. These problems are avoided if the number is written using powers of ten:

2.7×10^5 $(10^5 = 10 \times 10 \times 10 \times 10 \times 10 = 100\,000)$

'2.7×10^5' tells you that the figures 2 and 7 are important. The number is being given to *two significant figures*. If the population were known more accurately, to three significant figures, it might be written like this:

2.70×10^5

Numbers written using powers of ten are in **scientific notation** or **standard form**. The examples on the right are to one significant figure.

decimal	fraction	scientific notation
500		5×10^2
0.5	$\frac{5}{10}$	5×10^{-1}
0.05	$\frac{5}{100}$	5×10^{-2}
0.005	$\frac{5}{1000}$	5×10^{-3}

1 How many grams are there in 1 kilogram?
2 How many millimetres are there in 1 metre?
3 How many microseconds are there in 1 second?
4 This equation is used to work out the area of a rectangle: area = length × width.
   If a rectangle measures 3 m by 2 m, calculate its area, and include the units in your calculation.

5 Write down the following in km:
   2000 m   200 m 2×10^4 m
6 Write down the following in s:
   5000 ms 5×10^7 μs
7 Using scientific notation, write down the following to two significant figures:
   1500 m   1 500 000 m   0.15 m   0.015 m

A system of units

There are many different units – including those above. But in scientific work, life is much easier if everyone uses a common system of units.

SI units

Most scientists use **SI units** (full name: Le Système International d'Unités). The basic SI units for measuring mass, time, and length are the kilogram, the second, and the metre. From these **base units** come a whole range of units for measuring volume, speed, force, energy, and other quantities.

Other SI base units include the ampere (for measuring electric current) and the kelvin (for measuring temperature).

Mass

Mass is a mysterious property. It affects how objects behave in two ways:
- All objects are attracted to the Earth. The greater the mass of an object, the stronger is the Earth's gravitational pull on it.
- All objects resist attempts to make them go faster, slower, or in a different direction. The greater the mass, the greater is the resistance to change in motion.

The SI base unit of mass is the **kilogram** (symbol **kg**). The standard kilogram is a block of platinum alloy kept at the Office of Weights and Measures in Paris. Other units based on the kilogram are shown below:

The mass of an object can be found using a **balance** like this. The balance really detects the gravitational pull on the object on the pan, but the scale is marked to show the mass.

mass	comparison with base unit	scientific notation	approximate size
1 tonne (t)	1000 kg	10^3 kg	medium-sized car
1 kilogram (kg)	1 kg		bag of sugar
1 gram (g) — 1 g	$\frac{1}{1\,000}$ kg	10^{-3} kg	banknote
1 milligram (mg) — $\frac{1}{1\,000}$ g	$\frac{1}{1\,000\,000}$ kg	10^{-6} kg	human hair

Note: the SI base unit of mass is the **kilogram**, not the gram

Time

The SI base unit of time is the **second** (symbol **s**). Here are some shorter units based on the second:

1 millisecond (ms) $= \dfrac{1}{1000}$ s $= 10^{-3}$ s

1 microsecond (μs) $= \dfrac{1}{1\,000\,000}$ s $= 10^{-6}$ s

1 nanosecond (ns) $= \dfrac{1}{1\,000\,000\,000}$ s $= 10^{-9}$ s

To keep time, clocks and watches need something that beats at a steady rate. Some old clocks used the swings of a pendulum. Modern digital watches count the vibrations made by a tiny quartz crystal.

> The second was originally defined as $\dfrac{1}{60 \times 60 \times 24}$ of a day, one day being the time it takes the Earth to rotate once. But the Earth's rotation is not quite constant. So, for accuracy, the second is now defined in terms of something that never changes: the frequency of an oscillation which can occur in the nucleus of a caesium atom.

Length

The SI base unit of length is the **metre** (symbol **m**). At one time, the standard metre was the distance between two marks on a metal bar kept at the Office of Weights and Measures in Paris. A more accurate standard is now used, based on the speed of light, as on the right.

> By definition, one metre is the distance travelled by light in a vacuum in $\dfrac{1}{299\,792\,458}$ of a second.

There are larger and smaller units of length based on the metre:

distance	comparison with base unit	scientific notation	approximate size
1 kilometre (km)	1 000 m	10^3 m	10 football pitches
1 metre (m)	1 m		
1 centimetre (cm)	$\dfrac{1}{100}$ m	10^{-2} m	cm 1 2 3 4 / mm 10 20 30 40
1 millimetre (mm)	$\dfrac{1}{1\,000}$ m	10^{-3} m	
1 micrometre (μm)	$\dfrac{1}{1\,000\,000}$ m	10^{-6} m	bacteria
1 nanometre (nm)	$\dfrac{1}{1\,000\,000\,000}$ m	10^{-9} m	atoms

Q

1 What is the SI unit of length?
2 What is the SI unit of mass?
3 What is the SI unit of time?
4 What do the following symbols stand for?

    g   mg   t   μm   ms

5 Write down the value of
   a) 1564 mm in m   **b)** 1750 g in kg
   c) 26 t in kg   **d)** 62 μs in s
   e) 3.65×10^4 g in kg   **f)** 6.16×10^{-7} mm in m

6 The 500 pages of a book have a mass of 2.50 kg. What is the mass of each page **a)** in kg **b)** in mg?

7 km   μg   μm   t   nm   kg   m
   ms   s   mg   ns   μs   g   mm

Arrange the above units in three columns as below. The units in each column should be in order, with the largest at the top.

	mass	length	time
largest → unit			

1.03 Volume and density

Volume

The quantity of space an object takes up is called its volume.

The SI unit of volume is the **cubic metre** (**m³**). However, this is rather large for everyday work, so other units are often used for convenience, as shown in the diagrams below:

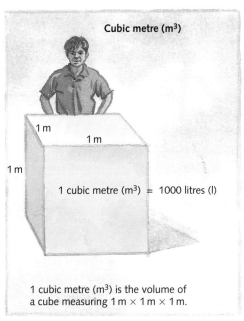

Cubic metre (m³)

1 m
1 m
1 m

1 cubic metre (m³) = 1000 litres (l)

1 cubic metre (m³) is the volume of a cube measuring 1 m × 1 m × 1 m.

Litre (l or L)

Note: the symbol l for litre can be confused with a 1 (one).

1 litre (L) = 1000 cubic centimetres (cm³)
= 1000 millilitres (ml)

1 litre is the same volume as 1 cubic decimetre (dm³)

Cubic centimetre (cm³) or millilitre (ml or mL)

1 cubic centimetre (cm³) is the volume of a cube measuring 1 cm × 1 cm × 1cm.
It is the same volume as 1 millilitre (ml)

Density

Is lead heavier than water? Not necessarily. It depends on the volumes of lead and water being compared. However, lead is more dense than water: it has more kilograms packed into every cubic metre.

The **density** of a material is calculated like this:

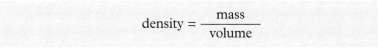

$$\text{density} = \frac{\text{mass}}{\text{volume}}$$

In the case of water:
a mass of 1000 kg of water has a volume of 1 m³
a mass of 2000 kg of water has a volume of 2 m³
a mass of 3000 kg of water has a volume of 3 m³, and so on.

Using any of these sets of figures in the above equation, the density of water works out to be 1000 kg/m³.

If masses are measured in grams (g) and volumes in cubic centimetres (cm³), it is simpler to calculate densities in g/cm³. Converting to kg/m³ is easy:

$1 \text{ g/cm}^3 = 1000 \text{ kg/m}^3$

The density of water is 1 g/cm³. This simple value is no accident. The kilogram (1000 g) was originally supposed to be the mass of 1000 cm³ of water (pure, and at 4 °C). However, a very slight error was made in the early measurement, so this is no longer used as a definition of the kilogram.

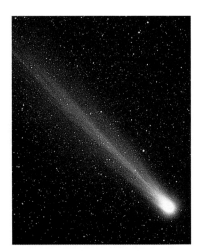

The glowing gas in the tail of a comet stretches for millions of kilometres behind the comet's core. The density of the gas is less than a kilogram per cubic *kilo*metre.

substance	density kg/m³	density g/cm³	substance	density kg/m³	density g/cm³
air	1.3	0.0013	granite	2700	2.7
expanded polystyrene	14	0.014	aluminium	2700	2.7
wood (beech)	750	0.75	steel (stainless)	7800	7.8
petrol	800	0.80	copper	8900	8.9
ice (0 °C)	920	0.92	lead	11 400	11.4
polythene	950	0.95	mercury	13 600	13.6
water (4 °C)	1000	1.0	gold	19 300	19.3
concrete	2400	2.4	platinum	21 500	21.5
glass (varies)	2500	2.5	osmium	22 600	22.6

The densities of solids and liquids vary slightly with temperature. Most substances get a little bigger when heated. The increase in volume reduces the density.

The densities of gases can vary enormously depending on how compressed they are.

The rare metal osmium is the densest substance found on Earth. If this book were made of osmium, it would weigh as much as a heavy suitcase.

Density calculations

The equation linking density, mass, and volume can be written in symbols:

$$\rho = \frac{m}{V}$$

where ρ = density, m = mass, and V = volume

This equation can be rearranged to give: $V = \dfrac{m}{\rho}$ and $m = V\rho$

These are useful if the density is known, but the volume or mass is to be calculated. On the right is a method of finding all three equations.

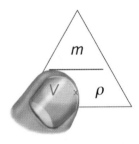

Cover V in the triangle and you can see what V is equal to. It works for m and ρ as well.

Example Using density data from the table above, calculate the mass of steel having the same volume as 5400 kg of aluminium.

First, calculate the volume of 5400 kg of aluminium. In this case, ρ is 2700 kg/m³, m is 5400 kg, and V is to be found. So:

$$V = \frac{m}{\rho} = \frac{5400 \text{ kg}}{2700 \text{ kg/m}^3} = 2 \text{ m}^3$$

This is also the volume of the steel. Therefore, for the steel, ρ is 7800 kg/m³, V is 2 m³, and m is to be found. So:

$$m = V\rho = 7800 \text{ kg/m}^3 \times 2 \text{ m}^3 = 15\,600 \text{ kg}$$

So the mass of steel is 15 600 kg.

1 How many cm³ are there in 1 m³?
2 How many cm³ are there in 1 litre?
3 How many ml are there in 1 m³?
4 A tankful of liquid has a volume of 0.2 m³. What is the volume in **a)** litres **b)** cm³ **c)** ml?
5 Aluminium has a density of 2700 kg/m³.
   a) What is the density in g/cm³?
   b) What is the mass of 20 cm³ of aluminium?
   c) What is the volume of 27 g of aluminium?

Use the information in the table of densities at the top of the page to answer the following:
6 What material, of mass 39 g, has a volume of 5 cm³?
7 What is the mass of air in a room measuring 5 m × 2 m × 3 m?
8 What is the volume of a storage tank which will hold 3200 kg of petrol?
9 What mass of lead has the same volume as 1600 kg of petrol?

Measuring volume and density

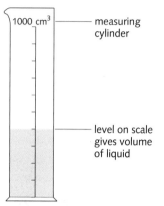

Measuring the volume of a liquid

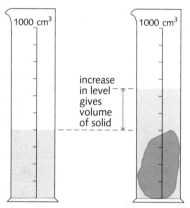

Measuring the volume of a small solid

Measuring volume

Liquid A volume of about a litre or so can be measured using a measuring cylinder. When the liquid is poured into the cylinder, the level on the scale gives the volume.

Most measuring cylinders have scales marked in millilitres (ml), or cubic centimetres (cm³).

Regular solid If an object has a simple shape, its volume can be calculated. For example:

volume of a rectangular block = length × width × height

volume of a cylinder = π × radius² × height

Irregular solid If the shape is too awkward for the volume to be calculated, the solid can be lowered into a partly filled measuring cylinder as shown on the left. The *rise* in level on the volume scale gives the volume of the solid.

If the solid floats, it can be weighed down with a lump of metal. The total volume is found. The volume of the metal is measured in a separate experiment and then subtracted from this total.

Measuring density

The density of a material can be found by calculation once the mass and the volume have been measured.

The mass of a small solid or of a liquid can be measured using a balance. In the case of a liquid, you must remember to allow for the mass of its container. The volume can be found as described above.

Archimedes and the crown

Archimedes, a Greek mathematician, lived in Syracuse (now in Sicily) around 250 BC. He made important discoveries about levers and liquids, but is probably best remembered for his clever solution to a problem set him by the King of Syracuse.

The King had given his goldsmith some gold to make a crown. But when the crown was delivered, the King was suspicious. Perhaps the goldsmith had stolen some of the gold and mixed in cheaper silver instead. The King asked Archimedes to test the crown.

Archimedes knew that the crown was the correct mass. He also knew that silver was less dense than gold. So a crown with silver in it would have a greater volume than it should have. But how could he measure the volume?

Stepping into his bath one day, so the story goes, Archimedes noticed the rise in water level. Here was the answer! He was so excited that he lept from his bath and ran naked through the streets, shouting "Eureka!", which means "I have found it!".

Later, Archimedes put the crown in a container of water and measured the rise in level. Then he did the same with an equal mass of pure gold. The rise in level was different. So the crown could not have been pure gold.

Relative density

The relative density of a substance tells you how the density compares with that of water. It is calculated like this:

$$\text{relative density} = \frac{\text{density of substance}}{\text{density of water}}$$

For example, lead has a density of 11 300 kg/m³ (11.3 g/cm³) and water has a density of 1000 kg/m³ (1 g/cm³). So:

$$\text{relative density of lead} = \frac{11\ 300\ \text{kg/m}^3}{1000\ \text{kg/m}^3} = \frac{11.3\ \text{g/cm}^3}{1\ \text{g/cm}^3} = 11.3$$

Relative density has no units. It is a number whose value is the same as that of the density in g/cm³. It used to be known as 'specific gravity'.

substance	density	relative density
water	1.0 g/cm³	1.0
aluminium	2.7 g/cm³	2.7
copper	8.9 g/cm³	8.9
lead	11.4 g/cm³	11.4
mercury	13.6 g/cm³	13.6
gold	19.3 g/cm³	19.3

Planet density

The density of a planet increases towards the centre. However, the average density can be found by dividing the total mass by the total volume. The mass of a planet affects its gravitational pull and, therefore, the orbit of any moon circling it. The mass can be calculated from this. The volume can be calculated once the diameter is known.

The average density gives clues about a planet's structure:

Earth

Average density 5520 kg/m³

This is about double the density of the rocks near the surface, so the Earth must have a high density core – probably mainly iron.

Jupiter

Average density 1330 kg/m³

The low average density is one reason why scientists think that Jupiter is a sphere mostly of hydrogen and helium gas, with a small, rocky core.

not to scale

Q

	crown A	crown B	crown C
mass/ g	3750	3750	3750
volume/ cm³	357	194	315

density: gold 19.3 g/cm³; silver 10.5 g/cm³

empty   liquid added   stone added

90 g   170 g   100 cm³   290 g   148 cm³

1 Use the information above to decide which crown is gold, which is silver, and which is a mixture.

2 Use the information above to calculate:
   a) the mass, volume, and density of the liquid,
   b) the mass, volume, and density of the stone.

1 In each of the following pairs, which quantity is the larger?

 a) 2 km or 2500 m?

 b) 2 m or 1500 mm?

 c) 2 tonnes or 3000 kg?

 d) 2 litres or 300 cm³? [4]

2 Which of the following statements is/are correct?

 A One milligram equals one million grams.

 B One thousand milligrams equals one gram.

 C One million milligrams equals one gram.

 D One million milligrams equals one kilogram. [2]

3 The table shows the density of various substances.

substance	density/ g/cm³
copper	8.9
iron	7.9
kerosene	0.87
mercury	13.6
water	1.0

Consider the following statements:

 A 1 cm³ of mercury has a greater mass than 1 cm³ of any other substance in this table – true or false?

 B 1 cm³ of water has a smaller mass than 1 cm³ of any other substance in this table – true or false?

 C 1 g of iron has a smaller volume than 1 g of copper – true or false?

 D 1 g of mercury has a greater mass than 1 g of copper – true or false? [2]

4 Which block is made of the densest material? [1]

block	mass/ g	length/ cm	breadth/ cm	height/ cm
A	480	5	4	4
B	360	10	4	3
C	800	10	5	2
D	600	5	4	3

5 The mass of a measuring cylinder and its contents are measured before and after putting a stone in it.

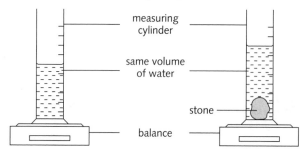

Which of the following could you calculate using measurements taken from the apparatus above?

 A the density of the liquid only

 B the density of the stone only

 C the densities of the liquid and the stone [2]

6 A plastic bag filled with air has a volume of 0.008 m³. When air in the bag is squeezed into a rigid container, the mass of the container (with air) increases from 0.02 kg to 0.03 kg. Use the formula

$$\text{density} = \frac{\text{mass}}{\text{volume}}$$

to calculate the density of the air in the bag. [2]

Photocopy the list of topics below and tick the boxes of the ones that are included in your examination syllabus. (Your teacher should be able to tell you which they are.) Use your list when you revise. The spread number in brackets tells you where to find more information.

❑ **1** How to use units. (1.01)

❑ **2** Making bigger or smaller units using prefixes. (1.01)

❑ **3** Writing numbers in scientific notation. (1.01)

❑ **4** SI units, including the metre, kilogram, and second. (1.02)

❑ **5** Units for measuring volume. (1.03)

❑ **6** How density is defined. (1.03)

❑ **7** Methods of measuring volume and density. (1.04)

❑ **8** The meaning of relative density. (1.04)

2

Forces and Motion

- SPEED AND VELOCITY
- ACCELERATION
- EQUATIONS OF MOTION
- FREE FALL
- FORCE AND MASS
- GRAVITY AND WEIGHT
- ACTION AND REACTION
- VECTORS AND SCALARS
- MOMENTUM
- CIRCULAR MOTION

A bungee jumper leaps more than 180 metres from the top of the Sky Tower in Auckland, New Zealand. With nothing to oppose his fall, he would hit the ground at a speed of 60 metres per second. However, his fall is slowed by the resistance of the air rushing past him, and eventually stopped by the pull of the bungee rope. Side ropes are also being used to stop him crashing into the tower.

2.01 Speed, velocity, and acceleration

▲ *Thrust* supersonic car travelling faster than sound. For speed records, cars are timed over a measured distance (either one kilometre or one mile). The speed is worked out from the average of two runs – down the course and then back again – so that the effects of wind are cancelled out.

Travel times

	time taken to travel 1 kilometre (1000 m)
runner	150 s
Grand Prix car	10 s
jet car	3 s
Concorde	1.5 s
Space Shuttle	0.1 s

Speed

If a car travels between two points on a road, its average speed can be calculated like this:

$$\text{average speed} = \frac{\text{distance moved}}{\text{time taken}}$$

If distance is measured in metres (m) and time in seconds (s), speed is measured in metres per second (m/s). For example: if a car moves 90 m in 3 s, its average speed is 30 m/s.

On most journeys, the speed of a car varies, so the actual speed at any moment is usually different from the average speed. To find an actual speed, you need to discover how far the car moves in the shortest time you can measure. For example, if a car moves 0.20 metres in 0.01 s:

$$\text{speed} = \frac{0.20 \, \text{m}}{0.01 \, \text{s}} = 20 \, \text{m/s}$$

Velocity

Velocity means the speed of something *and* its direction of travel. For example, a cyclist might have a velocity of 10 m/s due east. On paper, this velocity can be shown using an arrow:

10 m/s →

For motion in a straight line you can use a + or - to indicate direction. For example:

+10 m/s (velocity of 10 m/s *to the right*)
-10 m/s (velocity of 10 m/s *to the left*)

Note: +10 m/s may be written without the +, just as 10 m/s.

Quantities, such as velocity, which have a direction as well as a magnitude (size) are called **vectors**.

Acceleration

Something is accelerating if its velocity is *changing*. Acceleration is calculated like this:

$$\text{average acceleration} = \frac{\text{change in velocity}}{\text{time taken}}$$

For example, the car on the right increases its velocity from zero to 12 m/s in 4 s. So:

$$\text{average acceleration} = \frac{12\,\text{m/s}}{4\,\text{s}} = 3\,\text{m/s}^2$$

Note that acceleration is measured in metres per second² (m/s²).

Acceleration is a vector. It can be shown using an arrow (usually double-headed). Alternatively, a + or - sign can be used to indicate whether the velocity is increasing or decreasing. For example:

$+3$ m/s² (velocity *increasing* by 3 m/s every second)
-3 m/s² (velocity *decreasing* by 3 m/s every second)

A *negative* acceleration is called a **deceleration** or a **retardation**.
A *uniform* acceleration means a constant (steady) acceleration.

time	velocity
0 s	0 m/s
1 s	3 m/s
2 s	6 m/s
3 s	9 m/s
4 s	12 m/s

The velocity of this car is increasing by 3 m/s every second. The car has a steady acceleration of 3 m/s².

Solving a problem

Example The car on the right passes post A with a velocity of 12 m/s. If it has a steady acceleration of 3 m/s², what is its velocity 5 s later, as it passes B?

The car is gaining 3 m/s of velocity every second. So in 5 s, it gains an extra 15 m/s on top of its original 12 m/s. Therefore its final velocity is 27 m/s. Note that the result is worked out like this:

final velocity = original velocity + extra velocity

So: final velocity = original velocity + (acceleration × time)

The above equation also works for retardation. If a car has a retardation of 3 m/s², you treat this as an acceleration of -3 m/s².

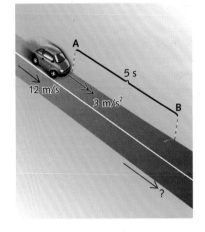

Q

1 A car travels 600 m in 30 s. What is its average speed? Why is its actual speed usually different from its average speed?
2 How is velocity different from speed?
3 A car has a steady speed of 8 m/s.
   a) How far does the car travel in 8 s?
   b) How long does the car take to travel 160 m?
4 Calculate the average speed of each thing in the chart of travel times on the opposite page.
5 A car has an acceleration of +2 m/s². What does this tell you about the velocity of the car? What is meant by an acceleration of -2 m/s²?

6 A car takes 8 s to increase its velocity from 10 m/s to 30 m/s. What is its average acceration?
7 A motor cycle, travelling at 20 m/s, takes 5 s to stop. What is its average retardation?
8 An aircraft on its take-off run has a steady acceleration of 3 m/s².
   a) What velocity does the aircraft gain in 4 s?
   b) If the aircraft passes one post on the runway at a velocity of 20 m/s, what is its velocity 8 s later?
9 A truck travelling at 25 m/s puts its brakes on for 4 s. This produces a retardation of 2 m/s². What does the truck's velocity drop to?

Motion graphs

Distance–time graphs

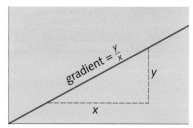

On a straight line graph like this, the gradient has the same value wherever you measure *y* and *x*.

Graphs can be useful when studying motion. Below, a car is travelling along a straight road, away from a marker post. The car's distance from the post is measured every second. The charts and graphs show four different examples of what the car's motion might be.

On a graph, the line's rise on the vertical scale divided by its rise on the horizontal scale is called the **gradient**, as shown on the left. With a distance–time graph, the gradient tells you how much extra distance is travelled every second. So:

> On a distance–time graph, the gradient of the line is numerically equal to the speed.

A Car travelling at steady speed

time/ s	0	1	2	3	4	5
distance/ m	0	10	20	30	40	50

The line rises 10 m on the distance scale for every 1 s on the time scale.

B Car travelling at higher steady speed

time/ s	0	1	2	3	4	5
distance/ m	0	20	40	60	80	100

The line is steeper than before. It rises 20 m on the distance scale for every 1 s on the time scale.

C Car accelerating

time/ s	0	1	2	3	4	5
distance/ m	0	10	25	45	70	100

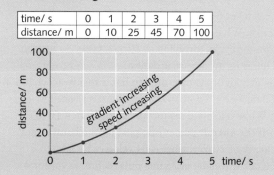

The speed rises. So the car travels further each second than the one before, and the line curves upwards.

D Car stopped

time/ s	0	1	2	3	4	5
distance/ m	50	50	50	50	50	50

The car is parked 50 m from the post, so this distance stays the same.

Speed–time graphs

Each speed–time graph below is for a car travelling along a straight road. The gradient tells you how much extra speed is gained every second. So:

> On a speed–time graph, the gradient of the line is numerically equal to the acceleration.

In graph E, the car travels at a steady 15 m/s for 5 s, so the distance travelled is 75 m. The area of the shaded rectangle, calculated using the scale numbers, is also 75. This principle works for more complicated graph lines as well. In graph F, the area of the shaded triangle, $1/2 \times$ base $\times$ height, equals 50. So the distance travelled is 50 metres.

> On a speed–time graph, the area under the line is numerically equal to the distance travelled.

E Car travelling at steady speed

time/ s	0	1	2	3	4	5
speed/ m/s	15	15	15	15	15	15

The speed stays the same, so the line stays at same level.

F Car with steady acceleration

time/ s	0	1	2	3	4	5
speed/ m/s	0	4	8	12	16	20

As car gains speed, the line rises 4 m/s on speed scale for every 1 s on time scale.

Q

1

2

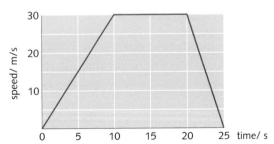

The distance–time graph above is for a motor cycle travelling along a straight road.

a) What is the motor cycle doing between points D and E on the graph?
b) Between which points is it accelerating?
c) Between which points is its speed steady?
d) What is this steady speed?
e) What is the distance travelled between A and D?
f) What is the average speed between A and D?

The speed–time graph above is for another motor cycle travelling along the same road.

a) What is the motor cycle's maximum speed?
b) What is the acceleration during the first 10 s?
c) What is its deceleration during the last 5 s?
d) What distance is travelled during the first 10 s?
e) What is the total distance travelled?
f) What is the time taken for the whole journey?
g) What is the average speed for the whole journey?

Related Topics: speed, velocity, and acceleration **2.01**; braking distance **4.04**

Equations of motion

2.03

Displacement

3 m

A displacement vector
(a vector is any quantity which has
direction as well as size).

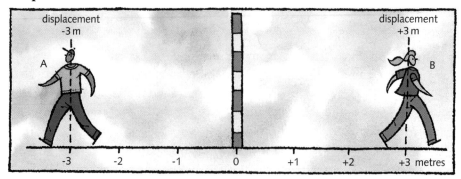

Distance moved in a particular direction is called **displacement**. It is a vector. In simple cases, the vector direction can be shown using a + or a - . Above, for example, one person has a displacement of -3 m from the post; the other has a displacement of +3 m (often written without the + sign).

Equations linking *s, u, v, a,* and *t*

Many problems involving moving objects can be solved using just four equations. They apply if the motion is in a straight line and the acceleration is uniform (steady).

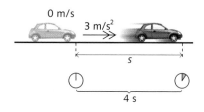

s = displacement (m)

u = initial velocity (m/s)

v = final velocity (m/s)

a = acceleration (m/s²)

t = time (s)

Be careful not to confuse s, the displacement in metres, with s, the symbol for second.

Five symbols are used in the equations. The diagram on the left shows what they mean. The car has an acceleration *a*. It passes the first marker (A) with a velocity *u*, its *initial velocity*. Time *t* later, it passes the second marker (B) with velocity *v*, its *final velocity*. It then has a displacement *s*.

These are the equations. Each one links four out of the five quantities:

$v = u + at$	(does not include *s*)
$s = ut + \frac{1}{2}at^2$	(does not include *v*)
$s = \frac{1}{2}(u + v)t$	(does not include *a*)
$v^2 = u^2 + 2as$	(does not include *t*)

If values of three of the quantities *s, u, v, a,* and *t* are known, you can calculate the value of a fourth by using the appropriate equation.

Example A car accelerates from rest at 3 m/s² along a straight road. How far has the car travelled after 4 s?

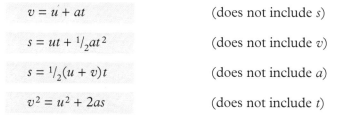

In this case: *s* is the quantity to be found

u is zero because the car starts at rest

a is 3 m/s²

t is 4 s

So, choosing the equation which includes *s, u, a,* and *t*, but not *v*, and omitting some of the units for simplicity:

$$s = ut + \frac{1}{2}at^2 = (0 \times 4) + (\frac{1}{2} \times 3 \times 4^2) = 24\,\text{m}$$

So: distance travelled = 24 m

Negatives and positives

u, v, a, and s are vectors, so you must allow for their direction when substituting numbers in the equations. The equations assume that all four vectors are in the same direction (for example, to the right), so if any are in the opposite direction you count them as negative (-).

These mean the same thing.

A deceleration is a negative acceleration. Mathematically, it is the same as an acceleration in the opposite direction.

> *Example* The car on the right is travelling at 20 m/s along a straight road. The driver puts the brakes on for 5 s. If this causes a deceleration of 3 m/s², what is the car's final velocity?

In this case: u is 20 m/s (positive, because it is to the right)
v is the quantity to be found
a is -3 m/s² (negative, because it is to the left)
t is 5 s

So, choosing the equation which includes u, v, a, and t, but not s, and omitting some of the units for simplicity:

$$v = u + at = 20 + (-3 \times 5) = 20 - 15 = 5 \text{ m/s}$$

So: final velocity = 5 m/s (to the right, because it is positive)

The car's deceleration has been shown as an acceleration to the left.

Explaining the equations

$v = u + at$

at, acceleration x time, is the gain in speed. So this equation is, in effect, telling you that:

final speed = initial speed + gain in speed

$s = \frac{1}{2}(u + v)t$

$\frac{1}{2}(u + v)$ is the average speed. So this equation is, in effect, telling you that:

distance travelled = average speed x time taken

$v^2 = u^2 + 2as$

This equation can be found by combining the two equations above, and eliminating t from them.

$s = ut + \frac{1}{2}at^2$

This equation can be found by working out the area under a speed–time graph for an object accelerating from one speed to another. The area gives the distance travelled and, therefore, the displacement.

Use the equations of motion to solve the following. In each case, assume that the motion is in a straight line and that the acceleration is uniform (steady).

1 A motor cycle travelling at 10 m/s accelerates at 4 m/s² for 8 s.
   a) What is its final velocity?
   b) How far does it travel during the 8 s?
2 A car accelerates from 8 m/s to 20 m/s in 10 s.
   a) What is its acceleration?
   b) How far does it travel during the 10 s?

3 A train is travelling at 40 m/s when its brakes are applied. This produces a deceleration of 2 m/s².
   a) How long does the train take to come to rest? (Hint: if the train comes to rest, what does this tell you about its final speed?)
   b) How far does the train travel before stopping?
4 An aircraft accelerates at 2.5 m/s². Its take-off speed is 60 m/s.
   a) What length of runway does it need to take off?
   b) How long does it take to reach its take-off speed?

Related topics: speed, velocity, and acceleration **2.01**; motion graphs **2.02**; acceleration of free fall **2.05 – 2.06**; vectors **2.11**

2.04 Recording motion

Using ticker-tape

trolley pulled across bench

paper tape

ticker-tape timer

50 dots punched on tape every second

Speed, velocity, and acceleration essentials

$$speed* = \frac{distance\ moved}{time\ taken}$$

velocity is speed in a particular direction

$$acceleration* = \frac{change\ in\ velocity}{time\ taken}$$

*average

In the laboratory, motion can be investigated using a trolley like the one above. As the trolley travels along the bench, it pulls a length of paper tape (ticker-tape) behind it. The tape passes through a ticker-tape timer which punches carbon dots on the tape at regular intervals. A typical timer produces 50 dots every second.

Together, the dots on the tape form a complete record of the motion of the trolley. The further apart the dots, the faster the trolley is moving. Here are some examples:

start

steady speed — distance between dots stays the same

higher steady speed — distance between dots greater than before

acceleration — distance between dots increases

acceleration ———— then ———— retardation

▼ Motion can also be recorded by taking lots of photographs one after another, like this. These pictures were taken at hour intervals, at midsummer, in Norway. Even at midnight (extreme left) the sun is still above the horizon.

Calculations from tape

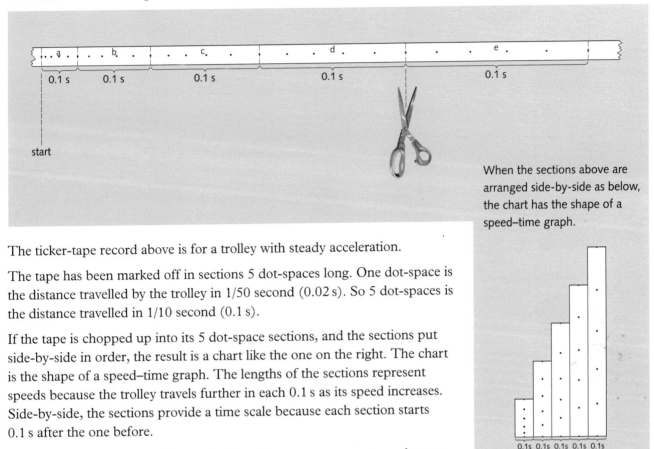

When the sections above are arranged side-by-side as below, the chart has the shape of a speed–time graph.

The ticker-tape record above is for a trolley with steady acceleration.

The tape has been marked off in sections 5 dot-spaces long. One dot-space is the distance travelled by the trolley in 1/50 second (0.02 s). So 5 dot-spaces is the distance travelled in 1/10 second (0.1 s).

If the tape is chopped up into its 5 dot-space sections, and the sections put side-by-side in order, the result is a chart like the one on the right. The chart is the shape of a speed–time graph. The lengths of the sections represent speeds because the trolley travels further in each 0.1 s as its speed increases. Side-by-side, the sections provide a time scale because each section starts 0.1 s after the one before.

The acceleration of the trolley can be found from measurements on the tape. Do questions 2 and 3 below to discover how.

1

Describe the motion of the trolley that produced the ticker-tape record above.

2 The dots on the tape below were made by a ticker-tape timer producing 50 dots per second.
a) Count the number of dot-spaces between A and B. Then calculate the time it took the tape to move from A to B.
b) Using a ruler, measure the distance from A to B in mm. Then calculate the average speed of the trolley between A and B, in mm/s.

c) Measure the distance from C to D, then calculate the average speed of the trolley between C and D.
d) Section CD was completed exactly one second after section AB. Calculate the acceleration of the trolley in mm/s^2.

3 Look at the chart above.
a) Using a ruler, measure the distance travelled by the trolley in the first 0.1 s recorded on the tape.
b) Calculate the trolley's average speed during this first 0.1 s.
c) Measure the distance travelled by the trolley in the last 0.1s recorded on the tape.
d) Calculate the average speed during this last 0.1 s.
e) Calculate the gain in speed during the 0.4 s.
f) Calculate the acceleration of the trolley in mm/s^2.

2.05 Free fall (1)

In the experiment above, all the air has been removed from the tube. Without air resistance, a light object falls with the same acceleration as a heavy one.

The acceleration of free fall, *g*

If you drop a lead weight and a feather, both fall downwards because of gravity. However, the feather is slowed much more by the air.

The diagram on the left shows what would happen if there were no air resistance. Both objects would fall with the same downward acceleration: 9.8 m/s². This is called the **acceleration of free fall**. It is the same for *all* objects falling near the Earth's surface, light and heavy alike.

The acceleration of free fall is represented by the symbol **g**. Its value varies slightly from one place on the Earth's surface to another, because the Earth's gravitational pull varies. However, the variation is less than 1%. Moving away from the Earth and out into space, *g* decreases.

Note that the value of *g* near the Earth's surface is close to 10 m/s². This simple figure is accurate enough for many calculations, and will be the one used in this book.

On the Moon, the acceleration of free fall is only 1.6 m/s². And as there is no atmosphere, a feather would fall with the same acceleration as a lead weight.

Measuring *g*

An experiment to find *g* is shown on the left. The principle is to measure the time taken for a steel ball to drop through a known height, and to calculate the acceleration from this. Air resistance has little effect on a small, heavy ball falling only a short distance, so the ball's acceleration is effectively *g*.

The ball is dropped by cutting the power to the electromagnet. The electronic timer is automatically switched on when the ball passes through the upper light beam, and switched off when it passes through the lower beam. If the height of the fall is *h* and the time taken is *t*, then *g* can be calculated using this equation (explained on the next spread):

$$g = \frac{2h}{t^2}$$

Experiment to measure *g*

Up and down

In the following example, assume that g is 10 m/s², and that there is no air resistance.

The ball on the right is thrown upwards with a velocity of 30 m/s. The diagram shows the velocity of the ball every second as it rises to its highest point and then falls back to where it started.

As an *upward* velocity of 30 m/s is the same as a *downward* velocity of -30 m/s, the motion of the ball can be described like this:

At 0 s....	the downward velocity is -30 m/s	
After 1 s....	the downward velocity is -20 m/s	10 m/s is
After 2 s....	the downward velocity is -10 m/s	being added
After 3 s....	the downward velocity is 0 m/s	to the
After 4 s....	the downward velocity is +10 m/s	downward
After 5 s....	the downward velocity is +20 m/s	velocity
After 6 s....	the downward velocity is +30 m/s	every second

Whether the ball is travelling up or down, it is gaining downward velocity at the rate of 10 m/s per second. So it always has a downward acceleration of 10 m/s², which is g. Even when the ball is moving upwards, or is stationary at its highest point, it still has downward acceleration.

Below, you can see a velocity–time graph for the motion.

▲ A ball in flight. As g is 10 m/s², the ball's velocity changes by 10 m/s every second.

◄ The velocity–time graph for the ball's motion is shown on the left.

Q

Assume that $g = 10$ m/s² and that there is no air resistance.

1 A stone is dropped from rest. What is its speed
   a) after 1 s **b)** after 2 s **c)** after 5 s?

2 A stone is thrown downwards at 20 m/s. What is its speed
   a) after 1 s **b)** after 2 s **c)** after 5 s?

3 A stone is thrown upwards at 20 m/s. What is its speed
   a) after 1 s **b)** after 2 s **c)** after 5 s?

4 This question is about the three points, A, B, and C, on the graph above left.
   a) In which direction is the ball moving at point C?
   b) At which point is the ball stationary?
   c) At which point is the ball at its maximum height?
   d) What is the ball's acceleration at point C?
   e) What is the ball's acceleration at point A?
   f) What is the ball's acceleration at point B?
   g) At which point does the ball have the same speed as when it was thrown?

Related topics: acceleration **2.01**; motion graphs **2.02**; g and equations of motion **2.06**; gravitational force **2.09**

2.06 Free fall (2)

height
h

acceleration
g

time
t

For an object falling with acceleration g, the following equations apply:

$$v = u + at$$
$$s = ut + \tfrac{1}{2}at^2$$
$$s = \tfrac{1}{2}(u + v)t$$
$$v^2 = u^2 + 2as$$

where s = displacement
u = initial velocity
v = final velocity
t = time
a = acceleration (g)

Finding *g*

The second equation above can be used to find a value for g, if you know the time taken t for an object to fall through a height h, as on the left. In this case, $a = g$, $s = h$, and $u = 0$ because the ball falls from rest.

Using $s = ut + \tfrac{1}{2}at^2$ and substituting as above:

$$h = (0 \times t) + \tfrac{1}{2}gt^2$$

Rearranging this gives: $$g = \frac{2h}{t^2}$$

With this equation, g can be calculated from measurements of h and t (see previous spread).

Solving problems

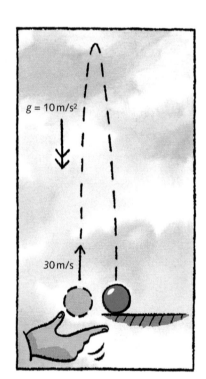

$g = 10\,\text{m/s}^2$

$30\,\text{m/s}$

Example On the left, a ball is thrown upwards from the ground with a velocity of 30 m/s. After how many seconds will it strike the ground again? (Assume that $g = 10\,\text{m/s}^2$, and that air resistance is negligible.)

When using the equations of motion to solve problems like this, you may find these guidelines helpful:

- Use a positive (+) sign to indicate the downward direction. In the problem above, the initial velocity of the ball is upwards, so $u = -30$ m/s. The acceleration of the ball is downwards, so $a = g = +10\,\text{m/s}^2$.
- Remember that s stands for displacement from the starting point rather than total distance travelled. The ball in the problem travels many metres, but when it returns to its starting point, its vertical displacement is 0.
- Look out for useful 'hidden' information. For example, if an object is at its highest point, its velocity is zero. If it has returned to its starting point, its displacement is zero.

In the problem above: $u = -30$ m/s, $a = 10\,\text{m/s}^2$, $s = 0$, and t is to be found.

So, using $s = ut + \tfrac{1}{2}at^2$ and omitting units for simplicity:

$$0 = -30t + (\tfrac{1}{2} \times 10 \times t^2)$$

Rearranged and simplified, this gives: $t(t - 6) = 0$

This has two solutions: $t = 6$ and $t = 0$

So the ball strikes the ground after 6 s. (The result $t = 0$ occurs because the ball also had zero displacement when it was first thrown.)

Downwards and sideways

Below, you can see what happens if one ball is dropped and another is thrown sideways at the same time (assuming no air resistance). The positions of the balls are shown at regular intervals of time.

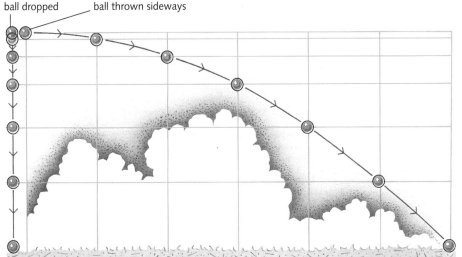

ball dropped   ball thrown sideways

Features of the motion

- The two balls have the same vertical motion. Both hit the ground at the same time, because both have the same downward acceleration (g).
- Horizontally, the second ball moves across the ground at a steady speed – it has a steady horizontal velocity.

The features of the motion are described above right. Results like this show that, if an object is falling freely, its vertical and horizontal motions are independent of each other.

Example Someone throws a stone horizontally from the top of a cliff, as shown on the right. Calculate the horizontal distance travelled by the stone before it hits the sea. (Assume that g is 10 m/s², and that there is no air resistance.)

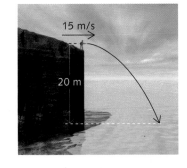

15 m/s

20 m

First, consider the *vertical* motion, and find the time it would take for the stone to fall straight down to the sea. In this case: $s = 20$ m (because the stone's vertical displacement equals the height of the cliff), $u = 0$ (because the stone has no vertical velocity at the start), and $a = g = 10$ m/s².

Using $s = ut + \frac{1}{2}at^2$: $20 = (0 \times t) + (\frac{1}{2} \times 10 \times t^2)$

Rearranged and simplified, this gives $t = 2$ seconds.

Next, consider the *horizontal* motion, and calculate how far the stone would travel in 2 s, at a steady horizontal velocity of 15 m/s:

horizontal distance travelled = horizontal velocity × time taken

So: horizontal distance travelled = 15 m/s × 2 s = 30 m

Q

Assume g is 10 m/s², and there is no air resistance.

1 A rock falls from a height of 45 m.
 a) How long does it take to reach the ground?
 b) What is its velocity as it hits the ground?
2 A stone is thrown upwards from the ground with a velocity of 40 m/s.
 a) How long does it take to reach its highest point?
 b) What is its height at this point?

3 Someone throws a stone horizontally from the top of a cliff and out to sea. The top of the cliff is 45 m above the sea. The initial speed of the stone is 30 m/s.
 a) If the stone had been dropped vertically, how long would it have taken to reach the sea?
 b) When the stone is thrown horizontally, how long does it take to reach the sea?
 c) What horizontal distance does the stone travel before hitting the sea?

Related topics: equations of motion 2.03; measuring g 2.05

2.07 Forces in balance

A **force** is a push or a pull, exerted by one object on another. It has direction as well as magnitude (size), so it is a vector.

The SI unit of force is the **newton** (**N**). Small forces can be measured using a spring balance like the one below. The greater the force, the more the spring is stretched and the higher the reading on the scale:

Typical forces in newtons

force to switch on a bathroom light.......	10 N
force to pull open a drinks can......	20 N
force to lift a heavy suitcase.....	200 N
force from a large jet engine....	250 000 N

Common forces

Here are some examples of forces:

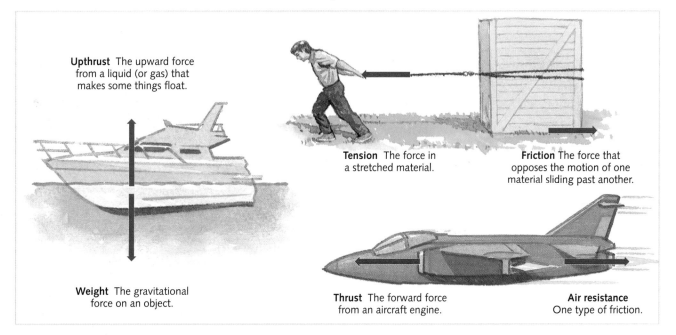

Upthrust The upward force from a liquid (or gas) that makes some things float.

Tension The force in a stretched material.

Friction The force that opposes the motion of one material sliding past another.

Weight The gravitational force on an object.

Thrust The forward force from an aircraft engine.

Air resistance One type of friction.

Motion without force

On Earth, unpowered vehicles soon come to rest because of friction. But with no friction, gravity, or other external force on it, a moving object will keep moving for ever – at a steady speed in a straight line. It doesn't need a force to keep it moving.

This idea is summed up in a law first put forward by Sir Isaac Newton in 1687:

> If no external force is acting on it, an object will
> – if stationary, remain stationary
> – if moving, keep moving at a steady speed in a straight line.

This is known as **Newton's first law of motion**.

Deep in space with no forces to slow it, a moving object will keep moving forever.

Balanced forces

An object may have several forces on it. But if the forces are in balance, they cancel each other out. Then, the object behaves as if there is no force on it at all. Here are some examples:

Stationary gymnast   Skater with steady velocity   Skydiver with steady velocity

With balanced forces on it, an object is *either* at rest, *or* moving at a steady velocity (steady speed in a straight line). That follows from Newton's first law.

Terminal velocity

When a skydiver falls from a hovering helicopter, as her speed increases, the air resistance on her also increases. Eventually, it is enough to balance her weight, and she gains no more speed. She is at her **terminal velocity**. Typically, this is about 60 m/s, though the actual value depends on air conditions, as well as the size, shape, and weight of the skydiver.

When the skydiver opens her parachute, the extra area of material increases the air resistance. She loses speed rapidly until the forces are again in balance, at a greatly reduced terminal velocity.

If air resistance balances her weight, why doesn't a skydiver stay still? If she wasn't moving, there wouldn't be any air resistance. And with only her weight acting, she would gain velocity.
Surely, if she is travelling downwards, her weight must be greater than the air resistance? Only if is she is gaining velocity. At a steady velocity, the forces must be in balance. That follows from Newton's first law.

If a skydiver is falling at a steady velocity, the forces on her are balanced: her weight downwards is exactly matched by the air resistance upwards.

> **Q**
> 1 What is the SI unit of force?
> 2 What does Newton's first law of motion tell you about the forces on an object that is **a)** stationary **b)** moving at a steady velocity?
> 3 The parachutist on the right is descending at a steady velocity.
>   **a)** What name is given to this velocity?
>   **b)** Copy the diagram. Mark in and label another force acting.
>   **c)** How does this force compare with the weight?
>   **d)** If the parachutist used a larger parachute, how would this affect the steady velocity reached? Explain why.

weight

Force, mass, and acceleration

Inertia and mass

▶ Once a massive tanker like this is moving it is extremely difficult to stop.

If an object is at rest, it takes a force to make it move. If it is moving, it takes a force to make it go faster, slower, or in a different direction. So all objects resist a change in velocity – even if the velocity is zero. This resistance to change in velocity is called **inertia**. The more mass something has, the more inertia it has.

Any change in velocity is an acceleration. So the more mass something has, the more difficult it is to make it accelerate.

Velocity is speed in a particular direction.

Resultant force

In the diagram on the left, the two forces are unbalanced. Together, they are equivalent to a single force. This is called the **resultant force**.

These two forces...

3 N   5 N

are equivalent to a single force of (5–3) N....

2 N

This is the **resultant force**

If forces are balanced, the resultant force is zero and there is no acceleration. Any other resultant force causes an acceleration – in the same direction as the resultant force.

Linking force, mass, and acceleration

There is a link between the resultant force acting, the mass, and the acceleration produced. For example:

If this resultant force...	acts on this mass...	then this is the acceleration...
1 N	1 kg	1 m/s^2
2 N	2 kg	1 m/s^2
4 N	2 kg	2 m/s^2
6 N	2 kg	3 m/s^2

In all cases, the following equation applies:

$$\text{resultant force} = \text{mass} \times \text{acceleration}$$

Symbols and units

F = force, in newtons (N)

m = mass, in kilograms (kg)

a = acceleration, in metres/second^2 (m/s^2)

In symbols:

$$F = ma$$

This relationship between force, mass, and acceleration is sometimes called **Newton's second law of motion**.

Example What is the acceleration of the model car on the right?

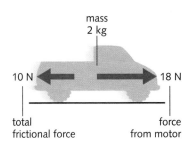

First, work out the resultant force on the car. A force of 18 N to the *right* combined with a force of 10 N to the *left* is equivalent to a force of (18-10) N to the *right*. So the resultant force is 8 N.

Next, work out the acceleration when $F = 8$ N and $m = 2$ kg:

$$F = ma$$

So: $8 = 2a$ (omitting units for simplicity)

Rearranged, this gives $a = 4$. So the car's acceleration is 4 m/s².

Finding the link

The link between force, mass, and acceleration can be found experimentally using the equipment shown above.

Different forces are applied to the trolley by pulling it along with one, two, or three elastic cords, stretched to the same length each time. During each run, the ticker-tape timer marks a series of dots on the paper tape. The acceleration can be calculated from the spacing of the dots.

To vary the mass, one, two, or three trolleys are used in a stack.

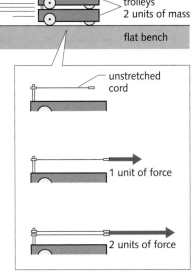

Defining the newton

A 1 N resultant force acting on 1 kg produces an acceleration of 1 m/s². This simple result is no accident. It arises from the way the newton is defined:

1 newton is the force required to give a mass of 1 kilogram an acceleration of 1 m/s².

Q

1 a) What equation links resultant force, mass, and acceleration?
b) Use this equation to calculate the resultant force on each of the stones shown below.

2 a) What is the resultant force on the car below?
b) What is the car's acceleration?
c) If the total frictional force rises to 1500 N, what happens to the car?

Force, weight, and gravity

Near the Earth's surface, a 1 kg mass has a gravitational force on it of about 10 newtons. This is its weight.

Gravitational force

If you hang an object from a spring balance, you measure a downward pull from the Earth. This pull is called a **gravitational force**.

No one is sure what causes gravitational force, but here are some of its main features:

● *All* masses attract each other.
● The greater the masses, the stronger the force.
● The closer the masses, the stronger the force.

The pull between small masses is extremely weak. It is less than 10^{-7} N between you and this book! But the Earth is so massive that its gravitational pull is strong enough to hold most things firmly on the ground.

Weight

Weight is another name for the Earth's gravitational force on an object. Like other forces, it is measured in newtons (N).

Near the Earth's surface, an object of mass 1 kg has a weight of 9.8 N, though 10 N is accurate enough for many calculations and will be used in this book. Greater masses have greater weights. Here are some examples:

mass	1 kg	2 kg	50 kg	m
weight (gravitational force)	10 N	20 N	500 N	mg

g = gravitational field strength = 10 N/kg

Gravitational field strength, g

The Earth has a **gravitational field** which exerts a force on any mass in it. Near the Earth's surface, there is a gravitational force of 10 newtons on each kilogram of mass: the Earth's **gravitational field strength** is 10 newtons per kilogram (N/kg).

Gravitational field strength is represented by the symbol g. So:

$$\text{weight} = \text{mass} \times g \qquad (g = 10 \text{ N/kg})$$

In symbols: $W = mg$

In everyday language, we often use the word 'weight' when it should be 'mass'. Even balances, which detect weight, are normally marked in mass units. But the person in the diagram above doesn't 'weigh' 50 kilograms. He has a *mass* of 50 kilograms and a *weight* of 500 newtons.

Symbols and units

W = weight, in newtons (N)

m = mass, in kilograms (kg)

g = gravitational field strength, 10 N/kg near the Earth's surface

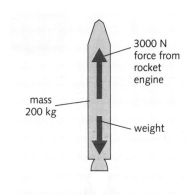

Example What is its acceleration of the rocket on the right?

To find the acceleration, you need to know the resultant force on the rocket. And to find that, you need to know the rocket's weight:

$$\text{weight} = mg = 200\,\text{kg} \times 10\,\text{N/kg} = 2000\,\text{N}$$

So: resultant force (upwards) = 3000 N - 2000 N = 1000 N

But :   resultant force = mass × acceleration
So: 1000 N = 200 kg × acceleration

Rearranged, this gives: acceleration = 5 m/s²

Changing weight, fixed mass

On the Moon, your weight (in newtons) would be less than on Earth, because the Moon's gravitational field is weaker.

Even on Earth, your weight can vary slightly from place to place, because the Earth's gravitational field strength varies. Moving away from the Earth, your weight decreases. If you could go deep into space, and be free of any gravitational pull, your weight would be zero.

Whether on the Earth, on the Moon, or deep in space, your body always has the same resistance to a change in motion. So your mass (in kg) doesn't change – at least, not under normal circumstances. But...

According to Einstein's theory of relativity, mass *can* change. For example, it increases when an object gains speed. However, the change is far too small to detect at speeds much below the speed of light. For all practical purposes, you can assume that mass is constant.

Two meanings for *g*

In the diagram opposite, the acceleration of each object can be worked out using the equation force = mass × acceleration. For example, the 2 kg mass has a 20 N force on it, so its acceleration is 10 m/s².

You get the same result for all the other objects. In each case, the acceleration works out at 10 m/s², or *g* (where *g* is the Earth's gravitational field strength, 10 N/kg).

So *g* has *two* meanings:
- *g* is the gravitational field strength (10 newtons per kilogram).
- *g* is the acceleration of free fall (10 metres per second²).

	mass	weight
deep in space	100 kg	zero
on Moon's surface	100 kg	160 N
on Earth's surface	100 kg	1000 N

Q

Assume that *g* = 10 N/kg and there is no air resistance.

5 kg   10 kg

1 The rocks above are falling near the Earth's surface.
   a) What is the weight of each rock?
   b) What is the acceleration of each rock?
   c) What is the gravitational field strength?

2 A spacecraft travels from Earth to Mars, where the gravitational field strength near the surface is 3.7 N/kg. The spacecraft is carrying a probe which has a mass of 100 kg when measured on Earth.
   a) What is the probe's weight on Earth?
   b) What is the probe's mass in space?
   c) What is the probe's mass on Mars?
   d) What is the probe's weight on Mars?
   e) When the probe is falling, near the surface of Mars, what is its acceleration?

2.10 Action and reaction

Action–reaction pairs

A single force cannot exist by itself. Forces are always pushes or pulls between *two* objects. So they always occur in pairs.

The experiment below shows the effect of a pair of forces. To begin with, the two trolleys are stationary. One of them contains a spring-loaded piston which shoots out when a release pin is hit.

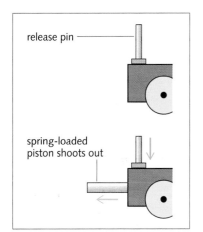

release pin

spring-loaded
piston shoots out

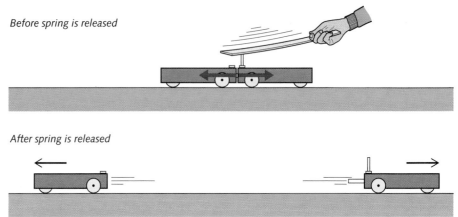

Before spring is released

After spring is released

When the piston is released, the trolleys shoot off in opposite directions. Although the piston comes from one trolley only, two equal but opposite forces are produced, one acting on each trolley. The paired forces are known as the **action** and the **reaction**, but it doesn't matter which you call which. One cannot exist without the other.

Here are some more examples of action–reaction pairs:

Earth pulls downwards
on skydiver

skydiver pulls
upwards on Earth

runner pushes   ground pushes
backwards on   forwards on
ground   runner

forward
force on
bullet: bullet
shoots out

backward
force on gun:
gun recoils

If forces always occur in pairs, why don't they cancel each other out?
The forces in each pair act on *different* objects, not the same object.

If a skydiver is pulled downwards, why isn't the Earth pulled upwards?
It is! But the Earth is so massive that the upward force on it has far too small an effect for any movement to be detected.

Newton's third law of motion

Sir Isaac Newton was the first to point out that every force has an equal but opposite partner acting on a different object. This idea is summed up by **Newton's third law of motion**:

> If object A exerts a force on object B, then object B will exert an equal but opposite force on object A.

Here is another way of stating the same law:

> To every action there is an equal but opposite reaction.

Rockets and jets

Rockets use the action–reaction principle. A rocket engine gets thrust in one direction by pushing out a huge mass of gas very quickly in the opposite direction. The gas is produced by burning fuel and oxygen. These are either stored as cold liquids, or the fuel may be stored in chemical compounds which have been compressed into solid pellets.

How can a rocket accelerate through space if there is nothing for it to push against? It *does* have something to push against – the huge mass of gas from its burning fuel and oxygen. Fuel and oxygen make up over 90% of the mass of a fully loaded rocket.

Jet engines also get thrust by pushing out a huge mass of gas. But the gas is mostly air that has been drawn in at the front:

▲ A rocket engine. In the combustion chamber, a huge mass of hot gas expands and rushes out of the nozzle. The gas is produced by burning fuel and oxygen.

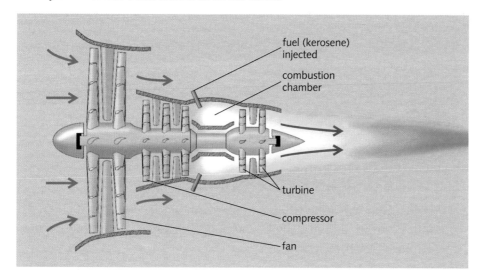

◄ A jet engine. The big fan at the front pushes out a huge mass of air. However, some of the air doesn't come straight out. It is compressed and used to burn fuel in a combustion chamber. As the hot exhaust gas expands, it rushes out of the engine, pushing round a turbine as it goes. The spinning turbine drives the fan and the compressor.

Q

1 The person on the right weighs 500 N. The diagram shows the force of his feet pressing on the ground.
   a) Copy the diagram. Label the size of the force (in newtons).
   b) Draw in the force that the ground exerts on the person's feet. Label the size of this force.
2 When a gun is fired, it exerts a forward force on the bullet. Why does the gun recoil backwards?
3 In the diagram on the opposite page, the forces on the runner and on the ground are equal. Why does the runner move forwards, yet the ground apparently does not move backwards?

2.11 More about vectors

Vectors and scalars

Quantities such as force, which have a direction as well as a magnitude (size), are called **vectors**.

Two vectors acting at a point can be replaced by a single vector with the same effect. This is their **resultant**. On the left, you can see how to find it in two simple cases. Finding the resultant of two or more vectors is called *adding* the vectors.

Quantities such as mass and volume, which have magnitude but no direction, are called **scalars**. Adding scalars is easy. A mass of 30 kg added to a mass of 40 kg always gives a mass of 70 kg.

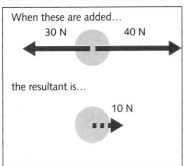

Adding vectors: the parallelogram rule

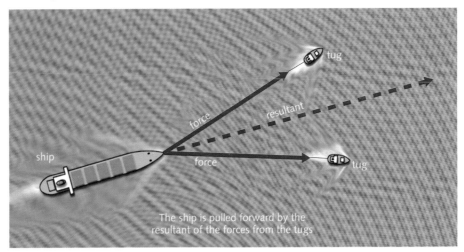

The ship is pulled forward by the resultant of the forces from the tugs

The **parallelogram rule** is a method of finding the resultant in situations like the one above, where the vectors are not in line. It works like this:

To find the resultant of two vectors (for example, forces of 30 N and 40 N acting at a point O, as in the diagram below):

1 On paper, draw two lines from O to represent the vectors. The directions must be accurate, and the length of each line must be in proportion to the magnitude of each vector.
2 Draw in two more lines to complete a parallelogram.
3 Draw in the diagonal from O and measure its length. The diagonal represents the resultant in both magnitude and direction. (Below, for example, the resultant is a force of 60 N at 26° to the horizontal.)

Why the rule works

To see why the parallelogram rule works, consider this simple example using displacement vectors:

Above, someone starts at O, walks 40 m east, then 30 m north. From Pythagoras' theorem, the person must end up 50 m from O.

Above, the journey has been shown as the sum of two displacement vectors. When the parallelogram is drawn, its diagonal gives the correct displacement.

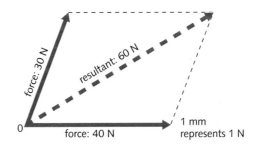

+++

Components of a vector

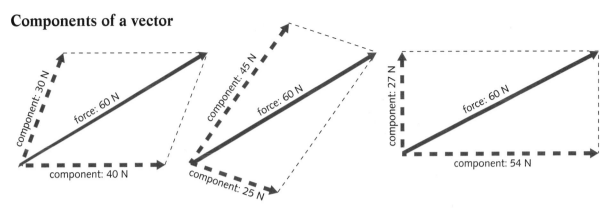

The parallelogram rule also works in reverse: a single vector can be replaced by two vectors having the same effect. Scientifically speaking, a single vector can be **resolved** into two **components**. When using the parallelogram rule in this way, the single vector forms the diagonal.

Above, you can see some of the ways in which a 60 N force can be resolved into two components. There are endless other possibilities.

Components at right angles   In working out the effects of a force, it sometimes helps to resolve the force into components at right angles. For example, when a helicopter tilts its main rotor, the force has vertical and horizontal components which lift the helicopter and move it forward:

Calculating components

The horizontal and vertical components of a force F can be calculated using trigonometry:

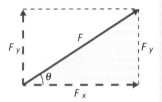

In the tinted triangle above:

$$\cos \theta = \frac{F_x}{F} \quad \text{and} \quad \sin \theta = \frac{F_y}{F}$$

So: $F_x = F \cos \theta$ and $F_y = F \sin \theta$

The horizontal and vertical components of F are therefore as shown below:

Q

1 How is a scalar different from a vector? Give an example of each.

2 Forces of 12 N and 5 N both act at the same point, but their directions can be varied.
   a) What is their greatest possible resultant?
   b) What is their least possible resultant?
   c) If the two forces are at right angles, find by scale drawing or otherwise the size and direction of their resultant.

3 On the right, someone is pushing a lawnmower.
   a) By scale drawing or otherwise, find the vertical and horizontal components of the 100 N force.

b) If the lawnmower weighs 300 N, what is the total downward force on the ground?

c) If the lawnmower is pulled rather than pushed, how does this affect the total downward force?

Related topics: force vectors 2.08

+++

2.12 # Momentum (1)

Momentum = mass x velocity, and this Australian 'road train' has lots of it.

People say that a heavy vehicle travelling fast has lots of **momentum**. However, momentum has an exact scientific definition:

$$\text{momentum} = \text{mass} \times \text{velocity}$$

For example, if a model car has a mass of 2 kg and a velocity of 3 m/s, its

momentum = mass × velocity = 2 kg × 3 m/s = 6 kg m/s

Like velocity, momentum is a vector, so a + or a - is often used to indicate its direction. For example:

momentum of car moving to the *right* = +6 kg m/s

momentum of car moving to the *left* = -6 kg m/s

Linking force and momentum: Newton's second law of motion

With a resultant force on it, an object will accelerate. Therefore, its velocity will change, and so will its momentum. The force and the momentum change are linked by this equation:

$$\text{resultant force} = \frac{\text{change in momentum}}{\text{time}} \qquad \frac{m(v-u)}{t}$$

or: resultant force = rate of change of momentum

The link between a resultant force and the rate of change of momentum it produces is known as **Newton's second law of motion**.

The above equation is really another way of saying that 'force = mass × acceleration'. The panel on the left explains why.

Impulse

From the previous equation, it follows that:

$$\text{resultant force} \times \text{time} = \text{change in momentum}$$

The quantity 'force × time' is called an **impulse**.

Newton noted that, when the same force acted for the same time on different masses, a large mass would gain less velocity than a smaller one, but the change in 'mass × velocity' was the same in every case. It was this observation that led to the concept of momentum and the second law.

Two versions of the same law

A resultant force *F* acts on an object of mass *m* for a time *t*. As a result, its velocity increases from *u* to *v*, its acceleration over this time being *a*.

From Newton's second law of motion:

$$\text{resultant force} = \frac{\text{change in momentum}}{\text{time}}$$

So: $F = \dfrac{mv - mu}{t}$

$= m\left(\dfrac{v - u}{t}\right)$

But: $a = \left(\dfrac{v - u}{t}\right)$

So: $F = ma$

In words:

resultant force = mass x acceleration

++

Handwritten: $a = \dfrac{v-u}{t} = \dfrac{6}{4} = 1.5 \, m/s^2$

Solving problems

Example 1 A model car of mass 2 kg is travelling in a straight line. If its velocity increases from 3 m/s to 9 m/s in 4 s, what is the resultant force on it?

---

mass
2 kg

velocity increases
from 3 m/s
to 9 m/s
in 4 s

To begin with:

momentum = mass × velocity = 2 kg × 3 m/s = 6 kg m/s

4 seconds later:

momentum = mass × velocity = 2 kg × 9 m/s = 18 kg m/s

So: change in momentum = 12 kg m/s

But: resultant force $= \dfrac{\text{change in momentum}}{\text{time}} = \dfrac{12 \, \text{kg m/s}}{4 \, \text{s}}$

So: resultant force = 3 N

Handwritten notes (right margin):
$F = ma$
$\Rightarrow a = \dfrac{F}{m}$
$a = \dfrac{3}{2} = 1.5 \, m/s^2$
$F = \dfrac{12}{4} = 3$
$F = ma = 1.5 \times 2 = 3$

The problem can also be solved by working out the car's acceleration and then using the equation: resultant force = mass × acceleration.

Handwritten:
change
$m = M \times v = 2kg \times 100 m/s$
$= 200 \, kg \, m/s$

Example 2 A small rocket pushes out 2 kg of exhaust gas every second at a velocity of 100 m/s. What thrust (force) is produced by the engine?

---

thrust

100 m/s

2 kg of gas
pushed out
every second

By Newton's third law of motion, the forward force on the engine is equal to the backward force pushing out the exhaust gas. That force can be calculated by finding the rate of change of momentum of the gas:

In 1 second, 2 kg of gas increases its velocity from 0 to 100 m/s.

So: change in momentum = mass × velocity change
                             = 2 kg × 100 m/s = 200 kg m/s

force on gas $= \dfrac{\text{change in momentum}}{\text{time}} = \dfrac{200 \, \text{kg m/s}}{1 \, \text{s}}$

So: thrust = 200 N

Handwritten:
$\dfrac{1}{2} \times \dfrac{1}{4} = \dfrac{1}{8}$
$\dfrac{2 \, m/s}{3 \, s} = \qquad A = 0.6666666 \, m/s^2$

Q

1 What equation is used to calculate momentum?
2 What equation links the resultant force with the change in momentum it produces?
3 When a resultant force acts for 3 seconds on the trolley below, its velocity increases to 6 m/s.
  a) What is the momentum of the trolley before the force acts?
  b) What is the momentum after the force has acted?

total mass:
12 kg

4 m/s

c) What is the change in momentum?
d) What is the change in momentum every second?
e) What is the resultant force on the trolley?
Now you will calculate the resultant force on the trolley using different steps:
f) What is the trolley's change in velocity?
g) What is the trolley's acceleration?
h) What equation links force, mass, and acceleration?
i) What is the resultant force on the trolley?
4 A jet engine pushes out 50 kg of gas (mainly air) every second, at a velocity of 150 m/s. *Handwritten:* $\text{mom} = 7500 \, kgm/s^2$
  a) What thrust (force) does the engine produce?
  b) If the engine pushed out twice the mass of gas at half the velocity, what would the thrust be?
  Handwritten: 100 kgs @ 75 m/s
  Handwritten: mom = 7500 kg m/s

Momentum (2)

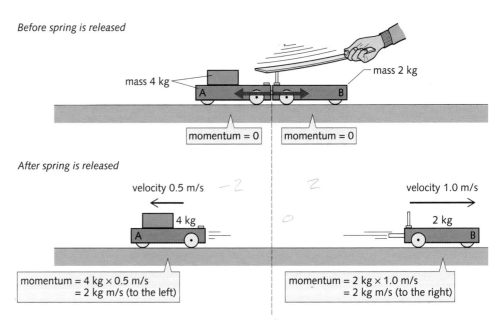

Before spring is released

mass 4 kg

mass 2 kg

A ← → B

momentum = 0   momentum = 0

After spring is released

velocity 0.5 m/s

4 kg

A

velocity 1.0 m/s

2 kg

B

momentum = 4 kg × 0.5 m/s
= 2 kg m/s (to the left)

momentum = 2 kg × 1.0 m/s
= 2 kg m/s (to the right)

Velocity and momentum essentials

Velocity is speed in a particular direction.

momentum = mass × velocity
(kg m/s)   (kg)   (m/s)

Velocity and momentum are vectors. They have direction as well as magnitude (size). Their direction can be shown using an arrow, or a + or -.

To begin with, the trolleys above are stationary. But when a spring-loaded piston is released between them, they shoot off in opposite directions. Their velocities can be measured using ticker-tape timers.

When the trolleys shoot apart, the trolley with least mass has most velocity. The diagram shows typical mass and velocity values. These illustrate a rule which applies in all such experiments:

mass × velocity to the left = mass × velocity to the right
(trolley A)   (trolley B)

This result is to be expected. From Newton's third law of motion, the forces on the two trolleys are equal but opposite. Also, the forces act for the same time. So they should cause equal but opposite changes in momentum (as force × time = change in momentum).

Conservation of momentum

With the mass and velocity values above, the total momentum of the trolleys before and after separation can be found. As momentum is a vector, its direction must be allowed for. In the following calculations, a momentum gain to the *right* is counted as *positive* (+):

Before the spring is released: total momentum of trolleys = 0

After the spring is released:
momentum of trolley A = mass × velocity = 4 kg × -0.5 m/s = -2 kg m/s
momentum of trolley B = mass × velocity = 2 kg × 1.0 m/s = +2 kg m/s
So: total momentum of trolleys = 0

So the total momentum (zero) is unchanged by the release of the spring. This is an example of the **law of conservation of momentum**:

When two or more objects act on each other, their total momentum remains constant, provided no external forces are acting.

Collision problem

handwritten: Total Mom pre crash = -10 kgm/s

handwritten: Mom = m×v = -12 kg/s

Before the collision

handwritten: m×v = 2×1 = 2 kgm/s.

velocity 2 m/s

mass 1 kg

A

velocity 3 m/s

sticky material

mass 4 kg

B

After the collision

handwritten: Mom = V × m
-10 = V × 5
V = -10/5 = -2 m/s

velocity ?

combined mass
5 kg

A   B

Example When the two trolleys above collide, they stick together. What is their velocity after the collision?

According to the law of conservation of momentum, the total momentum of the trolleys is the same after the collision as before:

Before the collision:
momentum of trolley A = mass × velocity = 1 kg × 2 m/s = +2 kg m/s
momentum of trolley B = mass × velocity = 4 kg × -3 m/s = -12 kg m/s
So: total momentum of trolleys A and B = -10 kg m/s

After the collision:
total momentum of trolleys A and B = -10 kg m/s   (as above)
So: combined mass × velocity = -10 kg m/s
So: 5 kg × velocity = -10 kg m/s
So: velocity of trolleys = -2 m/s

handwritten: Post coll +60 kgms.

Therefore the trolleys have a velocity of 2 m/s to the left.

handwritten: R.T.F.Q

handwritten: Tot RES Mom = +60 kgms.

handwritten: 16 +80 kgms   4 Mom = -20 kgms

Q

1 A trolley of mass 2 kg rests next to a trolley of mass 3 kg on a flat bench. When a spring is released between the trolleys, and they are pushed apart, the 2 kg trolleys travels to the left at 6 m/s.
handwritten: -12 mom
Before separation:
a) What is the total momentum of the trolleys?
After separation:
b) What is the total momentum of the trolleys?
c) What is the momentum of the 2 kg trolley?
d) What is the momentum of the 3 kg trolley?
e) What is the velocity of the 3 kg trolley?

2 A 16 kg mass travelling to the right at 5 m/s collides with a 4 kg mass travelling to the left, also at 5 m/s. When the masses collide, they stick together and move along the same line as before.
Before the collision:
a) What is the momentum of the 16 kg mass?
b) What is the momentum of the 4 kg mass?
c) What is the total momentum of the masses?
After the collision:
d) What is the total momentum of the masses?
e) What is the velocity of the masses?

Related topics: velocity and vectors **2.01**; using ticker-tape **2.04**; Newton's 3rd law **2.10**

2.14 # Moving in circles

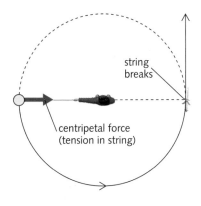

centripetal force
(tension in string)

string breaks

▶ When a motorcycle goes round a corner like this, the sideways friction between the tyres and the road provides the necessary centripetal force.

Centripetal force...

Centripetal force isn't produced by circular motion. It is the force that must be *supplied* to make something move in a circle rather than in a straight line.

...and centrifugal force

When you whirl a ball around on the end of some string, you feel an outward pull on your hand. But there is no such thing as a 'centrifugal force' on the ball itself. If the string breaks, the ball moves off at a tangent. It isn't flung outwards.

Centripetal force

On the left, someone is whirling a ball around in a horizontal circle at a steady speed. An inward force is needed to make the ball follow a circular path. The tension in the string provides this force. Without it, the ball would travel in a straight line, as predicted by Newton's first law of motion. This is exactly what happens if the string breaks.

This inward force needed to make an object move in a circle is called the **centripetal force**. *More* centripetal force is needed if:

● the *mass* of the object is *increased*
● the *speed* of the object is *increased*
● the *radius* of the circle is *reduced*.

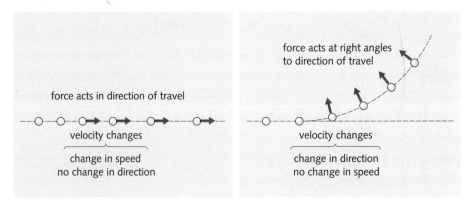

Changing velocity

An object needn't speed up or slow down to change its velocity. Velocity is speed in a particular direction. So a change in velocity can mean *either* a change in speed *or* a change in direction:

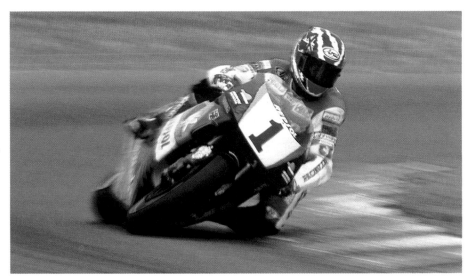

force acts in direction of travel

velocity changes

change in speed
no change in direction

force acts at right angles to direction of travel

velocity changes

change in direction
no change in speed

Above, you can see two ways in which a resultant force can produce a change in velocity. The second one is what happens in circular motion.

If an object's velocity changes in any way, the object is accelerating. The acceleration is in the same direction as the resultant force.

Inward acceleration

Motion in a circle is one example of a force producing acceleration.

When something is moving in a circle, the inward centripetal force produces an inward acceleration as on the right. It may be difficult to imagine a ball accelerating towards the centre of a circle without getting any closer to it, but the ball is constantly moving inwards from the position it would have had if it travelled in a straight line.

Satellites in orbit

Gravitational pull provides the centripetal force needed to make a satellite move in a circle around the Earth. When a satellite is put into a circular orbit, its speed is carefully chosen so that its weight supplies exactly the right amount of centripetal force required.

The mass of a satellite does not affect the speed required for a particular orbit. If the mass is doubled, twice as much centripetal force is needed, but that is supplied by the doubled gravitational pull of the Earth.

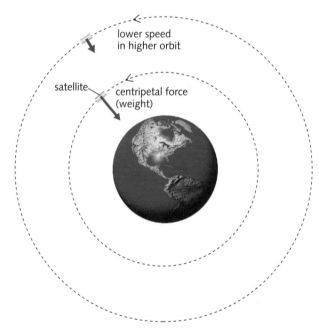

For a satellite orbiting close to the Earth, an orbital speed of about 8000 m/s (29 000 km per hour) is needed. The further out the orbit, the lower the gravitational pull, and the less speed is required.

Calculating...

...centripetal acceleration

There is an equation for calculating centripetal acceleration. If an object moves at speed v in a circle of radius r:

$$\text{centripetal acceleration} = \frac{v^2}{r}$$

Note: if the object moves *faster* in a circle of *smaller* radius, its centripetal acceleration *increases*.

...and centripetal force

Force = mass x acceleration. So, if the object moving in a circle has a mass m:

$$\text{centripetal force required} = \frac{mv^2}{r}$$

---

1 A piece of clay is stuck to the edge of a potter's wheel. Draw a diagram to show the path of the clay if it comes unstuck while the wheel is rotating.

2 A car travels round a bend in the road. What supplies the centripetal force needed?

3 In question 2, how does the centripetal force change if the car
   a) has less mass
   b) travels at a slower speed
   c) travels round a tighter curve?

4 A satellite is in a circular orbit around the Earth.
   a) Draw a diagram to show any forces on the satellite. On your diagram, show the direction of the satellite's acceleration.
   b) If the satellite had more mass, how would this affect the speed required for the orbit?
   c) If the satellite had a higher orbit, how would this affect the speed required?
   d) If the satellite had a higher orbit, how would this affect the centripetal force required?

---

1 a) Write down, **in words**, the equation connecting speed, distance and time. [1]

b) A car travels at a steady speed of 20 m/s. Calculate the distance travelled in 5 s. [2]

WJEC

2

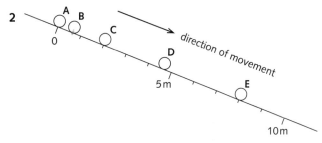

The diagram shows the positions of a ball as it rolled down a track. The ball took 0.5 s to roll from one position to the next. For example, it rolled from **A** to **B** in 0.5 s and from **B** to **C** in 0.5 s and so on.

a) Write down:

(i) the distance travelled by the ball from **A** to **E**; [1]

(ii) the time taken by the ball to reach **E**. [1]

b) Calculate the average speed of the ball in rolling from **A** to **E**. Write down the formula that you use and show your working. [3]

c) Explain:

(i) how you can tell from the diagram that the ball is speeding up; [1]

(ii) why the ball speeds up. [1]

WJEC

3

A student measures the acceleration of a trolley using the apparatus above. The light sensors are connected to a computer which is programmed to calculate the acceleration. The results obtained are shown on the acceleration-force graph.

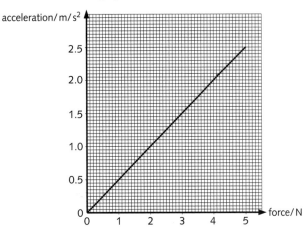

a) (i) Describe how changing the force affects the acceleration. [2]

(ii) Write down, **in words**, the equation connecting force, mass and acceleration. [1]

(iii) Use the data from the graph to calculate the mass of the trolley. [2]

b) Sketch the graph and draw the line that would have been obtained for a trolley of larger mass. [1]

WJEC

4 A car has a mass of 900 kg. It accelerates from rest at a rate of 1.2 m/s².

a) Calculate the time taken to reach a velocity of 30 m/s. [3]

b) Calculate the force required to accelerate the car at a rate of 1.2 m/s². [3]

c) Even with the engine working at full power, the car's acceleration decreases as the car goes faster. Why is this? [3]

MEG

5 The diagram below shows some of the forces acting on a car of mass 800 kg.

a) State the size of the total drag force when the car is travelling at constant speed. [1]

b) The driving force is increased to 3200 N.

(i) Find the resultant force on the car at this instant. [1]

(ii) Write down, **in words**, the equation connecting mass, force and acceleration. [1]

(iii) Calculate the initial acceleration of the car. [2]

c) Explain why the car will eventually reach a new higher constant speed. [2]

WJEC

6

A student investigated the motion of a marble as it rolled down a curved track and was projected over the edge of a bench top as shown.

When the marble was released from rest at a height h above the bench top, it landed 2 m away from the bottom of the bench 0.5 s after it left the bench top.

a) (i) Calculate the horizontal velocity **X** of the marble as it leaves the bench. Write down the formula that you use and show your working. [3]

(ii) What is the horizontal velocity of the marble as it hits the floor? [1]

b) (i) What is the vertical velocity of the marble as it leaves the bench? [1]

(ii) If the acceleration due to gravity is 10 m/s², calculate the vertical velocity with which the marble hits the floor.

[You may use the equation $v^2 = u^2 + 2as$ or some other method.] [2]

c) The student repeated the experiment by increasing the value of h.
State what effect this had on:

(i) the horizontal velocity **X**; [1]

(ii) the point where the marble hit the floor; [1]

(iii) the time of flight; [1]

(iv) the vertical velocity of the marble at the point of impact. [1]

WJEC

7 Two ice skaters stand facing each other just before they start an ice dance routine.
The man has a mass of 60 kg and the woman has a mass of 45 kg.

45 kg   60 kg

The man pushes the woman away and they move apart in opposite directions on the ice.

a) (i) How does the change in momentum of the man compare with that of the woman? [1]

(ii) The combined momentum of the man and the woman **before** they start to move is zero. What will it be just after they move apart? [1]

(iii) Use ideas about momentum to explain how you arrived at your answers to (i) and (ii). [2]

(iv) What assumption have you made in making these answers? [1]

b) Just after they part the speed of the man is 0.6 m/s. Calculate the speed of the woman. [3]

MEG

8 During a journey through space, to make a velocity correction, a rocket must increase its emission of exhaust gases.

a) Explain how this causes an increase in velocity of the rocket. [2]

b) The rocket has a mass of 20 000 kg and fires 6 kg of burnt fuel out of its engines as hot gases travelling at 10 000 m/s.
Use the equation
momentum (kg m/s) = *mass* (kg) × *velocity* (m/s)
to calculate the change in

(i) momentum of the hot gases, [1]

(ii) momentum of the rocket, [1]

(iii) velocity of the rocket. [1]

WJEC

9 a) In a collision or an explosion, **momentum is conserved**.
Explain what you understand by:

(i) the *momentum* of a body; [1]

(ii) the phrase *momentum is conserved*. [2]

b)

Trolleys **A** and **B**, mounted on a frictionless track, are held together so that the spring between them is fully compressed. When released they move apart as shown below.

Compare the speeds V_1 and V_2 of each trolley at the moment they separate when:

(i) **A** and **B** both have the same mass, [2]

(ii) the mass of **A** is twice that of **B**. [2]

c) Explain why the smallest fragments from an explosion can cause damage over a wide area. [2]

WJEC

10

mass of the rocket	radius of the orbit	speed of the rocket

Copy and complete the following sentence by selecting phrases from **the above list**. You may use each phrase once, more than once or not at all.
The force required to keep a rocket in orbit is smaller if the _____ is greater or if the _____ is smaller. [2]

WJEC

Photocopy the list of topics below and tick the boxes of the ones that are included in your examination syllabus. (Your teacher should be able to tell you which they are.) Use your list when you revise. The spread number in brackets tells you where to find more information.

❏ 1 Measuring speed. (2.01)

❏ 2 The difference between speed and velocity. (2.01)

❏ 3 How acceleration is defined. (2.01)

❏ 4 The meaning of retardation. (2.01)

❏ 5 Representing motion using distance-time and speed-time graphs. (2.02)

❏ 6 Calculating
- speed from a distance-time graph.
- acceleration from a speed-time graph.
- distance travelled from a speed-time graph. (2.02)

❏ 7 The equations linking s, u, v, a, and t, and how to use them. (2.03)

❏ 8 Recording the motion of a trolley using ticker-tape, and calculating an acceleration from the data collected. (2.04)

❏ 9 The acceleration of free fall, g. (2.05)

❏ 10 Measuring g. (2.05)

❏ 11 Carrying out calculations on the motion of an object in free fall using the s, u, v, a, and t, equations. (2.06)

❏ 12 The motion of an object that is falling while travelling sideways. (2.06)

❏ 13 Measuring force. (2.07)

❏ 14 How an object moves if the forces on it are balanced: Newton's first law of motion. (2.07)

❏ 15 Terminal velocity. (2.07)

❏ 16 The meaning of resultant force. (2.08)

❏ 17 The link between force, mass, and acceleration: Newton's second law of motion. (2.08)

❏ 18 Defining the SI unit of force: the newton. (2.08)

❏ 19 The properties of gravitational force. (2.09)

❏ 20 The difference between weight and mass. (2.09)

❏ 21 Defining gravitational field strength. (2.09)

❏ 22 Why the weight of an object can vary but, under normal circumstances, the mass does not change. (2.09)

❏ 23 Two meanings of g. (2.09)

❏ 24 How all forces exist in pairs: Newton's third law of motion. (2.10)

❏ 25 How rockets and jets produce a force. (2.10)

❏ 26 The difference between vectors and scalars. (2.11)

❏ 27 Adding vectors using the parallelogram rule. (2.11)

❏ 28 Resolving a vector into two components. (2.11)

❏ 29 Defining momentum. (2.12)

❏ 30 The link between force and momentum. (2.12)

❏ 31 The meaning of impulse. (2.12)

❏ 32 The law of conservation of momentum. (2.13)

❏ 33 Applying the law of conservation of momentum to objects which are springing apart or colliding. (2.13)

❏ 34 The meaning of centripetal force. (2.14)

❏ 35 The factors on which centripetal force depends. (2.14)

❏ 36 Why an object moving in a circle has an inward acceleration. (2.14)

❏ 37 The conditions required for a satellite to move in a circular orbit around the Earth. (2.14)

3

Forces and Pressure

- TURNING EFFECT OF A FORCE
- CENTRE OF GRAVITY
- ELASTIC AND PLASTIC BEHAVIOUR
- STRETCHING AND COMPRESSING MATERIALS
- PRESSURE
- HYDRAULIC MACHINES
- ATMOSPHERIC PRESSURE
- FLOATING AND SINKING
- FLUID FLOW

Sharks like this are among the most efficient swimmers and hunters in the sea. However, unlike most other fish, they do not have an air-filled swim bladder to adjust their buoyancy. To descend or climb, a shark must keep swimming forward and alter the angle of the two wing-like fins at the front. If it stops beating its tail and loses forward motion, it will sink to the seabed.

3.01 Forces and turning effects

A large force at the end of a long spanner gives a large turning effect.

Moment of a force

It is difficult to tighten a nut with your fingers. But with a spanner, you can produce a larger turning effect. The turning effect is even greater if you increase the force or use a longer spanner. The turning effect of a force is called a **moment**. It is calculated like this:

> moment of a force = force × perpendicular distance
> about a point   from the point

Below, there are some examples of forces and their moments. Moments are described as **clockwise** or **anticlockwise**, depending on their direction. The moment of a force is also called a **torque**.

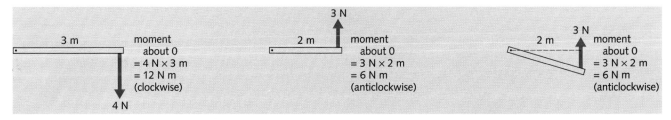

3 m

moment
about O
= 4 N × 3 m
= 12 N m
(clockwise)

4 N

3 N

2 m

moment
about O
= 3 N × 2 m
= 6 N m
(anticlockwise)

3 N

2 m

moment
about O
= 3 N × 2 m
= 6 N m
(anticlockwise)

The principle of moments

In diagram A below, the bar is in a state of balance, or **equilibrium**. Note that the anticlockwise moment about O is equal to the clockwise moment. One turning effect balances the other. In diagram B, there are more forces acting but, once again, the bar is in equilibrium. This time, the *total* clockwise moment about O is equal to the anticlockwise moment.

These examples illustrate the **principle of moments**:

> If an object is in equilibrium:
> the sum of the clockwise moments about any point is equal to the sum of the anticlockwise moments about that point.

Taking moments

Calculating the moments about a point is called *taking moments* about the point.

A

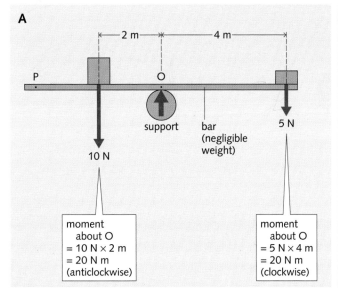

2 m — 4 m

P

O

support

bar
(negligible
weight)

5 N

10 N

moment
about O
= 10 N × 2 m
= 20 N m
(anticlockwise)

moment
about O
= 5 N × 4 m
= 20 N m
(clockwise)

B

4 m — 4 m
2 m — 1 m

P

O

3 N

10 N

8 N

moment
about O
= 10 N × 2 m
= 20 N m
(anticlockwise)

moment
about O
= 8 N × 1 m
= 8 N m

moment
about O
= 3 N × 4 m
= 12 N m

total moment
= 20 N m
(clockwise)

Conditions for equilibrium

If an object is in equilibrium, the forces on it must balance as well as their turning effects. So:

- The sum of the forces in one direction must equal the sum of the forces in the opposite direction.
- The principle of moments must apply.

For example, in diagram A on the opposite page, the upward force from the support must be 15 N, to balance the 10 N + 5 N total downward force. Also, if you take moments about *any* point – P, for example – the total clockwise moment must equal the total anticlockwise moment.

When taking moments about P, you need to include the moment of the upward force from the support. This doesn't arise when taking moments about O because the force has no moment about that point.

Solving a problem

> *Example* Below right, someone of weight 500 N is standing on a plank supported by two trestles. Calculate the upward forces, *X* and *Y*, exerted by the trestles on the plank. (Assume the plank has negligible weight.)

The system is in equilibrium, so the principle of moments applies. You can take moments about any point. But taking moments about A or B gets rid of one of the unknowns, *X* or *Y*.

Taking moments about A:
clockwise moment = 500 N × 2 m = 1000 N m
anticlockwise moment = Y × 5 m
As the moments balance, $5Y$ m = 1000 N m
So: $Y = 200$ N

From here, there are two methods of finding X. *Either* take moments about B and do a calculation like the one above. *Or* use the fact that $X + Y$ must equal the 500 N downward force. By either method: $X = 300$ N

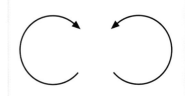

Clockwise .... or anticlockwise?

In the diagram below, the 500 N force has a *clockwise* moment about A, but an *anticlockwise* moment about B.

To decide whether a moment is clockwise or anticlockwise about a point, imagine that the diagram is pinned to the table through the point, then decide which way the force arrow is trying to turn the paper.

500 N

---

1 The moment (turning effect) of a force depends on two factors. What are they?

2 What is the principle of moments? What other rule also applies if an object is in equilibrium?

3 Below, someone is trying to balance a plank with stones. The plank has negligible weight.
a) Calculate the moment of the 4 N force about O.
b) Calculate the moment of the 6 N force about O.

c) Will the plank balance? If not, which way will it tip?
d) What extra force is needed at point P to balance the plank?
e) In which direction must the force at P act?

4 In *diagram* **B** on the opposite page:
a) What is the upward force from the support?
b) If moments are taken *about point P*, which forces have clockwise moments? What is the total clockwise moment about P?
c) Which force or forces have anticlockwise moments about P? What is the total anticlockwise moment about P?
d) Comparing moments about P, does the principle of moments apply?

Centre of gravity

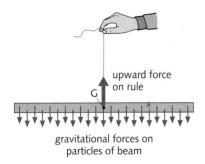

upward force
on rule

G

gravitational forces on
particles of beam

Like other objects, the beam on the left is made up of lots of tiny particles, each with a small gravitational force on it. The beam balances when suspended at one particular point, G, because the gravitational forces have turning effects about G which cancel out.

Together, the small gravitational forces act like a single force at G. In other words, they have a resultant at G. This resultant is the beam's **weight**. G is the **centre of gravity** (or **centre of mass**).

Finding a centre of gravity

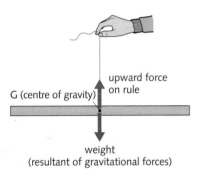

G (centre of gravity)

upward force
on rule

weight
(resultant of gravitational forces)

In diagram 1 below, the card can swing freely from the pin. When the card is released, the forces on it turn the card until its centre of gravity is vertically under the pin, as in diagram 2. Whichever point the card is suspended from, it will always hang with its centre of gravity vertically under the pin. This fact can be used to find the centre of gravity.

In diagram 3, the centre of gravity lies somewhere along the plumb line, whose position is marked by the line AB. If the card is suspended at a different point, a second line CD can be drawn. The centre of gravity must also lie along this line, so it is at the point where AB crosses CD.

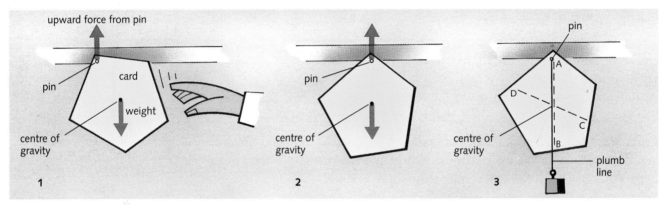

upward force from pin

pin
card
weight
centre of
gravity

1

pin
centre of
gravity

2

pin
A
D
C
centre of
gravity
B
plumb
line

3

Heavy bar problem

In simple problems, you are often told that a balanced bar has negligible weight. In more complicated problems, you have to include the weight.

Example If a uniform bar balances, as on the left, with a 1.5 kg mass attached to one end, what is its weight? ($g = 10$ N/kg)

To solve the problem, redraw the diagram to show all the forces and distances, as in the lower diagram. As $g = 10$ N/kg, the 1.5 kg mass has a weight of 15 N. 'Uniform' means that the bar's weight is evenly distributed, so the centre of gravity of the bar (by itself) is at the mid-point, 0.5 m from one end. The bar's weight W acts at this point.

Now take moments about the support, O. The upward force has no moment about this point, but there is an anticlockwise moment of 15 N × 0.2 m and a clockwise moment of W × 0.3 m. As the bar is in equilibrium:

$$15 \text{ N} \times 0.2 \text{ m} = W \times 0.3 \text{ m}$$

So: the bar's weight W is 10 N.

Stability

This box is in equilibrium. The forces on it are balanced, and so are their turning effects.

With a small tilt, the forces will turn the box back to its original position.

With a large tilt, the forces will tip the box over.

A box with a wider base and a lower centre of gravity can be tilted further before it falls over.

If the box above is pushed a little and then released, it falls back to its original position. Its position was **stable**. If the box is pushed much further, it topples. It starts to topple as soon as its centre of gravity passes over the edge of its base. From then on, the forces on the box have a turning effect which tips it even further. A box with a wider base and/or a lower centre of gravity is more stable. It can be tilted to a greater angle before it starts to topple.

States of equilibrium

Here are three types of equilibrium:

Stable equilibrium If you tip the cone a little, the centre of gravity stays over the base. So the cone falls back to its original position.

Unstable equilibrium The cone is balanced, but only briefly. Its pointed 'base' is so small that the centre of gravity immediately passes beyond it.

Neutral equilibrium Left alone, the ball stays where it is. When moved, it stays in its new position. Wherever it lies, its centre of gravity is always exactly over the point which is its 'base'.

This gymnast will stay balanced – as long as she keeps her centre of gravity over the beam.

Q

1 The stool on the right is about to topple over.
   a) Copy the diagram, showing the position of the centre of gravity.
   b) Give *two* features which would make the stool more stable.
2 A uniform metre rule has a 4 N weight hanging from one end. The rule balances when suspended from a point 0.1 m from that end.
   a) Draw a diagram to show the rule and the forces on it.
   b) Calculate the weight of the rule.
3 Draw diagrams to show a drawing pin in positions of stable, unstable, and neutral equilibrium.

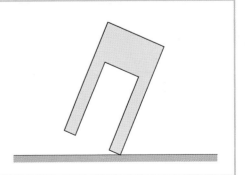

Related topics: resultant force **2.08** and **2.11**; mass, weight, and g **2.09**; turning effects, moments, and equilibrium **3.01**

3.03 Stretching and compressing

Elastic and plastic

If you bend a ruler slightly and release it, it springs back to its original shape. Materials that behave like this are **elastic**. However, they stop being elastic if bent or stretched too far. They either break or become permanently deformed (out of shape).

If you stretch or bend Plasticine, it keeps its new shape. Materials that behave like this are **plastic**. (The materials we call 'plastics' were given that name because they are plastic and mouldable when hot.)

Force and weight essentials

Force is measured in newtons (N).

Weight is a force.

On Earth, the weight of an object is 10 N for each kilogram of mass.

Stretching a spring

In the experiment below, a steel spring is stretched by hanging masses from one end. The force applied to the spring is called the **load**. As *g* is 10 N/kg, the load is 1 N for every 100 g of mass hung from the spring.

As the load is increased, the spring stretches more and more. Its **extension** is the difference between its stretched and unstretched lengths.

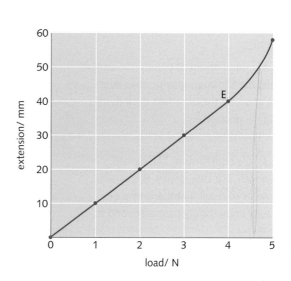

load	extension
N	mm
0	0
1	10
2	20
3	30
4	40
5	58

The readings on the left can be plotted as a graph, as above. Up to point E, the graph line has these features:

● The line is straight, and passes through the origin.
● If the load is doubled, the extension is doubled, and so on.
● Extension ÷ load always has the same value (10 mm/N).
● Every 1 N increase in load produces the same extra extension (10 mm).

Mathematically, these can be summed up as follows:

Up to point E, the extension is proportional to the load.

Point E marks another change in the spring's behaviour. Up to E, the spring behaves elastically and returns to its original length when the load is removed. E is its **elastic limit**. Beyond E, the spring is left permanently stretched when the load is removed.

Hooke's law

In the 1660s, Robert Hooke investigated how springs and wires stretched when loads were applied. He found that, for many materials, the extension and load were in proportion, provided the elastic limit was not exceeded:

> A material obeys Hooke's law if, beneath its elastic limit, the extension is proportional to the load.

Steel wires do not stretch as much as steel springs, but they obey Hooke's law. Glass and wood also obey the law, but rubber does not.

Extension–load graph for rubber

Compressing, bending, and twisting

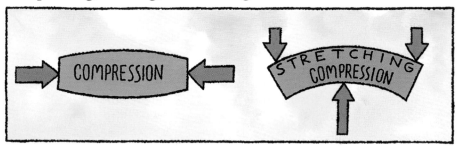

Materials can be compressed as well as stretched. If the compression is elastic, the material will return to its original shape when the forces are removed.

When a material is bent, the applied forces produce compression on one side and stretching on the other. If the elastic limit is exceeded, the bending is permanent. This can happen when a metal sheet is dented.

Steel is strong whether compressed or stretched. Concrete, on the other hand, is strong under compression, but weak under tension. So it breaks easily when stretched or bent. For tensile (stretching) strength, concrete can be reinforced with steel rods:

▲ The CN Tower in Toronto is over half a kilometre high. In high winds, its top can sway by half a metre. But, being elastic, its steel and concrete structure always returns to its original shape.

Q

1 What is meant by an *elastic* material?

2 What is meant by the *elastic limit* of a material?

3 Look at the small graph at the top of the page. Does rubber obey Hooke's law? Explain how you can tell from the graph whether this law is obeyed or not.

4 The table on the right shows the readings taken in a spring-stretching experiment:
   a) What is the unstretched length of the spring?
   b) Copy and complete the table.
   c) Plot a graph of extension against load.
   d) Mark the *elastic limit* on your graph.

e) Over which section of the graph line is the extension proportional to the load?

f) What load would produce a 35 mm extension?

g) What load would make the spring stretch to a length of 65 mm?

load/ N	0	1	2	3	4	5	6
length/ mm	40	49	58	67	76	88	110
extension/ mm	0	9	18	27	36	48	70

3.04 Pressure

A

force: 200 N
area: 2 m²
100 N on each m²
pressure = 100 N/m²
= 100 Pa

B

force: 200 N
area: 4 m²
50 N on each m²
pressure = 50 N/m²
= 50 Pa

Blocks A and B on the left are resting on soft ground. Both weigh the same and exert the same force on the ground. But the force from block B is spread over a larger area, so the force *on each square metre* is reduced. The **pressure** under block B is less than that under block A.

For a force acting at right angles to a surface, the pressure is calculated like this:

$$\text{pressure} = \frac{\text{force}}{\text{area}} \qquad \text{In symbols: } p = \frac{F}{A}$$

If force is measured in newtons (N) and area in square metres (m²), pressure is measured in newton/square metre (N/m²). 1 N/m² is called 1 **pascal** (Pa):

If a 100 N force is spread over an area of   1 m², the pressure is   100 Pa.
If a 100 N force is spread over an area of   2 m², the pressure is   50 Pa.
If a 100 N force is spread over an area of 0.2 m², the pressure is   500 Pa.
If a 200 N force is spread over an area of 0.2 m², the pressure is 1000 Pa.

For most pressure measurements, the pascal is a very small unit. In practical situations, it is often more convenient to use the **kilopascal (kPa)**.
1 kPa = 1000 Pa

Increasing **the pressure by** *reducing* **the area**

The studs on a football boot have only a small area of contact with the ground. The pressure under the studs is high enough for them to sink into the ground, which gives extra grip.

The area under the edge of a knife's blade is extremely small. Beneath it, the pressure is high enough for the blade to push easily through the material.

Under the tiny area of the point of a drawing pin, the pressure is far too high for the wood to withstand.

Reducing **the pressure by** *increasing* **the area**

Skis have a large area to reduce the pressure on the snow so that they do not sink in too far.

Wall foundations have a large horizontal area. This reduces the pressure underneath so that the walls do not sink further into the ground.

A load-spreading washer ensures that the nut is not pulled into the wood when tightened up.

Typical pressures

20 kPa

2000 kPa

1000 kPa

5 000 000 kPa

Pressure problems

Example 1 The wind pressure on the wall on the right is 100 Pa. If the wall has an area of 6 m², what is the force on it?

To solve this problem, you need to rearrange the pressure equation:

    force = pressure × area
          = 100 Pa × 6 m² = 600 N

So the force on the wall is 600 N.

area: 6 m²
pressure: 100 Pa

Example 2 A concrete block has a mass of 2600 kg. If the block measures 0.5 m by 1.0 m by 2.0 m, what is the maximum pressure it can exert when resting on the ground? ($g = 10$ N/kg)

As g is 10 N/kg, the 2600 kg block has a weight of 26 000 N, so the force on the ground is also 26 000 N.

To exert *maximum* pressure, the block must be resting on the side with the *smallest* area. This is the side measuring 1.0 m × 0.5 m, as shown on the right. Its area = 1.0 m × 0.5 m = 0.5 m². So:

$$\text{pressure} = \frac{\text{force}}{\text{area}} = \frac{26\,000\,\text{N}}{0.5\,\text{m}^2} = 52\,000\,\text{Pa}$$

So the maximum pressure is 52 000 Pa, or 52 kPa.

2.0 m

1.0 m

0.5 m

Q

Assume that $g = 10$ N/kg, and that all forces are acting at right angles to any area mentioned.

1 A force of 200 N acts on an area of 4 m².
  a) What pressure is produced?
  b) What would the pressure be if the same force acted on half the area?

2 What force is produced if:
  a) a pressure of 1000 Pa acts on an area of 0.2 m²?
  b) a pressure of 2 kPa acts on an area of 0.2 m²?

3 Explain why a tractor's big tyres stop it sinking too far into soft soil.

4 A rectangular block of mass 30 kg measures 0.1 m by 0.4 m by 1.5 m.
  a) Calculate the weight of the block.
  b) Draw a diagram to show how the block must rest to exert the *maximum* pressure on the ground. Calculate this pressure.
  c) Draw another diagram showing the position of *minimum* pressure. Calculate this pressure.

3.05 Pressure in liquids

Pressure acts in all directions.

Pressure increases with depth.

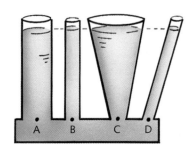

The pressure at points A, B, C, and D is the same.

A liquid is held in its container by its weight. This causes pressure on the container, and pressure on any object in the liquid.

The following properties apply to any stationary liquid in an open container. The experiments on the left demonstrate three of them.

Pressure acts in all directions The liquid pushes on every surface in contact with it, no matter which way the surface is facing. For example, the deep-sea vessel below has to withstand the crushing effect of sea water pushing in on it from all sides, not just downwards.

Pressure increases with depth The deeper into a liquid you go, the greater the weight of liquid above and the higher the pressure. Dams are made thicker at the bottom to withstand the higher pressure there.

Pressure depends on the density of the liquid The more dense the liquid, the higher the pressure at any particular depth.

Pressure doesn't depend on the shape of the container Whatever the shape or width, the pressure at any particular depth is the same.

▶ Deep-sea diving vessels are built to withstand the crushing effect of sea water whose pressure pushes inwards from all directions.

Useful connections

For calculations like those below, you need to know the connections between these:

 volume (in m³)   density (in kg/m³)   mass (in kg)   weight (in N)   g (10 N/kg)

For example, you might know the volume and density of a liquid, but need to find its weight. For this, the equations required are:

$$\text{density} = \frac{\text{mass}}{\text{volume}} \qquad \text{weight} = \text{mass} \times g$$

From these equations, it follows that:

$$\text{mass} = \text{density} \times \text{volume} \qquad \text{weight} = \text{density} \times \text{volume} \times g$$

Pressure and weight essentials

For a force acting at right angles to a surface:

$$\text{pressure} = \frac{\text{force}}{\text{area}}$$

If force is in newtons (N) and area in square metres (m²), then pressure is in pascals (Pa).

Calculating the pressure in a liquid

The container on the right has a base area A. It is filled to a depth h with a liquid of density ρ (Greek letter 'rho'). To calculate the pressure on the base due to the liquid, you first need to know the weight of the liquid on it:

$$\begin{aligned}
\text{volume of liquid} &= \text{base area} \times \text{depth} = Ah \\
\text{mass of liquid} &= \text{density} \times \text{volume} = \rho Ah \\
\text{weight of liquid} &= \text{mass} \times g \qquad = \rho gAh \quad (g = 10\,\text{N/kg})
\end{aligned}$$

So: force on base $= \rho gAh$

This force is acting on an area A.

So: $\text{pressure} = \dfrac{\text{force}}{\text{area}} = \dfrac{\rho gAh}{A} = \rho gh$

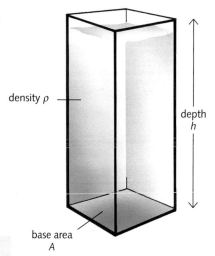

density ρ

depth h

base area A

At a depth h in a liquid of density ρ:

$$\text{pressure} = \rho gh$$

Example If the density of water is 1000 kg/m³, what is the pressure due to the water at the bottom of a swimming pool 2 m deep?

$$\text{pressure} = \rho gh = 1000\,\text{kg/m}^3 \times 10\,\text{N/kg} \times 2\,\text{m} = 20\,000\,\text{Pa}$$

$g = 10$ N/kg; density of water = 1000 kg/m³; density of paraffin = 800 kg/m³

1 In the diagram on the right:
   a) How does the pressure at A compare with the pressure at B?
   b) How does the pressure at B compare with the pressure at D?
   c) How does the pressure at A compare with the pressure at C?
   d) If the water in the system were replaced with paraffin, how would this affect the pressure at B?
2 A rectangular storage tank 4 m long by 3 m wide is filled with paraffin to a depth of 2 m. Calculate:
   a) the volume of paraffin   **b)** the mass of paraffin
   c) the weight of paraffin   **d)** the pressure at the bottom of the tank due to the paraffin
3 In the diagram on the right, calculate the pressure at B due to the water.

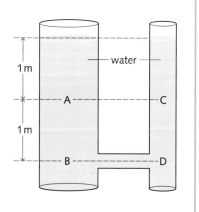

water

1 m

1 m

A

C

B

D

Hydraulic machines

In some machines, the forces are transmitted by liquids under pressure rather than by levers or cogs. Machines like this are called **hydraulic** machines. They make use of these properties of liquids:

● Liquids are virtually incompressible – they cannot be squashed.
● If a trapped liquid is put under pressure, the pressure is transmitted to all parts of the liquid.

Hydraulic brakes

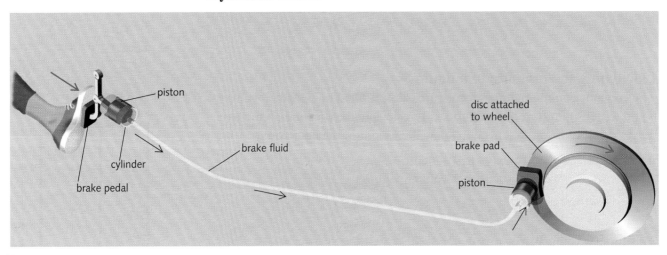

Car brakes work hydraulically. The diagram above shows the principle. When the brake pedal is pressed, a piston forces brake fluid from one cylinder along a connecting pipe to another cylinder. There, the fluid pushes on another piston. This presses a brake pad against a metal disc attached to the rotating wheel of the car. The friction slows the wheel.

In practical braking systems, there are pipes to all four wheels, pads on either side of each disc, and usually 'power assistance' as well.

Hydraulic jack

A load is easier to lift if you use a jack. The diagram at the top of the next page shows a simple hydraulic jack. A downward force on the input piston puts pressure on the oil. The pressure is transmitted by the oil. It produces a larger upward force on the output piston.

Knowing the input force and piston areas, the output force can be calculated:

In the input cylinder:
An input force of 12 N acts on an area of 0.01 m².

So: pressure on oil $= \dfrac{\text{force}}{\text{area}} = \dfrac{12\,\text{N}}{0.01\,\text{m}^2} = 1200\,\text{Pa}$

In the connecting pipe:
The pressure, 1200 Pa, is transmitted by the oil.

In the output cylinder:
The pressure, 1200 Pa, acts on a piston of area 0.1 m².
So: output force = pressure × area = 1200 Pa × 0.1 m² = 120 N

Pressure essentials

For a force acting at right angles to a surface:

$$\text{pressure} = \frac{\text{force}}{\text{area}}$$

If force is in newtons (N) and area in square metres (m²), pressure is in pascals (Pa).

simple hydraulic jack

input force

acts on

small area

causing

high pressure

12 N

oil

input...
piston
cylinder
area: 0.01 m²

high pressure transmitted

output...
piston
cylinder
area: 0.1 m²

object being lifted

120 N

high output force

caused because

large area

has high pressure acting on it

A force multiplier With the jack above, you put in a force of 12 N and get out a force of 120 N. The jack is a **force multiplier**. In this case, it multiplies the input force by a factor 10. But there is a price to be paid for the gain in force: the output piston is raised only $\frac{1}{10}$ of the distance that the input piston is pushed down.

The calculation of output force assumes that the jack is frictionless. In a real jack, there is friction to overcome. This reduces the output force.

Hydraulic jack

For a *frictionless* jack:

$$\frac{\text{output force}}{\text{input force}} = \frac{\text{output piston area}}{\text{input piston area}}$$

In the case of the jack above:

$$\frac{120\,\text{N}}{12\,\text{N}} = \frac{0.1\,\text{m}^2}{0.01\,\text{m}^2}$$

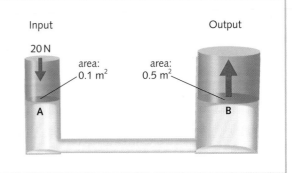

◀ The shovel and arm on this digger are operated hydraulically, and the caterpillar tracks are moved by 'hydraulic motors'. The high-pressure oil comes from a pump driven by a diesel engine.

Q

1 The diagram on the right shows a simple hydraulic jack. Assuming that the jack is frictionless:
   a) What is the pressure at A?
   b) What is the pressure at B?
   c) What is the output force?
   d) Explain why the jack can be called a *force multiplier*.
2 In the jack on the right, what would be the effect of
   a) increasing the area of the output piston?
   b) decreasing the area of the input piston?

Input

20 N

area: 0.1 m²

A

Output

area: 0.5 m²

B

Related topics: pressure **3.04**; pressure in liquids **3.05**; machines **4.10 – 4.11**

3.07 Pressure from the air

▲ **Demonstrating atmospheric pressure** When the air is removed from the can, there is nothing to resist the outside pressure, and the can is crushed.

The atmosphere is a deep ocean of air which surrounds the Earth. In some ways, it is like a liquid:

● Its pressure acts in all directions.
● Its pressure becomes less as you rise up through it (because there is less and less weight above).

Unlike a liquid, air can be compressed (squashed). This makes the atmosphere denser at lower levels. The atmosphere stretches hundreds of kilometres into space, yet the bulk of the air lies within about 10 kilometres of the Earth's surface.

Atmospheric pressure

At sea level, atmospheric pressure is about 100 kPa (100 000 newtons per square metre) – equivalent to the weight of ten cars pressing on every square metre. But you aren't crushed by this huge pressure because it is matched by the pressure in your lungs and blood system.

Drinking through a straw You expand your lungs to reduce the air pressure inside the straw. As a result atmospheric pressure pushes the liquid up the straw.

Vacuum cleaner A fan lowers the air pressure just beyond the bag. The atmosphere rushes in, carrying dust and dirt with it. The bag acts as a filter, stopping the dust and dirt, but not the air.

++

The mercury barometer

Instruments that measure atmospheric pressure are called **barometers**. The barometer on the right contains the liquid metal mercury. Atmospheric pressure has pushed mercury up the tube because the space at the top of the tube has no air in it. It is a **vacuum**. At sea level, atmospheric pressure will support a column of mercury 760 mm high, on average. For convenience, scientists sometimes describe this as a pressure of 760 'millimetres of mercury'. However, it is easily converted into pascals and other units, as you can see below.

The actual value of atmospheric pressure varies slightly depending on the weather. Rain clouds form in large areas of lower pressure, so a fall in the barometer reading may mean that rain is on the way. Atmospheric pressure also decreases with height above sea level. This idea is used in the **altimeter**, an instrument fitted in aircraft to measure altitude.

Standard atmospheric pressure

The pressure that will support a column of mercury 760.0 mm high is known as **standard atmospheric pressure**, or 1 **atmosphere** (1 atm). Its value in pascals can be found by calculating the pressure due to such a column.

At a depth h in a liquid of density ρ, the pressure = $\rho g h$, where g is 9.807 N/kg (or 10 N/kg if less accuracy is needed). As the density of mercury is 13 590 kg/m³, and the height of the column is 0.760 0 m:

$$1\ \text{atm} = \rho g h = 13\,590\ \text{kg/m}^3 \times 9.807\ \text{N/kg} \times 0.760\,0\ \text{m} = 101\,300\ \text{Pa}$$

In calculators, for simplicity, you can assume that 1 atm = 100 000 Pa. In weather forecasting, the **millibar** (**mb**) is often used as a pressure unit. 1 mb = 100 Pa, so standard atmospheric pressure is approximately 1000 millibars.

Barometer

- vacuum
- mercury
- glass tube

Manometer

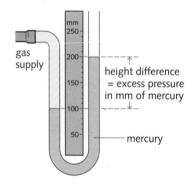

gas supply

height difference
= excess pressure
in mm of mercury

mercury

The manometer

A **manometer** measures pressure *difference*. The one in the diagram on the right is filled with mercury. The height difference shows the *extra* pressure that the gas supply has in addition to atmospheric pressure. This extra pressure is called the **excess pressure**. To find the actual pressure of the gas supply, you add atmospheric pressure to this excess pressure.

---

1 Write down *two* ways in which the pressure in the atmosphere is like the pressure in a liquid.

2 Explain why, when you 'suck' on a straw, the liquid travels up it.

3 If a mercury barometer were carried up a mountain, how would you expect the height of the mercury column to change?

4 Look at the diagram of the manometer on this page. If atmospheric pressure is 760 mm of mercury:
a) What is the excess pressure of the gas supply (in mm of mercury)?
b) What is the actual pressure of the gas supply (in mm of mercury)?

c) What is the actual pressure of the gas supply (in Pa)?

5 If, on a particular day, atmospheric pressure is 730 mm of mercury, what is this **a)** in pascals **b)** in atmospheres **c)** in millibars?

6 The density of mercury is 13 590 kg/m³, the density of water is 1000 kg/m³, and g is 9.81 N/kg.
a) What is the pressure (in Pa) at the bottom of a column of water 1 metre long?
b) If a barometer is made using water instead of mercury, and a very long tube, how high is the water column when atmospheric pressure is 1 atm (760 mm of mercury)?

Related topics: density **1.03**; pressure **3.04**; calculating the pressure in a liquid **3.05**

Floating and sinking

A **displacement can** can be used to find out how much liquid an object displaces. The object is carefully lowered into the full can, and the displaced liquid collected in a beaker.

When an object is in water, the water pressure pushes in on all sides, as shown on the left. However, the pressure underneath is greater than the pressure above because of the greater depth. The result is an upward force called an **upthrust**. To feel an upthrust for yourself, try pushing an empty plastic bottle down into some water.

Archimedes' principle

The block below weighs 25 N. But when immersed in water, it seems to weigh only 15 N, because of a 10 N upthrust from the water.

When immersed, the block takes up space once occupied by the water. It **displaces** water. Experiments show that the displaced water weighs 10 N, exactly the same as the upthrust. This principle works for any fluid (liquid or gas), not just water. It is called **Archimedes' principle**:

> When an object is immersed (totally or partially) in a fluid, the upthrust on it is equal to the weight of fluid displaced.

Force and weight essentials

Force is measured in newtons (N).

Weight is a force.

On Earth, the weight of an object is 10 N for each kilogram of mass.

The law of flotation

An object will float if the upthrust on it is enough to support its weight.

The model boat below weighs 10 N. As the forces on it are balanced, the upthrust is also 10 N. But the upthrust is equal to the weight of water displaced. So the weight of water displaced is 10 N, the same as the weight of the boat. This is an example of the **law of flotation**:

> If an object is floating freely, the weight of fluid it displaces is equal to its own weight.

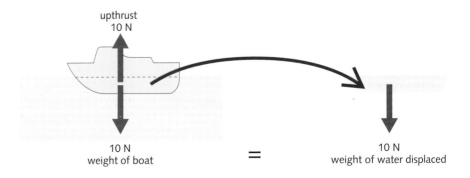

+++

With extra weight in it, a boat floats lower in the water. It displaces more water so that there is a greater upthrust to support the extra weight. But if too much extra weight is added, the boat will sink.

Floating and density

water

tar

density of tar = density of water

Tar floats in water, but only just. The law of flotation tells you that it has the same weight (and therefore the same mass) as the water it displaces. Being completely immersed, it also has the same volume. So its density must be the same (because density = mass/volume). If its density were any greater, it would sink:

> If a material floats, its density must be less than (or equal to) that of the fluid supporting it.

Wood floats in water because it has a lower density than water. A steel boat also floats in water. Solid steel is more dense than water, but a boat is hollow and full of air, so its *average* density is less than that of water.

Floating in air

In large volumes, air is heavy. The hot-air balloon on the right displaces more than 3 tonnes of air. It will rise upwards if its total weight (including the air inside) is less than the weight of air it displaces.

Before take-off, air in the balloon is heated by gas burners to over 100 °C. This makes the air expand so that over half a tonne is pushed out through the hole in the bottom. With less air to carry, the upthrust can support the fabric, burners, basket, and crew. So the balloon starts to rise.

A balloon will rise upwards if its total weight is less than the weight of the air it displaces.

Q

1 A small boat weighs 1000 N. It is floating in water.
   a) What is the upthrust on the boat?
   b) What weight of water is displaced by the boat?
   c) If extra weight is put into the boat, why will the boat float lower in the water?

2 Which of polythene, steel, and pine will float in
   a) water b) paraffin? Explain your answers.

   Densities in kg/m³: granite 2700; paraffin 800; polythene 950; water 1000; pine 500

3 Explain why a 1 tonne boat made of steel will float in water, but a 1 tonne block of steel will sink.

4 A hot-air balloon displaces air weighing 20 000 N. If the balloon, basket, and burners together weigh 2000 N, and the balloon contains hot air weighing 15 000 N, what is the maximum load (in N) it can lift?

5 A block of granite has a volume of 0.2 m³. It is resting on a hard, flat surface at the bottom of a lake. Using data from question 2, and g = 10 N/kg:
   a) What is the weight of the block (in N)?
   b) What weight of water is displaced by the block?
   c) What is the upthrust on the block?
   d) What is the minimum upward force needed to lift the block clear of the bottom?

Related topics: density **1.03**; balanced forces **2.07**; mass, weight and g **2.09**; pressure in liquids **3.05**

++

3.09 Fluid flow

Gases and liquids are called **fluids**. 'Fluid' means something that can flow.

Viscosity

Water flows easily, but treacle does not. Scientists say that treacle is more **viscous** than water: it has a higher **viscosity**.

Viscosity is caused by friction. When treacle runs off a spoon, the inner layer of treacle sticks to the spoon, so the other layers have to slide over each other. Friction between the layers stops them sliding easily, so the treacle flows slowly.

Viscosity also has another effect. A fluid with a high viscosity resists the motion of objects through it. For example, if you drop a heavy steel ball into treacle, it sinks only slowly through the treacle.

Lubricants

In machinery, too much friction between the moving parts can cause overheating and rapid wear. To reduce friction, **lubricants** such as oil and grease are used. The lubricant is trapped between the moving surfaces so that they can slide over each other without actually touching.

For minimum friction, a lubricant should have a low viscosity. But it must not be *too* low. If an oil flows away too easily, the moving surfaces may come into contact and rub. Grease has a higher viscosity than oil. But because of this, it does not flow away or need seals to trap it.

The viscosity of most liquids decreases with temperature. For example, hot oil flows more easily than cold oil. Engineers have to allow for this when designing engines and choosing lubricants for them.

oil or grease

Flow rate through a pipe

Below, a hosepipe is connected to a tap. The pressure difference between the ends of the pipe causes a flow of water through it.

high pressure

flow

lower pressure

The volume of water flowing per second is called the **flow rate**. It is the same throughout the pipe. The following changes would *reduce* the flow rate:
● a lower pressure difference between the ends of the hosepipe
● a longer pipe
● a narrower pipe
● a fluid of higher viscosity in the pipe.

If the hosepipe narrows at any point, the *speed* of flow rises, though the flow rate (volume per second) is unchanged.

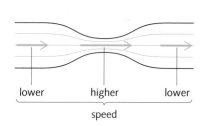

lower   higher   lower

speed

+++

The Bernoulli effect

If a fluid is flowing, and its speed increases, its pressure falls. This is known as the **Bernoulli effect**. Here are some examples:

An aircraft's wing is shaped so that the air flow speeds up across the top. This reduces the pressure above the wing, causing an upward force which contributes to the total **lift**. (Most of the lift is due to the slight upward angle of the wing.)

In a **Venturi tube**, the fluid speeds up where the tube narrows, so its pressure drops. The faster the flow, the greater the pressure drop. In aircraft, this principle is used to measure air speed. It is also used in meters that measure fluid flow rate.

Streamline and turbulent flow

Air is flowing slowly past this ball. Smooth flow like this is called **streamline** flow.

Now the airflow is faster. The flow has become **turbulent**. In most practical situations, the flow is turbulent – cars moving through the air, for example. With turbulent flow, air resistance rises sharply as the speed rises.

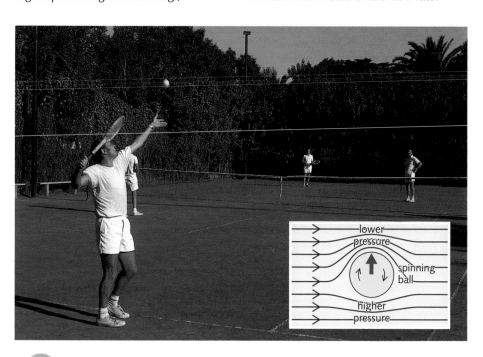

◀ In some sports, spin is used to make the ball swing. As a spinning ball moves through the air, its surface drags air round with it. So the air flow is speeded up on one side of the ball but slowed down on the other. This causes a pressure difference and, therefore, a sideways force on the ball.

Q

1 A pump (at fixed pressure) pushes water through a long pipe and out of the far end. What is the effect on the flow rate of using **a)** a shorter pipe **b)** a wider pipe?
2 What is the difference between *streamline* flow and *turbulent* flow?
3 In the paint spray on the right, the flow of air makes paint flow up the tube. As the paint meets the air flow, it is blown away in droplets.
   a) As the air flows from A to B, what happens to its speed? Why?
   b) As the air flows from A to B, what happens to its pressure?
   c) How does the air pressure at B compare with that at C?
   d) Why does the paint flow up the tube?

1 The diagram shows a pair of nutcrackers. Forces **F** are applied to the handles of the nutcrackers.

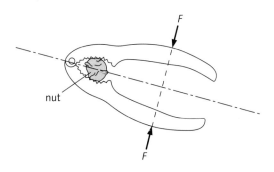

nut

F

F

a) The forces on the nut are bigger than **F**. Explain this. [1]

b) The nut does not crack. State **two** changes that could be made to crack the nut. [2]

MEG

2 The diagram below shows a uniform metre rule, weight *W*, pivoted at the 75 cm mark and balanced by a force of 2 N acting at the 95 cm mark.

0 cm   50 cm   75 cm   95 cm

W   2 N

a) Calculate the moment of the 2 N force about the pivot. [2]

b) Use the principle of moments to calculate the value of *W* in N. [2]

UCLES (O)

3 The diagram below shows a balance in use. The object on the right is balanced by the mass on the left. (Assume that $g = 10\,\text{N/kg}$)

16 cm   16 cm

pivot

200 g

object

a) Calculate the **weight** of the object. [2]

b) Calculate the moment of the weight of the object about the pivot. [2]

c) (i) What would the object weigh on the Moon, where $g = 1.7\,\text{N/kg}$?

  (ii) Explain why the object would still be balanced by the same mass if the balance was on the Moon. [3]

UCLES (O)

4 The figure shows an empty wheelbarrow which weighs 80 N.

The operator pulls upwards on the handles with a force of 20 N to keep the handles horizontal.

The point marked M is the centre of mass of the wheelbarrow.

upwards pull
20 N

1.5 m

M   A

level ground

a) Copy the figure and draw arrows to show the other two vertical forces that act on the wheelbarrow. [2]

b) Determine

  (i) the moment of the 20 N force about the centre of the wheel A,

  (ii) the distance between points A and M. [3]

UCLES (O)

5 The following results were obtained when a spring was stretched.

load/N	1.0	3.0	4.5	6.0	7.5
length of spring/cm	12.0	15.5	19.0	22.0	25.0

a) Use the results to plot a graph of length of spring against load. [1]

b) Use the graph to find the

  (i) unloaded length of the spring, [1]
  (ii) extension produced by a 7.0 N load, [1]
  (iii) load required to increase the length of the spring by 5.0 cm. [1]

WJEC

6 a) A glass window pane covers an area of 0.6 m². The force exerted by air pressure on the outside of the glass window pane is 60 000 N. Calculate the pressure of the air. Write down the formula that you use and show your working. [3]

b) Explain why the window does not break under this force. [1]

WJEC

7 A fitness enthusiast is trying to strengthen his calf muscles.

He uses the exercise machine below. His heels apply a force to the padded bar. This lifts the heavy weights.

a) The centre of mass of the weights is at **C**.
Copy the diagram and draw an arrow to show **where** and in which **direction** the force of gravity acts on the weights. Label this arrow **W**. [2]
b) The narrow steel bar is padded. Why does this feel more comfortable when lifting the weights? [2]
c) The heels press against the pad with a force **F** and cause a turning effect about the pivot. Calculate the value of **F** when the weights are in the position shown in the diagram. Show your working. [3]
d) Why does it become harder to lift the weights when they move to the right? [2]

MEG

8 Three concrete blocks can be stacked in two different ways as shown below.

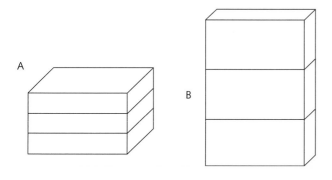

a)

less than	the same as	more than

Copy and complete the paragraph below using a phrase from the boxes above. Each phrase may be used once, more than once or not at all.
The force of stack **A** on the ground is _____ the force of stack **B**.

The pressure on the ground from stack **B** is _____ the pressure from stack **A**, because the area in contact with the ground for **B** is _____ for **A** [3]
b) Write down, **in words**, the equation connecting pressure, force and area. [1]
c) If the weight of stack **A** is 500 N and the area in contact with the ground is 200 cm², calculate the pressure on the ground in N/cm². [2]

WJEC

9 The figure shows a tyre used on a large earth-moving vehicle.

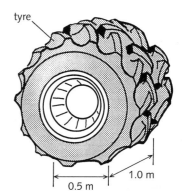

a) When the vehicle is loaded, the area of **each** tyre in contact with the ground is a rectangle of sides 1.0 m and 0.5 m.
   (i) Calculate the area in m² of contact of **one** tyre with the ground.
   (ii) The vehicle has four of these tyres. Calculate the total area in m² of contact with the ground. [4]
b) When the vehicle is loaded, it weighs 100 000 N. Calculate the pressure in N/m² exerted on the ground by the tyres. [3]

NEAB

10

upthrust

sea level — tanker

weight

a) A loaded tanker weighing 1 200 000 N is shown floating on the sea. What is the size of the upthrust on the loaded tanker? [1]
b) 200 000 N of oil is pumped out at an oil terminal.
   (i) Calculate the size of the upthrust on the tanker after unloading the oil. [1]
   (ii) Explain what happens to the tanker when the oil is unloaded. [2]

WJEC

Photocopy the list of topics below and tick the boxes of the ones that are included in your examination syllabus. (Your teacher should be able to tell you which they are.) Use your list when you revise. The spread number in brackets tells you where to find more information.

❏ 1 The factors affecting the moment of a force. (3.01)

❏ 2 Calculating the moment of a force. (3.01)

❏ 3 The principle of moments. (3.01)

❏ 4 The conditions applying when an object is in a state of equilibrium. (3.01)

❏ 5 The meaning of centre of gravity. (3.02)

❏ 6 Finding the centre of gravity of an object by experiment. (3.02)

❏ 7 Allowing for weight and the position of the centre of gravity in calculations using the principle of moments. (3.02)

❏ 8 The different types of equilibrium. (3.02)

❏ 9 The conditions necessary for stability. (3.02)

❏ 10 The difference between elastic and plastic behaviour. (3.03)

❏ 11 The meaning of elastic limit. (3.03)

❏ 12 How the extension changes with load when a spring is stretched. (3.03)

❏ 13 Hooke's law, and how it applies to metal springs and wires. (3.03)

❏ 14 How compression, bending, and twisting are produced. (3.03)

❏ 15 The definition of pressure. (3.04)

❏ 16 The SI unit of pressure: the pascal. (3.04)

❏ 17 Using the equation linking pressure, force, and area. (3.04)

❏ 18 The factors affecting the pressure in a liquid. (3.05)

❏ 19 Calculating the pressure at a particular depth in a liquid. (3.05)

❏ 20 How hydraulic machines work. (3.06)

❏ 21 Carrying out calculations showing that a hydraulic jack is force multiplier. (3.06)

❏ 22 Atmospheric pressure and the factors affecting it. (3.07)

❏ 23 The evidence that atmospheric pressure has a high value. (3.07)

❏ 24 Using atmospheric pressure in a drinking straw and in a vacuum cleaner. (3.07)

❏ 25 The mercury barometer. (3.07)

❏ 26 Standard atmospheric pressure. (3.07)

❏ 27 Using a manometer. (3.07)

❏ 28 Why a liquid (or gas) produces an upthrust on any object in it. (3.08)

❏ 29 Archimedes' principle. (3.08)

❏ 30 The law of flotation. (3.08)

❏ 31 The link between density, floating, and sinking. (3.08)

❏ 32 The conditions necessary for a hot-air balloon to float in the surrounding cooler air. (3.08)

❏ 33 The meaning of viscosity. (3.09)

❏ 34 The properties of lubricants. (3.09)

❏ 35 The factors affecting the rate of flow of a liquid through a pipe. (3.09)

❏ 36 The Bernoulli effect and its applications. (3.09)

❏ 37 The difference between streamline and turbulent flow. (3.09)

4

Forces and Energy

○ WORK ○ ENERGY ○ CONSERVATION OF ENERGY ○ POTENTIAL AND KINETIC ENERGY

○ FRICTION ○ EFFICIENCY ○ POWER ○ POWER STATIONS ○ ENERGY RESOURCES

○ RENEWABLE AND NON-RENEWABLE ENERGY ○ ENERGY FROM THE SUN ○ MACHINES

The Niagara falls, on the USA-Canada border. The photograph shows the highest section of the falls, where the water tumbles over 30 metres to the river below. Nearly three million litres of water flow over the falls every second. Most of the energy is wasted, but some is harnessed by a hydroelectric power station which generates electricity for the surrounding area.

Work and energy

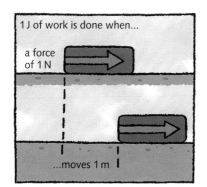

1 J of work is done when...

a force of 1 N

...moves 1 m

Work

In everyday language, work might be writing an essay or digging the garden. But to scientists and engineers, work has a precise meaning: work is done whenever a force makes something move. The greater the force and the greater the distance moved, the more work is done.

The SI unit of work is the **joule** (**J**):

> 1 joule of work is done when a force of 1 newton (N) moves an object 1 metre in the direction of the force.

Work is calculated using this equation:

> work done = force × distance moved in the direction of the force

For example, if a 4 N force moves an object 3 m, the work done is 12 J.

Energy

Things have energy if they can be used to do work. A compressed spring has energy, so does a tankful of petrol. Like work, energy is measured in joules (J).

Although people talk about energy being stored or given out, energy isn't a 'thing'. If, say, a compressed spring stores 100 joules of energy, this is just a measurement of how much work can be done by the spring.

Energy can take different forms. These are described on the opposite page. To understand them, you need to know the following:

Atoms vibrating in a solid. The atoms have energy because of their motion.

- Moving objects have energy. For example, a moving ball can do work by knocking something over.
- Materials are made up of atoms or molecules (groups of atoms). These are continuously on the move. For example, in a solid such as iron, the atoms are vibrating. If the solid is heated and its temperature rises, the atoms move faster. So a material has more energy when it is hot than when it is cold.

▶ A fully flexed bow stores about 300 joules of energy.

Forms of energy

When describing different forms of energy, the following names are sometimes used:

Kinetic energy This is energy due to motion. All moving objects have kinetic energy.

Potential energy This is energy which an object has because of its position, shape, or state. There are several different types of potential energy. Here are some of the terms used to describe them:

Gravitational potential energy A stone held up in the air can do work when dropped because gravity will pull it downwards. The stone has gravitational potential energy.

Elastic potential energy A stretched rubber band can do work when released, so can a compressed spring. Both have elastic potential energy.

Chemical potential energy When a fuel burns, its energy is released by chemical reactions. The energy stored in the fuel is called chemical potential energy, or chemical energy for short. Batteries also store it. So do foods. Without it, your muscles could not move.

Electrical potential energy In circuits, the current is a flow of tiny charged particles called electrons. These come from atoms. Electrons can transfer energy from, for example, a battery to a light bulb. They have electrical potential energy, or electrical energy for short.

Nuclear potential energy An atom has a nucleus at its centre. This is made up of particles, held there by strong forces. In some atoms, the particles become rearranged, or the nucleus splits, and energy is released. This is called nuclear potential energy, or nuclear energy for short.

The following terms are sometimes used when describing energy which is being transferred from one place to another, or from one object to another:

Thermal energy When hot objects cool down, their atoms and molecules slow down and lose energy. This is known as thermal energy, or heat. Engines use thermal energy to do work. For example, in a car engine, burning fuel produces hot gases which expand, push on pistons, and make them move. The motion is used to turn the wheels of a car.

Radiated energy The Sun radiates light. Loudspeakers radiate sound. Light and sound both travel in the form of waves. These carry energy.

Typical energy values

kinetic energy of a
football when kicked .... 50 J

potential energy
of a skier at the top
of a ski jump .... 15 000 J

chemical energy in
a chocolate biscuit .... 300 000 J

kinetic energy of
a car travelling at
70 mph (30 m/s) .... 500 000 J

thermal energy
needed to boil a
kettleful of water .... 700 000 J

electrical energy
supplied by a fully
charged car battery ...... 2 000 000 J

chemical energy
in all the food you
eat in one day .... 11 000 000 J

chemical energy in
one litre of petrol .... 35 000 000 J

1 kilojoule (kJ)	= 1000 J
	(10^3 J)
1 megajoule (MJ)	= 1 000 000 J
	(10^6 J)

1 How much work is done if a force of 12 N moves an object a distance of 5 m?
2 If you use a 40 N force to lift a bag, and do 20 J of work, how far do you lift it?
3 Express the following amounts of energy in joules:
   a) 10 kJ   **b)** 35 MJ   **c)** 0.5 MJ   **d)** 0.2 kJ
4 Using information in the chart of energy values on this page, estimate how many fully charged car batteries are needed to store the same amount of energy as one litre of petrol.
5 **a)** Write down three forms of energy which the apple on the right has.
   b) Using the energy chart on this page as a guide, decide in which form you think the apple has most energy.

Related topics: scientific notation **1.01**; SI units **1.02**; force **2.07**; particles **5.01**; electrons in circuits **8.03**

73

Energy transformation

4.02

Conservation of energy

To do work, you have to spend energy. But, like money, energy doesn't vanish when you spend it. It goes somewhere else! People talk about 'using energy', but energy is never used up. It just changes into different forms, as in the example below.

A stone is thrown upwards ...   ... and falls to the ground

Units

Energy is measured in joules (J).

Work is also measured in joules.

When energy changes from one form to another, scientists say that energy is **transformed**. The diagram above shows a sequence of energy transformations. The last one is from kinetic energy into thermal energy (heat). When the stone hits the ground, it makes the atoms and molecules in the stone and the ground move faster, so the materials warm up a little.

During each transformation, the *total amount* of energy stays the same. This is an example of the **law of conservation of energy**:

Energy cannot be made or destroyed, but it can change from one form to another.

Transform or transfer?

When energy changes form, some scientists describe this as an energy 'transfer'. However, in this book, 'transfer' will only be used if energy moves from one place to another – for example, radiant energy travelling from the Sun to the Earth. A change in form will be a 'transformation'.

Wasting energy

The above diagram shows the energy transformations as a simple chain. In reality, energy is lost from the system at different stages. For example, muscles convert less than $1/5$th of the stored energy in food into kinetic energy. The rest is wasted as thermal energy – which is why exercise makes you sweat. And when objects move through the air, some of their kinetic energy is changed into thermal energy because of friction (air resistance). Even sound is eventually 'absorbed', which leaves the absorbing materials a little warmer than before.

The diagram at the top of the next page shows how all of the original energy of the thrower eventually ends up as thermal energy – although most of it is far too spread out to detect. Despite the apparent loss of energy from the system, the law of conservation of energy still applies. The *total amount* of energy is unchanged.

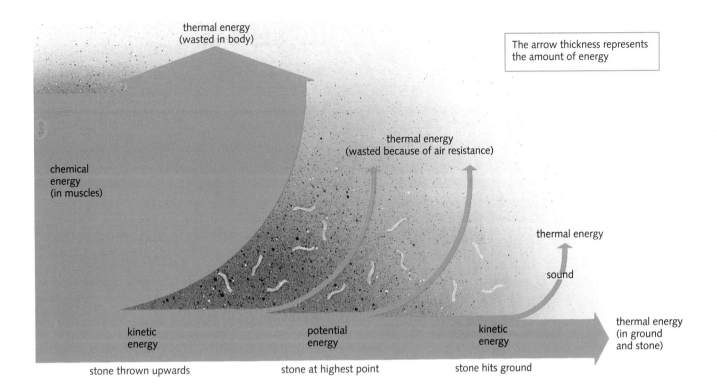

thermal energy
(wasted in body)

The arrow thickness represents
the amount of energy

thermal energy
(wasted because of air resistance)

chemical
energy
(in muscles)

thermal energy

sound

kinetic
energy

potential
energy

kinetic
energy

thermal energy
(in ground
and stone)

stone thrown upwards   stone at highest point   stone hits ground

Work done and energy transformed

Whenever work is done, energy is transformed. In the diagram on the right, for example, a falling brick loses 20 J of potential energy. Assuming no air resistance, this is changed into 20 J of kinetic energy. So 20 J of work is done in accelerating the brick. If the brick hits the ground and comes to rest, 20 J of kinetic energy is changed into thermal energy. Again 20 J of work is done as the brick flattens the ground beneath it.

In all cases:

20 J potential
energy

20 J kinetic
energy

20 J thermal
energy

work done = energy transformed

20 J
energy
in one form

20 J
work
done

20 J
energy in
another form

1 50 J of work must be done to lift a vase from the ground up on to a shelf.
   a) How much potential energy does the vase have when it is on the shelf?
   b) If the vase falls from the shelf, how much kinetic energy does it have just
   before it hits the ground? (Assume that air resistance is negligible.)
   c) What happens to this energy after the vase has hit the ground?
2 What is the law of conservation of energy?
3 On the right, you can see someone's idea for an electric fan that costs nothing to
   run. The electric motor which turns the fan also turns a generator. This produces
   electricity for the motor, so no battery or mains supply is needed! Explain why
   this idea will not work.

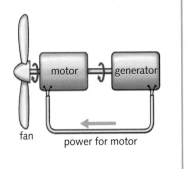

motor   generator

fan   power for motor

Calculating PE and KE

The ball below has potential energy because of the Earth's gravitational pull on it and its position above the ground. This is called gravitational potential energy (PE). If the ball falls, it gains kinetic energy (KE). Both PE and KE can be calculated.

Calculating PE

The gravitational potential energy of the ball on the left is equal to the work which would be done if the ball were to fall to the ground. Assuming no air resistance, it is also equal to the work done in lifting the ball a distance h up from the ground in the first place:

downward force on ball = weight of ball = mg

So: upward force needed to lift ball = mg

So: work done in lifting ball = force × distance moved

$$= mgh$$

For an object of mass m at a vertical height h above the ground:

> gravitational potential energy = mgh

For example, if a 2 kg mass is 3 m above the ground, and g is 10 N/kg:
gravitational PE = 2 kg × 3 m × 10 N/kg = 60 J

mass m

weight mg

h

Calculating KE

speed zero

speed v

mass m

The kinetic energy of the ball above is equal to the work which the ball could do by losing all of its speed. Assuming no air resistance, it is also equal to the work done on the ball in increasing its speed from zero to v in the first place:

$$
\begin{aligned}
\text{work done} &= \text{force} && \times \text{distance moved} \\
&= \text{mass} \times \text{acceleration} && \times \text{distance moved} \\
&= \text{mass} \times \frac{\text{gain in speed}}{\text{time taken}} && \times \text{average speed} \times \text{time taken} \\
&= \text{mass} \times \text{gain in speed} && \times \text{average speed} \\
&= m \quad\times\quad v && \times \quad \tfrac{1}{2}v \\
&= \tfrac{1}{2}mv^2
\end{aligned}
$$

For an object of mass m and speed v:

> kinetic energy = $\tfrac{1}{2}mv^2$

For example, if a 2 kg mass has a speed of 3 m/s:
kinetic energy = $\tfrac{1}{2} \times 2\,\text{kg} \times (3\,\text{m/s})^2 = \tfrac{1}{2} \times 2 \times 3^2\,\text{J} = 9\,\text{J}$

Units

Mass is measured in kilograms (kg).

Force is measured in newtons (N).
Weight is a force.

Work is measured in joules (J).
Energy is measured in joules (J).

Useful equations

$$\text{average speed} = \frac{\text{distance moved}}{\text{time taken}}$$

$$\text{acceleration} = \frac{\text{gain in speed}}{\text{time taken}}$$

force = mass x acceleration

weight = mass x g (g = 10 N/kg)

work done = force x distance moved

work done = energy transformed

Scalar energy

Energy is a **scalar** quantity: it has magnitude (size) but no direction. So you do not have to allow for direction when doing energy calculations.

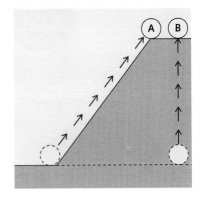

On the right, objects A and B have the same mass and are at the same height above the ground. B was lifted vertically but A was moved up a smooth slope. Although A had to be moved further, less force was needed to move it, and the work done was the same as for B. As a result, both objects have the same PE. The PE (*mgh*) depends on the vertical gain in height *h* and not on the particular path taken to gain that height.

KE and PE problems

Example If the stone on the right is dropped, what is its kinetic energy when it has fallen half-way to the ground? (*g* = 10 N/kg)

In problems like this, you don't necessarily have to use KE = $\frac{1}{2}mv^2$. When the stone falls, its *gain in KE* is equal to its *loss in PE*, so you can calculate that instead:

$$\text{height lost by stone} = 2\,\text{m}$$

So: gravitational PE lost by stone = mgh = 4 kg × 10 N/kg × 2 m = 80 J

So: KE gained by stone = 80 J

As the stone started with no KE, this is the stone's KE half-way down.

Example The stone on the right slides down a smooth slope. What is its speed when it reaches the bottom? (*g* = 10 N/kg)

This problem can also be solved by considering energy changes. At the top of the slope, the stone has extra gravitational PE. When it reaches the bottom, all of this PE has been transformed into KE.

$$\text{gravitational PE at top of slope} = mgh = 4\,\text{kg} \times 10\,\text{N/kg} \times 5\,\text{m} = 200\,\text{J}$$

So: kinetic energy at bottom of slope = 200 J

So: $\frac{1}{2}mv^2 = 200\,\text{J}$

So: $\frac{1}{2} \times 4\,\text{kg} \times v^2 = 200\,\text{J}$

This gives: $v = 10\,\text{m/s}$

So the stone's speed at the bottom of the slope is 10 m/s.

Note: if the stone fell vertically, it would start with the same gravitational PE and end up with the same KE, so its final speed would still be 10 m/s.

Assume that *g* is 10 N/kg and that air resistance and other frictional forces are negligible.

1 An object has a mass of 6 kg. What is its gravitational potential energy
   a) 4 m above the ground **b)** 6 m above the ground?

2 An object of mass 6 kg has a speed of 5 m/s.
   a) What is its kinetic energy?
   b) What is its kinetic energy if its speed is doubled?

3 A ball of mass 0.5 kg has 100 J of kinetic energy. What is the speed of the ball?

4 A ball has a mass of 0.5 kg. Dropped from a cliff top, the ball hits the sea below at a speed of 10 m/s.
   a) What is the kinetic energy of the ball as it is about to hit the sea?
   b) What was the ball's gravitational potential energy before it was dropped?
   c) From what height was the ball dropped?
   d) A stone of mass 1 kg also hits the sea at 10 m/s. Repeat stages a, b, and c above to find the height from which the stone was dropped.

Friction and braking

Friction is the force that tries to stop materials sliding across each other. There is friction between your hands when you rub them together, and friction between your shoes and the ground when you walk along. Friction prevents machinery from moving freely and heats up its moving parts. To reduce friction, wheels are mounted on ball or roller bearings, with oil or grease to make the moving surfaces slippery.

Friction is not always a nuisance. It gives shoes and tyres grip on the ground, and it is used in most braking systems. On a bicycle, for example, rubber blocks are pressed against the wheels to slow them down.

Static and dynamic friction

When the block below is pulled gently, friction stops it moving. As the force is increased, the friction rises until the block is about to slip. This is the starting or **static** friction. With a greater downward force on the block, the static friction is higher. Once the block starts to slide, the friction drops: moving or **dynamic** friction is less than static friction.

reducing friction
roller bearing + grease

brake pad   tyre gripping road

using friction

static friction is greater than. . .

. . . dynamic friction

Dynamic friction heats materials up. When something is moved against the force of friction, work is done and kinetic energy is transformed into thermal energy. Brakes and other machinery must be designed to get rid of this thermal energy. Otherwise their moving parts may become so hot that they seize up.

▼ Air resistance is a form of dynamic friction. When a car is travelling fast, it is the largest of all the frictional forces opposing motion.

Air resistance wastes energy, so less air resistance means better fuel consumption. Car bodies are specially shaped to smooth the air flow past them and reduce air resistance. A low frontal area also helps.

Stopping distance

In an emergency, the driver of a car may have to react quickly and apply the brakes. The car's **stopping distance** is the sum of the following:

- the **thinking distance**. This is how far the car travels *before* the brakes are applied, while the driver is still reacting.
- the **braking distance**. This is how far the car travels *after* the brakes have been applied.

It takes an average driver about half a second to react and press the brake pedal. This is the driver's **reaction time**. During this time, the car does not slow down, and the more speed it has, the further it travels.

The chart below shows how the stopping distance depends on speed:

> **Speed and kinetic energy**
> For a car to lose all of its speed, it must lose all of its kinetic energy. As kinetic energy is $\frac{1}{2} \times$ mass $\times$ speed^2 ($\frac{1}{2}mv^2$), a car with double the speed has *four* times as much kinetic energy and needs about four times the braking distance. It is the greatly increased kinetic energy that makes high-speed crashes so destructive.

◄ The stopping distances on the left are average figures for a dry road. If the road is wet or icy, or the car is heavily loaded, or the driver's reaction time is slow, the stopping distances will be greater. And if the brakes are applied too strongly, the car will skid.

◄ The front section of a car is a 'crumple zone', designed to collapse steadily in the event of a crash. It absorbs energy during the impact and reduces the deceleration of the passengers. Seat belts stop the passengers hitting inside parts of the car, while air bags cushion the effects of the impact.

1 In a car, friction is essential in some parts, but needs to be reduced in others. Give *two* examples of where friction is **a)** essential **b)** needs to be reduced.

2 A fast car has kinetic energy. What happens to this energy when the brakes are applied?

3 A car is travelling at 30 m/s. Suddenly, the driver sees a danger ahead and decides to do an emergency stop. The driver's reaction time is 0.6 s.
   a) Calculate how far the car travels before the driver starts pressing the brake pedal.

b) Using data from the chart on this page, estimate the car's stopping distance.
c) Re-estimate the stopping distance assuming that the driver is tired and has a reaction time of 1.2 s.
d) Give *two* other factors that could affect the stopping distance.

4 A car has a mass of 1000 kg. What is its kinetic energy at **a)** 10 m/s **b)** 20 m/s?

5 Explain why, if the speed of a car is doubled, its braking distance is much more than doubled.

Related topics: speed **2.01**; brakes **3.06**; fluid friction, lubricants **3.09**; work, KE, thermal energy **4.01 – 4.03**

Efficiency and power

Engines and motors do work by making things move. Petrol and diesel engines spend the energy stored in their fuel. Electric motors spend energy supplied by a battery or generator. The human body is also a form of engine. It spends the energy stored in food.

Efficiency

An engine does useful work with some of the energy supplied to it, but the rest is wasted as thermal energy (heat). The **efficiency** of an engine can be calculated as follows:

$$\text{efficiency} = \frac{\text{useful work done}}{\text{energy input}} \quad or \quad \text{efficiency} = \frac{\text{useful energy output}}{\text{energy input}}$$

For example, if a petrol engine does 25 J of useful work for every 100 J of energy supplied to it, then its efficiency is $\frac{1}{4}$, or 25%. In other words, its useful energy output is $\frac{1}{4}$ of its total energy input.

energy supplied		useful work done	efficiency
100 J	petrol engine	25 J	25%
100 J	diesel engine	35 J	35%
100 J	electric motor	80 J	80%
100 J	human body	15 J	15%

The chart above shows the efficiencies of some typical engines and motors. The low efficiency of fuel-burning engines is not due to poor design. When a fuel burns, it is impossible to transform its thermal energy into kinetic (motion) energy without wasting much of it.

Power

A small engine can do just as much work as a big engine, but it takes longer to do it. The big engine can do work at a faster rate. The rate at which work is done is called the **power**.

The SI unit of power is the **watt** (**W**). A power of 1 watt means that work is being done (or energy transformed) at the rate of 1 joule per second. Power can be calculated as follows:

$$\text{power} = \frac{\text{useful work done}}{\text{time taken}} \quad or \quad \text{power} = \frac{\text{energy transformed}}{\text{time taken}}$$

For example, if an engine does 1000 joules of useful work in 2 seconds, its power output is 500 watts (500 joules per second).

Force, work, and energy essentials

Work is measured in joules (J).

Energy is measured in joules (J).

work done = energy transformed

Force is measured in newtons (N).

work done = force x distance moved

Typical power outputs

washing machine motor	250 W
athlete	400 W
small car engine	35 000 W
large car engine	150 000 W
large jet engine	75 000 000 W

---

1 kilowatt (kW)	= 1000 W

The **horsepower** (**hp**) is a power unit which dates back to the days of the early steam engines:

1 hp = 746 W (about $\frac{3}{4}$ kilowatt)

As energy and power are related, there is another way of calculating the efficiency of an engine:

$$\text{efficiency} = \frac{\text{useful power output}}{\text{power input}}$$

Power problems

Example 1 The car on the right has a steady speed of 30 m/s. If the total frictional force on the car is 700 N, what useful power output does the engine deliver to the driving wheels?

steady speed
30 m/s
700 N
total frictional force (air resistance etc)
forward force due to engine

As the speed is steady, the engine must provide a forward force of 700 N to balance the total frictional force. In 1 second, the 700 N force moves 30 m, so: work done = force × distance = 700 N × 30 m = 21 000 J.

As the engine does 21 000 J of useful work in 1 second, its useful power output must be 21 000 W, or 21 kW.

Problems of this type can also be solved with this equation:

$$\text{useful power output} = \text{force} \times \text{speed}$$

Example 2 The crane on the right lifts a 100 kg block of concrete through a vertical height of 16 m in 20 s. If the power input to the motor is 1000 W, what is the efficiency of the motor?

mass 100 kg
time taken 20 s
16 m
power input 1000 W

On Earth, g is 10 N/kg, so a 100 kg block has a weight of 1000 N. Therefore, a force of 1000 N is needed to lift the block. When the block is lifted:

$$\text{work done} = \text{force} \times \text{distance} = 1000\,\text{N} \times 16\,\text{m} = 16\,000\,\text{J}$$

$$\text{useful power output} = \frac{\text{useful work done}}{\text{time taken}} = \frac{16\,000\,\text{J}}{20\,\text{s}} = 800\,\text{W}$$

$$\text{efficiency} = \frac{\text{useful power output}}{\text{power input}} = \frac{800\,\text{W}}{1000\,\text{W}} = 0.8$$

So the motor has an efficiency of 80%.

$g = 10$ N/kg

1 An engine does 1500 J of useful work with each 5000 J of energy supplied to it.
   a) What is its efficiency?
   b) What happens to the rest of the energy supplied?
2 If an engine does 1500 J of work in 3 seconds, what is its useful power output?
3 A motor has a useful power output of 3 kW.
   a) What is its useful power output in watts?
   b) How much useful work does it do in 1 s?
   c) How much useful work does it do in 20 s?
   d) If the power input to the motor is 4 kW, what is the efficiency?

4 Someone hauls a load weighing 600 N through a vertical height of 10 m in 20 s.
   a) How much useful work does she do?
   b) How much useful work does she do in 1 s?
   c) What is her useful power output?
5 A crane lifts a 600 kg mass through a vertical height of 12 m in 18 s.
   a) What weight (in N) is the crane lifting?
   b) What is the crane's useful power output?
6 With frictional forces acting, a forward force of 2500 N is needed to keep a lorry travelling at a steady speed of 20 m/s along a level road. What useful power is being delivered to the driving wheels?

Energy for electricity (1)

▶ Part of a coal-burning power station. The large, round towers with clouds of steam coming from them are cooling towers.

Industrial societies spend huge amounts of energy. Much of it is supplied by electricity which comes from **generators** in **power stations**.

Thermal power stations

high pressure steam

burning fuel:
    coal
    oil
    natural gas
or
nuclear reactor

water

(condensed steam)

cables

thermal energy source   boiler   turbines   generator

A turbine

In most power stations, the generators are turned by **turbines**, blown round by high pressure steam. To produce the steam, water is heated in a boiler. The thermal energy comes from burning fuel (coal, oil, or natural gas) or from a **nuclear reactor**. Nuclear fuel does not burn. Its energy is released by nuclear reactions which split uranium atoms.

Once steam has passed through the turbines, it is cooled and condensed (turned back into a liquid) so that it can be fed back to the boiler. Some power stations have huge cooling towers, with draughts of air up through them. Others use the cooling effect of nearby sea or river water.

In a **combined cycle gas turbine** power station, natural gas is used as the fuel for a jet engine. The shaft of the engine turns one generator. The hot gases from the jet are used to make steam to drive another generator. Units like this are small and produce less power than larger types. However, they can be brought up to speed, or shut off, very quickly. So they are useful when the demand for electricity varies.

Energy spreading

Thermal power stations waste more energy than they deliver. Most is lost as thermal energy in the cooling water and waste gases. For example, the efficiency of a typical coal-burning power station is only about 35% – in other words, only about 35% of the energy in its fuel is transformed into electrical energy. The diagram below shows what happens to the rest:

$$\text{efficiency} = \frac{\text{useful energy output}}{\text{energy input}}$$

$$= \frac{\text{useful power output}}{\text{power input}}$$

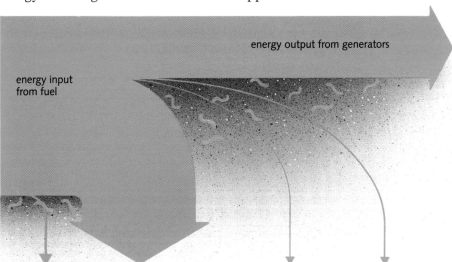

energy output from generators

energy input from fuel

energy loss in boilers | energy loss in turbines | energy loss in generators | energy to run power station

◀ Typical energy-flow chart for a thermal power station. A chart like this is called a **Sankey diagram**. The thickness of each arrow represents the amount of energy.

Engineers try to make power stations as efficient as possible. But once energy is in thermal form, it cannot all be used to drive the generators. Thermal energy is the energy of randomly moving particles (such as atoms and molecules). It has a natural tendency to spread out. As it spreads, it becomes less and less useful. For example, the concentrated energy in a hot flame could be used to make steam for a turbine. But if the same amount of thermal energy were spread through a huge tankful of water, it would only warm the water by a few degrees. This warm water could not be used as an energy source for a turbine.

District heating The unused thermal energy from a power station does not have to be wasted. Using long water pipes, it can heat homes, office, and factories in the local area. This works best if the power station is run at a slightly lower efficiency so that hotter water is produced.

1 Write down *four* different types of fuel used in thermal power stations.
2 In a thermal power station:
a) What is the steam used for?
b) What do the cooling towers do?
3 The table on the right gives data about the power input and losses in two power stations, X and Y.
a) Where is most energy wasted?
b) In what form is this wasted energy lost?
c) What is the electrical power output of each station? (You can assume that the table shows all the power losses in each station.)
e) What is the efficiency of each power station?

	power station	
	X	**Y**
	coal	nuclear
power input from fuel in MW	5600	5600
power losses in MW:		
– in reactors/boilers	600	200
– in turbines	2900	3800
– in generators	40	40
power to run station in MW	60	60
electrical power output in MW	?	?

4.07 Energy for electricity (2)

Reactions for energy

When fuels burn, they combine with oxygen in the air. With most fuels, including fossil fuels, the energy is released by this chemical reaction:

$$\underbrace{\text{fuel} + \text{oxygen}}_{\substack{\text{these are}\\\text{used up}}} \xrightarrow{\text{burning}} \underbrace{\text{carbon dioxide} + \text{water}}_{\substack{\text{these waste gases}\\\text{are made}}} + \textit{thermal energy}$$

There may be other waste gases as well. For example, burning coal produces some sulphur dioxide. Natural gas, which is mainly methane, is the 'cleanest' (least polluting) of the fuels burned in power stations.

In a nuclear power station, the nuclear reactions produce no waste gases like those above. However, they do produce radioactive waste.

Pollution problems

Thermal power stations can cause pollution in a variety of ways:

- Fuel-burning power stations put carbon dioxide gas into the atmosphere. The carbon dioxide traps the Sun's energy and may be adding to **global warming**.
- The sulphur dioxide from coal-burning power stations causes acid rain. This can damage stonework and harm wildlife. One solution is to burn expensive low-sulphur coal. Another is to fit costly flue gas desulphurization (FGD) units to the power stations.
- Transporting fuels can cause pollution. For example, there may be a leak from an oil tanker.
- The radioactive waste from nuclear power stations is highly dangerous. It must be carried away and stored safely in sealed containers for many years – in some cases, thousands of years.
- Nuclear accidents are rare. But when they do occur, radioactive gas and dust can be carried thousands of kilometres by winds.

One effect of acid rain

Power from water and wind

Some generators are turned by the force of moving water or wind. There are three examples on the next page. Power schemes like this have no fuel costs, and give off no polluting gases. However, they can be expensive to build, and need large areas of land. Compared with fossil fuels, moving water and wind are much less concentrated sources of energy:

1 kWh of electrical energy can be supplied using…

…0.5 litres of oil (burning)

…5000 litres of fast-flowing water (20 m/s)

Hydroelectric power scheme River and rain water fill up a lake behind a dam. As water rushes down through the dam, it turns turbines which turn generators.

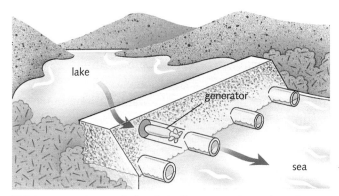

Tidal power scheme A dam is built across a river where it meets the sea. The lake behind the dam fills when the tide comes in and empties when the tide goes out. The flow of water turns the generators.

Wind farm This is a collection of **aerogenerators** – generators driven by giant wind turbines ('windmills').

power station ▶	A	B	C	D	E
	coal	combined	nuclear	wind farm	large tidal
(1 MW = 1 000 000 W)	(non-FGD)	cycle gas			scheme
power output in MW	1800	600	1200	20	6000
efficiency (fuel energy – electrical energy)	35%	45%	25%	–	–
The following are on a scale 0–5					
build cost per MW output	2	1	5	3	4
fuel cost per kWh output	5	4	2	0	0
atmospheric pollution per kWh output	5	3	<1	0	0

1 What is the source of energy in a hydroelectric power station?

2 The table above gives data about five different power stations, A–E.

a) C has an efficiency of 25%. What does this mean?

b) Which power station has the highest efficiency? What are the other advantages of this type of power station?

c) Which power station cost most to build?

d) Which power station has the highest fuel cost per kWh output?

e) Which power station produces most atmospheric pollution per kWh output? What can be done to reduce this problem?

g) Why do two of the power stations have a zero rating for fuel costs and atmospheric pollution?

4.08 Energy resources

How energy is spent in the UK

| industry 35% | domestic 30% | transport 20% | other 15% |

Most of the energy that we use comes from fuels which are burned in power stations, factories, homes, and vehicles.

Nearly all of the world's energy originally came from the Sun. To find out how, you need to study the illustration on the next spread, 4.09.

The energy resources we use on Earth can be **renewable** or **non-renewable**. For example, wood is a renewable fuel. Once used, more can be grown to replace it. Oil, on the other hand is non-renewable. It took millions of years to form in the ground. Once used, it cannot be replaced.

Non-renewable energy resources

Fossil fuels Coal, oil, and natural gas are called fossil fuels because they formed from the remains of plants and tiny sea creatures which lived millions of years ago. They are a very concentrated source of energy. Oil is especially useful because petrol, diesel, and jet fuel can be extracted from it. It is also the raw material from which most plastics are made.

Problems Supplies are limited. When the fuels burn, their waste gases pollute the atmosphere. Probably the most serious concern is the amount of carbon dioxide produced. This may be adding to global warming.

Nuclear fuels Most contain uranium. 1 kg of nuclear fuel stores as much energy as 25 tonnes of coal.

Problems High safety standards are needed. The waste from nuclear fuel is very dangerous and stays radioactive for thousands of years. Nuclear power stations are expensive to build, and expensive to decommission (close down and dismantle at the end of their working life).

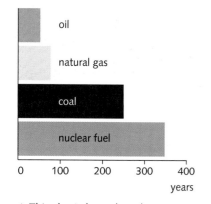

▲ This chart shows how long our *known* reserves of non-renewable fuels might last at present rates of consumption. However, it does not allow for the results of further exploration.

Location of the world's fossil fuel reserves

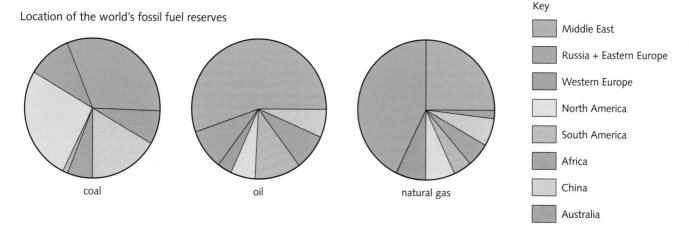

coal   oil   natural gas

Key
- Middle East
- Russia + Eastern Europe
- Western Europe
- North America
- South America
- Africa
- China
- Australia

Renewable energy resources

Hydroelectric energy A river fills a lake behind a dam. Water flowing down from the lake turns generators.

Problems Expensive to build. Few areas of the world are suitable. Flooding land and building a dam causes environmental damage.

Tidal energy Similar to hydroelectric energy, but a lake fills when the tide comes in and empties when it goes out.

Problems As for hydroelectric energy.

Wind energy Generators are driven by wind turbines ('windmills').

Problems Large, remote, windy sites are needed. Winds are variable. The wind turbines are noisy and can spoil the landscape.

Wave energy Generators are driven by the up-and-down motion of waves at sea.

Problems Difficult to build – few devices have been successful.

Geothermal energy Steam comes from hot underground springs. Or water is pumped down to hot rocks deep underground and rises as steam.

Problems Deep drilling is difficult and expensive.

Solar energy Solar panels absorb radiant energy from the Sun and use it to heat water. Solar (photovoltaic) cells produce electricity directly.

Problems Variable amounts of sunshine. Solar cells are expensive.

Biofuels These are fuels made from plant or animal matter, sometimes called **biomass**. They include wood, alcohol made from sugar cane, and methane gas from rotting waste.

Problems Huge areas of land are needed to grow sufficient plants.

In Brazil, many cars use alcohol as a fuel instead of petrol. The alcohol is made from sugar cane, which is grown as a crop.

Saving energy

Burning fossil fuels causes pollution. But the alternatives have their own environmental problems. That is why many people think that we should be less wasteful with energy. Methods could include greater use of public transport and bicycles instead of cars, better insulation in buildings, manufacturing goods that last longer, and recycling more waste materials.

To answer these questions, you may need information from the illustration on the next spread, 4.09.

1 Some energy resources are *non-renewable*. What does this mean? Give *two* examples.
2 Give *two* ways of generating electricity in which no fuel is burned and the energy is renewable.
3 The energy in petrol originally came from the Sun. Explain how it got into the petrol.
4 Describe *two* problems caused by using fossil fuels.

5 Look at the pie-charts on the opposite page.
 a) Which region has the largest oil reserves?
 b) What other fuel does this region have plentiful reserves of?
 c) Which region has the largest natural gas reserves?
 c) The USA needs to import oil but not coal. Can you suggest reasons why?
 d) Which regions of the world do you think consume most fossil fuels?

Related topics: power stations **4.06 – 4.07**; energy from the Sun **4.09**; nuclear reactors **11.06**

4.09 How the world gets its energy

Solar panels

These absorb energy radiated from the Sun and use it to heat water.

Solar cells

These use the energy in sunlight to produce small amounts of electricity.

The Sun

The Sun radiates energy because of nuclear reactions deep inside it. Its output is equivalent to that from 3×10^{26} electric hotplates. Just a tiny fraction of this reaches the Earth.

Energy in food

We get energy from the food we eat. The food may be from plants, or from animals which fed on plants.

Energy in plants

Plants take in energy from sunlight falling on their leaves. They use it to turn water and carbon dioxide from the air into new growth. The process is called photosynthesis. Animals eat plants to get the energy stored in them.

Biofuels from plants

Wood is an important fuel in many countries. When wood is burned, it releases energy that the tree once took in from the Sun. In some countries, sugar cane is grown and fermented to make alcohol. This can be used as a fuel instead of petrol.

Fossil fuels

Fossil fuels (coal, oil, and natural gas) were formed from the remains of plants and tiny sea creatures which lived many millions of years ago. Industrial societies rely on fossil fuels for most of their energy. Many power stations burn fossil fuels.

Biofuels from waste

Rotting animal and plant waste can give off methane gas. This is similar to natural gas and can be used as a fuel. Marshes, rubbish tips, and sewage treatment works are all sources of methane. Some waste can also be used directly as fuel by burning it.

Batteries

Some batteries (e.g. car batteries) have to be given energy by charging them with electricity. Others are manufactured from chemicals which already store energy. But energy is needed to produce the chemicals in the first place.

Fuels from oil

Many fuels can be extracted from oil (crude). These include: petrol, diesel fuel, jet fuel, paraffin, central heating oil, bottled gas.

The tides

The gravitational pull of the Moon (and to a lesser extent, the Sun) creates gentle bulges in the Earth's oceans. As the Earth rotates, different places have high and low tides as they pass in and out of the bulges. The motion of the tides carries energy with it.

Tidal energy

In a tidal energy scheme, an estuary is dammed to form an artificial lake. Incoming tides fill the lake; outgoing tides empty it. The flow of water in and out of the lake turns generators.

Nucleus of the atom

Radioactive materials have atoms with unstable nuclei (centres) which break up and release energy. The material gives off the energy slowly as thermal energy. With some nuclei, energy can be released much more quickly by nuclear reactions.

Nuclear energy

In a reactor, nuclear reactions release energy from the nuclei of uranium atoms. This heats water to make steam for driving generators.

Weather systems

These are driven by energy radiated from the Sun. Heated air rising above the equator causes belts of wind around the Earth. Winds carry water vapour from the oceans and bring rain and snow.

Geothermal energy

Deep underground, the rocks are hotter than they are on the surface. The thermal energy comes from radioactive materials naturally present in the rocks. It can make steam for heating buildings or driving generators.

Wave energy

Waves are caused by the wind (and partly by tides). Waves cause a rapid up-and-down movement on the surface of the sea. This movement can be used to drive generators.

Hydroelectric energy

An artificial lake forms behind a dam. Water rushing down from this lake is used to turn generators. The lake is kept full by river water which once fell as rain or snow.

Wind energy

For centuries, people have been using the power of the wind to move ships, pump water, and grind corn. Today, huge wind turbines are used to turn generators.

Machines (1)
4.10

Machines make jobs easier. They can be complicated like a gearbox, or simple like a lever. The ones described below have no motors. You 'put in' a force, and the machine 'puts out' a force which does the job.

A simple machine – the lever

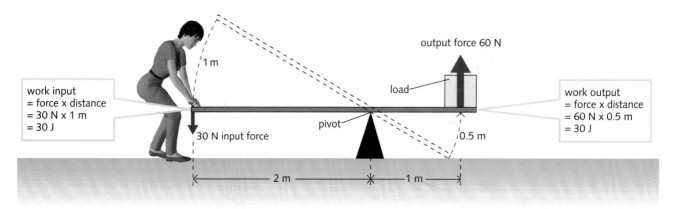

output force 60 N

load

work input
= force x distance
= 30 N x 1 m
= 30 J

work output
= force x distance
= 60 N x 0.5 m
= 30 J

30 N input force

pivot

0.5 m

1 m

2 m   1 m

1 m

Force and work essentials

Force is measured in newtons (N).

Work and energy are measured in joules (J).

work done = energy transformed

work done = force x distance moved

$$\text{efficiency} = \frac{\text{useful work output}}{\text{work input}}$$

The lever above is a simple machine. When you push down at one end, the load is lifted at the other end. In this particular case:

- The output force is twice the input force: in other words, the lever *multiplies* the input force by two. (This result follows from the principle of moments and assumes that the lever is of negligible weight.)
- There is a price to pay for the gain in force: the output force moves only half the distance of the input force.
- The useful work output is the same as the work input. So no energy is wasted, and the efficiency of the lever is 100%.

Most machines waste energy because of friction. So their useful work output is less than the work input, and the efficiency is less than 100%.

Force multipliers

Some machines are **force multipliers**: they put out a greater force out than is put in. The lever above is one example. Here are two others:

input force

output force

input force

output force

Pliers A small force on the handles produces a larger force at the jaws – although the jaws do not move as far as the handles.

Car jack A small downward force on the handle produces a large upward force on the car. But you have to move the handle a long way to raise the car just a little.

+++

Distance multipliers

Some machines are **distance multipliers**: the output force moves further than the input force – although the size of the force is reduced as a result. Here are two examples:

Human arm A small movement of the muscle causes a large movement of the hand. So the arm can make large, rapid movements – although the force is reduced.

Bicycle When you push on a pedal, the bicycle moves further forwards than your foot moves downwards – although the forward force is less than the force from your foot.

Mechanical advantage...

A machine's **mechanical advantage** is calculated like this:

$$\text{mechanical advantage} = \frac{\text{output force}}{\text{input force}}$$

The lever on the opposite page has a mechanical advantage of 2 because the output force is twice the input force.

The mechanical advantage depends partly on the design of the machine, and partly on how much the output force is reduced by frictional forces.

...and velocity ratio

A machine's **velocity ratio** is calculated like this:

$$\text{velocity ratio} = \frac{\text{distance moved by input force}}{\text{distance moved by output force}}$$

The lever on the opposite page has a velocity ratio of 2 because the input force moves twice as far as the output force.

The velocity ratio depends only on the design of the machine. With the lever opposite, for example, one side is twice as long as the other, and it is this which sets the velocity ratio at 2.

For the lever on the opposite page, the mechanical advantage and velocity ratio are equal. This is true for any machine with an efficiency of 100%. If a machine wastes energy, and has an efficiency less than 100%, the mechanical advantage is always less than the velocity ratio – because the output force is always less than its 'ideal' value.

1 Decide whether each of the following machines is a *force multiplier* or a *distance multiplier* (you may have to look at an example of each to find out):
   a) bottle opener **b)** nail clippers **c)** door handle
   d) bathroom scales (with pointer) **e)** tin opener.
2 A lever is used to lift a load weighing 200 N. When the handle is pushed down 1 m, the load rises 0.25 m. The lever has an efficiency of 100%.
   a) How much work is done on the load in lifting it?
   b) How much work must be done on the handle?
   c) What force must be used on the handle?

3 A car is lifted using a jack. The table below gives some information about the load and the jack.
   a) How much work is done on the car in lifting it?
   b) How much work must be done on the handle?
   c) What force must be used on the handle?

> load lifted (weight): 4000 N   distance lifted: 0.5 m
>
> handle pushed down: 100 times
> distance moved by handle each time: 1.0 m
>
> efficiency of jack: 50%

+++

Machines (2)

The ramp

A ramp is a machine, even if it doesn't look like one. You can pull a load up a ramp using less force than you would need to lift it vertically. So the ramp is a force multiplier.

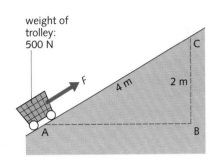

weight of trolley: 500 N

> *Example* The trolley on the left weighs 500 N. What force F is needed to pull it up the ramp from A to C, assuming that there is no friction?

To raise the trolley vertically from B to C, a force of 500 N is needed.
So: work done = force × distance moved = 500 N × 2 m = 1000 J
Treating the ramp as a lifting machine, this is its useful work output.

If the trolley is pulled up the ramp from A to C:
work done = force × distance moved = F × 4 m
This is the work input.

As there is no friction: useful work output = work input
So, leaving out the units for simplicity: F × 4 = 1000.
This gives F = 250, so the force needed to pull the trolley is 250 N.

The pulley

A pulley like the one below is also a force multiplier. You can deduce this from the diagram. When you pull on the rope, the tension provides *two* upward forces to lift the load because the lower pulley block is supported by *two* sections (a and b) of the rope.

This particular pulley has a velocity ratio of 2 – you have to pull the end of the rope twice the distance that the load is lifted. Again, you can deduce this from the diagram. To lift the load 0.5 m, sections a and b each have to shorten by 0.5 m. But both are part of one long rope. So the end of the rope has to be pulled down a total of 1 m.

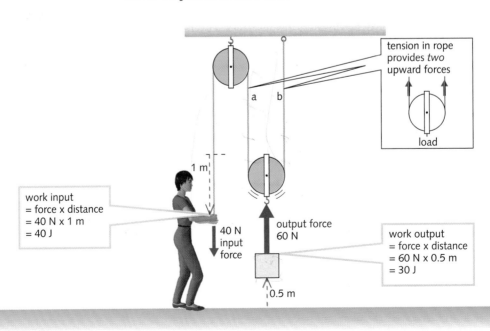

tension in rope provides *two* upward forces

load

work input
= force x distance
= 40 N x 1 m
= 40 J

40 N input force

output force 60 N

work output
= force x distance
= 60 N x 0.5 m
= 30 J

0.5 m

Efficiency The efficiency of the pulley can be calculated from the figures on the diagram:

$$\text{efficiency} = \frac{\text{useful work output}}{\text{work input}} = \frac{30\,\text{J}}{40\,\text{J}} = 0.75 = 75\%$$

The pulley is only 75% efficient because one quarter of the energy input is wasted in lifting the lower pulley block and overcoming friction. As the load is increased, the energy wasted becomes a smaller proportion of the energy input, and the efficiency rises. If the pulley were 100% efficient, it would waste no energy, and its mechanical advantage would be 2: in other words, the output force would be twice the input force.

Gears

Linked gearwheels do for torques (turning moments) what levers do for forces: they multiply or reduce their strength.

The gearwheels on the right are similar to those used on a bicycle. In this example, the output shaft turns at twice the speed of the input shaft. But, it only delivers half the torque (assuming no friction).

On many bicycles, when you change gear, the chain is moved so that it fits over a different combination of gearwheels.

◄ When you change down a gear on a bicycle, you have to pedal faster to keep moving at the same speed. However, the torque on the rear wheel is increased, so it is easier to cycle uphill.

1 This question is about the ramp on the right. If no energy is wasted because of friction:
   a) How much work must be done to lift the trolley directly from B to C?
   b) How much work must be done to pull the trolley up the ramp from A to C?
   c) What force is needed to pull the trolley?
2 This question is about the pulley on the right:
   a) How far does the rope have to be pulled down to lift the load 1 m?
   b) Assuming an efficiency of 100%, what input force is needed to lift a 200 N load?
   c) Why, in reality, is more force than this needed?

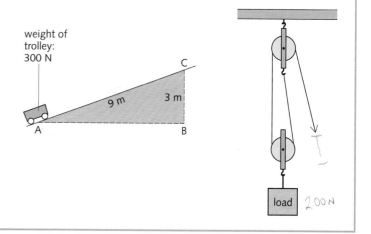

1

wound up spring	batteries connected to motors
rotating flywheel	stretched rubber bands

a) State which of the above **change shape** when their stored energy is transferred. [2]
b) Describe how the energy from a rotating flywheel can be transferred to moving parts of a child's toy. [2]

WJEC

2 The diagram below shows a pendulum which was released from position **A**.

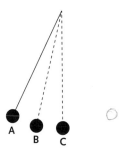

a) What form(s) of energy did the pendulum have at
(i) **A**, (ii) **B**, (iii) **C**? [3]
b) Eventually the pendulum would stop moving. Explain what has happened to the initial energy of the pendulum. [2]

UCLES (O)

3

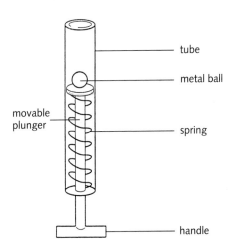

A type of toy catapult consists of a movable plunger which has a spring attached as shown above. The handle was pulled down to fully compress the spring and on release the metal ball of mass 0.1 kg (weight 1 N) was projected 0.75 m vertically.
a) (i) What type of energy is stored in a compressed spring? [1]
   (ii) What happens to this stored energy when the handle of the plunger is released? [2]

b) Calculate the maximum potential energy acquired by the metal ball from the catapult. Write down the formula that you use and show your working. Take the acceleration due to gravity to be 10 m/s². [3]
c) Explain why the maximum potential energy gained by the metal ball is less than the original stored energy of the spring. [3]

WJEC

4 a) Name **four** renewable energy sources that are used to generate electricity in this country. [4]
b) The main advantage of using renewable sources to generate electricity is that there are no fuel costs. Give **two** major **disadvantages** of using renewable energy. [2]
c) The fuel costs for nuclear energy are low. State the main **financial** drawbacks in the use of nuclear energy to generate electricity. [2]

WJEC

5 A drop hammer is used to drive a hollow steel post into the ground. The hammer is placed inside the post by a crane. The crane lifts the hammer and then drops it so that it falls onto the baseplate of the post.

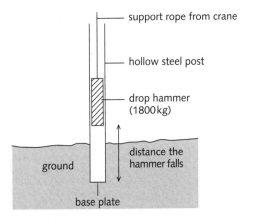

The hammer has a mass of 1800 kg. Its velocity is 5 m/s just before it hits the post.
a) Calculate the kinetic energy of the hammer just before it hits the post. [3]
b) How much potential energy has the hammer lost as it falls? Assume that it falls freely. [1]
c) Calculate the distance the hammer has fallen. (Assume g = 10 N/kg) [3]
d) The steel post has a mass of 1200 kg. The hammer strikes the post and remains in contact with it. The post is driven into the ground. Use the principle of conservation of momentum to calculate the speed of the hammer and post immediately after the impact. [3]
[To answer part (d) you will need information from section 2 in this book.]

MEG

6

electrical appliance	power rating/ kW	power rating/ W
television	0.2	200
electric kettle		2000
food mixer	0.6	

The table above shows the power rating of three electrical appliances.
a) Copy the table and fill in the blank spaces.   [2]
b) State which appliance transfers the least amount of energy per second.   [1]
c) State which appliance converts electrical energy into heat and kinetic energy.   [1]

WJEC

7 a) Explain what you understand by the phrase *non-renewable energy resources*.   [2]
b) Explain why most non-renewable energy resources are burned.   [1]
c) Name a non-renewable energy resource which is not burned.   [1]

WJEC

8 a) The chemical energy stored in a fossil fuel produces heat energy when the fuel is burned. Describe how this heat energy is then used to produce electrical energy at a power station.   [2]
b) Identify and compare the financial and environment costs of generating electricity using fossil fuels and wind.   [4]

WJEC

9 a)

fuel/energy resource	renewable fuel	must be burned to release energy	found in the Earth's crust
coal	no	yes	yes
wood		yes	
uranium			yes

The table above shows that coal is **not** a renewable fuel. It releases energy when burned and is found in the Earth's crust.

Copy and complete the table for the other fuels/energy resources named.   [2]
b) (i) Explain how fossil fuels were produced.   [1]
    (ii) State **two** reasons why we should use less fossil fuels.   [2]

WJEC

10 a) Most of the energy available on Earth comes, or has come, from the Sun. Some energy resources on Earth store the Sun's energy from millions of years ago. Name one of these resources.   [1]

b) Copy and complete the sentence below to say what a fuel does.   [2]
A fuel is a material which supplies _____ when it _____
c) Explain the difference between renewable and non-renewable fuels.   [1]
d) Copy and complete the following table to give examples of some fuels and their uses. The first one has been done for you.   [?]

description	example	use
a gaseous fuel	hydrogen	rocket fuel
a liquid fuel		
a solid fuel		
a renewable fuel		
a non-renewable fuel		

NEAB

11 a) Copy and complete the following sentences about household electrical devices. Use words from the list below. Each word may be used once, more than once or not at all.

chemical   electrical   heat   kinetic   light   sound

(i)   In an iron, electrical energy is transferred into mainly _____ energy.
(ii) In a vacuum cleaner, electrical energy is transferred into mainly _____ energy and unwanted _____ energy.
(iii) In a torch, electrical energy is transferred into mainly _____ and _____ energy.
(iv) In a Hi-fi system, electrical energy is transferred into mainly _____ energy, and some unwanted _____ energy is also produced.   [7]
b) The list below contains some types of potential energy.

chemical   elastic   gravitational   nuclear

Copy and complete the table below by naming the potential energy stored in each one. Use words from the list. Each word may be used once, more than once or not at all.   [3]

a bow about to fire an arrow	
water at the top of a waterfall	
a birthday cake	

NEAB

Photocopy the list of topics below and tick the boxes of the ones that are included in your examination syllabus. (Your teacher should be able to tell you which they are.) Use your list when you revise. The spread number in brackets tells you where to find more information.

❏ 1 Calculating work done. (4.01)

❏ 2 Defining energy. (4.01)

❏ 3 The SI unit of work and energy: the joule. (4.01)

❏ 4 The different forms of energy. (4.01)

❏ 5 Energy transformations. (4.02)

❏ 6 The law of conservation of energy. (4.02)

❏ 7 How energy transformations eventually result in thermal energy. (4.02)

❏ 8 The link between work done and energy transformed. (4.02)

❏ 9 Calculating gravitational potential energy (PE) and kinetic energy (KE). (4.03)

❏ 10 Energy a scalar quantity. (4.03)

❏ 11 Solving problems on PE and KE. (4.03)

❏ 12 How friction can be useful. (4.04)

❏ 13 How friction can be a nuisance. (4.04)

❏ 14 How friction can be reduced in machinery. (4.04)

❏ 15 The difference between static and dynamic friction. (4.04)

❏ 16 The factors affecting the stopping distance of a moving vehicle. (4.04)

❏ 17 Calculating the efficiency of a machine. (4.05)

❏ 18 Defining power. (4.05)

❏ 19 The SI unit of power: the watt. (4.05)

❏ 20 Carrying out calculations on power. (4.05)

❏ 21 The link between efficiency and power. (4.05)

❏ 22 How thermal power stations (nuclear power stations and fuel-burning power stations) work. (4.06)

❏ 23 The limited efficiency of thermal power stations. (4.06)

❏ 24 How thermal energy wasted by a power station can be used. (4.06)

❏ 25 The pollution problems caused by thermal power stations. (4.07)

❏ 26 Why fuel-burning power stations may be contributing to global warming. (4.07)

❏ 27 The alternatives to thermal power stations, including hydroelectric and tidal power stations and wind farms. (4.07 – 4.09)

❏ 28 The difference between renewable and non-renewable energy resources. (4.08)

❏ 29 Different energy resources, and the advantages and disadvantages of each type. (4.08)

❏ 30 The benefits of energy saving. (4.08)

❏ 31 Why the Sun is the main source of energy on Earth. (4.09)

❏ 32 The properties of simple machines, including the lever. (4.10)

❏ 33 The difference between a force multiplier and a distance multiplier. (4.10)

❏ 34 Defining the mechanical advantage and velocity ratio of a machine. (4.10)

❏ 35 The properties of ramps and pulleys. (4.11)

❏ 36 Calculating the efficiency of a machine such as a pulley. (4.11)

❏ 37 The properties of linked gearwheels. (4.11)

Thermal Effects

Concorde about to take off. Forward thrust is produced when hot gases expand in the jet engines and rush out of the exhaust nozzles. At take off, the glow of the afterburners is also visible as extra fuel is burnt in the nozzles for additional thrust. Concorde is still the fastest airliner in scheduled service – and also one of the oldest. It first flew more than thirty years ago.

5.01 Moving particles

▶ Water can exist in three forms: solid, liquid, and gas. (The gas is called water vapour, and it is present in the air.) Like all materials, water is made up of tiny particles. Which form it takes depends on how firmly its particles stick together.

Solids, liquids, and gases

Every material is a solid, a liquid, or a gas. Scientists have developed a model (description) called the **kinetic theory** to explain how solids, liquids, and gases behave. According to this theory, matter is made up of tiny particles which are constantly in motion. The particles attract each other strongly when close.

Solid A solid, such as iron, has a fixed shape and volume. Its particles are held closely together by strong forces of attraction called **bonds**. They vibrate to and fro but cannot change positions.

Liquid A liquid, such as water, has a fixed volume but can flow to fill any shape. The particles are close together and attract each other. But they vibrate so vigorously that the attractions cannot hold them in fixed positions, and they can move past each other.

Gas A gas, such as hydrogen, has no fixed shape or volume and quickly fills any space available. Its particles are well spaced out, and virtually free of any attractions. They move about at high speed, colliding with each other and the walls of their container.

Solid Particles vibrate about fixed positions.

Liquid Particles vibrate, but can change positions.

Gas Particles move about freely.

What are the particles?

Everything is made from about 100 simple substances called **elements**. An **atom** is the smallest possible amount of an element. In some materials, the 'moving particles' of the kinetic theory are atoms. However, in most materials, they are groups of atoms called **molecules**. Below, each atom is shown as a coloured sphere. This is a simplified model (description) of an atom. Atoms have no colour or precise shape.

Iron atoms   **Water molecules**   **Hydrogen molecules**

oxygen atom   hydrogen atom

Brownian motion: evidence for moving particles

Smoke is made up of millions of tiny bits of ash or oil droplets. If you look at smoke through a microscope, as on the right, you can see the bits of smoke glinting in the light. As they drift through the air, they wobble about in zig-zag paths. This effect is called **Brownian motion**, after the scientist Robert Brown who first noticed the wobbling, wandering motion of pollen grains in water, in 1827.

The kinetic theory explains Brownian motion as follows. The bits of smoke are just big enough to be seen, but have so little mass that they are jostled about as thousands of particles (gas molecules) in the surrounding air bump into them at random.

microscope

glass cover

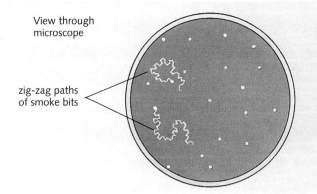

View through microscope

zig-zag paths of smoke bits

lamp   smoke   glass cell

Energy of particles

The particles (atoms or molecules) in solids, liquids, and gases have kinetic energy because they are moving. They also have potential energy because their motion keeps them separated and opposes the bonds trying to pull them together. The particles in gases have the most potential energy because they are furthest apart.

The total kinetic and potential energies of all the atoms or molecules in a material is called its **internal energy**. The hotter a material is, the faster its particles move, and the more internal energy it has.

If a hot material is in contact with a cold one, the hot one cools down and loses internal energy, while the cold one heats up and gains internal energy. The energy transferred is known as **heat**.

The term **thermal energy** is often used for both internal energy and heat.

> **Kinetic energy**
>
> Energy because of motion.
>
> **Potential energy**
>
> Energy stored because of a change in position or shape.

1 Say whether each of the following describes a *solid*, a *liquid*, or a *gas*:
   a) Particles move about freely at high speed.
   b) Particles vibrate and cannot change positions.
   c) Fixed shape and volume.
   d) Particles vibrate but can change positions.
   e) No fixed shape or volume.
   f) Fixed volume but no fixed shape.
   g) Virtually no attractions between particles.

2 Smoke is made up of millions of tiny bits of ash or oil droplets.
   a) What do you see when you use a microscope to study illuminated smoke floating in air?
   b) What is the effect called?
   c) How does the kinetic theory explain the effect?

3 If a gas is heated up, how does this affect the motion of its particles?

4 What is meant by the *internal energy* of an object?

5.02 Temperature

Sun's centre	15 000 000 °C
Sun's surface	6000 °C
bulb filament	2500 °C
bunsen flame	1500 °C
boiling water	100 °C
human body	37 °C
warm room	20 °C
melting ice	0 °C
food in freezer	-18 °C
liquid oxygen	-180 °C
absolute zero	-273 °C

The Celsius scale

A **temperature scale** is a range of numbers for measuring the level of hotness. Everyday temperatures are normally measured on the **Celsius** scale (sometimes called the 'centigrade' scale). Its unit of temperature is the **degree Celsius** (**°C**). The numbers on the scale were specially chosen so that pure ice melts at 0 °C and pure water boils at 100 °C (under standard atmospheric pressure of 101 325 pascals). These are its two **fixed points**. Temperatures below 0 °C have negative (-) values.

Thermometers

Temperature is measured using a **thermometer**. One simple type is shown below. The glass bulb contains a liquid – either mercury or coloured alcohol – which expands when the temperature rises and pushes a 'thread' of liquid further along the scale.

alcohol (or mercury)   'thread'   narrow tube

▼ **Clinical thermometers** like the one below measure the temperature of the human body very accurately. Their range is only a few degrees either side of the average body temperature of 37 °C. When removed from the body, they keep their reading until reset.

Every thermometer depends on some *property* (characteristic) of a material that varies with temperature. For example, the thermometer above contains a liquid whose volume increases with temperature. The two thermometers below use materials whose electrical properties vary with temperature.

All thermometers agree at the fixed points. However, at other temperatures, they may not agree exactly because their chosen properties may not vary with temperature in quite the same way.

digital meter measures current and converts to a temperature reading

37.2 C

probe contains thermistor

battery (inside) supplies current for thermistor

130 C

copper wire

constantan wire

cold junction

probe contains temperature-sensing junction

Thermistor thermometer The thermistor is a device which becomes a much better electrical conductor when its temperature rises. This means that a higher current flows from the battery, causing a higher reading on the meter.

Thermocouple thermometer Two different metals are joined to form two junctions. A temperature difference between the junctions causes a tiny voltage which makes a current flow. The greater the temperature difference, the greater the current.

What is temperature?

In any object, the particles (atoms or molecules) are moving, so they have kinetic energy. They move at varying speeds, but the higher the temperature, then – on average – the faster they move.

If a hot object is placed in contact with a cold one, as on the right, there is a transfer of thermal energy from one to the other. As the hot object cools down, its particles lose kinetic energy. As the cold object heats up, it particles gain kinetic energy. When both objects reach the same temperature, the transfer of energy stops because the average kinetic energy per particle is the same in both:

Objects at the *same temperature* have the *same average kinetic energy per particle*. The higher the temperature, the greater the average kinetic energy per particle.

Temperature is not the same as heat. For example, a spoonful of boiling water has exactly the same temperature (100 °C) as a saucepanful of boiling water, but you could get far less thermal energy (heat) from it.

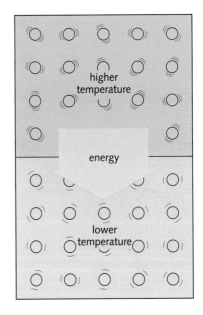

Absolute zero and the Kelvin scale

As the temperature falls, the particles in a material lose kinetic energy and move more and more slowly. At -273 °C, they can go no slower. This is the lowest temperature there is, and it called **absolute zero**. The rules of atomic physics do not allow particles to have zero energy, but at absolute zero, they would have the minimum energy possible.

In scientific work, temperatures are often measured using the **Kelvin scale**. Its temperature unit, the **kelvin (K)**, is the same size as the degree Celsius, but the scale uses absolute zero as its zero (0 K). You convert from one scale to the other like this:

The Kelvin scale is a **thermodynamic** scale. It is based on the average kinetic energy of particles, rather than on a property of a particular substance.

The **constant volume hydrogen thermometer** contains trapped hydrogen gas whose pressure increases with temperature. It gives the closest match to the thermodynamic scale and is used as a standard against which other thermometers are calibrated (marked).

> Kelvin temperature/K = Celsius temperature/°C + 273

	absolute zero	melting ice	boiling water
Celsius scale	-273 °C	0 °C	100 °C
Kelvin scale	0 K	273 K	373 K

Q

1 *-273   0   100   273   373*

Say which of the above is the temperature of
a) boiling water in °C   **b)** boiling water in K
c) absolute zero in °C   **d)** absolute zero in K
e) melting ice in °C   **f)** melting ice in K.

2 Every thermometer depends on some property of a material that varies with temperature. What property is used in each of the following?
a) A mercury-in-glass thermometer.
b) A thermistor thermometer.

A	B
lower temperature	higher temperature

3 Blocks A and B above are identical apart from their temperature.
a) How does the motion of the particles in A compare with that in B?
b) In what direction is thermal energy transferred?
c) When does the transfer of thermal energy cease?

Related topics: kinetic energy **4.01** and **4.03**; motion of particles in solids, liquids, and gases **5.01**; Kelvin scale and particles in a gas **5.08**; expansion of liquids **5.09**; thermistors **8.05** and **10.04**

5.03 Thermal conduction

high temperature

lower temperature

thermal energy transferred by conduction

All materials are made up of tiny, moving particles (atoms or molecules). The higher the temperature, the faster the particles move.

If one end of a metal bar is heated as above, the other end eventually becomes too hot to touch. Thermal energy (heat) is transferred from the hot end to the cold end as the faster particles pass on their extra motion to particles all along the bar. The process is called **conduction**.

More thermal energy is transferred every second if:
- the temperature difference across the ends of the bar is *increased*
- the cross-sectional ('end-on') area of the bar is *increased*
- the length of the bar is *reduced*.

Thermal conductors and insulators

Some materials are much better **conductors** of thermal energy than others. Poor conductors are called **insulators**.

Metals are the best thermal conductors. Non-metal solids tend to be poor conductors, so do most liquids. Gases are the worst of all. Many materials are insulators because they contain tiny pockets of trapped air. You use this idea when you put on lots of layers of clothes to keep you warm. There are some more examples at the top of the next page.

You can sometimes tell how well something conducts just by touching it. A metal door handle feels cold because it quickly conducts thermal energy away from your hand, which is warmer. A polystyrene tile feels warm because it insulates your hand and stops it losing thermal energy.

Good conductors

metals e.g.   copper
              aluminium
              iron

silicon

graphite

Poor conductors (insulators)

glass

water

plastics

rubber

wood

materials ⎡ wool
containing ⎢ glass wool (fibreglass)
trapped ⎢ plastic foam
air ⎣ expanded polystyrene

The materials above are arranged in order of conducting ability starting with the best.

boiling water

rods coated with a thin layer of wax when cold

steel

iron

aluminium

copper

melted wax

solid wax

▲ Comparing four good thermal conductors. Ten minutes or so after the boiling water has been tipped into the tank, the length of melted wax shows which material is the best conductor.

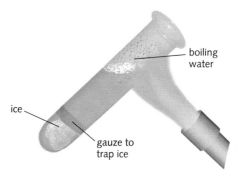

boiling water

ice

gauze to trap ice

▲ This experiment shows that water is a poor thermal conductor. The water at the top of the tube can be boiled without the ice melting.

Using insulating materials

▲ Feathers give good thermal insulation, especially when fluffed up to trap more air.

In a house, good insulation means lower fuel bills. Above are some of the ways in which insulating materials are used to reduce heat losses:
1 Plastic foam lagging round the hot water storage tank.
2 Glass or mineral wool insulation in the loft.
3 Wall cavity filled with plastic foam, beads, or mineral wool.
4 Double-glazed windows: two sheets of glass with air between them.

How materials conduct

When a material is heated, the particles move faster, push on neighbouring particles, and speed those up too. All materials conduct thermal energy like this, but the process is slow. In metals, energy is also transferred by another, much quicker method.

In atoms, there are tiny particles called **electrons**. Most are firmly attached, but in metals, some are 'loose' and free to drift between the atoms. When a metal is heated, these **free electrons** speed up. As they move randomly within the metal, they collide with atoms and make them vibrate faster. In this way, thermal energy is rapidly transferred to all parts.

An electric current is a flow of electrons – so metals are good electrical conductors as well as good thermal conductors.

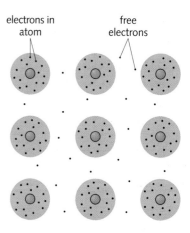

Atoms in a metal

Q

1 Explain each of the following:
   a) A saucepan might have a copper bottom but a plastic handle.
   b) Wool and feathers are good insulators.
   c) An aluminium window frame feels colder than a wooden window frame when you touch it.
   d) It is much safer picking up hot dishes with a dry cloth than a wet one.
2 Give *three* ways in which insulating materials are used to reduce thermal energy losses from a house.

3 A hot water tank loses thermal energy even when lagged. How could the energy loss be reduced?
4 Look at the experiment shown on the opposite page, comparing four thermal conductors.
   a) Which of the metals is the best conductor?
   b) In experiments like this, it is important to make sure that the test is fair. Write down *three* features of this experiment which make it a fair test.
5 Why are metals much better thermal conductors than most other materials?

5.04 Convection

Liquids and gases are poor thermal conductors, but if they are free to circulate, they can carry thermal energy (heat) from one place to another very quickly.

Convection in a liquid

In the experiment on the left, the bottom of the beaker is being gently heated in one place only. As the water above the flame becomes warmer, it expands and becomes less dense. It rises upwards as cooler, denser water sinks and displaces it (pushes it out of the way). The result is a circulating stream, called a **convection current**. Where the water is heated, its particles (water molecules) gain energy and vibrate more rapidly. As the particles circulate, they transfer energy to other parts of the beaker.

Convection does not occur if the water is heated at the top rather than at the bottom. The warmer, less dense water stays at the top.

Convection in air

Convection can occur in gases as well as liquids. For example, warm air rises when it is displaced by cooler, denser air sinking around it.

Heated by the Sun, warm air rises above the equator as it is displaced by cooler, denser air sinking to the north and south. The result is huge convection currents in the Earth's atmosphere. These cause winds across all oceans and continents. Convection also causes the onshore and offshore breezes which sometimes blow at the coast during the summer:

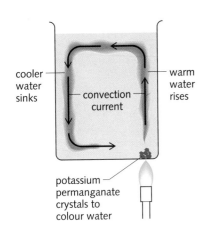

cooler water sinks

warm water rises

convection current

potassium permanganate crystals to colour water

During the daytime, in hot sunshine, the land heats up more quickly than the sea. Warm air rises above the land, as it is displaced by cooler air moving in from the sea.

air cools

warm air rises

cool air sinks

wind towards coast

land warmer than sea

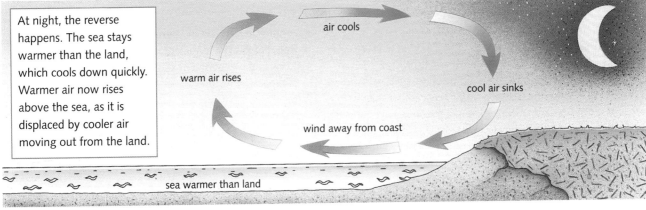

At night, the reverse happens. The sea stays warmer than the land, which cools down quickly. Warmer air now rises above the sea, as it is displaced by cooler air moving out from the land.

air cools

warm air rises

cool air sinks

wind away from coast

sea warmer than land

Using convection in the home

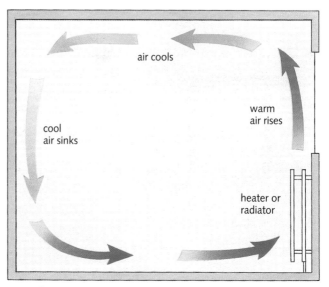

Room heating Warm air rising above a convector heater or radiator carries thermal energy all around the room – though unfortunately, the coolest air is always around your feet.

Hot water system Cold water in the storage tank sinks down to the boiler, where it is heated. The heated water in the boiler rises to the top of the storage tank. In this way, a supply of hot water collects in the storage tank from the top down. The storage tank is insulated to reduce thermal energy losses by conduction and convection. The header tank provides the pressure to push the water out of the taps.

Practical systems are more complicated than that shown. There may be separate circuits for the taps and radiators, and a pump to assist the flow of water.

Refrigerator Cold air sinks below the freezer compartment. This sets up a circulating current of air which cools all the food in the refrigerator.

Q

1 Explain the following:
 a) A radiator quickly warms all the air in a room, even though air is a poor thermal conductor.
 b) The smoke from a bonfire rises upwards.
 c) Anyone standing near a bonfire feels a draught.
 d) The freezer compartment in a refrigerator is placed at the top.
 e) A refrigerator does not cool the food inside it properly if the food is too tightly packed.
2 On a hot summer's day, coastal winds often blow in from the sea.
 a) What causes these winds?
 b) Why do the winds change direction at night?

3 Some hot water systems have an immersion heater – an electrical heating element in the storage tank. In the tank below, should the heating element be placed at A or at B? Explain your answer.

Related topics: density **1.03**; floating and sinking **3.08**; thermal conduction **5.03**; expansion of liquids **5.09**

5.05 Thermal radiation

Thermal radiation is mainly infrared waves, but very hot objects also give out light waves.

On Earth, we are warmed by the Sun. Its energy travels to us in the form of **electromagnetic waves**. These include invisible **infrared waves** as well as light, and they can travel through empty space. They heat up things that absorb them, so are often called **thermal radiation**.

All objects give out some thermal radiation. The higher their temperature, the more energy they radiate per second. Thermal radiation is a mixture of different **wavelengths**, as shown on the left. Warm objects radiate infrared. But if they become hotter, they also emit shorter wavelengths which may include light. That is why a radiant heater or grill starts to glow 'red hot' when it heats up.

Emitters and absorbers

Some surfaces are better at emitting (sending out) thermal radiation than others. For example, a black saucepan cools down more quickly than a similar white one because it emits energy at a faster rate.

Good emitters of thermal radiation are also good absorbers, as shown in the chart below. White or silvery surfaces are poor absorbers because they reflect most of the thermal radiation away. That is why, in hot, sunny countries, houses are often painted white to keep them cool inside.

▶ This chart shows how some surfaces compare as emitters, reflectors, and absorbers of thermal radiation.

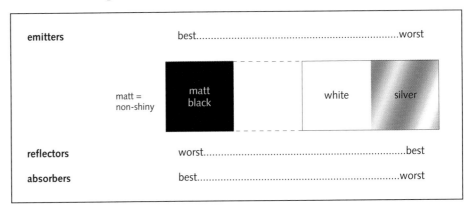

Comparing emitters The metal cube is filled with boiling water which heats the surfaces to the same temperature. The thermal radiation detector is placed in turn at the same distance from each surface and the meter readings compared.

Comparing absorbers The metal plates are placed at the same distance from a radiant heater. To find out which surface absorbs thermal radiation most rapidly, the rises in temperature are compared.

Greenhouse effects

On a sunny day, a greenhouse becomes a 'heat trap'. Short-wavelength thermal radiation from the Sun passes easily through the glass and warms up the materials inside. The warmed materials emit thermal radiation, but at longer wavelengths that do not pass through the glass so easily. Radiation is reflected back into the greenhouse, so the temperature rises.

The Earth's atmosphere contains a small amount of carbon dioxide gas. This has a similar effect to the glass in a greenhouse – it lets the Sun's thermal radiation through to warm the Earth, but reflects the Earth's radiation back. Without this natural **greenhouse effect**, the Earth would be about 30 °C colder than it is. Extra carbon dioxide from burning fuels may be adding to the effect and causing global warming.

Thermal radiation gets into a greenhouse more easily than it gets out.

The solar panel

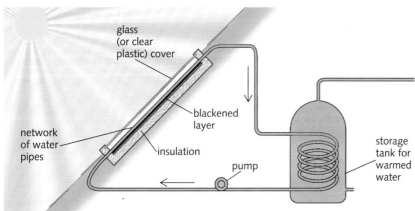

Some houses have a **solar panel** on the roof like the one above. It uses the Sun's thermal radiation to warm up water for the house. The blackened layer absorbs the radiant energy and warms up the water flowing through the pipes.

The vacuum flask

A vacuum flask can keep drinks hot (or cold) for hours. It has these features for reducing the rate at which thermal energy flows out (or in):
1 An insulated stopper to reduce *conduction* and *convection*.
2 A double-walled container with a gap between the walls. Air has been removed from the gap to reduce *conduction* and *convection*.
3 Walls with silvery surfaces to reduce *thermal radiation*.

A vacuum flask

1 *white   silvery   matt black*
   Which of the above surfaces is the best at
   a) absorbing thermal radiation
   b) emitting thermal radiation
   c) reflecting thermal radiation?
2 When a warm object is heated up, the thermal radiation it emits changes. Give *two* ways in which the thermal radiation changes.
3 What feature does a Thermos flask have to reduce the transfer of heat by thermal radiation?

4 In experiments like those on the opposite page, it is important to make sure that each test is fair.
   a) Write down *three* features of the *Comparing emitters* experiment that make it a fair test.
   b) Repeat for the *Comparing absorbers* experiment.
5 On a sunny day, why does thermal radiation get into a greenhouse more easily than it gets out?
6 In the solar panel above, why does the panel have
   a) a blackened layer at the back
   b) a network of water pipes?

Related topics: energy **4.01**, global warming **4.07**; solar energy **4.08 – 4.09**; thermal energy **5.01**; conduction **5.03**; convection **5.04**; electromagnetic waves **7.10 – 7.11**

5.06 Liquids and vapours

Evaporation

Even on a cool day, rain puddles can vanish and wet clothes dry out. The water becomes an invisible gas (called water vapour) which drifts away in the air. When a liquid below its boiling point changes into a gas, this is called **evaporation**. It happens because some particles in the liquid move faster than others. The faster ones near the surface have enough energy to escape and form a gas.

There are several ways of making a liquid evaporate more quickly:

Increase the temperature Wet clothes dry faster on a warm day because more of the particles (water molecules) have enough energy to escape.

Increase the surface area Water in a puddle dries out more quickly than water in a cup because more of its molecules are close to the surface.

Reduce the humidity If air is very *humid*, this means that it already has a high water vapour content. In humid air, wet washing dries slowly because molecules in the vapour return to the liquid almost as fast as those in the liquid escape. In less humid air, wet washing dries more quickly.

Blow air across the surface Wet clothes dry faster on a windy day because the moving air carries escaping water molecules away before many of them can return to the liquid.

▶ When a liquid **evaporates**, faster particles escape from its surface to form a gas. However, unless the gas is removed, some of the particles will return to the liquid.

Boiling

Boiling is a very rapid form of evaporation. When water boils, as in the photograph on the left, vapour bubbles form deep in the liquid. They expand, rise, burst, and release large amounts of vapour.

Even cold water has tiny vapour bubbles in it, but these are squashed by the pressure of the atmosphere. At 100 °C, the vapour pressure in the bubbles is strong enough to overcome atmospheric pressure, so the bubbles start to expand and boiling occurs. At the top of Mount Everest, where atmospheric pressure is less, water would boil at only 70 °C.

The cooling effect of evaporation

Evaporation has a cooling effect. For example, if you wet your hands, the water on them starts to evaporate. As it evaporates, it takes thermal energy away from your skin. So your hands feel cold.

The kinetic theory explains the cooling effect like this. If faster particles escape from the liquid, slower ones are left behind, so the temperature of the liquid is less than before.

Refrigerators use the cooling effect of evaporation. In the refrigerator on the right, the process works like this:

1 In the pipes in the freezer compartment, a liquid called a **refrigerant** evaporates and takes thermal energy from the food and air.

2 The vapour is drawn away by the pump, which compresses it and turns it into a liquid. This releases thermal energy, so the liquid heats up.

3 The hot liquid is cooled as it passes through the pipes at the back, and the thermal energy is carried away by the air.

Overall, thermal energy is transferred from the things inside the fridge to the air outside.

① refrigerant
vapour   liquid

freezer
compartment

② pump   ③ cooling pipes

Sweating also uses the cooling effect of evaporation. You start to sweat if your body temperature rises more than about 0.5 °C above normal. The sweat, which is mainly water, comes out of tiny pores in your skin. As it evaporates, it takes thermal energy from your body and cools you down.

On a humid ('close') day, sweat cannot evaporate so easily, so it is more difficult to stay cool and comfortable.

Condensation

When a gas changes back into a liquid, this is called **condensation**. For example, cold air can hold less water vapour than warm air, so if humid air is suddenly cooled, some of the water vapour may condense. It may become billions of tiny water droplets in the air – we see these as clouds, mist, or fog. Or it may become condensation on windows or other surfaces. If condensation freezes, the result is frost.

Gas and vapour

A gas is called a vapour if it can be turned back into a liquid by compressing it.

Condensation can be seen   ...on windows   ...as clouds in the sky   ...and as clouds of 'steam' from a kettle
(the vapour itself is invisible)

Q

1 A puddle and a small bowl are next to each other. There is the same amount of water in each.
a) Explain why the puddle dries out more rapidly than the water in the bowl.
b) Give *two* changes that would make the puddle dry out even more rapidly.

2 If you are wearing wet clothes, and the water evaporates, it cools you down. How does the kinetic theory explain the cooling effect?

3 Give *two* practical uses of the cooling effect of evaporation.

4 Explain why, on a humid day
a) you may feel hot and uncomfortable
b) you do not feel so uncomfortable if there is a breeze blowing.

5 What is the difference between evaporation and boiling?

6 Why does condensation form on cold windows?

Related topics: atmospheric pressure **3.07**; kinetic theory **5.01**; latent heat of vaporization **5.11**

5.07 The gas laws (1)

▲ When this balloon rises, the pressure, volume, and temperature can all change.

When dealing with a fixed mass of gas, there are always three factors to consider: *pressure*, *volume*, and *temperature*. A change in one of these factors always produces a change in at least one of the others. Often all three change at once. This happens, for example, when a balloon rises through the atmosphere.

To find the laws linking the pressure, volume, and temperature of a gas experimentally, each factor must be kept constant in turn while the link between the other two is investigated. In the experiments described on this spread and the next, the gas being studied is a *fixed mass* of *dry air*.

Linking pressure and volume (at constant temperature)

In the experiment below, air is trapped in a glass tube. Its volume is reduced in stages by pumping air into the reservoir so that oil is pushed further up the tube. Each time the volume is reduced, the pressure of the trapped air is measured on the gauge.

pressure	volume
kPa	cm³
200	50
250	40
400	25
500	20
1000	10

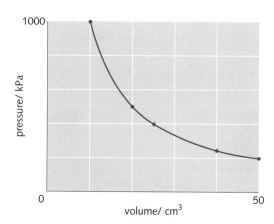

Squashing the air warms it up slightly. So before taking each reading, you have to wait a few moments for the air to return to its original temperature. The gauge actually measures the pressure in the reservoir, but this is the same as in the tube because the oil transmits the pressure.

Above, you can see some typical readings and the graph they produce. Results like this show that the relationship between the pressure and volume is an **inverse proportion**. It has these features:

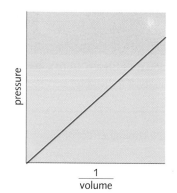

1 If the volume *halves*, the pressure *doubles*, and so on.

2 *Pressure × volume* always has the same value (10 000 in this case).

3 If *pressure* is plotted against $\frac{1}{volume}$, the graph is a straight line through the origin, as shown on the left.

The findings can be expressed as a law:

> For a fixed mass of gas at constant temperature, the pressure is inversely proportional to the volume.

This is known as **Boyle's law**.

Here is another way of writing Boyle's law. If the pressure of a gas changes from p_1 to p_2 when the volume is changed from V_1 to V_2:

$$p_1 \times V_1 = p_2 \times V_2 \quad \text{(at constant temperature)}$$

Example An air bubble has a volume of $2\,cm^3$ when released at a depth of $20\,m$ in water. What will its volume be when it reaches the surface? Assume that the temperature does not change and that atmospheric pressure is equivalent to the pressure from a column of water $10\,m$ deep.

In this case: p_1 = atmospheric pressure + pressure due to $20\,m$ of water
$$= 1\,\text{atm} + 2\,\text{atm} = 3\,\text{atm}$$
Also: $p_2 = 1\,\text{atm}$, $V_1 = 2\,cm^3$, and V_2 is to be found.

As the temperature does not change, Boyle's law applies. So:
$$p_1 \times V_1 = p_2 \times V_2 \quad \text{(at constant temperature)}$$
So: $3 \times 2 = 1 \times V_2$ (omitting units for simplicity)

This gives $V_2 = 6$, so on the surface, the volume of the bubble is $6\,cm^3$.

Boyle's law and the kinetic theory

The kinetic theory explains Boyle's law as follows. In a gas, the molecules are constantly striking and bouncing off the walls of the container. The force of these impacts causes the pressure. If the volume of the gas is halved, as shown below, there are twice as many molecules *in each cubic metre*. So, every second, there are twice as many impacts with each square metre of the container walls. So the pressure is doubled.

A gas that exactly obeys Boyle's law is called an **ideal gas**. Real gases come close to this provided they have a low density, a temperature well above their liquefying point, and are not full of water vapour. Unless these conditions are met, attractions between molecules affect their behaviour. An ideal gas has no attractions between its molecules.

Pressure essentials

$$\text{pressure} = \frac{\text{force}}{\text{area}}$$

If force is measured in newtons (N) and area in square metres (m^2), pressure is measured in pascals (Pa): $1\,\text{Pa} = 1\,N/m^2$.

Standard atmospheric pressure, called 1 atmosphere (atm), is approximately $100\,000\,\text{Pa}$.

Kinetic theory essentials

According to the kinetic theory, a gas is made up of tiny, moving particles (usually molecules). These are spaced out with almost no attractions between them, and move about freely at high speed. The higher the temperature, then on average, the faster they move.

volume halved

pressure doubled

Q

1 If you squash a balloon, the pressure inside it rises. How does the kinetic theory explain this?

2 A balloon contains $6\,m^3$ of helium at a pressure of $100\,kPa$. As the balloon rises through the atmosphere, the pressure falls and the balloon expands. Assuming that the temperature does not change, what is the volume of the balloon when the pressure has fallen to
a) $50\,kPa$ **b)** $40\,kPa$?

3 The readings below are for a fixed mass of gas at constant temperature:

pressure/atm	5.0	4.0	2.0	1.0	0.5	0.4
volume/cm³	4	5	10	20	40	50

a) How can you tell that the gas obeys Boyle's law?
b) Use a calculator to work out values for 1/volume. Plot a graph of pressure against 1/volume and describe its shape.

Related topics: pressure **3.04**; air pressure **3.07**; kinetic theory **5.01**; temperature **5.02**; water vapour **5.06**

111

+++

The gas laws (2)

Linking pressure and temperature (at constant volume)

In the experiment below left, air is trapped in a flask of fixed volume. The temperature of the air is changed in stages by heating the water – or putting a hotter or colder material (melting ice, for example) in the container. At each stage, the pressure is measured on the gauge.

thermometer   pressure gauge   water (or other material)

27 C

trapped air

thermal energy

pressure	temperature	temperature
kPa	°C	K
100	-73	200
150	27	300
200	127	400
250	227	500
300	327	600

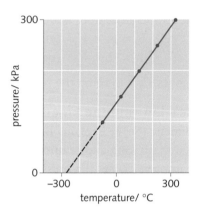

Above, you can see some typical readings and the graph they produce. The graph is a straight line which, if extended backwards, cuts the temperature axis at -273 °C. Other gases give the same result – provided conditions are such that they behave as ideal gases.

Absolute zero and the kinetic theory According to the kinetic theory, if the temperature of a gas is reduced, the molecules move more slowly. As a result, they strike the container walls with less force, so the pressure drops. If you could go on cooling a gas, its molecules would eventually stop moving and cause no pressure. The graph shows that this would happen at -273 °C. This is the lowest possible temperature and it is called **absolute zero**. (Because of attractions between their molecules, real gases turn liquid before absolute zero is reached.)

On the Kelvin scale, temperature is directly proportional to the average kinetic energy per molecule of an ideal gas. At 0 K (absolute zero), an ideal gas molecule has no kinetic energy.

Kelvin temperature scale This uses absolute zero as its zero (0 K). Its unit, the kelvin (K), is the same size as the degree Celsius (°C). To convert from °C to kelvin (K), you just add 273.

The pressure law On the left, you can see what happens if the graph above is redrawn using Kelvin temperatures. The straight line now passes through the origin and the features of a **direct proportion** can be seen:

1 If the Kelvin temperature *doubles*, the pressure *doubles*, and so on.
2 *pressure ÷ Kelvin temperature* always has the same value (0.5 in this case).

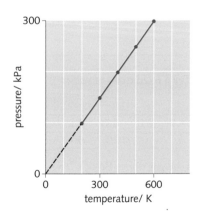

These results are summed up by the **pressure law**:

> For a fixed mass of gas at constant volume, the pressure is directly proportional to the Kelvin temperature.

++

Linking volume and temperature (at constant pressure)

When dry air is heated and allowed to expand at constant pressure, experiments show that *volume ÷ Kelvin temperature* always has the same value for any particular sample. This result can be expressed as a law, often called **Charles's law**:

> For a fixed mass of gas at constant pressure, the volume is directly proportional to the Kelvin temperature.

Combined gas equation

The results of the experiments so far can be combined into a single equation. If the pressure, volume, and Kelvin temperature of a fixed mass of (ideal) gas change as shown on the right:

$$\frac{p_1 V_1}{T_1} = \frac{p_2 V_2}{T_2}$$

All three gas laws can be obtained from this equation:

If T is constant, $T_1 = T_2$, so: $p_1 V_1 = p_2 V_2$ (Boyle's law)

If V is constant, $V_1 = V_2$, so: $\dfrac{p_1}{T_1} = \dfrac{p_2}{T_2}$ (pressure law)

If P is constant, $P_1 = P_2$, so: $\dfrac{V_1}{T_1} = \dfrac{V_2}{T_2}$ (Charles's law)

initial conditions

pressure p_1
volume V_1
temperature T_1
(in kelvin)

pressure p_2
volume V_2
temperature T_2
(in kelvin)

final conditions

> *Example* Some trapped air, of volume $4\,m^3$, has a pressure of 3 atm when its temperature is 27 °C. What will its pressure be if it is compressed into half the volume and heated to 127 °C?

Remembering that temperatures must be converted into kelvin:

$P_1 = 3\,atm$ P_2 is to be found
$V_1 = 4\,m^3$ $V_2 = {}^1/_2 \times V_1 = 2\,m^3$
$T_1 = (27 + 273)\,K = 300\,K$ $T_2 = (127 + 273)\,K = 400\,K$

$$\frac{p_1 V_1}{T_1} = \frac{p_2 V_2}{T_2}$$

So: $\dfrac{3 \times 4}{300} = \dfrac{P_2 \times 2}{400}$ (omitting units for simplicity)

This gives $P_2 = 8$, so the final pressure of the gas is 8 atm.

1 How does the kinetic theory explain the following?
   a) A gas exerts a pressure on its container walls.
   b) The pressure increases with temperature (assuming that the volume does not change).
2 According to the kinetic thory, what is the pressure of an ideal gas at absolute zero? Why?
3 A gas in a fixed container is at a pressure of 4 atm and a temperature of 27 °C. What will its pressure be if it is heated to a temperature of 177 °C?

4 The readings below are for a fixed mass of gas at constant volume:

pressure/ atm	0.78	0.96	1.13	1.31	1.48
temperature/°C	-50	0	50	100	150

a) By plotting a graph, estimate a value for absolute zero.
b) Does the graph obey the pressure law? Explain your answer.

5.09 Expanding solids and liquids

If a concrete or steel bar is heated, its volume will increase slightly. The effect is called **thermal expansion**. It is usually too small to notice, but unless space is left for it, it can produce enough force to crack the concrete or buckle the steel. Most solids expand when heated. So do most liquids – and by more than solids. If a liquid is stored in a sealed container, a space must be left at the top to allow for expansion.

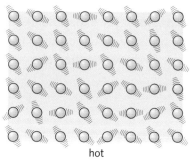

cold   hot

The kinetic theory explains thermal expansion as follows. When, say, a steel bar is heated, its particles speed up. Their vibrations take up more space, so the bar expands slightly in all directions. If the temperature falls, the reverse happens and the material contracts (gets smaller).

Comparing expansions

The chart on the left shows how much 1 metre lengths of different materials expand when their temperature goes up by 100 °C. For greater lengths and higher temperature increases, the expansion is more.

invar (metal)	0.1 mm
Pyrex glass	0.3 mm
platinum alloy	0.9 mm
glass	0.9 mm
concrete	1 mm
steel	1 mm
brass	2 mm
aluminium	3 mm

increase in length of a 1 m bar for a 100 °C rise in temperature

When choosing materials for particular jobs, it can be important to know how much they will expand. Here are two examples:

Steel rods can be used to reinforce concrete because both materials expand equally. If the expansions were different, the steel might crack the concrete on a hot day.

If an ordinary glass dish is put straight into a hot oven, the outside of the glass expands before the inside and the strain cracks the glass. Pyrex expands much less than ordinary glass, so should not crack.

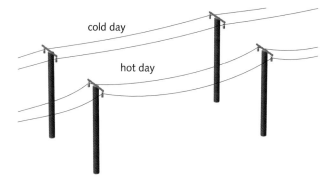

Allowing for expansion...

Gaps are left at the ends of bridges to allow for expansion. One end of the bridge is often supported on rollers so that movement can take place.

... and contraction

When overhead cables are suspended from poles or pylons, they are left slack, partly to allow for the contraction that would happen on a very cold day.

Using expansion

In the **thermometer** above, the liquid in the bulb expands when the temperature rises. The tube is made narrow so that a small increase in volume of the liquid produces a large movement along the tube.

bimetal strip: cold

invar

brass

...hot

brass expands most

In the **bimetal strip** above, thin strips of two different metals are bonded together. When heated, one metal expands more than the other, which makes the bimetal strip bend. Bimetal strips are used in some **thermostats** – devices for keeping a steady temperature. The thermostat shown on the right is controlling an electric heater.

▲ **Bimetal thermostat** When the temperature rises, the bimetal strip bends, the contacts separate, and the current to the heater is cut off. When the temperature falls, the bimetal strip straightens, and the current is switched on again. In this way, an approximately steady temperature is maintained.

Water and ice

When hot water cools, it contracts. However, when water freezes it *expands* as it turns into ice. The force of the expansion can burst water pipes and split rocks with rainwater trapped in them.

Water expands on freezing for the following reason. In liquid water, the particles (water molecules) are close together. But in ice, the molecules link up in a very open structure that actually takes up *more* space than in the liquid – as shown in the diagram on the right.

Ice has a lower *density* than liquid water – in other words, each kilogram has a greater volume. Because of its lower density, ice floats on water. When liquid water is cooled, the molecules start forming into an open structure at 4 °C, just before freezing point is reached. As a result, water expands very slightly as it is cooled from 4 °C to 0 °C. It takes up least space, and therefore has its maximum density, at 4 °C.

molecules in liquid water

molecules in ice

1 Explain the following:
  a) A metal bar expands when heated.
  b) Overhead cables are hung with plenty of slack in them.
  c) It would *not* be a good idea to reinforce concrete with aluminium rods.
  d) A bimetal strip bends when heated.
  e) Water expands when it freezes.

2 This question is about the thermostat in the diagram at the top of the page.
  a) Why does the power to the heater get cut off if the temperature rises too much?
  b) To maintain a *higher* temperature, which way would you move the control knob? – to the *right* so that it moves towards the contacts, or to the *left*? Explain your answer.

5.10 Specific heat capacity

If a material absorbs thermal energy, then unless it is melting or boiling, its temperature rises. However, some materials have a greater capacity for absorbing thermal energy than others. For example, if you heat a kilogram each of water and aluminium, the water must be supplied with nearly five times as much energy as the aluminium for the same rise in temperature:

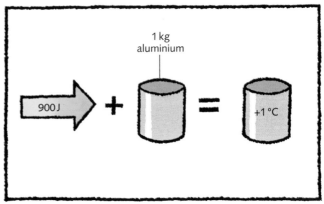

▲ 4200 joules of energy are needed to raise the temperature of 1 kg of water by 1 °C.

▲ 900 joules of energy are needed to raise the temperature of 1 kg of aluminium by 1 °C.

Units

Energy is measured in joules (J).

Temperature is measured in °C or in kelvin (K). Both scales have the same size 'degree', so a 1 °C *change* in temperature is the same as a 1 K change.

	specific heat capacity
	J/(kg °C)
water	4200
alcohol	2500
ice	2100
aluminium	900
concrete	800
glass	700
steel	500
copper	400

Scientifically speaking, water has a **specific heat capacity** of 4200 J/(kg °C). Aluminium has a specific heat capacity of only 900 J/(kg °C). Other specific heat capacities are shown in the table below left.

The energy that must be transferred to an object to increase its temperature can be calculated using this equation:

energy transferred = mass × specific heat capacity × temperature change

In symbols: energy transferred = $mc\Delta T$

where m is the mass in kg, c is the specific heat capacity in J/(kg °C), and ΔT represents the temperature *change* in °C (or in K).

The same equation can also be used to calculate the energy transferred when a hot object cools down.

Example If 2 kg of water cools from 70 °C to 20 °C, how much thermal energy does it lose?

In this case, the temperature change is 50 °C.
So: energy transferred = $mc\Delta T$ = 2 × 4200 × 50 J
= 420 000 J

Heat capacity

The quantity *mass × specific heat capacity* is called the **heat capacity**. For example, if there is 2 kg of water in a kettle:
heat capacity of the water = 2 kg × 4200 J/(kg °C) = 8400 J/°C

This means that, for each 1 °C rise in temperature, 8400 joules of energy must be supplied to the water in the kettle. A greater mass of water would have a higher heat capacity.

+++

Linking energy and power

$$\text{power} = \frac{\text{energy}}{\text{time}}$$

So: energy = power × time

Energy is measured in joules (J).

Power is measured in watts (W).

Time is measured in seconds (s).

Measuring specific heat capacity

thermometer

cover

power supply

electric heater

water

insulation

Water   A typical experiment is shown on the right. Here, the beaker contains 0.5 kg of water. When the 100 watt electric heater is switched on for 230 seconds, the temperature of the water rises by 10 °C. From these figures, a value for the specific heat capacity of water can be calculated:

(Omitting some of the units for simplicity)

energy transferred to water $= mc\Delta T = 0.5 \times c \times 10$

energy supplied by heater   = power × time = $100 \times 230 = 23\,000$ J

so: $0.5 \times c \times 10 = 23\,000$

Rearranged and simplified, this gives $c = 4600$

so the specific heat capacity of water is 4600 J/(kg °C).

This method makes no allowance for any thermal energy lost to the beaker or the surroundings, so the value of c is only approximate.

Aluminium (or other metal)   The method is as above, except that a block of aluminium is used instead of water. The block has holes drilled in it for the heater and thermometer. As before, c is calculated from this equation:

   power × time = $mc\Delta T$ (assuming no thermal energy losses)

Storing thermal energy

Because of its high specific heat capacity, water is a very useful substance for storing and carrying thermal energy. For example, in central heating systems, water carries thermal energy from the boiler to the radiators around the house. In car cooling systems, water carries unwanted thermal energy from the engine to the radiator.

water gives out thermal energy

radiator

water takes in thermal energy

boiler

In most central heating systems, water is used to carry the thermal energy.

Night storage heaters use concrete blocks to store thermal energy. Although concrete has a lower specific heat capacity than water, it is more dense, so the same mass takes up less space. Electric heating elements heat up the blocks overnight, using cheap, 'off-peak' electricity supplied through a special meter. The hot blocks release thermal energy through the day as they cool down.

 Q

The specific heat capacities of copper and water are given in the table on the opposite page.

1 Water has a very high specific heat capacity. Give *two* practical uses of this.

2 a) How much thermal energy is needed to raise the temperature of 1 kg of copper by 1 °C?
   b) If a 10 kg block of copper cools from 100 °C to 50 °C, how much thermal energy does it give out?

c) If, in part b, the copper were replaced by water, how much thermal energy would this give out?

3 A 210 W heater is placed in 2 kg of water and switched on for 200 seconds.
   a) How much energy is needed to raise the temperature of 2 kg of water by 1 °C?
   b) How much energy does the heater supply?
   c) Assuming that no thermal energy is lost, what is the temperature rise of the water?

Latent heat

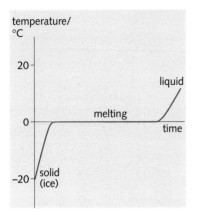

Water can be a solid (ice), a liquid, or a gas called water vapour (or steam). These are its three **phases**, or **states**.

Latent heat of fusion

If ice from a cold freezer is put in a warm room, it absorbs thermal energy. The graph on the left shows what happens to its temperature. While melting, the ice goes on absorbing energy, but its temperature does not change. The energy absorbed is called the **latent heat of fusion**. It is needed to separate the particles so that they can form the liquid. If the liquid changes back to a solid, the energy is released again.

Ice has a **specific latent heat of fusion** of 330 000 J/kg. This means that 330 000 joules of energy must be transferred to change each kilogram of ice into liquid water at the same temperature (0 °C). For any known mass, the energy transferred can be calculated using this equation:

energy transferred = mass × specific latent heat

In symbols: energy transferred = mL

For example, if 2 kg of ice is melted (at 0 °C):
energy transferred = mL = 2 kg × 330 000 J/kg = 660 000 J

Measuring the specific latent heat of fusion of ice In the experiment on the left, a 100 watt heater is switched on for 300 seconds. By weighing the water collected in the beaker, it is found that 0.10 kg of ice has melted. From these figures, a value for L can be calculated:

(Omitting some of the units for simplicity)
energy transferred when ice melts = mL = 0.10L
energy supplied by heater = power × time = 100 W × 300 s = 30 000 J
So: 0.10L = 30 000, which gives L = 300 000
So the specific latent heat of fusion of ice is 300 000 J/kg.

This method makes no allowance for any thermal energy received from the funnel or surroundings, so the value of L is only approximate.

Kinetic theory essentials

According to the kinetic theory, materials are made up of tiny, moving particles (usually molecules). In solids, the particles are held together by strong attractions. In liquids, they have more energy and are less strongly held. In gases, they have enough energy to overcome the attractions, stay spaced out, and move around freely.

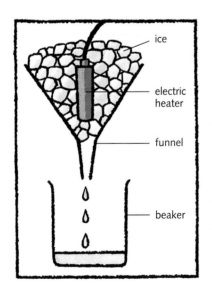

Linking energy and power

$$power = \frac{energy}{time}$$

So: energy = power × time

Energy is measured in joules (J).

Power is measured in watts (W).

Time is measured in seconds (s).

++

Latent heat of vaporization

If you heat water in a kettle, the temperature rises until the water is boiling at 100°C, then stops rising. If the kettle is left switched on, the water absorbs more and more thermal energy, but this just turns more and more of the boiling water into steam, still at 100°C. The energy absorbed is called **latent heat of vaporization**. Most is needed to separate the particles so that they can form a gas, but some is required to push back the atmosphere as the gas forms.

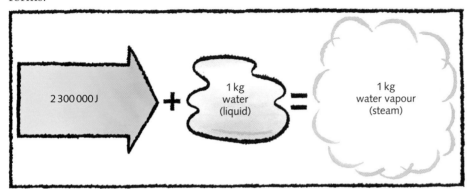

▲ A jet of steam releases latent heat when it condenses (turns liquid). This idea can be used to heat drinks quickly.

Water has a **specific latent heat of vaporization** of 2 300 000 J/kg. This means that 2 300 000 joules of energy must be transferred to change each kilogram of liquid water into steam at the same temperature (100°C).

To calculate the energy transferred when any known mass of liquid changes into a gas at the same temperature, you use the equation on the opposite page. However, L is now the specific latent heat of *vaporization*.

Measuring the specific latent heat of vaporization of water

In the experiment on the right, the can contains boiling water. When the 100 watt heater has been switched on for 500 seconds, the change in the mass balance's reading shows that 0.020 kg of water has boiled away. From these figures, a value for L can be calculated:

(Omitting some of the units for simplicity)
energy transferred when water is vaporized = mL = 0.020L
energy supplied by heater = power × time = 100 W × 500 s = 50 000 J
So: 0.020L = 50 000, which gives L = 2 500 000
So the specific latent heat of vaporization of water is 2 500 000 J/kg.

This method makes no allowance for any thermal energy lost to the surroundings, so the value of L is only approximate.

 Q

Specific latent heat of fusion of ice = 330 000 J/kg; specific latent heat of vaporization of water = 2 300 000 J/kg

1 Some crystals were melted to form a hot liquid, which was then left to cool. As it cooled, the readings in the table below were taken.
   a) What was happening to the liquid between 10 and 20 minutes after it started to cool?
   b) What is the melting point of the crystals in °C?

2 Energy is needed to turn water into water vapour (steam). How does the kinetic theory explain this?

3 How much energy is needed to change
   a) 10 kg of ice into water at the same temperature
   b) 10 kg of water into water vapour at the same temperature?

4 A 460 watt water heater is used to boil water. Assuming no thermal energy losses, what mass of steam will it produce in 10 minutes?

Time/minutes	0	5	10	15	20	25	30
Temperature/°C	90	75	68	68	68	62	58

Related topics: kinetic theory and thermal energy **5.01**; evaporation, boiling, and condensation **5.06**; electrical power **8.10**

1 Explain in terms of molecules:

a) the process of evaporation; [3]

b) why the pressure of the air inside a car tyre increases when the car is driven at high speed. [2]

WJEC

2 The figure shows an outdoor water storage tank.

a) (i) For the water molecules in the tank,

1. describe the distance between the molecules compared to those in solids and gases,

2. describe the movement of the water molecules.

(ii) Explain in molecular terms why water is a liquid, and not a solid, at a temperature of 20 °C. [3]

b) In terms of molecular movement, explain how evaporation takes place. [2]

c) Water tank designers wished to reduce the amount of water evaporating during hot weather. They investigated three factors, which they thought would affect evaporation. In each case write down the most likely conclusion reached, explaining your answer in terms of the water molecules. All other factors were kept constant.

(i) changing the depth of the tank (assuming it is always full)

(ii) fitting a lid

(iii) changing the temperature of the water. [3]

d) In further tests, open-topped tanks of the same size were constructed and placed in the shade for the whole of the day. These tanks were made of steel, concrete and a rigid plastic, only one material being used for each tank. The tanks were all filled, at the beginning of the day, with water at a temperature of 15 °C. Suggest which one would have the lowest rate of evaporation during a day when the air temperature averaged 35 °C, and explain your answer. [2]

e) On a hot day the water level in an open tank of cross-sectional area 100 m², dropped by 0.005 m in 8 hours. The density of water is 1000 kg/m³ and the average specific latent heat of vaporisation of the water is 2×10^6 J/kg. Calculate the average rate at which energy is taken from the Sun's rays to evaporate the water. [3]

UCLES (I)

3 The scale of a mercury-in-glass thermometer is linear. One such thermometer has a scale extending from -10 °C to 110 °C. The length of that scale is 240 mm.

a) What is meant by the statement that *the scale is linear?* [2]

b) Calculate the distance moved by the end of the mercury thread when the temperature of the thermometer rises

(i) from 0.0 °C to 1.0 °C

(ii) from 1.0 °C to 100.0 °C [3]

UCLES (O)

4 a) The table gives the melting and boiling points for lead and oxygen.

	melting point in °C	*boiling point in °C*
lead	327	1744
oxygen	-219	-183

(i) At 450 °C will the lead be a solid, a liquid or a gas? [1]

(ii) At -200 °C will the oxygen be a solid, liquid or a gas? [1]

b) The graph shows how the temperature of a pure substance changes as it is heated.

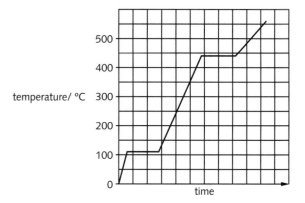

(i) At what temperature does the substance boil? [1]

(ii) Sketch the graph and mark with an **X** any point where the substance exists as both a liquid and gas at the same time. [1]

c) (i) All substances consist of particles. What happens to the average kinetic energy of these particles as the substance changes from a liquid to a gas. [1]

(ii) Explain, in terms of particles, why energy must be given to a liquid if it is to change to a gas. [2]

SEG

5 A glass bottle was heated. State whether the following properties were unchanged, decreased or increased.

a) mass of the bottle

b) density of the bottle

c) external diameter of the bottle

d) volume inside the bottle [4]

UCLES (O)

6

volume increases	volume decreases	volume stays the same
pressure increases	pressure decreases	pressure stays the same

Copy the following statements about how gases behave and select **one** phrase from the above boxes to complete them correctly. Each phrase may be used once, more than once or not at all.

a) When the pressure on a gas increases and its temperature stays the same, its _____   [1]

b) When the temperature of a gas increases and its pressure stays the same its _____   [1]

c) When the _____ and the volume stays the same the temperature of a gas decreases.   [1]

WJEC

7 a) Describe an experiment to show that a brass rod expands when it is heated. Draw a labelled diagram of the apparatus you would use.   [4]

b) The diagram below shows a thermostat. It contains a bimetallic strip made of brass and steel. When heated brass expands more than steel. The bimetallic strip is used to switch the heater off when the temperature rises above the pre-set value.

(i) When the bimetallic strip is heated the heater is switched off. Explain why.

(ii) How would you use the control knob to make the heater switch off at a higher temperature?   [3]

NEAB

8

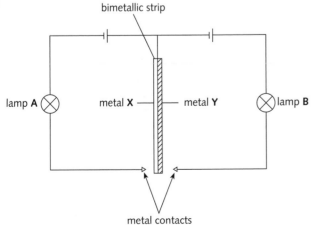

The diagram shows a warning system containing a bimetallic strip. The bimetallic strip has two metals **X** and **Y** firmly joined together.

a) Explain how and why
   (i) lamp **B** lights when the temperature of the strip increases by 20 °C,   [3]
   (ii) lamp **A** lights when the temperature falls by 20 °C   [2]

b) State what effect moving the metal contacts nearer to the bimetallic strip would have on the warning system. [1]

WJEC

9 The diagram below shows a type of heater used in schools.

Hot water is pumped from the boiler into pipes inside the heater. Fins are attached to those pipes. Cold air is drawn into the base of the heater by an electric fan.

a) Why are fins attached to the pipes inside the heater? [2]

b) 600 kg of water pass through the heater every hour. The temperature of the water falls by 5 °C as it passes through the heater.
Calculate the amount of heat energy transferred from the water every hour. The specific heat capacity of water is 4200 J/(kg °C).   [3]

MEG

10 The graph below shows how the temperature of some liquid in a beaker changed as it was heated until it was boiling.

a) What was the boiling point of the liquid?   [1]

b) State and explain what difference, if any, there would be in the final temperature if the liquid was heated more strongly.   [2]

c) State **one** difference between boiling and evaporation.   [1]

UCLES (O)

Photocopy the list of topics below and tick the boxes of the ones that are included in your examination syllabus. (Your teacher should be able to tell you which they are.) Use your list when you revise. The spread number in brackets tells you where to find more information.

❏ **1** The kinetic theory of matter. (5.01)

❏ **2** The different properties of solids, liquids, and gases. (5.01)

❏ **3** The motion of particles in solids, liquids, and gases. (5.01)

❏ **4** Atoms and molecules. (5.01)

❏ **5** Brownian motion. (5.01)

❏ **6** The meaning of internal energy. (5.01)

❏ **7** The Celsius temperature scale. (5.02)

❏ **8** The principles of
    - liquid-in-glass thermometers
    - electrical thermometers. (5.02)

❏ **9** The difference between heat (thermal energy) and temperature. (5.02)

❏ **10** The Kelvin temperature scale. (5.02)

❏ **11** The link between the Kelvin and Celsius scales. (5.02)

❏ **12** The factors affecting thermal conduction. (5.03)

❏ **13** Examples of good and poor thermal conductors. (5.03)

❏ **14** Uses of thermally insulating materials. (5.03)

❏ **15** Why some materials are better thermal conductors than others. (5.03)

❏ **16** Convection currents and why they occur. (5.04)

❏ **17** Examples and uses of convection in liquids and gases. (5.04)

❏ **18** The nature of thermal radiation. (5.05)

❏ **19** How different surfaces compare as emitters, reflectors, and absorbers of thermal radiation. (5.05)

❏ **20** Thermal radiation and the greenhouse effect. (5.05)

❏ **21** How a vacuum flask works. (5.05)

❏ **22** The difference between evaporation and boiling. (5.06)

❏ **23** Factors affecting the rate at which a liquid evaporates. (5.06)

❏ **24** The cooling effect of evaporation its uses. (5.06)

❏ **25** Why condensation occurs. (5.06)

❏ **26** Boyle's law. (5.07)

❏ **27** How the kinetic theory explains Boyle's law. (5.07)

❏ **28** The pressure law. (5.08)

❏ **29** How the kinetic theory explains the pressure law. (5.08)

❏ **30** Absolute zero and the kinetic theory explanation. (5.08)

❏ **31** Charles's law. (5.08)

❏ **32** The combined gas equation. (5.08)

❏ **33** Why solids and liquids normally expand whn heated. (5.09)

❏ **34** Effects and uses of thermal expansion. (5.09)

❏ **35** How water changes volume when it freezes, and the effects this can produce. (5.09)

❏ **36** Specific heat capacity. (5.10)

❏ **37** Calculating the thermal energy changes that occur when the temperature of an object changes. (5.10)

❏ **38** Using materials to store thermal energy. (5.10)

❏ **39** Specific latent heat of fusion (of ice) and its measurement. (5.11)

❏ **40** Specific latent heat of vaporization (of water) and its measurement. (5.11)

6

Waves, Sounds, and Vibrations

- TRANSVERSE AND LONGITUDINAL WAVES
- DIFFRACTION AND OTHER WAVE EFFECTS
- SOUND WAVES
- SPEED, FREQUENCY, AND WAVELENGTH
- ECHOES
- ULTRASOUND
- SEISMIC WAVES
- VIBRATIONS IN STRINGS AND PIPES
- HEARING
- NOISE

This hyla tree frog from South America uses the large, inflatable sac under its throat to amplify the sound of its voice. Only the males can do this, and their calls can travel ten times further than sounds from other frogs. The sound itself is generated when air from the sac is blown past two stretched membranes in the bottom of the frog's mouth, making them vibrate.

6.01 Transverse and longitudinal waves

If you drop a stone into a pond, ripples spread across the surface. The tiny waves carry energy, as you can tell from the movements they cause at the water's edge. But there is no flow of water across the pond. The wave effect is just the result of up-and-down motions in the water.

Waves are not only found on water. Sound travels as waves, so does light. Waves can also travel along stretched springs like those in the experiments below. These show that there are two main types of waves.

Transverse waves

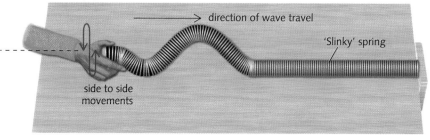

When the end coil of the spring is moved sideways, it pulls the next coil sideways a fraction of a second later... and so on along the spring. In this way, the sideways motion (and its energy) is passed from coil to coil, and a travelling wave effect is produced.

The to-and-fro movements of the coils are called **oscillations**. When the oscillations are up and down or from side to side like those above, the waves are called **transverse waves**. In transverse waves, the oscillations are at right-angles to the direction of travel.

Light waves are transverse waves, although it is electric and magnetic fields which oscillate, rather than any material.

Longitudinal waves

Moving the end coil of the spring backwards and forwards also produces a travelling wave effect. However, the waves are bunched-up sections of coils with stretched-out sections in between. These sections are known as **compressions** and **rarefactions**.

When the oscillations are backwards-and-forwards like those above, the waves are called **longitudinal waves**. In longitudinal waves, the oscillations are in the direction of travel.

Sound waves are longitudinal waves. When you speak, compressions and rarefactions travel out through the air.

Describing waves

On the right, transverse waves are being sent along a rope. Here are some of the terms used to describe these and other waves:

Speed The speed of the waves is normally measured in metres per second (m/s).

Frequency This is the number of waves passing any point per second. The SI unit of frequency is the **hertz** (**Hz**). For example, if the hand on the right makes 4 oscillations per second, then 4 waves pass any point per second, and the frequency is 4 Hz.

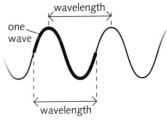

Wavelength This is the distance between any point on a wave and the equivalent point on the next.

Amplitude This is the maximum distance a point moves from its rest position when a wave passes.

The wave equation

The speed, frequency, and wavelength of any set of waves are linked by this equation:

$$\text{speed} = \text{frequency} \times \text{wavelength}$$

In symbols: $v = f\lambda$ (λ = Greek letter *lambda*)

where speed is in m/s, frequency in Hz, and wavelength in m.

The following example shows why the equation works:

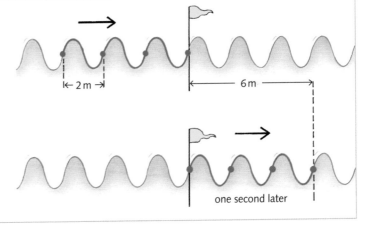

The waves on the right are travelling across water.

Each wave is 2 m long, so the *wavelength* is 2 m.

One second later...

3 waves have passed the flag, so the *frequency* is 3 Hz.

The waves have moved 3 wavelengths (3 × 2 m) to the right so their *speed* is 6 m/s.

Therefore: 6 m/s =   3 Hz   ×   2 m
           (speed) (frequency)   (wavelength)

Q

1 The waves in A below are travelling across water.
   a) Are the waves *transverse* or *longitudinal*?
   b) What is the wavelength of the waves?
   c) What is the amplitude of the waves?
   d) If 2 waves pass the flag every second, what is the frequency?

   e) Use the wave equation to calculate the speed of the waves in A.
   f) What is the wavelength of the waves in diagram B below?
   g) If the waves in B have the same speed as those in A, what is their frequency?

6.02 Wave effects

The properties of waves can be studied using a **ripple tank** like the one below. Ripples (tiny waves) are sent across the surface of water. Obstacles are put in their path to see what effects are produced.

Reflection

A vertical surface is put in the path of the waves. The waves are reflected from the surface at the same angle as they strike it.

Refraction

A flat piece of plastic makes the water more shallow, which slows the waves down. When the waves slow, they change direction. The effect is called **refraction**.

Refraction can be explained as follows.

The waves keep oscillating up and down at the same rate (frequency), so when they slow, the wavefronts close up on each other. That follows from the wave equation on the right. As the frequency is unchanged, a decrease in speed must cause a decrease in wavelength. From the last diagram on the opposite page, you can see that if the wavefronts close up on each other, their direction of travel must change, unless they are travelling at right-angles to the boundary.

The wave equation

speed = frequency × wavelength

distance	number of	distance
per	oscillations	between
second	per second	wavefronts
(m/s)	(Hz)	(m)

Diffraction

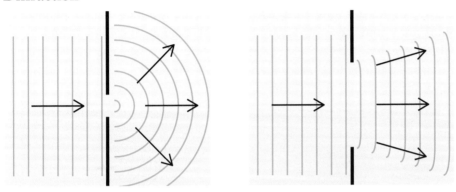

The waves bend round the sides of an obstacle, or spread out as they pass through a gap. The effect is called **diffraction**.

Diffraction is only significant if the size of the gap is about the same as the wavelength. Wider gaps produce less diffraction.

Wave evidence

Sound, light, and radio signals all undergo reflection, refraction, and diffraction. This suggests that they travel as waves. For example:

a Light reflects from mirrors; sound reflects from hard surfaces.
b Light bends when it passes from air into glass or water (refraction).
c Sound bends round obstacles such as walls and buildings, which is why you can hear round corners (diffraction).
d Light spreads when it passes through tiny holes and slits. This suggests that light waves must have much shorter wavelengths than sound.
e Some radio signals can bend round very large obstacles such as hills. This suggests that radio waves must have long wavelengths.

Q

1 Say whether each of the effects b to e above is an example of *reflection*, *refraction*, or *diffraction*.
2 On the right, waves are moving towards a harbour.
  a) What will happen to waves striking the harbour wall at A?
  b) What will happen to waves slowed by the submerged sandbank at B?
  c) What will happen to waves passing through the harbour entrance at C?
  d) If the harbour entrance were wider, what difference would this make?

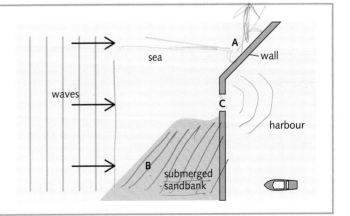

Related topics: waves and the wave equation **6.01**; reflection of sound **6.04**; reflection of light **7.01–7.02**; refraction of light **7.03**; light waves **7.01** and **7.12**; radio waves **7.11**

Sound waves

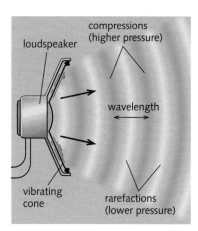

When a loudspeaker cone vibrates, it moves forwards and backwards very fast. This squashes and stretches the air in front. As a result, a series of compressions ('squashes') and rarefactions ('stretches') travel out through the air. These are **sound waves**. When they reach your ears, they make your ear-drums vibrate and you hear a sound.

The nature of sound waves

Sound waves are caused by vibrations Any vibrating object can be a source of sound waves. As well as loudspeaker cones, examples include vibrating guitar strings, the vibrating air inside a trumpet, and the vibrating prongs of a tuning fork. Also, when hard objects (such as cymbals and blocks of wood) are struck, they vibrate and produce sound waves.

Sound waves are longitudinal waves The air oscillates backwards and forwards as the compressions and rarefactions pass through it. When a compression passes, the air pressure rises. When a rarefaction passes, the pressure falls. The distance from one compression to the next is the **wavelength**.

Sound waves need a material to travel through This material is called a **medium**. Without it, there is nothing to pass on any oscillations. Sound cannot travel through a vacuum (completely empty space).

Sound waves can travel through solids, liquids, and gases Most sound waves reaching your ear have travelled through air. But you can also hear when swimming underwater, and walls, windows, doors, and ceilings can all transmit (pass on) sound.

Diffraction of sound waves

You can hear someone through an open window even if you cannot see them. That is because sound waves spread through gaps, or bend round obstacles, of a similar size to their wavelength. The effect is called **diffraction**. Most sound waves have wavelengths between a few centimetres and a few metres, so they are diffracted by everyday objects.

Sound cannot travel through a vacuum. When the air is removed from this jar, the bell goes quiet, even though the hammer is still striking the metal. (The rubber bands reduce the sound transmitted by the connecting wires.)

Interference of sound waves

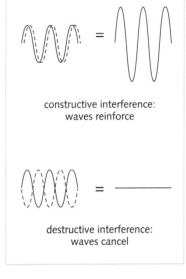

constructive interference:
waves reinforce

destructive interference:
waves cancel

On the left, for simplicity, the sound waves have been shown as lines called **wavefronts**. Each wavefront marks the position of a compression.

When identical sets of sound waves overlap, they may reinforce each other or cancel each other out, depending on whether they are **in phase** ('in step') or out of phase. This effect is called **interference**.

If two loudspeakers are giving out steady, identical sets of sound waves as above, and you walk along in front of them, you can find loud positions where the waves reinforce and quiet positions where they cancel.

Displaying sounds

Sound waves can be displayed graphically using a microphone and an **oscilloscope** as on the right. When sound waves enter the microphone, they make a crystal or a metal plate inside it vibrate. The vibrations are changed into electrical oscillations, and the oscilloscope uses these to make a spot oscillate up and down on the screen. It moves the spot steadily sideways at the same time, producing a wave shape called a **waveform**. The waveform is really a graph showing how the air pressure at the microphone varies with time. It is *not* a picture of the sound waves themselves: sound waves are *not* transverse (up-and-down).

Q

1 Give an example which demonstrates each of the following:
   a) Sound can travel through a gas.
   b) Sound can travel through a liquid.
   c) Sound can travel through a solid.

2 Explain each of the following:
   a) Sound cannot travel though a vacuum.
   b) It is possible to hear round corners.

3 **a)** Sound waves are *longitudinal* waves. Explain what this means.
   b) If sound waves are longitudinal, why are transverse (up-and-down) 'waves' seen on the screen of the oscilloscope above when someone whistles into the microphone?

4 What is the difference between *constructive interference* and *destructive interference*?

Related topics: air pressure **3.07**; longitudinal waves **6.01**; diffraction **6.02**; loudspeaker **9.05**; oscilloscope **10.10**

6.04 Speed of sound and echoes

▶ Sound is much slower than light, so you hear lightning after you see it. Sound takes about 3 seconds to travel one kilometre. Light does it in almost an instant, so a 3 second gap between the flash and the crash means that the lightning is about a kilometre away.

Sound wave essentials

Sound waves are a series of compressions ('squashes') and rarefactions ('stretches') that travel through the air or other material.

Speed of sound

through...

air (dry) at 0 °C	330 m/s
air (dry) at 30 °C	350 m/s
water (pure) at 0 °C	1400 m/s
concrete	5000 m/s

The speed of sound

In air, the speed of sound is about 330 metres per second (m/s), or 760 mph. That is slower than Concorde but about four times faster than a racing car.

The speed of sound depends on the temperature of the air

Sound waves travel faster through hot air than through cold air.

The speed of sound does not depends on the pressure of the air

If atmospheric pressure changes, the speed of sound waves stays the same.

The speed of sound is different through different materials

Sound waves travel faster through liquids than through gases, and fastest of all through solids. There are some examples on the left.

Measuring the speed of sound

The speed of sound in air can be measured as shown below. A sound is made by hitting a metal block or plate with a hammer. When the control unit receives a pulse of sound from microphone A, it starts the clock. When it receives a pulse from microphone B, it stops it.

If B is 1.00 metre further away from the source of sound than A, and the clock records a time of 3.0 milliseconds (0.003 s):

$$\text{speed of sound} = \frac{\text{distance travelled}}{\text{time taken}} = \frac{1.00\,\text{m}}{0.003\,\text{s}} = 330\,\text{m/s}$$

Refraction of sound

Distant trains and traffic often sound louder (and closer) at night. The reason is this. During the night time, when the ground cools quickly, air layers near the ground become colder than those above. Sound waves travel more slowly through this colder air. As a result, waves leaving the ground tend to bend back towards it, instead of spreading upwards. A bending effect like this, caused by a change in speed, is called **refraction**.

Echoes

Hard surfaces such as walls reflect sound waves. When you hear an **echo**, you are hearing a reflected sound a short time after the original sound. In the diagram on the right, the sound has to travel to the wall *and back again*. The time it takes is the **echo time**. So:

$$\text{speed of sound} = \frac{\text{distance travelled}}{\text{time taken}} = \frac{2 \times \text{distance to wall}}{\text{echo time}}$$

If the speed of sound is known, and the echo time is measured accurately, the distance to the wall can be calculated from the above equation. The principle is used in several devices, including the following:

- **Echo-sounder** This measures the depth of water under a boat. It sends pulses of sound waves towards the sea-bed and measures the echo time. The longer the time, the deeper the water.

- **Electronic tape-measure** A surveyor can use this to measure the distance between two walls. It works like an echo-sounder.

- **Radar** This uses the echo-sounding principle, but with microwaves instead of sound waves. It detects the positions of aircraft by measuring the 'echo times' of microwave pulses reflected from them.

handwritten annotations:
$d = vt$
$= 330 \times 0.5$
$= 165\,m$
$0.5\,s$

$\dfrac{440}{330} = 1.3\,s$

220

Q

Assume that the speed of sound in air is 330 m/s.

1 **a)** Why do you hear lightning after you see it?
   b) If lightning strikes, and you hear it 4 seconds after you see it, how far away is it?
2 Does sound travel faster through
   a) *cold air* or *warm air*? **b)** a *solid* or a *gas*?
3 When sound waves change direction because their speed changes, what is this effect called?

4 A ship is 220 metres from a large cliff when it sounds its foghorn.
   a) When the echo is heard on the ship, how far has the sound travelled?
   b) What time delay is there before the echo is heard?
   c) The ship changes its distance from the cliff. When the echo time is 0.5 seconds, how far is the ship from the cliff?

6.05 Characteristics of sound waves

Sound wave essentials

Sound waves are a series of compressions ('squashes') and rarefactions ('stretches') that travel through the air or other material.

wavelength

Frequency and pitch

Sound waves are caused by vibrations – for example, the rapid, backwards-and-forwards oscillations of a loudspeaker cone.

The number of oscillations per second is called the **frequency**. It is measured in **hertz** (**Hz**). If a loudspeaker cone has a frequency of 100 Hz, it is oscillating 100 times per second and giving out 100 sound waves per second.

Different frequencies sound different to the ear. You hear *high* frequencies as *high* notes: musicians say that they have a **high pitch**. You hear *low* frequencies as *low* notes: they have a **low pitch**.

The human ear can detect frequencies ranging from about 20 Hz up to 20 000 Hz, although the ability to hear high frequencies decreases with age.

	1 octave		1 octave		1 octave		1 octave	
C		C		middle C		C		C
64 Hz		128 Hz		256 Hz		512 Hz		1024 Hz

pitch		frequency
high	upper limit of hearing	20 000 Hz
	whistle	10 000 Hz
	high note (soprano)	1000 Hz
	low note (bass)	100 Hz
low	drum note	20 Hz

1000 Hz = 1 kilohertz (kHz)

Musical scales are based on **octaves**. If the pitch of a note increases by one octave, the frequency doubles, as shown on the keyboard above. This keyboard is tuned to **scientific pitch**. Bands and orchestras normally use frequencies that differ slightly from those shown.

The diagrams below show what happens if two steady notes, an octave apart, are picked up by a microphone and displayed on the screen of an oscilloscope. As the higher note has double the frequency of the lower note, the peaks occur twice as often and are only half as far apart.

▶ The **waveform** on each screen is a graph showing how the air pressure varies with time as the sound waves enter the microphone. The horizontal line is the time axis.

waveform

This sound has a higher pitch (and frequency)

...than this sound

The wave equation

This equation applies to sound waves:

$$\text{speed} = \text{frequency} \times \text{wavelength}$$

In symbols: $v = f\lambda$ (λ = Greek letter *lambda*)

For example, if the speed of sound in air is 330 m/s:
sound waves of frequency 110 Hz have a wavelength of 3 m;
sound waves of frequency 330 Hz have a wavelength of 1 m;
so the *higher* the frequency, the *shorter* the wavelength.

> **Why the equation works**
>
> If 110 waves are sent out in one second, and each wave is 3 m long, then the waves must travel 330 metres in one second. In other words, if the frequency is 110 Hz and the wavelength is 3 m, the speed is 330 m/s.

Amplitude and loudness

The sounds displayed on the oscilloscope screens above have the same frequency, but one is *louder* than the other. The oscillations in the air are bigger and the **amplitude** of the waveform is greater.

Sound waves carry energy. *Doubling* the amplitude means that *four* times as much energy is delivered per second.

Quality

Middle C on a guitar does not sound quite the same as middle C on a piano, and its waveform looks different. The two sounds have a different **quality** or **timbre**. Each sound has a strong **fundamental frequency**, giving middle C. But other weaker frequencies are mixed in as well, as shown on the right. These are called **overtones**, and they differ from one instrument to another. With a synthesizer, you can select which frequencies you mix together, and produce the sound of a guitar, piano, or any other instrument.

fundamental frequency...

...plus overtones

...gives the final waveform

Assume that the speed of sound in air is 330 m/s.

1 Here are the frequencies of four sounds:

A: 400 Hz   B: 150 Hz   C: 500 Hz   D: 200 Hz

a) Which sound has the highest pitch?
b) Which two sounds are one octave apart?
c) Which sound has the longest wavelength?

2 Why does a piano not sound quite like a guitar, even if both play the same note?

3 A sound is picked up by a microphone and displayed as a waveform on an osclloscope. How would the waveform change if
a) the sound had a higher pitch?
b) the sound was louder?

4 The lower limit of human hearing is 20 Hz; the upper limit is 20 000 Hz.
a) What is the upper limit in kHz?
b) What is the wavelength at the lower limit?
c) What is the wavelength at the upper limit?

Related topics: speed **2.01**; waves and the wave equation **6.01**; sound waves **6.03**; speed of sound **6.04**; oscilloscope **10.10**

6.06 Ultrasound

| 20 | frequency/Hz | 20 000 | 50 000 | | 120 000 |

range of human hearing

ultrasound

upper limit for... | ...humans | ...dogs | ...bats

Sound wave essentials

Sound waves are a series of compressions ('squashes') and rarefactions ('stretches') that travel through the air or other material.

wavelength

The number of waves per second is called the **frequency**. It is measured in hertz (Hz).

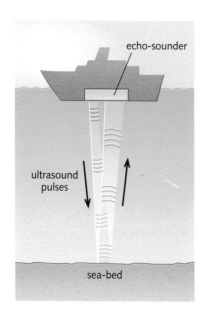

echo-sounder

ultrasound pulses

sea-bed

▶ This bat uses ultrasound to locate insects and other objects in front of it. It sends out a series of ultrasound pulses and uses its specially shaped ears to pick up the reflections. The process is called **echo-location**. It works like echo-sounding.

The human ear can detect sounds up to a frequency of about 20 000 Hz. Sounds above the range of human hearing are called **ultrasonic sounds**, or **ultrasound**. Here are some of the uses of ultrasound:

Cleaning and breaking

Using ultrasound, delicate machinery can be cleaned without dismantling it. The machinery is immersed in a tank of liquid, then the vibrations of high-power ultrasound are used to dislodge the bits of dirt and grease.

In hospitals, concentrated beams of ultrasound can be used to break up kidney stones and gall stones without patients needing surgery.

Echo-sounding

Ships use **echo-sounders** to measure the depth of water beneath them. An echo-sounder sends pulses of ultrasound downwards towards the sea-bed, then measures the time taken for each echo (reflected sound) to return. The longer the time, the deeper the water. For example:

If a pulse of ultrasound takes 0.1 second to travel to the sea-bed and return, and the speed of sound in water is 1400 m/s:

$$\text{distance travelled} = \text{speed} \times \text{time} = 1400 \text{ m/s} \times 0.1 \text{ s} = 140 \text{ m}$$

But the ultrasound has to travel down *and back*:
So: depth of water = $\frac{1}{2} \times 140$ m = 70 m

Most echo-sounders **scan** the area beneath them – they sweep their ultrasound beam backwards and forwards and from side to side. A computer displays the depth information as a picture on a screen.

Metal testing

The echo-sounding principle can be used to detect flaws in metals. A pulse of ultrasound is sent through the metal as on the right. If there is a flaw (tiny gap) in the metal, *two* reflected pulses are picked up by the detector. The pulse reflected from the flaw returns first, followed by the pulse reflected from the far end of the metal. The pulses can be displayed using an oscilloscope. The trace on the screen is a graph showing how the amplitude ('strength') of the ultrasound varies with time.

Scanning the womb

The pregnant mother in the photograph below is having her womb scanned by ultrasound. Again, the echo-sounding principle is being used. A transmitter sends pulses of ultrasound into the mother's body. The transmitter also acts as a detector and picks up pulses reflected from the baby and different layers inside the body. The signals are processed by a computer, which puts an image on the screen.

Using ultrasound is much safer than using X-rays because X-rays can cause cell damage inside a growing baby. Also, ultrasound can distinguish between different layers of soft tissue, which an ordinary X-ray machine cannot.

◄ An ultrasound scan of the womb. The nurse is moving an ultrasound transmitter/detector over the mother's body. A computer uses the reflected pulses to produce an image.

1 What is *ultrasound*?
2 Give *two* examples of the medical use of ultrasound.
3 **a)** What is an *echo-sounder* used for?
   b) How does an echo-sounder work?
4 To answer this question, you will need the information on the right.
   A boat is fitted with an echo-sounder which uses ultrasound with a frequency of 40 kHz.
   a) What is the frequency of the ultrasound in Hz?
   b) If ultrasound pulses take 0.03 seconds to travel from the boat to the sea-bed and return, how deep is the water under the boat?
   c) What is the wavelength of the ultrasound in water?

$$speed = \frac{distance\ travelled}{time\ taken}$$

speed of sound in water = 1400 m/s

$$\begin{matrix} speed & = & frequency & \times & wavelength \\ (m/s) & & (Hz) & & (m) \end{matrix}$$

1 kilohertz (kHz) = 1000 Hz

6.07 Seismic waves

Earthquakes are caused by sudden rock movements underground. The vibrations send **seismic waves** (shockwaves) through the Earth.

Seismic waves get weaker as they travel through the ground. However, they can be detected many thousands of kilometres away by a sensitive instrument called a **seismometer**. A simple type is shown below left. The incoming vibrations are recorded as a graph on a slowly revolving drum. Together, the detector and recording equipment are known as a **seismograph**. The graph produced is a **seismogram**:

seismograph

seismometer

heavy mass (stays still)

revolving drum

pen

vibrating rock

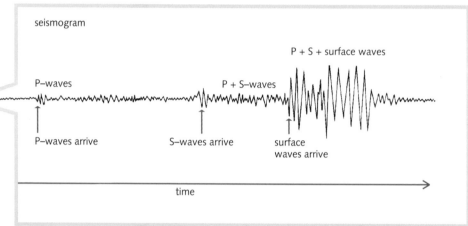

seismogram

P–waves

P + S–waves

P + S + surface waves

P–waves arrive

S–waves arrive

surface waves arrive

time

Recordings like the one above show that there are three main types of seismic waves. These leave the **focus** (site) of the earthquake together, but travel at different speeds and reach the seismometer at different times.

P-waves (primary waves) are longitudinal waves. They are the fastest and arrive first. They travel through solids and liquids deep in the Earth at speeds of several kilometres per second. Their speed is highest through solids.

S-waves (secondary waves) are transverse waves. They arrive after the P-waves because they are slower. They can pass through solids deep in the Earth, but not through liquids such as molten (melted) rock.

Surface waves are the slowest and arrive last. They travel round the Earth's surface. In the earthquake zone itself, they are the most destructive. Some produce a rolling motion, rather like waves at sea. Huge fissures (cracks) can appear on the crests, and close again seconds later when the crests become troughs. Whole buildings may be swallowed up.

Longitudinal waves

Waves in which the vibrations are in the direction of travel (i.e. backwards and forwards).

Transverse waves

Waves in which the vibrations are at right-angles to the direction of travel (e.g. up and down or from side to side).

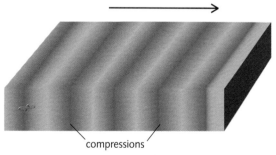

P-waves (<u>P</u>rimary waves) are longitudinal or 'Push-pull' waves. The rock vibrates backwards and forwards.

S-waves (<u>S</u>econdary waves) are transverse or 'Shake' waves. The rock vibrates up and down.

Inside the Earth: evidence from seismic waves

P and S-waves travel faster in denser rock. A gradual change in density causes a gradual change in speed and makes the waves follow a curved path. The bending effect is called **refraction**. A sudden change in density causes a sudden change in direction, and also some reflection.

By measuring the travel times of P and S-waves arriving at different seismic recording stations around the Earth, scientists can work out the paths of the waves through the Earth. The results give clues about the Earth's inner structure and density. For example:

- Some P and S-waves are reflected at a boundary 7 km – 70 km beneath the Earth's surface. This suggests that the Earth has an outer **crust** with a layer of denser rocks beneath it. This is called the **mantle**.
- The curving of the P and S-waves through the Earth suggests that the density of the rocks increases with depth.
- S-waves are blocked by the central part of the Earth. As S-waves cannot pass through liquids, this suggests that the Earth has a central **core** whose outer part must be liquid.
- There is a 'shadow zone' where no waves are detected. This suggests that liquid in the core must be slowing P-waves and refracting them inwards.

The **density** of surface rocks is about 2800 kg/m³. This means that each cubic metre has a mass of 2800 kg.

▲ Around the world, there is an international network of recording stations for monitoring seismic waves.

1 *P-waves* and *S-waves* can travel through the Earth:
  a) Which type is faster? How you can tell this from the seismogram on the opposite page?
  b) Which type is transverse?
2 Why do seismic waves bend when they travel through the Earth?
3 The graph on the right shows the speeds of P and S-waves at different depths down to the Earth's centre.
  a) Which line is for the P-waves? How can you tell?
  b) At what depth is the boundary between the mantle and the outer core?
  c) How can you tell that the Earth's outer core is liquid?

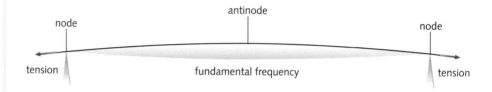

Sounds from strings and pipes (1)

Sound wave essentials

Sound waves are caused by vibrations. If a plucked string has a frequency of 100 hertz (Hz), it is vibrating 100 times per second and sending out 100 sound waves per second.

The sound waves are a series of compressions ('squashes') and rarefactions ('stretches') which travel through the air.

The higher the frequency, the higher the pitch of the note heard.

string vibrates at
fundamental frequency

length halves,
fundamental frequency doubles

Vibrating strings

If you pluck a guitar string, the simplest way it can vibrate is as shown below. The amplitude (size) of the oscillation varies along the string. A point where the amplitude is zero is called a **node**. A point where it is a maximum is called an **antinode**.

node   antinode   node

tension   fundamental frequency   tension

The string above is vibrating at its **fundamental frequency**. This frequency depends on several factors:

● **The tension** (stretching force) in the string. Increasing the tension increases the fundamental frequency. For example, on a guitar, changes in tension are used to make tuning adjustments.

● **The length** of the string. *Halving* the vibrating length of the string *doubles* the fundamental frequency – provided the tension does not change – and raises the pitch of the note by one octave.

● **The mass per metre** of the string. Heavy strings vibrate more slowly than light ones (of the same length and tension).

A stretched string can vibrate in various ways, or **modes**, depending on how it is plucked. The one above is the fundamental mode. Others occur at 2, 3, and 4 times the fundamental frequency ...and so on. Simple multiples of the fundamental frequency are called **harmonics**.

Normally, when a guitar string is plucked, higher, weaker harmonics are produced on top of the fundamental frequency. The extra frequencies, called **overtones**, give the guitar its characteristic sound, or **quality**.

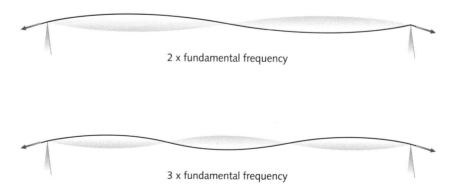

2 x fundamental frequency

3 x fundamental frequency

This guitar has six 'strings' (wires). The upper one has the lowest fundamental frequency. For a higher mass per metre and easy tension adjustment, the lower-frequency wires are made as narrow, coiled springs.

lower frequency string

higher frequency string

Making sounds louder

By themselves, guitar strings do not move enough air to make a loud sound. This problem can be overcome in two ways:

In an electric guitar, pick-ups under the strings change the vibrations into electrical signals. These are boosted by an amplifier and used to vibrate the cone of a loudspeaker.

In an acoustic guitar, the body of the instrument is a hollow box called a sound box. When the strings vibrate, they make the wooden surfaces of the sound box vibrate. These move more air, so the sound is louder.

The sound produced by a guitar also depends on an effect called resonance.

Resonance

When a bus starts its engine, the windows can vibrate strongly if the engine is ticking over at just the right speed. It happens because there is a source of vibration (the engine) whose frequency exactly matches the natural frequency of vibration of another object (the windows). As a result, the amplitude (size) of the vibrations builds up to a peak. The effect is called **resonance**. It occurs at the **resonant frequency**. Above and below this frequency, the vibrations are smaller.

When guitar strings are plucked, resonances in the body of the instrument amplify (boost) some frequencies but not others. This affects the strength of the different overtones present. In a well designed guitar, the result is a pleasant sound. But in a poorly designed guitar, some frequencies may be too strong and spoil the sound.

This strip…

… has a higher natural frequency of vibration…

… than this strip

The natural frequency of vibration of an object depends its mass and size. Heavier objects vibrate more slowly than lighter ones, and bigger objects vibrate more slowly than smaller ones.

Q

1

The guitar string above is vibrating at its fundamental frequency, which is 440 Hz.

a) Redraw the string to show the mode of vibration that has a frequency of 880 Hz. How many nodes does this mode have?

b) Give *two* ways of increasing the fundamental frequency of the string on the left.

c) If the string was replaced by a heavier one of the same length and tension, how would this affect the fundamental frequency?

2 Two strings on the same guitar are tuned to exactly the same frequency and one of them is plucked.

a) What happens to the other string?

b) What is this effect called?

Related topics: sound waves **6.03**; frequency, pitch, amplitude, loudness, and overtones **6.05**

++

 # Sounds from strings and pipes (2)

Air vibrating in a pipe

The air in a pipe, tube, or open container can vibrate and give out sound waves. This happens when you blow across the top of an empty bottle – or into a wind instrument such as trumpet, trombone, or flute.

Like a stretched string, the air in a pipe has a fundamental frequency of vibration. One way of making the air vibrate is to hold a tuning fork near the open end of the pipe, as shown below. If the frequency of the tuning fork exactly matches the frequency of the air in the pipe, resonance occurs and the sound coming from the pipe is at its loudest.

The air vibrations are longitudinal (backwards and forwards)

The air vibrations can be represented symbolically like this

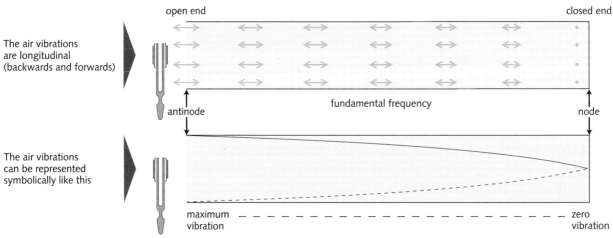

open end   closed end

antinode   fundamental frequency   node

maximum vibration   zero vibration

When the air in the pipe vibrates, it does so with an antinode (maximum vibration) at the open end and a node (zero vibration) at the closed end. As sound waves are longitudinal, the vibrations are backwards and forwards. This is difficult to show in a diagram, so a transverse waveform is normally drawn, as for a string. You can think of the wavy lines as a graph showing how the amplitude of the vibrations varies along the pipe.

Measuring the speed of sound by resonance

If a pipe is closed at one end, and the air inside is vibrating at its fundamental frequency:

length of the pipe = $\frac{1}{4}$ × wavelength of sound waves

This principle can be used to measure the speed of sound in air.

In the experiment on the left, a tuning fork of frequency 440 Hz is being held above the open end of a glass tube. The length of the air column is varied by changing the amount of water in the bottom of the tube. Starting with an almost full tube, water is slowly emptied until resonance occurs and the sound is at its loudest. On the left, this happens when the air column is 180 mm (0.18 m) long. So:

wavelength of sound = 4 × length of air column = 4 × 0.180 m = 0.72 m
But: speed of sound = frequency × wavelength
So: speed of sound =   440 Hz × 0.72 m   = 320 m/s

This value is only approximate. In reality, the pipe is not *exactly* a quarter wavelength long because the antinode occurs just beyond the open end.

The wave equation

speed = frequency × wavelength

(m/s)   (Hz)   (m)

---

frequency: 440 Hz

air | quarter wavelength: 180 mm

water

Modes of vibration in a pipe

As with stretched strings, air in a pipe can vibrate in various modes. Here are some examples:

Pipe open at one end
200 Hz
fundamental frequency
600 Hz
3 x fundamental frequency of pipe above

Pipe open at both ends
400 Hz
fundamental frequency 2 x that of pipe open at one end
800 Hz
2 x fundamental frequency of pipe above

Frequency and pipe length

If a pipe is shortened, its fundamental frequency increases. For example, *halving* the pipe length *doubles* the fundamental frequency and raises the pitch of the note by an octave.

▲ In this trombone, the length of the pipe is changed by sliding one section of pipe in or out of another.

▲ In this flute, the effective length of the pipe can be varied by covering or uncovering holes along it.

Q

1 In the diagram on the right, the air in the pipe is vibrating at its fundamental frequency.

a) Copy the diagram to show the positions of any nodes or antinodes.

b) What is the wavelength of the sound coming from the pipe?

c) If the speed of sound in air is 330 m/s, what is the frequency of the sound coming from the pipe?

d) If the pipe was double the length, what would its fundamental frequency be?

e) If the pipe (at its original length) was open at both ends, what would its fundamental frequency be?

0.3 m

6.10 Hearing, noise, and acoustics

Hearing

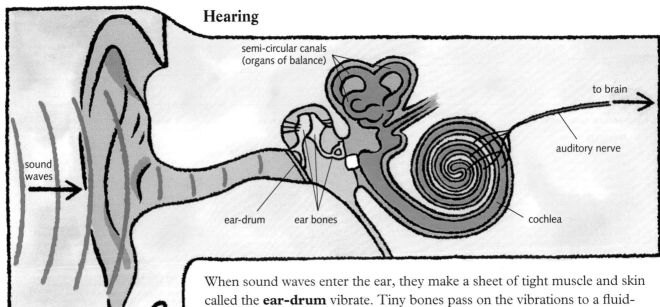

semi-circular canals
(organs of balance)

to brain

auditory nerve

sound
waves

ear-drum   ear bones

cochlea

When sound waves enter the ear, they make a sheet of tight muscle and skin called the **ear-drum** vibrate. Tiny bones pass on the vibrations to a fluid-filled tube called the **cochlea**. There, the vibrations are detected by tiny hair cells. These send signals along the **auditory nerve** to the brain.

The cochlea and auditory nerve can be damaged by very loud sounds. That is why you should not play a personal stereo at high volume. If you are exposed to loud sounds over a long period of time, the damage may be so gradual that you do not notice.

Noise

Unwanted sound is called **noise**. It is a form of pollution and, at high levels, can be damaging as well as annoying. Scientists check noise levels using meters marked in **decibels** (**dB**).

Noise can get into a room through gaps round doors and windows. But it can also pass through walls, floors, ceilings, and glass. Double glazing reduces the transmission of noise, so do carpets, curtains, and acoustic ceiling tiles. These all absorb the energy of sound waves.

Noise levels in decibels (dB)	
personal stereo, very loud	150
damage to hearing	140
rock concert	110
pneumatic drill, 3 metres away	90
busy street	70
normal conversation	60
whispering	30
threshold of hearing	0

▶ People who operate noisy vehicles or machinery wear **ear defenders** to cut down the noise. Too high a noise level causes stress and disturbs the concentration. Over a period of time, it can also cause hearing loss.

+++

Acoustics

When a band or orchestra is playing in a concert hall, the sound the audience hears depends partly on how the hall itself affects the sound waves – it depends on the **acoustics** of the hall.

A large, empty hall, with hard walls, floors, and ceiling, sounds 'echoey'. Sound is reflected from one surface to another, to another ...and so on, and it may take several seconds for the wave energy to be absorbed so that the sound dies away. This effect is called **reverberation**. If there is too much reverberation, it is difficult to hear sounds clearly.

Soft materials such as carpets, curtains, and even the audience themselves, reduce reverberation by acting as sound absorbers. Some halls also have specially designed sound absorbers suspended from the ceiling. However, it is important not to cut out reverberation altogether. Reflections make the performers sound louder. Without any reflected sounds, an orchestra may complain that the hall is 'dead'.

Multi-screen cinemas have an extra problem with acoustics. Their rooms have to be separated by thick, sound-absorbing materials so that the audience for one film does not hear sounds coming through from another.

Speed of sound

The speed of sound in air is about 330 m/s.

$$\text{speed of sound} = \frac{\text{distance travelled}}{\text{time taken}}$$

Echoes

Echoes are reflected sounds. In a large hall 40 metres long, it would take sound about $\frac{1}{4}$ second to travel right down the hall, reflect from a far wall, and return as an echo.

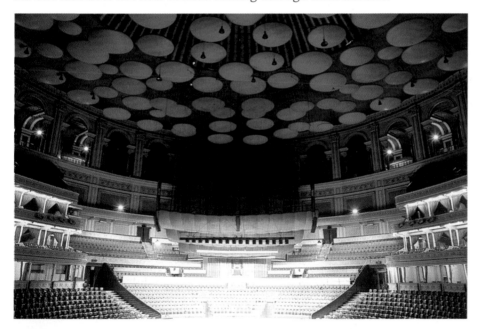

◀ Sound-absorbing 'mushrooms' on the ceiling of the Royal Albert Hall in London.

Q

1 Give *two* reasons why people who operate noisy machinery should wear ear defenders.
2 People living near airports can have problems with noise pollution. Give *two* ways in which the noise getting into a house can be reduced.
3 In the diagram on the right, someone is standing at one end of a large, bare, empty hall. The speed of sound in air is 330 m/s.
   a) If the person shouts, how long is it (in seconds) before a reflected sound reaches him from the wall at the far end?
   b) If the sound of the shout takes 2 seconds to die away, approximately how many reflections have there been before its energy is absorbed?
   c) What materials could be added to the hall to reduce the time it takes for the sound to die away?

← 30 m →

---

1 Kim and Sam are playing with a ball in the park. Unfortunately the ball finishes up in the middle of a pond, out of reach.

Kim thinks that hitting the water with a stick will make waves that will push the ball to the other side.

a) Which **two** of these words best describe the waves that are created on the water surface?

circular   longitudinal   plane   pressure   transverse [2]

b) Kim hits the water surface regularly so that waves travel out to the ball and beyond it.

  (i)   What happens to the ball?   [1]
       Sam throws a stick which hits the ball at **P**.
  (ii) Sam is successful at moving the ball across the pond. Kim is not. Explain why.   [2]

c) (i)   Kim hits the water surface regularly with the stick 20 times in 10 seconds. Calculate the frequency of the waves.   [2]
  (ii) The waves travel across the pond at 0.5 m/s. Calculate the wavelength.   [4]

MEG

2 a) The wave in the shallow tank of water shown in the figure moves at 0.08 m/s towards the left.

How long does it take for the wave to return to the position XY, but moving to the right?   [3]

b) A man is cutting down a tree with an axe. He hears the echo of the impact of the axe hitting the tree after 1.6 s.

  (i)   What sort of obstacle could have caused the echo?   [1]
  (ii) The speed of sound is 330 m/s. How far is the tree from the obstacle?

c) Distinguish between the nature of the sound wave in (b) and the water wave in (a).   [2]

UCLES (I)

3 The figure shows a cathode-ray oscilloscope trace for a sound wave produced by a loudspeaker.

a) Copy the figure and draw the trace for a louder sound of the same pitch.   [2]

b) It takes 1/50th of a second (0.02 s) for the whole trace to be produced.

  (i)   Show that the frequency of the sound produced by the loudspeaker is 100 Hz.
  (ii) Determine the wavelength in air of the sound produced by the loudspeaker. (The speed of sound in air is 330 m/s.)   [3]

UCLES (O)

4 a) A sound wave travelling through air can be represented as shown in the diagram.

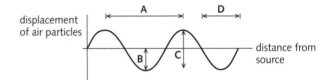

Which distance, **A**, **B**, **C**, or **D**, represents:

  (i)   one wavelength?
  (ii) the amplitude of the wave?   [2]

b) The cone of a loudspeaker is vibrating. The diagram shows how the air particles are spread out in front of the cone at a certain time.

P is a compression, **Q** is a rarefaction.

  (i)   Describe how the pressure in the air changes from **P** to **Q**.   [2]
  (ii) Describe the motion of the air particles as the sound wave passes.   [2]
  (iii) Copy the diagram of air particles above and mark and label a distance equal to one wavelength of the sound wave.   [1]

MEG

5 a) The first diagram on the next page shows a wave.

  (i)   Copy the diagram and mark the amplitude, and label it A.   [1]
  (ii) State the number of cycles ("wavelengths") shown in the diagram.   [1]

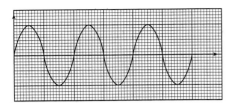

(iii) This complete wave was produced in 0.15 s. Calculate the period (time for one wave). [1]

(iv) Use the equation

frequency (Hz) = $\dfrac{1}{period~(s)}$

to calculate the frequency of the wave. [1]

b) (i) Sound is a *longitudinal wave*. Explain what is meant by a longitudinal wave. [2]

(ii) If the amplitude of a sound wave is increased, what difference would you hear? [1]

WJEC

6

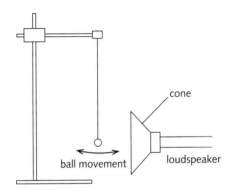

A light polystyrene ball is shown hanging very close to a loudspeaker. The loudspeaker gives out a sound of low frequency and the ball is seen to vibrate.

a) Explain how the sound from the loudspeaker causes the ball to move as described. [2]

b) Explain what will happen to the motion of the cone of the loudspeaker when:

(i) the sound is made louder; [1]

(ii) the pitch of the sound is increased. [1]

c) Calculate the frequency of a sound which has a wavelength of 0.5 m and travels at a speed of 340 m/s in air. Write down the formula that you use and show your working. [3]

WJEC

7 a) The figure shows a metal rod, 2.4 m long, being struck a sharp blow at one end using a light hammer. The time interval between the impact of the hammer and the arrival of the sound wave at the other end of the rod is measured electronically.

Four measurements of the time interval are 0.44 ms, 0.50 ms, 0.52 ms and 0.47 ms.

(i) Determine the average value of the four measurements.

(ii) Hence calculate a value for the speed of sound in the rod. [4]

UCLES (O)

8 a) When an earthquake occurs two types of shock waves, P and S, travel through the Earth.

(i) Which of these wave types travels faster?

(ii) Which of these wave types cannot travel through liquids? [2]

b) The figure shows the speed of P-waves inside the Earth.

The base of the Earth's crust occurs at the depth represented by line A.

(i) Which section of the graph represents the Earth's mantle? [1]

(ii) Explain the sudden change in P-wave speed at the depth represented by B. [2]

NEAB

9 Ultrasound waves are high frequency longitudinal waves. X-rays are high frequency transverse waves.

a) Explain the difference between transverse and longitudinal waves. [2]

b) The diagram shows an ultrasound probe used to obtain an image of an unborn baby.

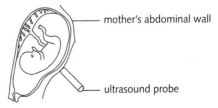

Give **two** reasons why ultrasound and not X-rays are used for this investigation. [2]

c) Describe **one** industrial use of ultrasonic waves. [2]

WJEC

145

Photocopy the list of topics below and tick the boxes of the ones that are included in your examination syllabus. (Your teacher should be able to tell you which they are.) Use your list when you revise. The spread number in brackets tells you where to find more information.

❑ 1 The difference between transverse and longitudinal waves. (6.01)

❑ 2 The meaning of wavelength. (6.01)

❑ 3 The meaning of amplitude. (6.01)

❑ 4 The meaning of frequency. (6.01)

❑ 5 The SI unit of frequency: the hertz. (6.01)

❑ 6 The equation linking speed, frequency, and wavelength. (6.01 and 6.05)

❑ 7 Demonstrating the following wave effects in a ripple tank:
- reflection
- refraction
- diffraction. (6.02)

❑ 8 How diffraction depends on the size of the gap through which the waves are passing. (6.02)

❑ 9 Evidence that sound is a form of wave motion. (6.02 – 6.03)

❑ 10 The production of sound waves. (6.03)

❑ 11 Why sound cannot travel through a vacuum. (6.03)

❑ 12 Interference of sound waves. (6.03)

❑ 13 Displaying waveforms on an oscilloscope screen. (6.03 and 6.05)

❑ 14 The speed of sound in air. (6.04)

❑ 15 Factors affecting the speed of sound. (6.04)

❑ 16 Measuring the speed of sound. (6.04 and 6.09)

❑ 17 The refraction of sound. (6.04)

❑ 18 Echoes. (6.04)

❑ 19 Uses of the echo-timing principle. (6.04)

❑ 20 The frequency range of sound waves. (6.05)

❑ 21 The link between frequency and pitch. (6.05)

❑ 22 The link between amplitude and loudness. (6.05)

❑ 23 Interpreting the waveforms on an oscilloscope screen. (6.05)

❑ 24 Fundamental frequency and overtones. (6.05, 6.08 – 6.09)

❑ 25 Ultrasound frequencies. (6.06)

❑ 26 Uses of ultrasound, including
- cleaning and breaking
- echo-sounding
- metal testing
- scanning the womb. (6.06)

❑ 27 Detecting seismic waves. (6.07)

❑ 28 The difference between P-waves, S-waves, and surface waves. (6.07)

❑ 29 Evidence for the Earth's inner structure. (6.07)

❑ 30 Nodes and antinodes in a vibrating string. (6.08)

❑ 31 Factors affecting the frequency of vibration of a stretched string. (6.08)

❑ 32 The different modes of vibration of a stretched string. (6.08)

❑ 33 Harmonics. (6.08)

❑ 34 Resonance and its effects. (6.08)

❑ 35 Resonance in the air in a pipe. (6.09)

❑ 36 Measuring the speed of sound by resonance. (6.09)

❑ 37 The different modes of vibration of the air in a pipe. (6.09)

❑ 38 The link between fundamental frequency and pipe length. (6.09)

❑ 39 The human ear. (6.10)

❑ 40 Noise, and decibels. (6.10)

❑ 41 Acoustics and reverberation. (6.10)

7

Rays and Waves

● LIGHT RAYS AND SHADOWS ● REFLECTION ● REFRACTION ● SPECTRUM OF LIGHT
● OPTICAL FIBRES ● LENSES ● CAMERA AND PROJECTOR ● THE HUMAN EYE ● COLOUR
● ELECTROMAGNETIC WAVES ● INTERFERENCE OF LIGHT WAVES ● REFRACTIVE INDEX

A rainbow over a rock formation in Monument Valley, Utah, USA. Raindrops, acting like tiny prisms, are splitting the white sunlight into its different spectral colours and reflecting them back. Because the Sun is behind the camera and the rainbow appears to extend to the ground, the rain must be falling between the camera and the distant rock.

Light and shade

▶ If you can see a beam of light, this is because tiny particles of dust, smoke, or mist in the air are reflecting some of the light into your eyes.

For you to see something, light must enter your eyes. The Sun, lamps, lasers, and glowing TV screens all emit (send out) their own light. They are **luminous**. However, most objects are **non-luminous**. You see them only because daylight, or other light, bounces off them. They **reflect** light, and some of it goes into your eyes.

You can see this page because it reflects light. The white parts reflect most light and look bright. However, the black letters **absorb** nearly all the light striking them. They reflect very little and look dark.

Diffuse reflection

Regular reflection

Absorption

Transmission

Most surfaces are uneven, or contain particles that scatter light. As a result, they reflect light in all directions. The reflection is **diffuse**. However, mirrors are smooth and shiny. When they reflect light, the reflection is **regular**.

Transparent materials like glass and water let light pass right through them. They **transmit** light.

Features of light

Light is a form of radiation This means that light radiates (spreads out) from its source. In diagrams, lines called **rays** are used to show which way the light is going.

Light travels in straight lines You can see this if you look at the path of a sunbeam or a laser beam.

Light transfers energy Energy is needed to produce light. Materials gain energy when they absorb light. For example, solar cells use the energy in sunlight to produce electricity.

Light travels as waves Light radiates from its source rather as ripples spread across the surface of a pond. However, in the case of light, the 'ripples' are tiny, varying electric and magnetic fields. These 'ripples' are very small: about 2000 light waves would fit into a millimetre.

Some effects of light, however, are best explained by thinking of light as a stream of tiny 'energy particles'. Scientists call these particles **photons**.

Light can travel through empty space Electric and magnetic ripples do not need a material to travel through. That is why light can reach us from the Sun and stars.

Light is the fastest thing there is In a vacuum (in space, for example), the speed of light is 300 000 kilometres *per second*. Nothing can travel faster than this. The speed of light seems to be a universal speed limit.

This solar-powered car uses the energy in sunlight to produce electricity for its motor.

Shadows

In diagram A below, light from the small bulb can only reach part of the screen. The **shadow** is the darker region where the light is blocked. Light travels in straight lines, so it cannot reach this region.

In diagram B, the lamp is an extended (spread-out) source of light. This time, the shadow is blurred at the edges. This is because each point on the lamp causes a different shadow and they all overlap.

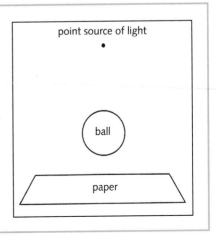

Related topics: speed **2.01**; energy **4.01**; electromagnetic waves **7.10**; photons **11.09**; Sun, Moon, and eclipses **12.01**

Q

1 Give *two* examples each of objects which
   a) emit their own light
   b) are only visible because they reflect light from another source.
2 Describe *two* pieces of evidence that light travels in straight lines.
3 If the Moon is 384 000 km from Earth, the Sun is 150 000 000 km from Earth, and the speed of light is 300 000 km/s, calculate the time taken for light to travel
   a) from the Moon to the Earth
   b) from the Sun to the Earth.
4 **a)** Copy the diagram on the right and draw the region on the paper where a shadow is formed.
   b) Explain why, if the bulb is replaced by a bright globe, the shadow becomes blurred at the edges.

Reflection in plane mirrors

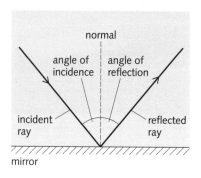

The laws of reflection

When a ray of light strikes a mirror, it is reflected as shown on the left. The incoming ray is the **incident ray**, the outgoing ray is the **reflected ray**, and the line at right-angles to the mirror's surface is called a **normal**. The mirror in this case is a **plane mirror**. This just means that it is a flat mirror, rather than a curved one.

There are two **laws of reflection**. They apply to all types of mirror:

1 The angle of incidence is equal to the angle of reflection.
2 The incident ray, the reflected ray, and the normal all lie in the same plane.

Put another way, light is reflected at the same angle as it arrives, and the two rays and the normal can all be drawn on one flat piece of paper.

Image in a plane mirror

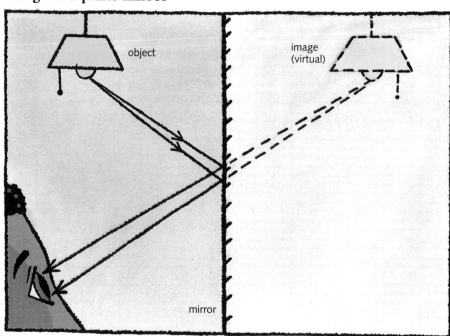

In the diagram above, light rays are coming from an **object** (a lamp) in front of a plane mirror. Thousands of rays could have been drawn but, for simplicity, only two have been shown. After reflection, some of the rays enter the girl's eye. To the girl, they seem to come from a position behind the mirror, so that is where she sees an **image** of the lamp. Dotted lines have been drawn to show the point where two of the reflected rays appear to come from. The dotted lines are *not* rays.

The image seen in the mirror looks exactly the same as the object, apart from one important difference. The image is **laterally inverted** (back to front).

Real and virtual images In a cinema, the image on the screen is called a **real image** because rays from the projector focus (meet) to form it. The image in a plane mirror is not like this. Although the rays *appear* to come from behind the mirror, no rays actually pass through the image and it cannot be formed on a screen. An image like this is called a **virtual image**.

The word AMBULANCE is laterally inverted so that it reads correctly when seen in a driving mirror.

Finding the position of an image in a mirror

The position of an image in a plane mirror can be found by experiment:

Put a mirror upright on a piece of paper. Put a pin (the object) in front of it. Mark the positions of the pin and the mirror.

Line up one edge of a ruler with the image of the pin. Draw a line along the edge to mark its position. Then repeat with the ruler in a different position.

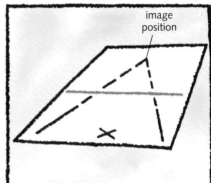

Take away the mirror, pin, and ruler. Extend the two lines to find out where they meet. This is the position of the image.

The result of the experiment can be checked like this. If a second pin is put *behind* the mirror, in the position found for the image, the pin should be in line with the image, as shown on the right. And it should stay in line when you move your head from side to side. Scientifically speaking, there should be **no parallax** (no relative movement) between the second pin and the image when you change your viewing position. If there is relative movement (parallax), then the two are not in the same position.

If a second pin is put in exactly the same position as the image of the first pin, it should stay in line with the image, wherever you view it from.

Rules for image size and position

When a plane mirror forms an image:
- The image is the same size as the object.
- The image is as far behind the mirror as the object is in front.
- A line joining equivalent points on the object and image passes through the mirror at right-angles.

1 a) Copy the diagram on the right. Draw in the image in its correct position.

b) From the object arrow's tip, A, draw two rays which reflect from the mirror and go into the person's eye.

c) The image cannot be formed on a screen. What name is given to this type of image?

d) Can the person see an image of the arrow's tail, B? If not, why not?

2 A man stands 10 m in front of a large, plane mirror. How far must he walk before he is 5 m away from his image?

7.03 Refraction of light

The 'broken pen' illusion on the left occurs because light is bent by the glass block. The bending effect is called **refraction**.

The diagram below shows how a ray of light passes through a glass block. The line at right-angles to the side of the block is called a **normal**. The ray is refracted towards the normal when it enters the block, and away from the normal when it leaves it. The ray emerges parallel to its original direction (provided the block has parallel sides).

Refraction would also occur if the glass were replaced with another transparent material, such as water or acrylic plastic, although the angle of refraction would be slightly different. The material that light is travelling through is called a **medium**.

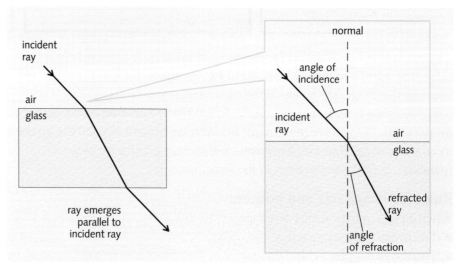

Real and apparent depth

Because of refraction, water (or glass) looks less deep than it really is. Its apparent depth is less than its real depth. This diagram shows why:

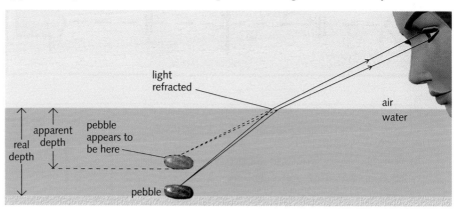

Why light is refracted

Scientists explain refraction as follows. Light is made up of tiny waves. These travel more slowly in glass (or water) than in air. When a light beam passes from air into glass, as shown on the left, one side of the beam is slowed before the other. This makes the beam 'bend'.

Refractive index

In a vacuum (empty space), the speed of light is 300 000 km/s. In air, it is effectively the same. However, in glass, light slows to 200 000 km/s.

The **refractive index** of a medium is defined like this:

$$\text{refractive index} = \frac{\text{speed of light in vacuum}}{\text{speed of light in medium}}$$

300, 000
300, 000

So, in the case of glass:

$$\text{refractive index} = \frac{300\,000 \text{ km/s}}{200\,000 \text{ km/s}} = 1.5$$

Some refractive index values are given on the right. The medium with the *highest* refractive index has the *greatest* bending effect on light because it slows the light the *most*.

medium	refractive index
diamond	2.42
glass (crown)	1.52
acrylic plastic (Perspex)	1.49
water	1.33

The above figures are based on more accurate values of the speed of light than those used on the left.

The refractive index of glass varies depending on the type of glass. Refractive index also varies slightly depending on the colour of the light.

RI = 1.52 = 200,000,
$\frac{1}{1.33}$ =
$S_m = \frac{300000}{1.333} = 225563$

Refraction by a prism

A **prism** is a triangular block of glass or plastic. The sides of a prism are not parallel. So, when light is refracted by a prism, it comes out in a different direction. It is **deviated**.

If a narrow beam of white light is passed through a prism, it splits into a range of colours called a **spectrum**, as shown below. The effect is called **dispersion**. It occurs because white is not a single colour but a mixture of all the colours of the rainbow. The prism refracts each colour by a different amount.

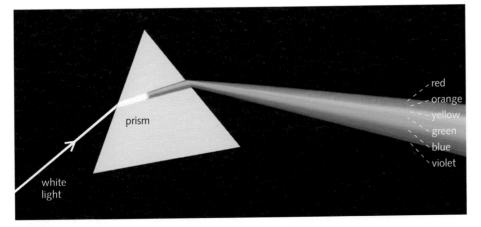

prism

white light

red
orange
yellow
green
blue
violet

◀ Most people think that they can see about six colours in the spectrum of white light. However, the spectrum is really a continuous change of colour from beginning to end.

Red light is deviated (bent off-course) least by a prism. Violet light is deviated most. However, in this diagram, the difference has been exaggerated.

Q

For questions 1b and 3, you will need to refer to the table at the top of the page. Assume that the speed of light in a vacuum is 300 000 km/s.

1 **a)** Copy the diagram on the right. Draw in and label the *normal*, the *refracted ray*, the *angle of incidence*, and the *angle of refraction*.
b) How would your diagram be different if the ray was passing into water rather than glass?
2 **a)** When white light passes through a prism, it spreads into a spectrum of colours. What is the spreading effect called?
b) Which colour is deviated most by a prism?
c) Which colour is deviated least?
3 Calculate the speed of light in water.

air | glass

7.04 Total internal reflection

The inside surface of water, glass, or other transparent material can act like a perfect mirror, depending on the angle at which the light strikes it.

The diagrams below show what happens to three rays leaving an underwater lamp at different angles. Angle c is called the **critical angle**. For angles of incidence greater than this, there is no refracted ray. All the light is reflected. The effect is called **total internal reflection**.

i = angle of incidence

The ray splits into a refracted ray and a weaker reflected ray.

c = critical angle

The rays splits, but the refracted ray only just leaves the surface.

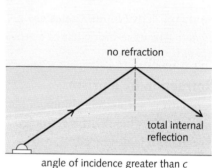

angle of incidence greater than *c*

There is no refracted ray. The surface of the water acts like a perfect mirror.

The value of the critical angle depends on the material. For example:

critical angle			
water 49°	acrylic plastic 42°	glass (crown) 41°	diamond 24°

Reflecting prisms

In the diagrams below, inside faces of prisms are being used as mirrors. Total internal reflection occurs because the angle of incidence on the face (45°) is greater than the critical angle for glass or acrylic plastic.

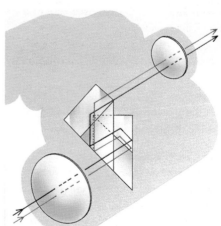

Periscope This is an instrument for looking over obstacles. Prisms reflect the light, although they can be be replaced with mirrors.

Rear reflectors (on cars and cycles) The direction of the incoming light is reversed by *two* total internal reflections.

Binoculars The lens system in each 'barrel' produces an upside-down image. Reflecting prisms are used to turn it the right way up.

Optical fibres

Optical fibres are very thin, flexible rods made of special glass or transparent plastic. Light put in at one end is total internally reflected until it comes out of the other end, as shown below. Although some light is absorbed by the fibre, it comes out almost as bright as it goes in – even if the fibre is several kilometres long.

core

Single optical fibre In the type shown above, the inner glass core is coated with glass of a lower refractive index.

Bundle of optical fibres Provided the fibres are in the same positions at both ends, a picture can be seen through them.

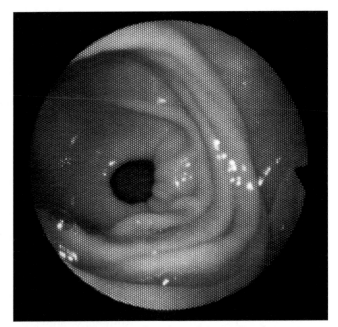

▲ Optical fibres can carry telephone calls. The signals are coded and sent along the fibre as pulses of laser light. Fewer booster stations are needed than with electrical cables.

▲ This photograph was taken through an **endoscope**, an instrument used by surgeons for looking inside the body. An endoscope contains a long, thin bundle of optical fibres.

1 Glass has a critical angle of 41°. Explain what this means.

2 **a)** Copy and complete the diagrams on the right to show where each ray will go after it strikes the prism.
   b) If the prisms on the right were transparent triangular tanks filled with water, would total internal reflection still occur? If not, why not?

3 **a)** Give *two* examples of the practical use of optical fibres.
   b) Give *two* other examples of the practical use of total internal reflection.

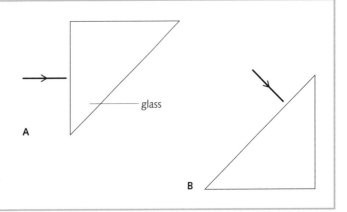

glass

A

B

Related topics: refraction **7.03**; calculating the critical angle **7.13**; optical fibres in communications **10.07**

155

7.05 Lenses (1)

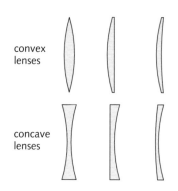

convex lenses

concave lenses

Lenses bend light and form images. There are two main types of lens. The diagram on the left shows some examples of each.

Convex lenses These are thickest in the middle and thin round the edge. When rays parallel to the principal axis pass through a convex lens, they are bent inwards. The point F where they converge (meet) is called the **principal focus**. Its distance from the centre of the lens is the **focal length**. A convex lens is known as a **converging lens**.

Rays can pass through the lens in either direction, so there is another principal focus F′ on the opposite side of the lens and the same distance from it.

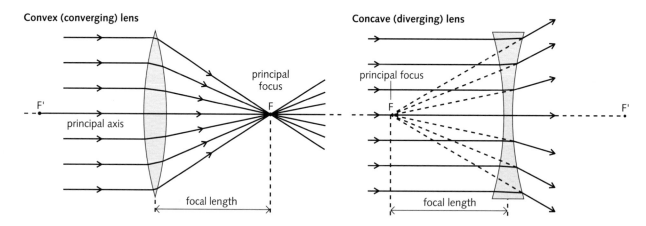

Convex (converging) lens

F′
principal axis
principal focus
F
focal length

Concave (diverging) lens

principal focus
F
F′
focal length

How lenses bend light

Lenses are made of glass, plastic, or other transparent material. Each section of a lens acts like a tiny prism, refracting (bending) light as it goes in and again as it comes out. Expensive lenses have special coatings to reduce the colour-spreading of the prisms.

Concave lenses are thin in the middle and thickest round the edge. When rays parallel to the principal axis pass through a concave lens, they are bent outwards. The principal focus is the point from which the rays appear to diverge (spread out). A concave lens is a **diverging lens**.

Real images formed by convex lenses

In the diagram below, rays from a very distant object are being brought to a focus by a convex lens. Rays come from all points on the object. However, for simplicity, only a few rays from one point have been shown. Together, the rays form an image which can be picked up on a screen. An image like this is called a **real image**. It is formed in the **focal plane**.

In a camera, a convex lens is used as below to form a real image on a piece of film. The image in the eye is formed in the same way.

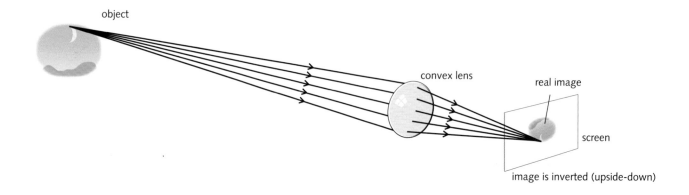

object

convex lens

real image

screen

image is inverted (upside-down)

The rays from a point on a very distant object are effectively parallel, so the image passes through the principal focus. However, for an object at any other distance, the image is in a different position.

You can predict where a convex lens will form an image by drawing a **ray diagram**. There are two examples below. Each has these features:

- For simplicity, rays are drawn from just one point on the object.
- The rays used are the **standard rays** described on the right. These are chosen because it is easy to work out where they go. Only two of them are needed to find where the image is.
- For simplicity, rays are shown bending at the line through the middle of the lens. In reality, bending takes place at each surface.

Standard rays

In ray diagrams, any two of the following rays are needed to fix the image position and size:

1 A ray through the centre passes straight through the lens.

2 A ray parallel to the principal axis passes through F after leaving the lens.

3 A ray through F′ leaves the lens parallel to the principal axis.

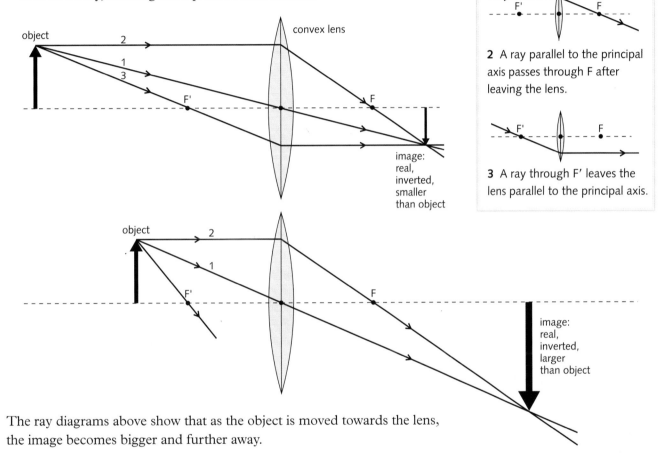

image:
real,
inverted,
smaller
than object

image:
real,
inverted,
larger
than object

The ray diagrams above show that as the object is moved towards the lens, the image becomes bigger and further away.

A film projector uses a convex lens to form a magnified, real image on a screen a long way away from it, as in the lower diagram.

Q

1 a) Which of the lenses on the right is a convex lens?
  b) Which one is a converging lens?
  c) What is meant by the *principal focus* of the convex lens?
  d) What is meant by the *focal length* of the convex lens?
2 a) If a convex lens picks up rays from a very distant object, where is the image formed?
  b) If the object is moved towards the lens, what happens to the position and size of the image?
3 Draw a ray diagram like one of those above, but with the object exactly 2 × focal length away from the lens. Draw in and describe the image.

A   B

7.06 Lenses (2)

Convex lens as a magnifying glass

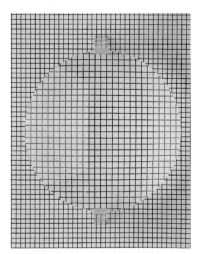

▲ Thick, bulging convex lenses have the shortest focal lengths and make the most powerful magnifying glasses.

Thin convex lenses have longer focal lengths and are much less powerful.

If an object is closer to a convex lens than the principal focus, the rays never converge. Instead, they appear to come from a position behind the lens. The image is upright and magnified. It is called a **virtual image** because no rays actually meet to form it and it cannot be picked up on a screen. Used like this, a convex lens is often called a **magnifying glass**.

Drawing accurate ray diagrams

Problems like the one below can be solved by doing a ray diagram as an accurate scale drawing on graph paper:

Example An object 2 cm high stands on the principal axis at a distance of 9 cm from a convex lens. If the focal length of the lens is 6 cm, what is the image's position, height, and type?

For accuracy, you need to choose a scale that makes the diagram as large as possible. In the drawing below, 1 cm on the paper represents 2 cm of actual distance. When the final measurements are scaled up, they show that the image is 18 cm from the lens, 4 cm high, and real.

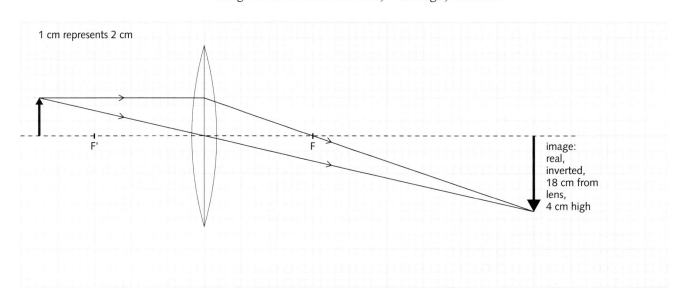

1 cm represents 2 cm

image: real, inverted, 18 cm from lens, 4 cm high

Measuring the focal length of a convex lens

You can find an approximate value for the focal length of a convex lens by forming an image of a distant window (or other distant bright object) on a screen. Rays from the window are almost parallel, so the image is close to the principal focus of the lens. Therefore the distance from the image to the lens is approximately the same as the focal length.

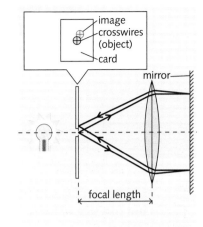

For a more accurate measurement, you can use the method shown on the right. Here, the object is a set of illuminated crosswires. Its position is adjusted until a clear image is picked up alongside it on the card. As the rays are being reflected back to the position they came from, they must be parallel when they strike the mirror. So the crosswires must be exactly at the principal focus of the lens.

Linear magnification

In the diagram on the right, the image distance is *twice* the object distance. As the two triangles formed are similar, the sizes of the image and object are in the same proportion as their distances. So, the image height is *twice* the object height. The **linear magnification** in this case is 2:

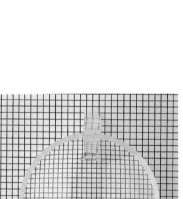

$$\text{linear magnification} = \frac{\text{image height}}{\text{object height}} = \frac{\text{image distance}}{\text{object distance}}$$

This equation applies whatever the type of lens or image.

Images formed by concave lenses

In the diagram below, two standard rays have been used to show how a concave lens forms an image. Wherever the object is positioned, the image is always small, upright, and virtual.

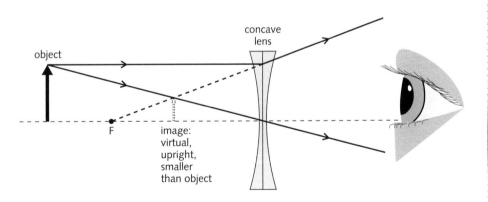

▲ A concave lens forms a small, upright, virtual image.

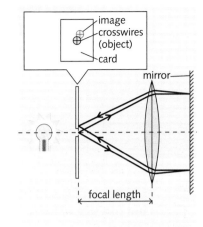

1 **a)** An object 2 cm high is placed 12 cm away from a convex lens of focal length 6 cm. By doing an accurate drawing on graph paper, find the position, height, and type of image.
b) The object is moved so that it is only 10 cm away from the lens. Use another drawing to find the new position, height, and type of image.
c) What is the linear magnification in part b?

2 Where should the object be placed if the image formed by a convex lens is to be
a) virtual, and larger than the object?
b) real, and the same size as the object?
c) real, and larger than the object?
3 Draw a labelled diagram to show how you could quickly find an approximate value for the focal length of a convex lens.

7.07 Camera and projector

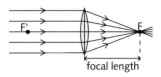
The camera

A camera uses a convex lens to form a small, inverted, real image on a piece of film at the back.

The lens is moved in or out to make focusing adjustments. In many cameras, this happens automatically. In cheaper cameras, the lens is fixed.

The shutter opens and shuts quickly to let a small amount of light into the camera. On some cameras, the speed of the shutter can be adjusted.

The film is kept in darkness until the shutter opens. It is coated with light-sensitive chemicals which are changed by the different shades and colours in the image. When the film is processed, these changes are 'fixed', and the developed film is used to print the photograph.

The diaphragm is a set of sliding plates between the lens and the film. It controls the **aperture** (diameter) of the hole through which the light passes. In bright sunshine, a small aperture might be used to cut down the amount of light reaching the film. Many cameras have automatic aperture adjustment. Cheaper cameras usually have a fixed aperture.

▲ For very distant objects, the film needs to be at the principal focus F of the lens.

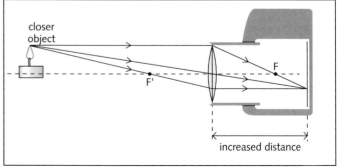

▲ For closer objects, the lens must be moved further away from the film.

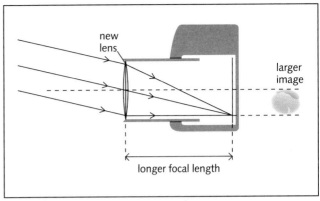

▲ On some cameras, the lens can be changed............................

▲ A longer focal length lens gives a larger image.

The projector

A projector uses a convex lens to form a large, inverted, real image on a screen. The object is a brightly lit piece of film with a picture on it.

The projection lens forms the image on the screen. To get a large image, the lens has to be a long way from the screen. The lens is moved backwards or forwards in its holder to make focusing adjustments.

The film or transparency must be upside down to get an upright picture on the screen. As the image is large and distant, the film must be positioned just outside the principal focus F′ of the projection lens.

The condenser lens concentrates light on the film so that it is very bright and evenly lit.

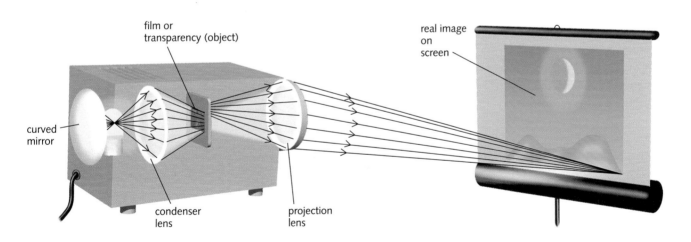

Q

1. Give *two* ways in which the amount of light entering a camera can be controlled.
2. An object moves closer to a camera. Which way must the lens be moved to keep the image in focus?
3. The original lens is removed from a camera and a new one of shorter focal length fitted.
   a) How will this affect the size of the image?
   b) What must the position of the new lens be compared with the original one?
4. In a projector, what job is done by
   a) the condenser lens
   b) the projection lens?
5. Why must the film or transparency be put into a projector upside-down?
6. Someone is using a projector when they decide to move the screen closer and re-focus the image.
   a) How will the size of the image be affected?
   b) Which way must the lens be moved?

Related topics: convex lenses and ray diagrams 7.05–7.06

7.08 The human eye

Like a camera, the human eye uses a convex lens system to form a small, inverted, real image of an object in front of it.

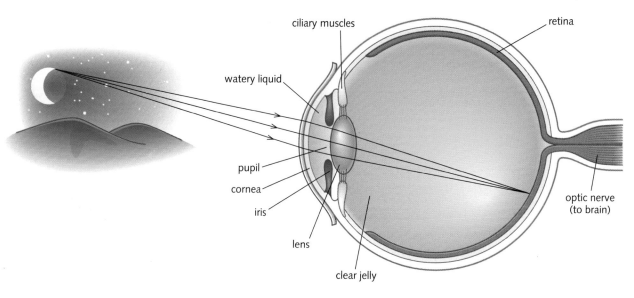

The cornea is a curved 'window' over the front of the eye. The cornea and the watery liquid behind do most of the converging of the light.

The lens is used to make focusing adjustments: the process is called **accommodation**. The lens does not move backwards and forwards as in a camera. Instead, it is flexible, and its shape is changed by the ring of **ciliary muscles** around it. When an object moves closer to the eye, the lens thickens so that the image stays in focus on the back.

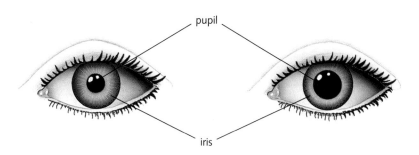

The iris is the bit that makes your eyes brown or blue. Its job is to control the amount of light entering the eye. The light passes through a gap in the middle, called the **pupil**. If you walk into a dark room, the pupil automatically becomes bigger to let in more light.

The retina is the 'screen' on the back of the eye where the image is formed. It contains over 100 million light-sensitive cells. These react to light by sending nerve impulses (electrical signals) along the **optic nerve** to the brain. The brain uses the nerve impulses to form a view of the outside world.

The image on the retina is upside-down. However, the brain is so used to this view, that it thinks of it as the right way up!

Convex lens essentials

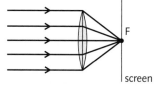

Rays from a distant point are effectively parallel. A convex lens makes them converge at its **principal focus** F.

If the rays come from a closer point, the lens makes them converge further away from it.

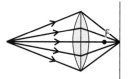

If a thicker lens is used, its focal length is shorter, so the rays converge nearer the lens.

The image formed when rays converge is called a **real image**.

Correcting defects in vision

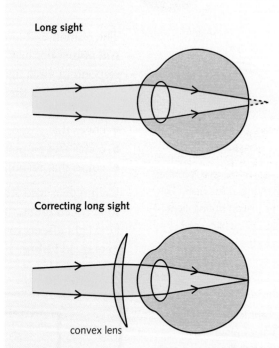

With many people, changes in the shape of the eye lens are not enough to produce sharp focusing on the retina. To overcome the problem, spectacles or contact lenses have to be worn.

Short sight In a short-sighted eye, the lens cannot be made thin enough for looking at distant objects. So the rays are bent inwards too much. They converge before they reach the retina. To correct the fault, a *concave* (diverging) lens is placed in front of the eye.

Long sight In a long-sighted eye, the lens cannot be made thick enough for looking at close objects. So the rays are not bent inwards enough. When they reach the retina, they have still not met. To correct the fault, a *convex* (converging) lens is placed in front of the eye.

From middle age onwards, the eye lens becomes less flexible and loses its ability to accommodate for objects at different distances. To overcome this difficulty, some people wear **bifocals** – spectacles whose lenses have a top part for looking at distant objects and a bottom part for close ones. If the spectacles have **progressive** lenses, the change is continuous from top to bottom.

▲ This person's eye has been fitted with a plastic lens because the natural lens had developed too many cloudy patches, called cataracts.

1 Which part of the eye
   a) is the 'screen' on which the image is formed
   b) does most of the converging of the light
   c) controls the amount of light entering the eye?
2 If an object moves closer to the eye, the lens has to adjust to refocus the image.
   a) What is this process called?
   b) How does the lens make focusing adjustments?

3 A short-sighted person cannot see distant objects clearly. Why not?
4 A long-sighted person cannot see close objects clearly. Why not?
5 What type of spectacle lens or contact lens is needed to correct for
   a) short sight
   b) long sight?

Related topics: convex and concave lenses, real images, ray diagrams **7.05–7.06**, camera **7.07**

Colour

The human eye contains millions of light-sensitive cells. These are called **rods** and **cones** because of their shape. There are far more rods than cones. Rods respond to weak light but cannot detect colour differences. Cones are mainly concentrated in the centre of the retina and are sensitive to colour. Humans can see hundreds of colours, yet the retina has only *three* types of cones:

- cones that respond to **red** light
- cones that respond to **green** light
- cones that respond to **blue** light.

Each type is also sensitive to other colours in the same part of the spectrum, so between them, they cover the full range. The brain senses *all* colours by how light affects each type of cell. So you see all colours in terms of **red**, **green**, and **blue**. These are called the **primary colours**.

Adding colours

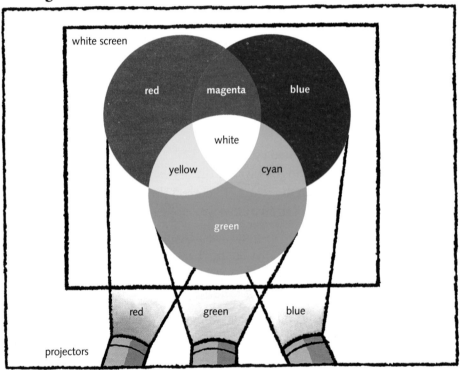

Above, beams of red, green, and blue light are overlapping on a white screen. Where all three primaries overlap, white is seen. So:

$$red + green + blue = white$$

Pure white contains all the colours of the rainbow. But a mixture of red, green, and blue can also give the eye the sensation of white. It makes all three types of colour-sensitive cell respond, just as pure white would.

Where any two primary colours overlap, a new colour is seen:

$$red + green = yellow$$
$$green + blue = cyan$$
$$red + blue = magenta$$

Yellow, cyan, and magenta are called the **secondary colours**.

The human eye

The image in the eye is formed on the **retina** at the back. This contains million of tiny, light-sensitive cells which send signals to the brain.

The spectrum

White light (such as daylight) is not a single colour but a mixture of all the colours of the rainbow. The range of colours is called a **spectrum**.

In the spectrum of white light, most people think they can see about six colours...

...however, the spectrum is really a continuous change of colour from beginning to end.

By adding red, green, and blue light in different proportions, the brain can be given the sensation of almost any colour. This effect is used in colour television, as shown on the right. The screen is covered with thousands of tiny red, green, and blue strips. These glow in different combinations, and at different intensities, to produce a full colour picture.

Part of a colour TV screen.

Subtracting colours

Most things do not give out their own light. We see them because they reflect light from the Sun (or some other source). To the eye, white daylight is a mixture of red, green, and blue. Most things look coloured in daylight because they reflect only some colours and absorb the rest. In other words, they *subtract* colours from white. For example:

In white light:

- A *red* cloth reflects red light but absorbs green and blue.
- A *yellow* cloth reflects red and green light but absorbs blue.
- A *white* cloth reflects red, green, and blue. It absorbs no colours.
- A *black* cloth reflects virtually no light. It absorbs red, green, and blue.

Coloured paints, inks, and dyes reflect some colours and absorb others. When paints are mixed together, more colours are absorbed, rather than added, so the final colour is not the same as when light beams overlap. That is why printers have a different set of colours which they call their 'primaries'.

The pictures in this book were printed using inks of just three colours: yellow, cyan, and magenta (with some black added in places as well). For example the red area below was produced by printing magenta ink on top of yellow. Red light is reflected because it is the only colour not absorbed by either the magenta ink or the yellow.

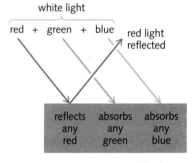

In white light, a red cloth looks red.

Filters are pieces of plastic or glass which transmit (let through) certain colours only. For example, a red filter *transmits* red light but *absorbs* green and blue.

Colour changes can happen when you shine coloured light on things. There is an example of this on the right. A red cloth looks black in green light because all the light is absorbed and none is reflected.

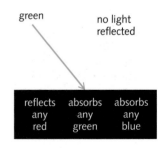

In green light, the same cloth looks black.

Q

1. What are the three primary colours?
2. What colour is produced when the three primaries are added together?
3. What colour is produced when red and green light beams overlap on a white screen?
4. What colours does a white coat reflect?

5. What colours does a black coat absorb?
6. **a)** What colour does a blue filter transmit?
   b) What colours does it absorb?
7. **a)** What colour does a green coat reflect?
   b) What colours does it absorb?
8. What colour will a green coat appear in red light?

Related topics: how surfaces reflect light **7.01**; producing a spectrum **7.03**; the human eye **7.08**; wavelength and colour **7.12**

Electromagnetic waves (1)

Wave essentials

Waves radiate (spread out) from their source. They are a form of **radiation**.

wavelength

With **transverse waves** as above, the oscillations (vibrations) are at right-angles to the direction of travel.

The number of waves sent out per second is called the **frequency**. It is measured in hertz (Hz).

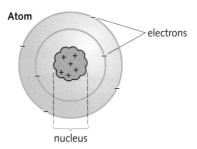

Atom

electrons

nucleus

In an atom, the electrons have negative (−) charge and the nucleus has positive (+) charge. Electromagnetic waves are emitted whenever charged particles oscillate or lose energy.

Wave equation

For any set of moving waves:

speed = frequency × wavelength
(m/s)   (Hz)   (m)

If the speed of the waves is unchanged, an *increase* in frequency means a *decrease* in wavelength, and vice versa.

1000 Hz = 1 kilohertz (kHz)

1 000 000 Hz = 1 megahertz (MHz)

Light waves belong to a whole family of **electromagnetic waves**. These have several features in common. For example:

- They can travel through a vacuum (for example, space).
- They travel through a vacuum at a speed of 300 000 kilometres per second. This is usually called the **speed of light**, although it is the speed of all electromagnetic waves.
- They are transverse waves – their oscillations are at right-angles to the direction of travel. It is electric and magnetic fields that are oscillating, not material.
- They transfer energy. A source loses energy when it radiates electromagnetic waves. A material gains energy when it absorbs them.

The electromagnetic spectrum

The full range of electromagnetic waves is called the **electromagnetic spectrum**. It is shown in the chart on the opposite page. The range of wavelengths is huge. At one end are the longest radio waves with wavelengths of several kilometres. At the other end are the shortest gamma rays with wavelengths of less than one-billionth of a millimetre.

Where electromagnetic waves come from

All matter is made of atoms. Atoms are themselves made up of a central **nucleus** with tiny particles called **electrons** orbiting around it. The nucleus and the electrons are electrically charged. Sometimes, electrons can escape from their atoms. For example, when an electric current passes through a wire, the current is a flow of free electrons.

Electromagnetic waves are emitted (sent out) whenever charged particles oscillate or lose energy in some way. For example, the vibrating atoms in a hot, glowing bulb filament emit infrared and light, and an oscillating electric current emits radio waves. The higher the frequency of oscillation, or the greater the energy change, the shorter the wavelength of the electromagnetic waves produced.

You may need information from the next spread, 7.11.

1 Give *three* properties (features) common to all electromagnetic waves.
2 Put the following in order of wavelength, starting with the longest:
   ultraviolet   X-rays   red light   violet light   microwaves   infrared
3 Name a type of electromagnetic radiation that
   a) is visible to the eye   **b)** is emitted by hot objects
   c) is diffracted by hills   **d)** can cause fluorescence
   e) is used for radar   **f)** can pass through dense metals.
4 A VHF radio station emits radio waves at a frequency of 100 MHz.
   a) What is the frequency in Hz?
   b) What is the wavelength? (speed of radio waves = 3 × 10⁸ m/s)
   c) What is the wavelength of radio waves from a long-wave transmitter, broadcasting at a frequency of 200 kHz?

The electromagnetic spectrum

frequency Hz	wavelength m	type of electromagnetic radiation	examples, uses, and effects

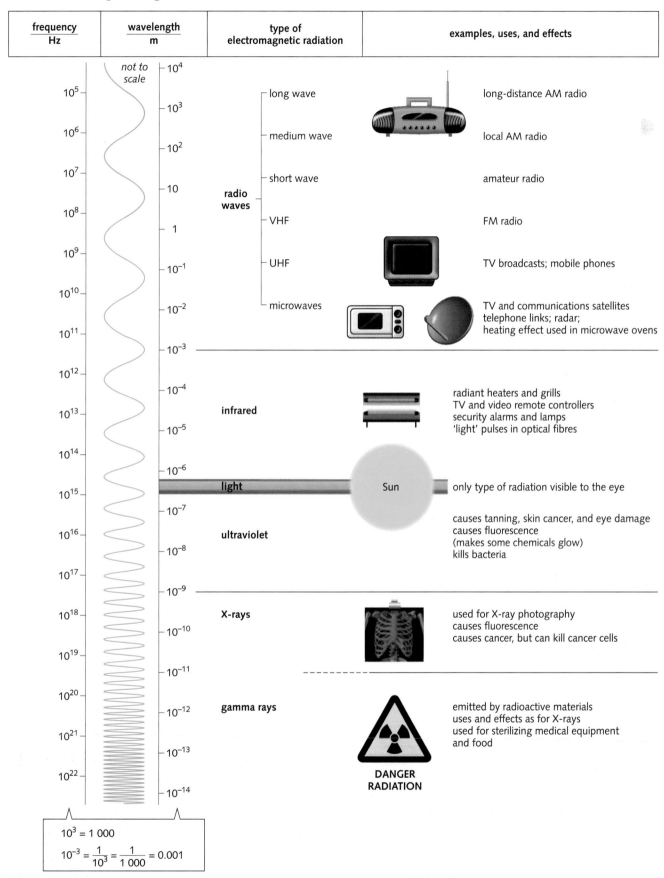

The diagram shows:

not to scale

frequency scale: 10^5, 10^6, 10^7, 10^8, 10^9, 10^{10}, 10^{11}, 10^{12}, 10^{13}, 10^{14}, 10^{15}, 10^{16}, 10^{17}, 10^{18}, 10^{19}, 10^{20}, 10^{21}, 10^{22}

wavelength scale: 10^4, 10^3, 10^2, 10, 1, 10^{-1}, 10^{-2}, 10^{-3}, 10^{-4}, 10^{-5}, 10^{-6}, 10^{-7}, 10^{-8}, 10^{-9}, 10^{-10}, 10^{-11}, 10^{-12}, 10^{-13}, 10^{-14}

radio waves
- long wave — long-distance AM radio
- medium wave — local AM radio
- short wave — amateur radio
- VHF — FM radio
- UHF — TV broadcasts; mobile phones
- microwaves — TV and communications satellites; telephone links; radar; heating effect used in microwave ovens

infrared — radiant heaters and grills; TV and video remote controllers; security alarms and lamps; 'light' pulses in optical fibres

light — Sun — only type of radiation visible to the eye

ultraviolet — causes tanning, skin cancer, and eye damage; causes fluorescence (makes some chemicals glow); kills bacteria

X-rays — used for X-ray photography; causes fluorescence; causes cancer, but can kill cancer cells

gamma rays — emitted by radioactive materials; uses and effects as for X-rays; used for sterilizing medical equipment and food

DANGER RADIATION

$10^3 = 1\ 000$

$10^{-3} = \dfrac{1}{10^3} = \dfrac{1}{1\ 000} = 0.001$

For more information about the different types of electromagnetic radiation, see the next spread, 7.11.

Related topics: thermal radiation **5.05**; transverse waves, frequency and wavelength **6.01**; radar **6.04**; light waves **7.01** and **7.12**; light spectrum **7.03**; gamma rays **7.11** & **11.02**; atoms and electric charge **8.01**; radio communication **10.08**

7.11 Electromagnetic waves (2)

Radio waves of long and medium wavelengths diffract (bend) round hills.

Microwave aerials

Radio waves

Stars are natural emitters of radio waves. However, radio waves can be produced artificially by making a current oscillate in a transmitting aerial (antenna). In a simple radio system, a microphone controls the current to the aerial so that the radio waves 'pulsate'. In the radio receiver, the incoming pulsations control a loudspeaker so that it produces a copy of the original sound. Radio waves are also used to transmit TV pictures.

Long and medium waves will diffract (bend) around hills, so a radio can still receive signals even if a hill blocks the direct route from the transmitting aerial. Long waves will also diffract round the curved surface of the Earth.

VHF and UHF waves have shorter wavelengths. VHF (very high frequency) is used for stereo radio and UHF (ultra high frequency) for TV broadcasts. These waves do not diffract round hills. So, for good reception, there normally needs to be a straight path between the transmitting and receiving aerials.

Microwaves have the shortest wavelengths (and highest frequencies) of all radio waves. Beams of microwaves, sent between dish aerials, carry telephone and TV signals to and from satellites and across country.

Like all electromagnetic waves, microwaves produce a heating effect when their energy is absorbed. Water will absorb microwaves of one particular frequency. This principle is used in microwave ovens, where microwaves penetrate deep into food and heat up the water in it.

Infrared radiation and light

When a radiant heater or grill is switched on, you can detect the infrared radiation coming from it by the heating effect it produces in your skin. In fact, *all* objects emit some infrared because of the motion of their atoms or molecules. Most radiate a wide range of wavelengths.

As an object heats up, it radiates more and more infrared, and shorter wavelengths. At about 700 °C, the shortest wavelengths radiated can be detected by the eye, so the object glows 'red hot'. Above about 1000 °C, the whole of the visible spectrum is covered, so the object is 'white hot'.

Short-wavelength infrared is often called 'infrared light', even though it is invisible. However, strictly speaking, light is just the part of the electromagnetic spectrum that is visible to the eye.

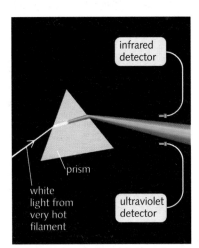

▲ Infrared and ultraviolet can be detected just beyond the two ends of the visible part of the spectrum.

Some security alarms and lamps are switched on by detectors which pick up infrared given off by the warm body of anyone who approaches. In telephone networks, speech and data are coded and sent along optical fibres as pulses of infrared 'light'. And remote controllers for TVs and video recorders work by transmitting infrared pulses.

Ultraviolet radiation

Very hot objects, such as the Sun, emit some of their radiation beyond the violet end of the visible spectrum. This is ultraviolet radiation. It is sometimes called 'ultraviolet light', even though it is invisible.

The Sun's ultraviolet is harmful to living cells. If too much penetrates the skin, it can cause skin cancer. If you have a black or dark skin, the ultraviolet is absorbed before it can penetrate too far. But with a fair skin, the ultraviolet can go deeper. Skin develops a tan to try to protect itself against ultraviolet. Ultraviolet can also damage the retina in the eye.

High in the atmosphere, a band of gases called the **ozone layer** absorbs some of the Sun's ultraviolet before it can reach the Earth's surface. Without this layer, sunlight would be much more harmful.

Fluorescence Some materials **fluoresce** when they absorb ultraviolet: they convert its energy into visible light and glow. Fluorescent paints look bright because the ultraviolet in sunlight makes them glow. In fluorescent lamps, the inside of the tube is coated with a white powder which gives off light when it absorbs ultraviolet. The ultraviolet is produced by passing an electric current through the gas (mercury vapour) in the tube.

The Sun's ultraviolet radiation causes tanning – and skin cancer.

X-rays

X-rays are given off when fast-moving electrons lose energy very quickly. For example, in an X-ray tube, the radiation is emitted when a beam of electrons hits a metal target. Short-wavelength X-rays are extremely penetrating. A dense metal like lead can reduce their strength, but not stop them. Long-wavelength X-rays are less penetrating. For example, they can pass through flesh but not bone, so bones will show up on an X-ray photograph.

All X-rays are dangerous because they damage living cells deep in the body and can cause cancer. However, concentrated beams of X-rays can be used to *treat* cancer by destroying abnormal cells.

An X-ray photograph

Gamma rays

Gamma rays come from radioactive materials. They are produced when the nuclei of unstable atoms break up or lose energy. They tend to have shorter wavelengths than X-rays because the energy changes that produce them are greater. However, there is no difference between X-rays and gamma rays of the same wavelength.

Like X-rays, gamma rays can be used in the treatment of cancer, and for taking X-ray-type photographs. As they kill harmful bacteria, they are also used for sterilizing food and medical equipment.

Ionizing radiations

Ultraviolet, X-rays, and gamma rays cause **ionization** – they strip electrons from atoms in their path. The atoms are left with an electric charge, and are then known as **ions**.

Ionization is harmful because it can kill or damage living cells, or make them grow abnormally as cancers.

For questions, see the previous spread, 7.10.

Related topics: infrared and thermal radiation **5.05**; diffraction **6.02**; light spectrum **7.03**; optical fibres **7.04** and **10.07**; X-ray tube **10.02**; radio communication **10.08**; radioactivity, gamma rays, and ionization **11.02**

7.12 Light waves

Wave essentials

Waves spread out as they pass through a gap. The effect is called **diffraction**. It is only significant if the size of the gap is about the same as the wavelength. Wider gaps cause less diffraction.

If identical sets of waves overlap, they may reinforce each other or cancel each other out, depending on whether they are in phase ('in step') or out of phase ('out of step'):

The waves above are in phase, so they reinforce each other. The effect is called **constructive interference**.

The waves above are out of phase, so they cancel each other out. The effect is called **destructive interference**.

Wavelength and colour

When light waves enter the eye, the brain senses different wavelengths as different colours. The wavelengths range from about 0.000 4 mm (violet light) to 0.000 7 mm (red light). Most light sources emit a mixture of wavelengths. However, **lasers** emit light of a single wavelength and colour. Light like this is called **monochromatic** light.

Laser light has other features as well. The beam is narrow. Also, the waves all match – they are in phase, or **coherent**. Light from an ordinary lamp is not coherent. It is emitted in random bursts of different wavelengths.

Diffraction through a single slit

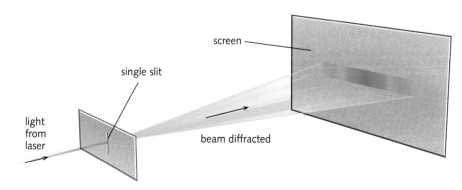

If the beam from a laser is passed through a slit, as above, the beam spreads because of diffraction. As the slit is very narrow, this suggests that the light waves must have a very short wavelength.

Interference caused by a double slit

The diagram above shows a modern version of an experiment first performed by Thomas Young in the early 1800s. Monochromatic light is passed through two narrow slits (typically about 0.5 mm apart). As a result, *two* spreading beams overlap on the screen.

The pattern on the screen is an **interference pattern**. It is caused by interference between the two sets of waves. The bright and dark lines are called **fringes**. The bright fringes are lines of constructive interference, where waves from the two slits reinforce each other. The dark fringes are lines of destructive interference, where the waves cancel each other out.

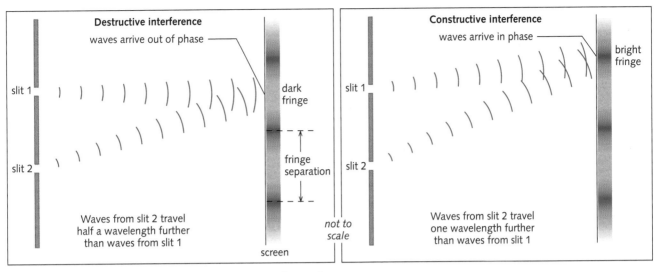

Destructive interference

waves arrive out of phase

slit 1

slit 2

dark fringe

fringe separation

Waves from slit 2 travel half a wavelength further than waves from slit 1

not to scale

screen

Constructive interference

waves arrive in phase

bright fringe

slit 1

slit 2

Waves from slit 2 travel one wavelength further than waves from slit 1

The diagram above shows how the fringes are formed.

To produce an interference pattern, the two sets of waves must be coherent. That happens in the experiment just described because both sets are from the same laser. However, if beams from two different light bulbs are overlapped, no interference pattern is seen because the beams are not coherent.

From a double-slit experiment, a value for the wavelength of the light can be found. This is because there is a simple geometrical relationship between the various distances in the experiment. For example, if the slit-to-screen distance is 1000 times the slit separation, then the fringe separation is 1000 times the wavelength. So, if the fringe separation is found by experiment to be 0.6 mm, the wavelength is 0.6 mm/1000, which is 0.000 6 mm.

◀ Light from a laser is monochromatic (single wavelength and colour) and coherent (the waves all match). Here, laser light is being used to measure the deflection of the rotating fan blades on an experimental jet engine.

 Q

1 For each of the following, give one piece of experimental evidence which suggests that
a) light is made up of waves
b) light wavelengths must be very small compared with the sizes of everyday objects.

2 In the spectrum of white light, most people think that they can see about six colours.
a) Which colour has the longest wavelength?
b) Which colour has the shortest wavelength?

3 a) What is meant by *monochromatic* light?
b) Name one source of monochromatic light.

4 Explain what is meant by
a) constructive interference
b) destructive interference.

5 In the double-slit experiment described on the opposite page
a) why are some of the lines on the screen dark?
b) why are some of the lines on the screen bright?

Related topics: diffraction **6.02**, interference of sound waves **6.03**; light spectrum **7.03**; colour **7.09**; electromagnetic spectrum **7.10–7.11**

7.13 Refraction calculations

Refraction essentials

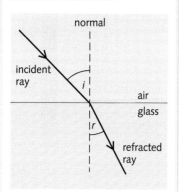

Above, a light ray bends as it enters a glass block. The bending effect is called **refraction**. The refracted ray and the incident ray are on opposite sides of the normal and in the same plane.

Refraction occurs because the light waves slow down when they pass from air into glass (or other **medium**). One side of the beam slows before the other, so the beam bends towards the normal.

When light waves pass from water back into air, they speed up again. This means that if the ray in the top diagram were reversed, it would pass back into the air along exactly the same path as it came in.

Snell's law

When light is refracted, an increase in the angle of incidence i produces an increase in the angle of refraction r. In 1620, the Dutch scientist Willebrord Snell discovered the link between the two angles: their *sines* are always in proportion.

When light passes from one medium into another:

$$\frac{\sin i}{\sin r} \text{ is constant}$$

This is known as **Snell's law**. It is illustrated by these examples:

$$\frac{\sin 15°}{\sin 10°} = \frac{0.26}{0.17} \qquad \frac{\sin 45°}{\sin 28°} = \frac{0.71}{0.47} \qquad \frac{\sin 60°}{\sin 35°} = \frac{0.87}{0.57}$$

$$= 1.5 \qquad\qquad = 1.5 \qquad\qquad = 1.5$$

Refractive index

The refractive index of a medium is defined like this:

$$\text{refractive index} = \frac{\text{speed of light in vacuum}}{\text{speed of light in medium}}$$

In a vacuum, the speed of light is 300 000 km/s – and effectively the same in air. In glass, it drops to 200 000 km/s. So, the refractive index of glass is 300 000 km/s ÷ 200 000 km/s, which is 1.5. This is the same as the value of $\sin i \div \sin r$ in the diagrams above.

Here is an alternative definition of refractive index:

$$\text{refractive index} = \frac{\sin i}{\sin r}$$

Example Light (in air) strikes water at an angle of incidence of 45°. If the refractive index of water is 1.33, what is the angle of refraction?

Applying the above equation: $1.33 = \dfrac{\sin 45°}{\sin r}$

Rearranged, this gives $\sin r = \sin 45°/1.33$. When calculated, this gives $\sin r = 0.532$. So the angle of refraction r is 32°.

Calculating the critical angle

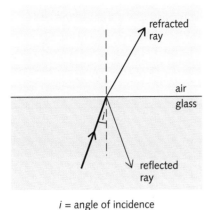

i = angle of incidence

c = critical angle

angle of incidence greater than *c*

In the diagrams above, rays are travelling from glass towards air at different angles. When the angle of incidence is greater than the **critical angle**, there is no refracted ray. All the light is reflected. There is **total internal reflection**.

Knowing the refractive index of a material, the critical angle can be calculated. For example:

On the right, the middle diagram above has been redrawn, but this time with the ray going back along its original path. This time, the angle of *incidence* is 90°, and angle *c* is now the angle of *refraction*. If the refractive index of glass is 1.5:

$$\text{refractive index} = 1.5 = \frac{\sin 90°}{\sin c}$$

so: $$1.5 = \frac{1}{\sin c} \qquad (\text{as } \sin 90° = 1)$$

rearranging: $$\sin c = \frac{1}{1.5} = 0.67$$

so *c*, the critical angle of glass, is 42°.

Note: the above figure differs slightly from that given on spread 7.04 because a simplified value for the refractive index of glass has been used in the calculation.

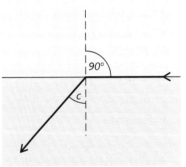

▲ Compare this with the middle diagram at the top of the page.

> Q
>
> To answer these questions, you will need a calculator (or set of tables) containing sine values.
>
> **1** The refractive index of water is 1.33. Calculate the angle of refraction if light (in air) strikes water at an angle of incidence of **a)** 24° **b)** 53°.
> **2** A transparent material has a refractive index of 2.0.
>   **a)** Calculate the critical angle.
>   **b)** If the refractive index were less than 2.0, would the critical angle be *greater* or *less* than before?
> **3** Diamond has a refractive index of 2.42. The speed of light in a vacuum (or in air) is 300 000 km/s. Calculate:
>   **a)** the speed of light in diamond **b)** the critical angle for diamond.

▲ When a diamond is cut, the facets (faces) are angled so that they produce total internal reflection. Reflected light gives the diamond its 'sparkle'.

Related topics: refraction and refractive index **7.03**; total internal reflection **7.04**

1 The diagram shows a light signal travelling through an optical fibre made of glass.

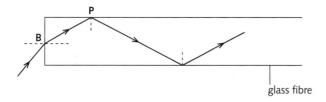

a) State **two** changes that happen to the light when it passes from air into the glass fibre at **B**.   [2]
b) Explain why the light follows the path shown after hitting the wall of the fibre at **P**.   [2]

WJEC

2 Lenses are used in many optical devices.
a) Copy and complete the table below about the images formed by some optical devices.   [6]

optical device	nature of image	size of image	position of image
eye	real		
projector		magnified	
magnifying glass			further from lens than the object

b) An object is placed closer to a converging (convex) lens than its principal focus. The figure shows an incomplete ray diagram for the formation of the image.

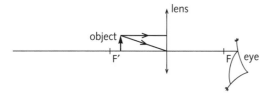

(i) Copy and complete the ray diagram and draw the image formed.
(ii) Use the ray diagram to help you describe **three** properties of this image formed by the lens.   [7]

NEAB

3 **a)** Copy the diagram and draw the path of the ray of yellow light as it passes through and comes out of the glass prism.   [2]

b) What do we call this effect?   [1]
c) State why light changes direction when it enters a glass prism.   [1]

WJEC

4 The figure shows an object OB in front of a converging lens. The principal focii of the lens are labelled F and F'. An image of OB will be formed to the right of the lens.

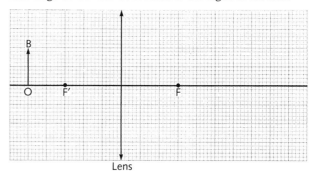

a) Copy the figure and draw two rays from the top of the object B which pass through the lens and go to the image.   [2]
b) Draw the image formed. Label this image I.   [1]
c) Calculate the linear magnification produced by the lens.   [3]

NEAB

5

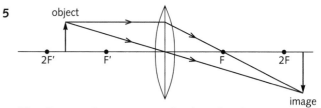

The diagram shows a converging lens forming a real image of an illuminated object.
State **two** things that happen to the image when the object is moved towards F.   [2]

WJEC

6

The diagram shows an object **O** placed in front of a convex (converging) lens and the passage of two rays from the top of the object through the lens.
a) Copy and complete the diagram (using the dimensions given) to show where the image is formed.   [1]
b) State **two** properties of the image.   [2]
c) Use the information from the completed diagram and the equation

$$linear\ magnification = \frac{height\ of\ image}{height\ of\ object}$$

to calculate the magnification produced by the lens.   [3]

WJEC

7 a)

long sight	short sight	converging lens	diverging lens

Copy and complete the table below using phrases selected from the above list.   [2]

defect of vision	name of defect	lens used to correct the defect
distant objects are seen clearly but near objects are not.		
near objects are seen clearly but distant objects are not.		

b) (i) State what change occurs to the eye when a person moves from sunlight to shade.   [1]
(ii) Name the part of the eye that causes this change. [1]

WJEC

8 a) Copy and complete the following sentence.
The secondary colours of light are cyan, magenta and
_____   [1]
b) Explain how secondary colours of light are made.   [2]

WJEC

9

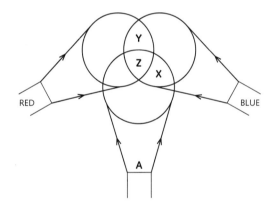

The diagram shows three lamps shining beams of light onto a white wall. The beams overlap as shown. Each beam is a different primary colour of light.
a) What is the colour of beam **A**?   [1]
b) State the colour seen, where the beams overlap at:
    (i) **X**;   [1]
    (ii) **Y**;   [1]
    (iii) **Z**.   [1]

WJEC

10

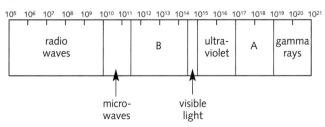

The diagram shows the main regions of the electromagnetic spectrum. The numbers show the frequencies of the waves measured in hertz (Hz).
a) Name the regions
    (i) **A**,   [1]
    (ii) **B**.   [1]
b) (i) Write down, **in words**, the equation connecting wave speed, wavelength and wave frequency.   [1]
    (ii) Calculate the frequency of the radiation with a wavelength of 0.001 m (10^{-3} m), given that all electromagnetic waves travel at a speed of 300 000 000 m/s (3×10^8 m/s) in space.   [2]
    (iii) State, to which part of the electromagnetic spectrum, the radiation in part (ii) belongs.   [1]
c) Explain how and why microwaves can cause damage to or even kill living cells.   [2]

WJEC

11 The figure shows a square block of glass JKLM with a ray of light incident on side JK at an angle of incidence of 60°. The refractive index of the glass is 1.50.

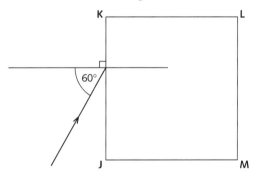

a) Calculate the angle of refraction of the ray.   [2]
b) Calculate the critical angle for a ray of light in this glass.   [2]
c) Explain why the ray shown cannot emerge from side KL but will emerge from side LM.   [3]

UCLES (O)

12 a)

less than	the same as	greater than

Copy the sentences below and use **one** of the three phrases above to complete each sentence. Each phrase may be used once, more than once or not at all.
    (i) The wavelength of radio waves is _____ the wavelength of ultraviolet radiation.   [1]
    (ii) In a vacuum the speed of ultraviolet radiation is _____ the speed of light.   [1]
    (iii) The frequency of ultraviolet radiation is _____ the frequency of infrared radiation. [1]
b) Name the part of the electromagnetic spectrum that is used to:
    (i) send information to and from satellites;   [1]
    (ii) kill harmful bacteria in food.   [1]

WJEC

175

Photocopy the list of topics below and tick the boxes of the ones that are included in your examination syllabus. (Your teacher should be able to tell you which they are.) Use your list when you revise. The spread number in brackets tells you where to find more information.

❏ 1   Luminous and non-luminous objects. (7.01)

❏ 2   The characteristics (features) of light. (7.01)

❏ 3   The speed of light. (7.01 and 7.10)

❏ 4   How shadows are formed. (7.01)

❏ 5   The laws of reflection. (7.02)

❏ 6   How and where an image is formed in a plane mirror. (7.02)

❏ 7   The difference between a real and virtual image. (7.02)

❏ 8   Finding the position of an image in a plane mirror. (7.02)

❏ 9   The refraction of light. (7.03)

❏ 10 Why water (or a glass block) looks less deep than it really is. (7.03)

❏ 11 Why light is refracted. (7.03)

❏ 12 The definition of refractive index. (7.03)

❏ 13 How a prism forms a spectrum. (7.03)

❏ 14 Total internal reflection. (7.04)

❏ 15 The meaning of critical angle. (7.04)

❏ 16 Uses of reflecting prisms. (7.04)

❏ 17 Optical fibres and their uses. (7.04)

❏ 18 The properties of convex lenses. (7.05)

❏ 19 The difference between a convex and a concave lens. (7.05)

❏ 20 The meanings of principal focus and focal length. (7.05)

❏ 21 Using a convex lens can form a real image. (7.05)

❏ 22 Using a convex lens as a magnifying glass. (7.06)

❏ 23 Drawing accurate ray diagrams for a convex lens. (7.06)

❏ 24 Measuring the focal length of a convex lens. (7.06)

❏ 25 Linear magnification. (7.06)

❏ 26 How a concave lens forms an image. (7.06)

❏ 27 The camera and its parts. (7.07)

❏ 28 The projector and its parts. (7.07)

❏ 29 The human eye and its parts. (7.08)

❏ 30 Short and long sight and their correction. (7.08)

❏ 31 How the eye sees colour. (7.09)

❏ 32 The primary colours. (7.09)

❏ 33 The effects of adding colours. (7.09)

❏ 34 Colour subtraction: the effects of paints, dyes, and filters. (7.09)

❏ 35 Electromagnetic waves. (7.10)

❏ 36 The electromagnetic spectrum. (7.10)

❏ 37 Radio waves and their properties. (7.11)

❏ 38 Microwaves and their properties. (7.11)

❏ 39 Infrared rays and their properties. (7.11)

❏ 40 Ultraviolet rays and their properties. (7.11)

❏ 41 X-rays and their properties. (7.11)

❏ 42 Gamma rays and their properties. (7.11)

❏ 43 Light waves and their properties. (7.12)

❏ 44 Diffraction of light through a single slit. (7.12)

❏ 45 Interference caused by a double slit. (7.12)

❏ 46 Snell's law for refraction. (7.13)

❏ 47 Using the refractive index in calculations. (7.13)

❏ 48 Calculating the critical angle. (7.13)

Electricity

○ CHARGE ○ CONDUCTORS AND INSULATORS ○ CURRENT, VOLTAGE, AND RESISTANCE

○ SERIES AND PARALLEL CIRCUITS ○ CONDUCTION THROUGH LIQUIDS AND GASES

○ ELECTRICAL POWER ○ MAINS ELECTRICITY ○ ELECTRIC FIELDS ○ CELLS AND BATTERIES

The city of Bogotá, Colombia, at night. Like other cities, it is so bright that it can even be seen from space. Modern industrial societies rely heavily on the use of electricity – not only for lighting, as shown here, but also for running factory machinery, information and communications systems, and heating. Typically, electricity accounts for about one sixth of an industrialized country's energy use.

Electric charge (1)

8.01

Electric charge, or 'electricity', can come from batteries and generators. But some materials become charged when they are rubbed. Their charge is sometimes called **electrostatic charge** or 'static electricity'. It causes sparks and crackles when you take off a pullover, and if you slide out of a car seat and touch the door, it may even give you a shock.

Negative and positive charges

Polythene and Perspex can be charged by rubbing them with a dry, woollen cloth.

When two charged polythene rods are brought close together, as shown below, they *repel* (try to push each other apart). The same thing happens with two charged Perspex rods. However, a charged polythene rod and a charged Perspex rod *attract* each other. Experiments like this suggest that there are two different and opposite types of electric charge. These are called **positive** (**+**) charge and **negative** (**-**) charge:

> Like charges repel; unlike charges attract.
> The closer the charges, the greater the force between them.

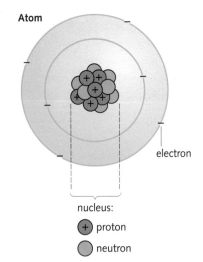

This person has been charged up. Her hairs all carry the same type of charge, so they repel each other.

Where charges come from

Everything is made of tiny particles called atoms. These have electric charges inside them. A simple model of the atom is shown on the left. There is a central **nucleus** made up of **protons** and **neutrons**. Orbiting the nucleus are much lighter electrons:

> Electrons have a negative (-) charge.
> Protons have an equal positive (+) charge.
> Neutrons have no charge.

Normally, atoms have equal numbers of electrons and protons, so the *net* (overall) charge on a material is zero. However, when two materials are rubbed together, electrons may be transferred from one to the other. One material ends up with more electrons than normal and the other with less. So one has a net negative charge, while the other is left with a net positive charge. Rubbing materials together does not *make* electric charge. It just *separates* charges that are already there.

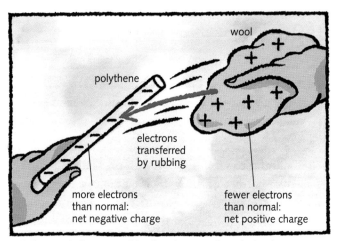

▲ When polythene is rubbed with a woollen cloth, the polythene pulls electrons from the wool.

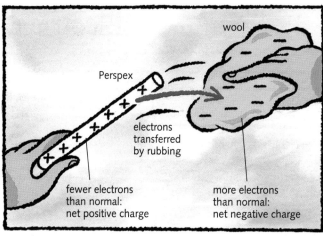

▲ When Perspex is rubbed with a woollen cloth, the wool pulls electrons from the Perspex.

Conductors and insulators

When some materials gain charge, they lose it almost immediately. This is because electrons flow through them or the surrounding material until the balance of negative and positive charge is restored.

Conductors are materials that let electrons pass through them. Metals are the best electrical conductors. Some of their electrons are so loosely held to their atoms that they can pass freely between them. These **free electrons** also make metals good thermal conductors.

Most non-metals conduct charge poorly or not at all, although carbon is an exception.

Insulators are materials that hardly conduct at all. Their electrons are tightly held to atoms and are not free to move – although they can be transferred by rubbing. Insulators are easy to charge by rubbing because any electrons that get transferred tend to stay where they are.

Semiconductors are 'in-between' materials. They are poor conductors when cold, but much better conductors when warm.

Conductors	
Good	*Poor*
metals	water
especially:	human body
silver	earth
copper	
aluminium	
carbon	

Semiconductors	
silicon	germanium

Insulators	
plastics	glass
e.g:	rubber
PVC	dry air
polythene	
Perspex	

conductor (copper)

insulator (PVC)

◄ The 'electricity' in a cable is a flow of electrons. Most cables have copper conducting wires with PVC plastic around them as insulation.

---

1 Say whether the following *attract* or *repel*:
   a) two negative charges
   c) a negative charge and a positive charge
   b) two positive charges.
2 In an atom, what kind of charge is carried by
   a) protons b) electrons c) neutrons?
3 What makes copper a better electrical conductor than polythene?

4 Why is it easy to charge polythene by rubbing, but not copper?
5 Name one non-metal that is a good conductor.
6 When someone pulls a plastic comb through their hair, the comb becomes negatively charged.
   a) Which ends up with more electrons than normal, the comb or the hair?
   b) Why does the hair become positively charged?

Electric charge (2)

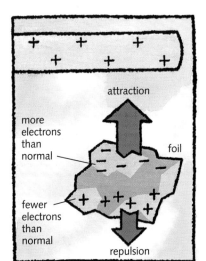

A charged object attracts an uncharged one.

Attraction of uncharged objects

A charged object will attract any uncharged object close to it. For example, the charged screen of a TV will attract dust.

The diagram on the left shows what happens if a positively charged rod is brought near a small piece of aluminium foil. Electrons in the foil are pulled towards the rod, which leaves the bottom of the foil with a net positive charge. As a result, the top of the foil is attracted to the rod, while the bottom is repelled. However, the attraction is stronger because the attracting charges are closer than the repelling ones.

Earthing

If enough charge builds up on something, electrons may be pulled through the air and cause sparks – which can be dangerous. To prevent charge building up, objects can be **earthed**: they can be connected to the ground by a conducting material so that the unwanted charge flows away.

▶ An aircraft and its tanker must be earthed during refuelling, otherwise charge might build up as the fuel 'rubs' along the pipe. One spark could be enough to ignite the fuel vapour.

Detecting charge

Electrostatic charge can be detected using a **leaf electroscope** as above. If a charged object is placed near the cap, charges are induced in the electroscope. Those in the gold leaf and metal plate repel, so the leaf rises.

Induced charges

Charges that 'appear' on an uncharged object because of a charged object nearby are called **induced charges**. In the diagram below, a metal sphere is being charged by induction. The sphere ends up with an *opposite* charge to that on the rod, which never actually touches the sphere.

Unit of charge

The SI unit of charge is the **coulomb** (**C**). It is equal to the charge on about 6 million million million electrons, although it is not defined in this way.

One coulomb is a relatively large quantity of charge, and it is often more convenient to measure charge in **microcoulombs**:

1 microcoulomb (μC) = 10^{-6} C   (one millionth of a coulomb)

The charge on a rubbed polythene rod is, typically, only about 0.005 μC.

Using electrostatic charge

In the following examples, the charge comes from an electricity supply rather than from rubbing.

Electrostatic precipitators are fitted to the chimneys of some power stations and factories. They reduce pollution by removing tiny bits of ash from the waste gases. They work like this. As the ash and waste gases pass through the chamber, the ash is given a negative charge by the wires. The charged ash is attracted to the positive plates and sticks to them. When shaken from the plates, it is collected in the tray at the bottom.

Photocopiers print copies of documents on paper. The principle of how they work is shown below:

An electrostatic precipitator

1 Inside the photocopier, a light-sensitive plate (or drum) is given a negative charge.

2 An image of the original document is projected onto the plate. The bright areas lose their charge but the dark areas keep it.

3 Powdered ink (called toner) is attracted to the charged (dark) areas.

4 A blank sheet of paper is pressed against the plate and picks up powdered ink.

5 The paper is heated so that the powdered ink melts and sticks to it. The result is a copy of the original document.

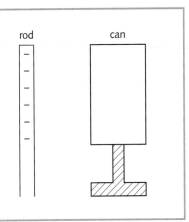

1 a) Give an example of where electrostatic charge might be a hazard.
   b) How can the build-up of electrostatic charge be prevented?
2 How many microcoulombs are there in one coulomb?
3 On the right, a charged rod is held close to a metal can. The can is on an insulated stand.
   a) Copy the diagram. Draw in any induced charges on the can.
   b) Why is the can attracted to the rod even though the net (overall) charge on the can is zero?
   c) If you touch the can with your finger, electrons flow through it. In which direction is the flow?
   d) What type of charge is left on the can after it has been touched?

Current in a simple circuit

An electric **cell** (commonly called a **battery**) can make electrons move, but only if there is a conductor connecting its two terminals. Then, chemical reactions inside the cell push electrons from the negative (-) terminal round to the positive (+) terminal.

The cell below is being used to light a bulb. As electrons flow through the bulb, they make a filament (thin wire) heat up so that it glows. The conducting path through the bulb, wires, switch, and battery is called a **circuit**. There must be a *complete* circuit for the electrons to flow. Turning the switch OFF breaks the circuit and stops the flow.

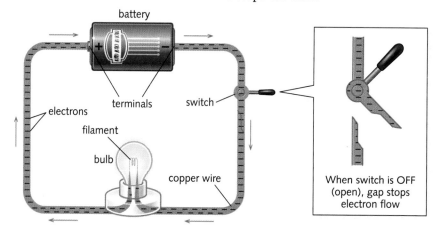

When switch is OFF (open), gap stops electron flow

The above circuit can be drawn using **circuit symbols**:

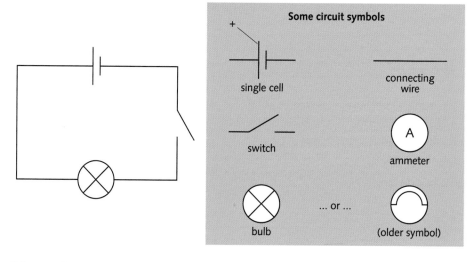

Some circuit symbols

single cell

connecting wire

switch

ammeter

bulb

... or ...

(older symbol)

An ammeter like this must be connected into the circuit the right way round. The red (+) terminal should be on the same side of the circuit as the positive (+) terminal of the battery.

Measuring current

A flow of charge is called an electric **current**. The higher the current, the greater the flow of charge.

The SI unit of current is the **ampere (A)**. About 6 million million million electrons flowing round a circuit every second would give a current of 1 A. However, the ampere is not defined in this way.

Currents of about an ampere or so can be measured by connecting an **ammeter** into the circuit. For smaller currents, a **milliammeter** is used. The unit in this case is the **milliampere (mA)**. 1000 mA = 1 A

Some typical current values

current through a small torch bulb   0.2 A   (200 mA)
current through a car headlight bulb   4 A
current through an electric kettle element   10 A

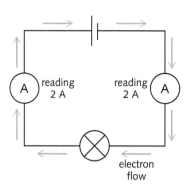

Putting ammeters (or milliammeters) into a circuit has almost no effect on the current. As far as the circuit is concerned, the meters act just like pieces of connecting wire.

The circuit on the right has two ammeters in it. Any electrons leaving the battery must flow through both, so both give the same reading:

> The current is the same at all points round a simple circuit.

Charge and current

There is a link between charge and current:

If charge flows at this rate...	then the current is...	
1 coulomb per second	1 ampere	
2 coulombs per second	2 amperes	...and so on.

The link can also be expressed as an equation:

$$\text{charge} = \text{current} \times \text{time}$$
$$(\text{C}) \qquad (\text{A}) \qquad (\text{s})$$

For example, if a current of 2 amperes flows for 3 seconds, the charge delivered is 3 coulombs.

Current direction

Some circuit diagrams have arrowheads marked on them. These show the **conventional current direction**: the direction from + to - round the circuit. Electrons actually flow the other way. Being negatively charged, they are repelled by negative charge, so are pushed out of the negative terminal of the battery.

The conventional current direction is equivalent to the direction of transfer of positive charge. It was defined before the electron was discovered and scientists realised that positive charge did not flow through wires. However, it isn't 'wrong'. Mathematically, a transfer of positive charge is the same as a transfer of negative charge in the opposite direction.

Definitions

Although it is convenient to think of 1 ampere as 1 coulomb per second, the coulomb is actually defined in terms of the ampere:

1 coulomb is the charge that passes when a current of 1 ampere flows for 1 second.

The ampere is one of the SI base units. It is defined in terms of the magnetic force produced by a current.

1 Convert these currents into amperes: **a)** 500 mA   **b)** 2500 mA
2 Convert these currents into milliamperes: **a)** 2.0 A   **b)** 0.1 A
3 **a)** Draw the circuit on the right using circuit symbols.
    b) On your diagram, mark in and label the conventional current direction and the direction of electron flow.
    c) The current reading on one of the ammeters is shown. What is the reading on the other one?
    d) Which bulb(s) will go out if the switch contacts are moved apart? Give a reason for your answer.
4 What charge is delivered if
    a) a current of 10 A flows for 5 seconds
    b) a current of 250 mA flows for 40 seconds?

Potential difference

Circuit essentials

A cell can make electrons flow round a circuit. The flow of electrons is called a current. Electrons carry a negative (-) charge. As like charges repel, electrons are pushed out of the negative (-) terminal of the cell.

Charge is measured in coulombs (C).

Energy essentials

Energy is measured in joules (J). Potential energy is the energy that something has because of its state or position.

A voltmeter

Symbol for voltmeter

cell gives electrons potential energy

electrons return to cell

electrons transfer energy to bulb

electrons lose potential energy: energy radiated

The cell above is pushing out electrons. The electrons repel each other, so, like the coils of compressed spring, they have potential energy. As the electrons slowly flow round the circuit, they transfer energy from the cell to the bulb. The energy is radiated by the hot filament.

PD (voltage) across a cell

A cell normally has a **voltage** marked on it. The higher its voltage, the more energy it gives to the electrons pushed out.

The scientific name for voltage is **potential difference** (**PD**). PD can be measured by connecting a **voltmeter** across the terminals of the cell. The SI unit of potential difference is the **volt** (**V**):

If the PD across a cell is 1 volt, then 1 joule of potential energy is given to each coulomb of charge.

If the PD across a cell is 2 volts, then 2 joules of potential energy are given to each coulomb of charge, ...and so on.

A cell produces its highest PD when not in a circuit and not supplying current. This maximum PD is called the **electromotive force** (**EMF**) of the cell. When a current is being supplied, the PD drops because of energy wastage inside the cell. For example, a car battery labelled '12 V' might only deliver 9 V when being used to turn a starter motor.

Cells in series

To produce a higher PD, several cells can be connected in **series** (in line) as shown below. The word 'battery' really means a collection of joined cells, although it is commonly used for a single cell as well.

+   1.5 V   1.5 V   1.5 V   1.5 V   −

——————— 6 V ———————

battery made up of several cells (symbol)

PDs around a circuit

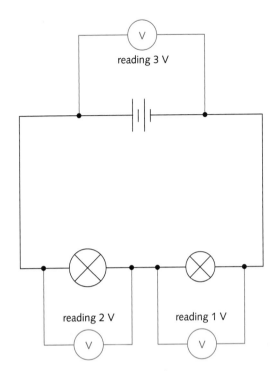

In the circuit above, the electrons flow through two bulbs. They lose some of their potential energy in the first bulb and the rest in the second. In total, all the energy supplied by the battery is radiated by the bulbs. Almost none is spent in the connecting wires.

Like the battery, each bulb has a PD across it:
If a bulb (or other component) has a PD of 1 volt across it, then 1 joule of potential energy is spent by each coloumb of charge passing through it.

The second diagram shows the same circuit with voltmeters connected across different sections (the voltmeters do not affect how the circuit works). The readings illustrate a principle which applies in any circuit:

Moving round a circuit, from one battery terminal to the other, the sum of the PDs across the components is equal to the PD across the battery.

Q

1 In what unit is each of these measured?
   a) PD b) EMF c) charge d) current e) energy
2 In the circuit on the right, the two bulbs are of different sizes and brightnesses.
   a) What type of meter is meter X?
   b) What type of meter is meter Y?
   c) What is the reading on meter Y?
   d) How much potential energy does each coulomb have as it leaves the battery?
   e) How much potential energy is lost by each coulomb passing through bulb A?
   f) How much charge passes through A every second?
   g) How much energy is radiated from A every second?

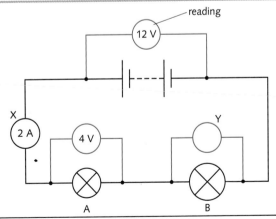

Current is measured in amperes (A) using an ammeter. If 1 ampere flows for 1 second, the charge passing is 1 coulomb.

8.05 Resistance (1)

To make a current flow through a conductor, there must be a potential difference (voltage) across it. Copper connecting wire is a good conductor and a current passes through it easily. However, a similar piece of nichrome wire is not so good and less current flows for the same PD. The nichrome wire has more **resistance** than the copper.

Resistance is calculated using the equation below. The SI unit of resistance is the **ohm** (Ω). (The symbol Ω is the Greek letter *omega*.)

$$\text{resistance } (\Omega) = \frac{\text{PD across conductor (V)}}{\text{current through conductor (A)}}$$

For example, if a PD of 6 V is needed to make a current of 3 A flow through a wire: resistance = 6 V/3 A = 2 Ω.

With a *lower* resistance, a *lower* PD would be needed to give the same current. Even copper connecting wire has some resistance. However, it is normally so low that only a very small PD is needed to make a current flow through it, and this can be neglected in calculations.

Some factors affecting resistance

The resistance of a conductor depends on several factors:

- **Length** Doubling the length of a wire doubles its resistance.
- **Cross-sectional area** Halving the 'end on' area of a wire doubles its resistance. So a thin wire has more resistance than a thick one.
- **Material** A nichrome wire has more resistance than a copper wire of the same size.
- **Temperature** For metal conductors, resistance increases with temperature. For semiconductors, it decreases with temperature.

Resistance and heating effect

There is a heating effect whenever a current flows through a resistance. This principle is used in heating elements, and also in the filaments of bulbs. The heating effect occurs because electrons collide with atoms as they pass through a conductor. The electrons lose energy. The atoms gain energy and vibrate faster. Faster vibrations mean a higher temperature.

high resistance

long, thin, nichrome wire

long, thin, copper wire

long, thick, copper wire

short, thick, copper wire

low resistance

▲ The filament of a bulb is made of very thin tungsten wire. Tungsten has a high melting point.

heating element
(nichrome wire)

Symbol for heating element

Heating elements are normally made of nichrome.

Resistance components

Resistors are specially made to provide resistance. In simple circuits, they reduce the current. In more complicated circuits, such as those in radios, TVs, and computers, they keep currents and PDs at the levels needed for other components (parts) to work properly.

Resistors can have values ranging from a few ohms to several million ohms. For measuring higher resistances, these units are useful:

1 kilohm (kΩ) = 1000 Ω   1 megohm (MΩ) = 1 000 000 Ω

Like all resistances, resistors heat up when a current flows through them. However, if the current is small, the heating effect is slight.

Variable resistors (rheostats) are used for varying current. The one on the right is controlling the brightness of a bulb. In hi-fi equipment, rotary (circular) variable resistors are used as volume controls.

Thermistors have a high resistance when cold but a much lower resistance when hot. They contain semiconductor materials. Some electrical thermometers use a thermistor to detect temperature change.

Light-dependent resistors (LDRs) have a high resistance in the dark but a low resistance in the light. They can be used in electronic circuits which switch lights on and off automatically.

Diodes have an extremely high resistance in one direction but a low resistance in the other. In effect, they allow current to flow in one direction only. They are used in electronic circuits.

Moving the slide control of the variable resistor to the right increases the length of resistance wire in the circuit. This reduces the current and dims the bulb.

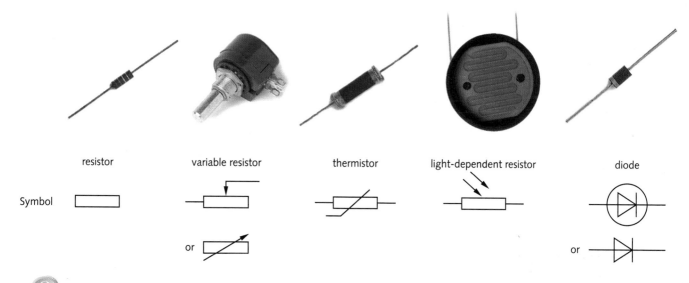

| resistor | variable resistor | thermistor | light-dependent resistor | diode |

Symbol

or   or

1 When a kettle is plugged into the 230 V mains, the current through its element is 10 A.
   a) What is the resistance of its element?
   b) Why does the element need to have resistance?

2 In the diagram at the top of this page, a variable resistor is controlling the brightness of a bulb. What happens if the slide control is moved to the left? Give a reason for your answer.

3 Which of the components in the photographs above has each of these properties?
   a) A high resistance in the dark but a low resistance in the light.
   b) A resistance that falls sharply when the temperature rises.
   c) A very low resistance in one direction, but an extremely high resistance in the other.

Related topics: SI units **1.02**; temperature, vibrating atoms, and thermometers **5.02**; conductors and semiconductors **8.01**; current, circuits and symbols **8.03**; potential difference **8.04**; diodes **10.02**; LDRs and thermistors **10.04**

Resistance (2)

Resistance equation

$$resistance = \frac{potential\ difference}{current}$$

Units:

resistance: ohm (Ω)

potential difference (PD): volt (V)

current: ampere (A)

This triangle gives the *V*, *I*, and *R* equations. To find the equation for *I*, cover up the *I*, ...and so on.

V, I, R equations

The resistance equation can be written using symbols:

$$R = \frac{V}{I}$$ where R = resistance, V = PD (voltage), and I = current

(Note the difference between the symbol V for PD and the symbol V for volt.)

The above equation can be rearranged in two ways:

$$V = IR \quad \text{and} \quad I = \frac{V}{R}$$

These are useful if the PD across a known resistance, or the current through it, is to be calculated.

Example A 12 Ω resistor has a PD of 6 V across it. What is the current through the resistor?

In this case: $V = 6\,V$, $R = 12\,\Omega$, and I is to be found. So:

$$I = \frac{V}{R} = \frac{6}{12} = 0.5 \quad \text{(omitting units for simplicity)}$$

So the current is 0.5 A.

How current varies with PD for a metal conductor

The circuit below left can be used to investigate how the current through a conductor depends on the PD across it. The conductor in this case is a coiled-up length of nichrome wire, kept at a steady temperature by immersing it in a large amount of water. The PD across the nichrome can be varied by adjusting the variable resistor.

Typical results are shown in the table and graph below. The experiment is also one method of measuring resistance.

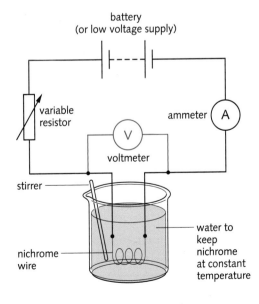

PD	current	PD/current
1.0 V	0.2 A	5.0 Ω
2.0 V	0.4 A	5.0 Ω
3.0 V	0.6 A	5.0 Ω
4.0 V	0.8 A	5.0 Ω
5.0 V	1.0 A	5.0 Ω

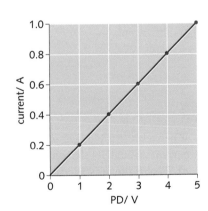

Ohm's law

In the experiment on the opposite page, the results have these features:
- A graph of current against PD is a straight line through the origin.
- If the PD doubles, the current doubles, ...and so on.
- PD ÷ current always has the same value ($5\,\Omega$ in this case).

Mathematically, these can be summed up as follows:

> The current is proportional to the PD.

This is known as **Ohm's law**, after George Ohm, the 19th century scientist who first investigated the electrical properties of wires.

Metal conductors obey Ohm's law, provided their temperature does not change. Put another way, a metal conductor has a constant resistance, provided its temperature is constant. This is not always the case with other types of conductor.

Current–PD graphs

Here are two more examples of current–PD graphs. In both, the resistance varies depending on the PD. In the case of the diode, the negative part of the graph is for readings obtained when the PD is reversed (i.e. when the diode is connected into the test circuit the opposite way round).

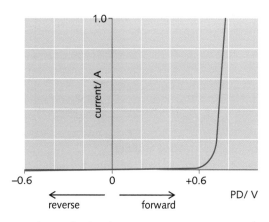

Tungsten filament As the current increases, the temperature rises and the resistance goes up. So the current is not proportional to the PD.

Semiconductor diode The current is not proportional to the PD. And if the PD is reversed, the current is almost zero. In effect, the diode 'blocks' current in the reverse direction.

1 The graph lines A and B on the right are for two different conductors. Which conductor has the higher resistance?

2 Using the left-hand graph above, calculate the resistance of the tungsten filament when its temperature is **a)** 1500 °C **b)** 3000 °C.

3 In the right-hand graph above, does the diode have its highest resistance in the forward direction or the reverse? Explain your answer.

4 A resistor has a steady resistance of $8\,\Omega$.
   a) If the current through the resistor is 2 A, what is the PD across it?
   b) What PD is needed to produce a current of 4 A?
   c) If the PD falls to 6 V, what is the current?

8.07 Series and parallel circuits (1)

Circuit essentials

Potential difference (PD), or voltage, is measured in volts (V). The greater the PD across a bulb or other component, the greater the current flowing through it. Current is measured in amperes (A).

Bulbs, resistors, and other components have resistance to a flow of current. Resistance is measured in ohms (Ω).

The bulbs above have to get their power from the same supply. There are two basic methods of connecting bulbs, resistors, or other components together. The circuits below demonstrate the differences between them.

Bulbs in series and parallel

These bulbs are connected in **series**.
● The bulbs share the PD (voltage) from the battery, so each glows dimly.
● If one bulb is removed, the other goes out because the circuit is broken.

These bulbs are connected in **parallel**.
● Each gets the full PD from the battery because each is connected directly to it. So each glows brightly.
● If one bulb is removed, the other keeps working because it is still part of an unbroken circuit.

Circuits and switches

If two or more bulbs have to be powered by one battery, as in a car lighting system, they are normally connected in parallel. Each bulb gets the full battery PD. Also, each can be switched on and off independently:

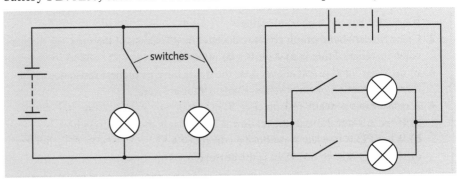

These diagrams show *two* different ways of drawing the *same* circuit for independently switched bulbs.

Basic circuit rules

There are some basic rules for all series and parallel circuits. They are illustrated by the examples below. The particular current values depend on the resistances and PDs. However, the equation on the right *always* applies to *every* resistor.

PD	=	current	×	resistance
(V)		(A)		(Ω)

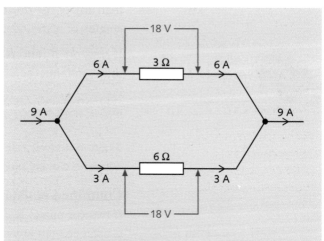

When resistors or other components are in **series**:
- the *current* through each of the components is the same
- the *total PD (voltage)* across all the components is the sum of the PDs across each of them.

When resistors or other components are in **parallel**:
- the *PD (voltage)* across each of the component is the same
- the *total current* in the main circuit is the sum of the currents in the branches.

Cell arrangements

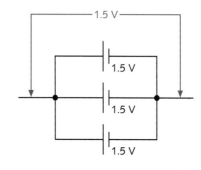

These cells are connected in series. The total PD (voltage) across them is the sum of the individual PDs.

Here, a mistake has occurred. One of the cells is the wrong way round, so it cancels out one of the others.

The PD across parallel cells is only the same as from one cell. But together, the cells can deliver a higher current.

1 When one of the lights on a Christmas tree breaks, the others go out as well. What does this tell you about the way the lights are connected?
2 Give *two* advantages of connecting bulbs to a battery in parallel.
3 Redraw either of the circuits on the left so that it has a single switch which turns both bulbs on and off together.
4 This question is about the circuit on the right:
   a) The readings on two of the ammeters are shown. What are the readings on ammeters X and Y?
   b) If the PD across the battery is 6 V, what is the PD across each of the bulbs? (Note: you can neglect the PD across an ammeter.)

Series and parallel circuits (2)

These resistors...

3 Ω   6 Ω

...are equivalent to this resistor...

9 Ω

resistance = 3 Ω + 6 Ω = 9 Ω

Combined resistance of resistors in series

If two (or more) resistors are connected in series, they give a *higher* resistance than any of the resistors by itself. The effect is the same as joining several lengths of resistance wire to form a longer length.

If resistors R_1 and R_2 are in series, their combined resistance R is given by this equation:

$$R = R_1 + R_2$$

There is an example on the left. For three or more resistors, the above equation can be extended by adding R_3 ... and so on.

Combined resistance of resistors in parallel

If two (or more) resistors are connected in parallel, they give a *lower* resistance than any of the resistors by itself. The effect is the same as using a thick piece of resistance wire instead of a thin one. There is a wider conducting path than before.

If two resistors R_1 and R_2 are in parallel, their combined resistance R is given by this equation (there is a proof at the bottom of the page):

$$\frac{1}{R} = \frac{1}{R_1} + \frac{1}{R_2}$$

For three or more resistors, the equation can be extended by adding $1/R_3$, ... and so on.

If the above equation for two resistors is rearranged, it becomes: $R = \dfrac{R_1 \times R_2}{R_1 + R_2}$

In words: combined resistance $= \dfrac{\text{resistances multiplied}}{\text{resistances added}}$

For example, if $3\,\Omega$ and $6\,\Omega$ resistors are in parallel:

$$\text{combined resistance} = \frac{6 \times 3}{6 + 3}\,\Omega = 2\,\Omega$$

Note: this method of calculation works only for *two* resistors in parallel.

These resistors...

3 Ω

6 Ω

...are equivalent to this resistor...

2 Ω

Omitting units for simplicity:

$$\frac{1}{\text{resistance}} = \frac{1}{3} + \frac{1}{6}$$
$$= \frac{2}{6} + \frac{1}{6}$$
$$= \frac{3}{6}$$
$$= \frac{1}{2}$$

So: resistance $= 2\,\Omega$

Proving the parallel resistor equation

In the circuit on the left, R_1 has the full battery PD of E across it. So does R_2.

As current $= \dfrac{\text{PD}}{\text{resistance}}$: $I_1 = \dfrac{E}{R_1}$ and $I_2 = \dfrac{E}{R_2}$

But $I = I_1 + I_2$ so $I = \dfrac{E}{R_1} + \dfrac{E}{R_2}$

If resistor R is equivalent to R_1 and R_2 in parallel, it must take the same current I from the battery: $I = \dfrac{E}{R}$ Therefore: $\dfrac{E}{R} = \dfrac{E}{R_1} + \dfrac{E}{R_2}$ so $\dfrac{1}{R} = \dfrac{1}{R_1} + \dfrac{1}{R_2}$

Solving circuit problems

To solve problems about circuits, you need to know the basic circuit rules on the previous spread. You also need to know the link between PD (voltage), current, and resistance. This is given on the right.

> PD = current × resistance
> (V)   (A)   (Ω)
>
> In symbols: $V = IR$

Example 1 Calculate the PDs across the $3\,\Omega$ resistor and the $6\,\Omega$ resistor in the circuit on the right.

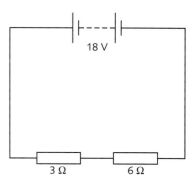

The first stage is to calculate the total resistance in the circuit, and then use this information to find the current:

total resistance $= 3\,\Omega + 6\,\Omega = 9\,\Omega$

so: current $I = \dfrac{\text{PD}}{\text{resistance}} = \dfrac{18\,\text{V}}{9\,\Omega} = 2\,\text{A}$

Knowing that the $3\,\Omega$ resistor has a current of $2\,\text{A}$ through it, you can calculate the PD across it:

PD = current × resistance $= 2\,\text{A} \times 3\,\Omega = 6\,\text{V}$

The PD across the $6\,\Omega$ resistor can be worked out in the same way. However, it can also be deduced from the fact that the PDs across the two resistors must add up to $18\,\text{V}$, the PD across the battery. By either method, the PD across the $6\,\Omega$ resistor is $12\,\text{V}$.

Example 2 Calculate the currents I, I_1, and I_2 in the circuit on the right.

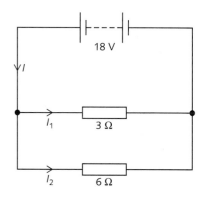

The $3\,\Omega$ resistor has the full battery PD of $18\,\text{V}$ across it. So:

$I_1 = \dfrac{\text{PD}}{\text{resistance}} = \dfrac{18\,\text{V}}{3\,\Omega} = 6\,\text{A}$

Using the same method: $I_2 = 3\,\text{A}$

The current I is the total of the currents in the two branches. So:

$I = I_1 + I_2 = 6\,\text{A} + 3\,\text{A} = 9\,\text{A}$

---

1 In circuit A on the right:
   a) What does the ammeter read?
   b) What is the PD across each of the resistors?
2 In circuit B on the right:
   a) What does the ammeter read when the switch is open (OFF)?
   b) What is the current through each of the $4\,\Omega$ resistors when the switch is closed (ON)?
   c) What does the ammeter read when the switch is closed?
   d) What is the combined resistance of the two resistors when the switch is closed?
3 Which resistor arrangement, C or D, on the right has the lower resistance? Check your answer by calculation.

8.09 Currents through gases and liquids

Gases and liquids can conduct an electric current if they contain **ions**. Ions are electrically charged atoms or groups of atoms. In other words, they are atoms or groups of atoms that have gained or lost electrons. A flow of ions is a current because it is a flow of charge.

▲ When atoms lose electrons, they become positive ions.

▲ When atoms gain electrons, they become negative ions.

Conduction through ionized air

Air is mainly a mixture of nitrogen and oxygen molecules. Most are uncharged, but not all. For example, radiation from space, radiation from radioactive materials in rocks, and the energy in flames can all wrench electrons from molecules in air so that positive ions are formed. Although these soon recombine with any free electrons around, more are being formed all the time, so there are always some ions present in the air.

With no ions in it, air is a good electrical insulator. But with ions present, it becomes a conductor. This example demonstrates how:

Spark conduction through ionized air.

The metal dome above has been negatively (-) charged with 'static electricity'. In other words, it has extra electrons on it. In time, the dome loses its charge because positive (+) ions in the air are attracted to it, touch it, and take electrons from it. So there is a flow of charge (in other words, a current) through the air because of the flow of ions.

If the PD (voltage) across air is high enough, moving ions and electrons collide with other molecules strongly enough to ionize them. The new ions cause more ions... and so on. The result is a sudden pulse of current which lights up the air in a spark.

Electrolysis

Some substances dissolve in water, forming a mixture called a solution. Copper(II) sulphate is an example. Copper(II) sulphate solution contains ions, so a current can flow through it. When this happens, a chemical change takes place and the liquid decomposes (splits) into simpler substances. The process is called **electrolysis**.

electrolyte: copper(II) sulphate solution

PD (voltage)

The graph above is for copper(II) sulphate solution with copper electrodes. The current is proportional to the PD, so Ohm's law is obeyed. With other electrodes and solutions, Ohm's law does not necessarily apply.

The diagram above shows the electrolysis of copper(II) sulphate solution. The liquid, called the **electrolyte**, has two electrodes in it: the **cathode** (-) and the **anode** (+). In this case, both are made of copper.

In the liquid, copper(II) sulphate splits to form positive copper ions and negative sulphate ions. The copper ions (+) are attracted to the cathode (-), where they collect electrons, become uncharged, and build up as a layer of copper. At the same time, copper from the anode dissolves in the electrolyte to replace the copper ions. Overall, copper is removed from the anode and deposited on the cathode.

Each copper ion carries the same amount of charge. So:

> The mass deposited is proportional to the total charge transferred.

Charge = current × time; therefore, if a higher current flows for a longer time, a greater mass of copper is deposited.

Depositing a metal by electrolysis is called electroplating. For example, food cans are made from steel electroplated with tin (which is safe for food). The jug on the right was electroplated with silver.

Here are some more uses of electrolysis:
- Splitting acidified water to form hydrogen and oxygen.
- Splitting molten sodium chloride to form sodium and chlorine.
- Extracting aluminium from its ore (the mineral bauxite).

Nickel cutlery, electroplated with silver.

1 What are *ions*?
2 Copy the diagram on the right. Then do the following:
   a) Label the *cathode*, the *anode*, and the *electrolyte*.
   b) Draw in and label the direction of electron flow through the wires.
   c) Label the ions to show which are + and which are - .
3 Give *two* practical uses of electrolysis.
4 Air with no ions in it is an electrical insulator. Why does air become a conductor when it is ionized?

ion

8.10 Electrical power

power = 5 W

battery supplies
5 J of energy per second

bulb receives and radiates
5 J of energy per second

power = 5 W

Circuit essentials

In a circuit like the one above, the charge is carried by electrons. Charge is measured in coulombs (C).

The flow of electrons is called a current. Current is measured in amperes (A).

Potential difference (PD), or voltage, is measured in volts (V). The greater the PD across a battery, the more potential energy each electron is given. The greater the PD aross a bulb or other component, the more energy each electron loses as it passes through.

Energy is measured in joules (J).

In the circuit on the left, the battery gives electrons potential energy. In the bulb, this is changed into thermal energy (heat) and then radiated.

Power is the rate at which energy is transformed (changed from one form to another). The SI unit of power in the **watt** (**W**):

$$\text{power} = \frac{\text{energy transformed}}{\text{time taken}}$$

The battery on the left is supplying 5 joules of energy every second, so its power is 5 watts. The bulb is taking energy at the same rate, so its power is also 5 watts.

Appliances such as toasters, irons, and TVs have a **power rating** marked on them, either in watts or in kilowatts:

1 kilowatt (kW) = 1000 watts

Some typical power ratings are shown below. Each figure tells you the power the appliance will take *if connected to a supply of the correct voltage*. For any other voltage, the actual power would be different.

1100 W
(1.1 kW)

400 W

80 W

2400 W
(2.4 kW)

60 W

Electrical power equation

For circuits, there is a more useful version of the power equation. If a battery, bulb, or other component has a PD (voltage) across it and a current through it, the power is given by this equation:

$$\begin{array}{ccc}
\text{power} = & \text{PD} & \times & \text{current} \\
\text{(W)} & \text{(V)} & & \text{(A)}
\end{array}$$

In symbols: $P = VI$

Example In the circuit on the left, what is the power of the battery and each of the bulbs?

For the battery: power = PD × current = 12 V × 2 A = 24 W
For bulb A: power = PD × current = 8 V × 2 A = 16 W
For bulb B: power = PD × current = 4 V × 2 A = 8 W
The bulbs are the only items getting power from the battery, so their total power (16 W + 8 W) is the same as that supplied by the battery (24 W).

Why the electrical power equation works

The equation power = PD × current is a result of how the volt, ampere, coulomb, joule, and watt are related. The following example should explain why.

Here are two ways of describing what is happening on the right:

General description	*Scientific description*
Each coulomb of charge gains 12 joules of energy from the battery	PD = 12 volts
2 coulombs of charge leave the battery every second	current = 2 amperes
So 12 x 2 joules of energy leave the battery every second	power = 24 watts

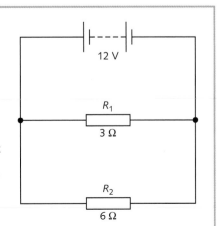

Power dissipated in a resistor

Although the following section is about resistors, it also applies to heating elements and any other components that have resistance.

When a current flows through a resistor, it has a heating effect. Electrons lose potential energy, which is changed into thermal energy. Scientifically speaking, energy is **dissipated** in the resistor.

For calculating the rate of energy dissipation, there is another useful version of the electrical power equation. It is found like this:

$$\text{power} = \text{PD} \times \text{current}$$

But: PD = current × resistance

So: power = current × resistance × current

So: $$\text{power} = \text{current}^2 \times \text{resistance}$$

In symbols: $$P = I^2R$$

> *Example* What power is dissipated in a 5 Ω resistor when the current through it is **a)** 2 A **b)** 4 A?

Omitting some of the units for simplicity:
a) Power = current² × resistance = 2² × 5 = 20 W
b) Power = current² × resistance = 4² × 5 = 80 W

Note that *doubling* the current produces *four times* the power dissipation.

Resistance essentials

Resistors have a resistance measured in ohms (Ω). The higher the resistance, the less current flows through the resistor for each volt of PD across it.

$$\text{resistance} = \frac{\text{PD}}{\text{current}}$$

---

1   In 5 seconds, a hairdrier takes 10 000 joules of energy from the mains supply. What is its power **a)** in watts **b)** in kilowatts?
2   If an electric heater takes a current of 4 A when connected to a 230 V supply, what is its power?
3   If a light bulb has a power of 36 W when connected to a 12 V supply, what is the current through it?
4   In the circuit on the right, both resistors receive the full battery PD.
    a) Use the resistance equation (in the box above right) to calculate the current through each of the resistors.
    b) Calculate the power dissipated in each of the resistors.
    c) Calculate the power of the battery.
    d) If a battery of twice the PD was used, what would its power be?

8.11 Mains electricity (1)

When you plug a kettle (or other appliance) into a mains socket, you are connecting it into a circuit, as shown below. The power comes from a generator in a power station. In the UK, the **supply voltage** is 230 V for mains sockets and other household circuits.

Mains current is **alternating current** (**AC**). It flows backwards and forwards, backwards and forwards,... 50 times per second in the UK, where the **mains frequency** is 50 hertz (Hz). In power stations, AC is easier to generate than one-way **direct current** (**DC**) like that from a battery.

Live wire The voltage of this goes alternately negative and positive, making the current flow backwards and forwards through the circuit.

Neutral wire This completes the circuit. It is kept at zero voltage by the electricity supply company.

Switch This is fitted in the live wire. It would work equally well in the neutral, but then wire in the cable would still be 'live' with the switch OFF. This would be dangerous if, for example, the cable was accidentally cut.

Fuse This is a thin piece of wire which overheats and melts if the current is too high. Like the switch, it is placed in the live wire, often as a cartridge inside the plug. If a fault develops, and the current gets too high, the fuse 'blows' and breaks the circuit before the cable can overheat and catch fire.

This table lamp has an insulating body and does not need an earth wire.

Earth wire This is a safety wire. It connects the metal body of the kettle to earth and stops it becoming live. For example, if the live wire comes loose and touches the metal body, a current immediately flows to earth and blows the fuse. This means that the kettle is then safe to touch.

Double insulation Some appliances – radios for example – do not have an earth wire. This is because their outer case is made of plastic rather than metal. The plastic acts as an extra layer of insulation around the wires.

Three-pin plugs

Plugs are a safe and simple way of connecting appliances to the mains. In the UK, fused, three-pin plugs are used:

earth wire
(green/yellow insulation)

fuse

neutral wire
(blue insulation)

live wire
(brown insulation)

cable grip

When wiring a plug, check the following:

● The wires are connected to the correct terminals, using the colour code on the left.
● The cable is held firmly by the grip.
● The correct fuse is fitted.

If the fuse in a plug blows:

● Switch off at the socket and pull out the plug.
● Fit a new fuse only when the fault has been traced and put right.

Fuse values The plug is usually fitted with either a 3 A, 5 A, or 13 A fuse. The value tells you the current needed to blow the fuse. It must be greater than the normal current through the appliance, but as close to it as possible – so that the fuse will blow as soon as the current gets too high.

If you know the power of an appliance, you can use the equation on the right to work out whether a 3 A, 5 A, or 13 A fuse is needed. For example:

Kettle: 2300 W 230 V

$$\text{current} = \frac{\text{power}}{\text{voltage}} = \frac{2300\,\text{W}}{230\,\text{V}} = 10\,\text{A} \qquad \text{So a 13 A fuse is needed.}$$

TV: 115 W 230 V

$$\text{current} = \frac{\text{power}}{\text{voltage}} = \frac{115\,\text{W}}{230\,\text{V}} = 0.5\,\text{A} \qquad \text{So a 3 A fuse is needed.}$$

The TV would still work with a 13 A fuse. But if a fault developed, its circuits might overheat and catch fire without the fuse blowing.

Electrical power equation

power	=	voltage	×	current
(watts)		(volts)		(amperes)
(W)		(V)		(A)

1 In a mains plug, which wire, *live, neutral,* or *earth,*
   a) has a brown covering   **b)** is a safety wire
   c) goes alternately + and -   **d)** has a yellow and green covering
   e) has a blue covering   **f)** forms part of the circuit but is at zero voltage?
2 What is a fuse, and how does it work?
3 Why should the switch always be in the live wire rather than the neutral?
4 Why do some appliances not have an earth wire?
5 Work out whether the plug for each appliance on the right should be fitted with a 3 A, 5 A, or a 13 A fuse.

Supply voltage: 230 V	
appliance	*power*
hairdrier	1500 W
drill	400 W
iron	1200 W
table lamp	60 W

Related topics: current and circuits **8.03**; voltage (PD) **8.04**; power **8.10**; generators **9.08**; electricity supply system **8.11**

199

8.12 Mains electricity (2)

earth

mains supply cable

neutral
live

electricity
supply company
fuse

| 4 | 2 | 9 | 1 | 9 |

energy
meter

main
switch

consumer
unit

fuses

30 A   30 A   15 A   5 A   5 A

lights (upstairs)
lights (downstairs)
immersion heater
cooker

ring main cable

mains socket
and switch

Circuits around the house

The electricity supply company's cable into each house contains a live and a neutral wire. At the **consumer unit** or 'fuse box', these wires branch into several parallel circuits for the lights, cooker, immersion heater, and mains sockets. The cable for each circuit also contains an earth wire.

In the consumer unit, each circuit passes through a fuse or, alternatively, a **circuit breaker**. A circuit breaker is an automatic switch which 'trips' (turns off) when the current rises above the specified value. It can be reset by turning the switch on or pressing a button.

For extra safety, some systems are fitted with a **residual current device** (**RCD**). This compares the currents in the live and neutral wires. These should be the same. If they are not, then current must be flowing to earth – perhaps through someone touching an exposed wire. The RCD senses the difference and switches off the current before any harm can be done.

Mains sockets

In many countries, each mains socket is protected by its own fuse or circuit breaker in the consumer unit. The plugs used in the sockets are unfused. In the UK, the mains sockets are connected to a **ring main**. This is a cable which begins and ends at the consumer unit, with the live, neutral and earth wires each forming a long loop or 'ring' around the house, as shown below. One advantage is that there are *two* conducting paths to each socket, so thinner (and cheaper) cable can be used. The ring main is protected by a 30 A fuse (or circuit breaker) in the consumer unit. Each plug connected to the ring has its own fuse.

Using two-way switches

In most houses, you can turn the landing lights on or off from upstairs or downstairs. For this, **two-way switches** are used:

▲ If both switches are up – or down – the circuit is complete and a current flows through the bulb.

▲ But if one switch is up and the other is down, the circuit is broken. Each switch reverses the effect of the other one.

Safety first

Mains electricity can be dangerous. Here are some of the hazards:

- Old, frayed wiring. Broken strands mean that a wire will have a higher resistance at one point. When a current flows through it, the heating effect may be enough to melt the insulation and cause a fire.
- Long extension leads. These may overheat if used when coiled up. The current warms the wire, but thermal energy is lost more slowly from the cable if it is in a tight bundle.
- Water in sockets or plugs. Water will conduct a current, so if electrical equipment gets wet, there is a risk that someone might be electrocuted.
- Accidentally cutting cables. With lawnmowers and hedgetrimmers, a plug-in RCD should always be used to avoid the risk of electrocution.

If an accident happens, and someone is electrocuted, you must switch off at the socket and pull out the plug before giving any help.

A plug-in RCD gives protection against the risk of electrocution.

1 If you use a hairdrier (or other appliance) in a UK mains system, as on the left, the current flows through three fuses. Where are these fuses?
2 What is the purpose of a circuit breaker?
3 a) What is the purpose of an RCD?
   b) Why should an RCD always be used with a lawnmower?
4 If an accident occurs and someone is electrocuted, what *two* things must you do before giving help?
5 Copy and complete the circuit diagram on the right so that the bulb can be controlled by either switch.

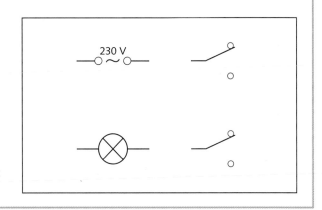

Related topics: resistance and heating effect **8.05**; parallel circuits **8.07**; how a circuit breaker works **9.04**

201

8.13 Electrical energy calculations

In a circuit, appliances such as kettles, toasters, and food mixers take energy from the supply and transform it (change it into other forms). For example, appliances with heating elements change it into thermal energy (heat).

Energy and power essentials

Energy is measured in joules (J).

$$power = \frac{energy\ transformed}{time\ taken}$$

Power is measured in watts (W).

For example, if a heating element is transforming energy at the rate of 1000 joules per second, it has a power of 1000 watts.

For circuits, this equation is more useful for calculating power:

power = PD × current

In the above equation:

PD (potential difference, or voltage) is measured in volts (V).

Current is measured in amperes (A).

Calculating energy

Energy and power are linked by the equation in the box on the left. If the power of an appliance is known, the energy transformed in any given time can be calculated by rearranging the equation like this:

energy transformed = power × time
(J)   (W)   (s)

For example, if a 1000 W heating element is switched on for 5 seconds (s): energy transformed = 1000 W × 5 s = 5000 J. So the heating element gives off 5000 J of thermal energy.

Electrical energy equation

As power = PD × current, the above equation can also be written like this:

energy transformed = PD × current × time
(J)   (V)   (A)   (s)

In symbols: $E = VIt$

> *Example* A 12 V water heater takes a current of 2 A. If it is switched on for 60 seconds, how much thermal energy does it produce?

Energy transformed = PD × current × time = 12 V × 2 A × 60 s = 1440 J

In this case, all the energy is transformed into thermal energy, so the heater produces 1440 J of thermal energy.

Measuring energy in kilowatt-hours

Electricity supply companies use the **kilowatt-hour**, rather than the joule, as their unit of energy measurement:

> One kilowatt-hour (kWh) is the energy supplied when an appliance whose power is 1 kW is used for 1 hour.

1 kW is 1000 W, and 1 hour is 3600 s. So, if a 1 kW appliance is used for 1 hour: energy supplied = power × time = 1000 W × 3600 s = 3 600 000 J. Therefore: 1 kWh = 3 600 000 J.

Energy in kilowatt hours is calculated like this:

energy supplied = power × time
(kWh)   (kW) (hours)

For example:
If a 2 kW heater is used for 3 hours, the energy supplied is 6 kWh.

Batteries are a very convenient, portable source of electricity, but their energy can cost over 200 times more per kilowatt-hour than energy from the mains.

Calculating the cost of electricity

◀ Part of an electricity bill, based on the meter readings below. On most bills, the cost is shown before tax is added, and there is usually an additional standing charge to pay.

CENTRAL ELECTRICITY BOARD   CUSTOMER ACCOUNT NO. **3742 463**

PRESENT METER READING	PREVIOUS METER READING	UNITS USED	COST PER UNIT (£) INCL. TAX	£
42935	41710	1225	0.10	122.50

The 'electricity meter' in a house is an energy meter. The more energy you take, the more you have to pay. The reading on the meter gives the total energy supplied in **Units**. The Unit is another name for the kilowatt-hour.

The diagrams on the right show the meter readings at the beginning and end of a quarter (three-month period). In this case:

energy supplied = 42935 kWh – 41710 kWh = 1225 kWh = 1225 Units

If the electricity supply company charges 10p per Unit:
cost of energy supplied = 1225 × 10p = 12250p = £122.50

The cost of running individual appliances can be calculated as follows:

> *Example 1* If energy is 10p per unit, what is the cost of running a 2 kW heater for 3 hours?

Energy supplied = power × time = 2 kW × 3 h = 6 kWh = 6 Units

As the cost per Unit is 10p:
total cost = 6 × 10p = 60p

> *Example 2* If energy costs 10p per unit, what is the cost of running a 100 W lamp for 30 minutes?

To calculate the number of kWh, the power must be in *kilo*watts and the time in *hours*. In this case: 100 W is 0.1 kW, and 30 minutes is 0.5 h. So:

energy supplied = power × time = 0.1 kW × 0.5 h = 0.05 kWh = 0.05 Units

As the cost per Unit is 10p:
total cost = 0.05 × 10p = 0.5p

1 Calculate the energy supplied to a 60 W bulb
   a) in 1 second **b)** in 1 minute.
2 A bulb takes a current of 3 A from a 12 V battery.
   a) What is the power of the bulb?
   b) How much energy is supplied in 10 minutes?
3 A 2 kW heater is switched on for 4 hours. Calculate the thermal energy given off by the heater
   a) in kWh **b)** in joules.

4 If energy costs 10p per Unit, calculate the cost of using
   a) a 3 kW electric fire for 5 hours
   b) five 60 W bulbs for 12 hours.
   c) a 1200 W hairdrier for 15 minutes.
5 Someone decides to replace six 60 W filament bulbs with six 15 W low-energy bulbs. If energy costs 10p per Unit and the bulbs are used, on average, for 4 hours per day, what will the annual saving be?

8.14 Electric fields

The girl on the right has given herself an electric charge by touching the dome of a van de Graaff generator. The dome can reach over 100 000 volts, although this is reduced when she touches it. However, the current that flows into her body (0.000 02 amperes or less) is far too small to be dangerous.

The force of repulsion between the charges on the girl's head and hairs is strong enough to make her hairs stand up. If electric charges feel a force, then, scientifically speaking, they are in an **electric field**. So there is an electric field around the dome and the girl.

Electric field patterns

In diagrams, lines with arrows on them are used to represent electric fields. There are some examples of field patterns below. In each case, the arrows show the direction in which the force on a *positive* (+) charge would act. As like charges repel, the field lines always point *away* from positive (+) charge and *towards* negative (-) charge.

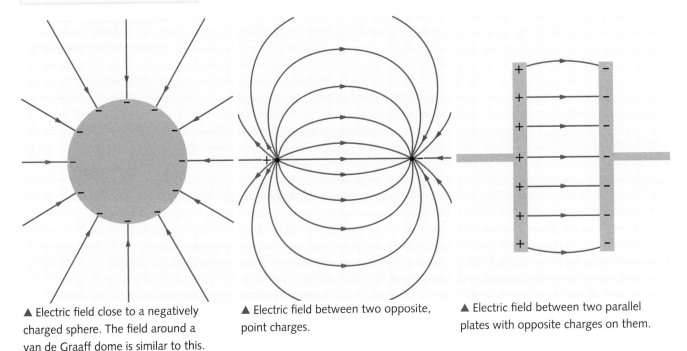

▲ Electric field close to a negatively charged sphere. The field around a van de Graaff dome is similar to this.

▲ Electric field between two opposite, point charges.

▲ Electric field between two parallel plates with opposite charges on them.

Curves and points

When a conductor is charged up, the charges repel each other, so they collect on the outside. The charges are most concentrated near the sharpest curve. This is where the electric field is strongest and the field lines closest together.

▲ The electric field is strongest where the charges are most concentrated and the field lines are closest together.

▲ At a sharp point, the electric field may be strong enough to ionize the air so that it will conduct charge away.

If a sharp spike is put on the dome of a van de Graaff generator, any charge on the dome immediately leaks away from the point. At the point, the metal is very sharply curved. Here, the charge is so concentrated that the electric field is strong enough to **ionize** the air. In other words, it is strong enough to wrench electrons always from molecules in the air so that ions are formed. Ionized air conducts, so the dome loses its charge through the air.

Lightning conductors

Thunderclouds carry charges. When a thundercloud passes over a building, it causes a build-up of opposite charge (an **induced** charge) on the roof. If the electric field between the opposite charges is strong enough, there may be a spark of lightning as the charges flow through the air towards each other.

Most tall buildings have **lightning conductors** on them. The sharp spikes at the top reduce the chance of a lightning strike by letting charge on the building leak away into the air before a spark can occur. However, if lightning does strike, the conductor provides a route for charge to flow to the ground without damaging the building.

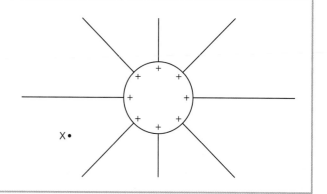

1 The diagram on the right shows electric field lines round a charged metal sphere (in air).
a) Copy the diagram. Draw in the direction of the electric field on each field line.
b) If a positive charge were placed at X, in which direction would it move?
c) If a negative charge were placed at X, in which direction would it move?
d) If a sharp spike were placed on top of the sphere, what would happen to the charge on the sphere?

8.15 Cells and batteries

Cells (commonly called batteries) are a convenient source of electricity for powering torches, watches, personal stereos, and car starter motors. The energy stored in a cell is released by chemical action.

The simple cell

The simple cell

The **simple cell** on the left has two plates (called **electrodes**) in dilute sulphuric acid (the **electrolyte**). One plate is copper, the other zinc. The two metals behave differently in the acid, and this causes a PD (voltage) of about 1 volt between them. The process works as follows.

The zinc slowly dissolves in the acid. However, it goes into the liquid as positive ions rather than complete atoms, so electrons get left behind on the plate. The copper does not dissolve. Instead, it loses electrons to positive hydrogen ions in the acid, turning them into molecules of hydrogen gas. Overall, because of the chemical reactions, the zinc plate is left with too many electrons and becomes negatively (-) charged. The copper plate loses electrons and becomes positively (+) charged. As a result, when the plates are linked by a conductor (such as a bulb and connecting wires), electrons flow from the zinc round to the copper to try to restore the balance.

The dry cell

The cell above is called a **dry cell**. The electrolyte, ammonium chloride solution, is in absorbent paper, so the cell does not have to be kept upright. The zinc container is the negative (-) electrode. Manganese dioxide acts as the positive (+) electrode. It is mixed with carbon to make it a better conductor and has a carbon rod through the middle. There are additional chemicals to keep the cell working properly. The EMF produced is about 1.5 volts.

Alkaline cells last longer than ordinary dry cells. They also use zinc and manganese dioxide, but in a different form and with a different electrolyte.

Cell and circuit essentials

Electrons are negatively (-) charged particles from the atom. A cell pushes electrons around a circuit. The flow of electrons is called a current.

The greater the PD (voltage) across a cell, the more energy the electrons are given.

A cell produces its highest PD when not in a circuit and not supplying current. This maximum PD is called its EMF. When a cell is supplying current, the PD across it is reduced.

Ion essentials

Normally, atoms have equal amounts of + and - charge. If atoms lose electrons, they become positive (+) ions.

Batteries

Most cells have an EMF of only a volt or so. To produce a higher EMF, several cells can be joined in series to form a **battery**. A 'battery' really means a collection of cells though the word is commonly used for a single cell as well. Some batteries are manufactured with several cells in the same case. For example, a 12 volt car battery has six 2 volt cells in it.

Primary and secondary cells

The simple cell and dry cell are **primary cells**. When a primary cell is made, its chemicals react immediately to produce an EMF. However, the reactions are not easily reversible and the cell cannot normally be recharged. When it is 'flat' (fully discharged), it must be replaced with a new one and the old one disposed of safely.

The lead–acid cells in car batteries are **secondary cells**. These must be charged before use by passing a current through them. However, they can be recharged over and over again because the chemical reactions are reversible.

▲ The six cells in a car battery.

◀ A simple charging circuit for a battery of secondary cells.

To charge (or recharge) secondary cells, a current must be passed back through them the 'wrong way'. The diagram above shows a simple charging circuit. The *positive* terminal of the DC supply is connected to the *positive* terminal of the battery being charged. Provided the EMF of the supply is *greater* than that of the battery, a current will flow back through the battery and charge it up. The current is controlled using the variable resistor.

'Overcharging' produces gases, which can be dangerous. To prevent it, modern battery chargers have electronic circuits to sense when the battery is approaching full charge and reduce or stop the charging current.

Nickel–cadmium cells are secondary cells. They must be charged before use (using the charger shown) but can be recharged over and over again.

---

1 In a dry cell, what is used as **a)** the negative electrode **b)** the positive electrode **c)** the electrolyte?
2 **a)** Give one advantage of a secondary cell over a primary cell.
  b) Give one disadvantage of a secondary cell.
  c) Give one example of a primary cell.
  d) Give one example of a secondary cell.
3 Copy and complete the diagram on the right to show how the battery should be connected to the charger.

battery charger

battery

Related topics: electrons in atoms **8.01**; current **8.03**; PD and EMF **8.04**; cells in series **8.04** and **8.07**; ions **8.09**

1 a) When a balloon is rubbed in your hair, the balloon becomes negatively charged.

    (i) Explain how the balloon becomes negatively charged. [2]

    (ii) State what you know about the size and sign of the charge left on your hair. [2]

b) The negatively charged balloon is brought up to the surface of a ceiling. The balloon sticks to the ceiling. Explain how and why this happens. [3]

WJEC

2 Read the following passage carefully before answering the questions.

Spraying crops with chemical fertilisers or insecticides has become more efficient. A portable high voltage generator gives the drops of liquid insecticide a small positive charge. This makes the liquid break up into smaller drops and causes the spray to become finer and spread out more.

The plants, which are all reasonable conductors, are in contact with the earth. As the droplets of spray get near the plants, the plants themselves become slightly charged and attract the droplets.

a) (i) Explain why the positive charge on the droplets makes the spray spread out. [1]

    (ii) State what charge appears on the plants as the droplets come near to them. [1]

b) Explain fully how the plants themselves become fully charged. [3]

c) Suggest two reasons why it is an advantage to both the farmer and the environment to use very small charged droplets during insecticide spraying. [2]

WJEC

3

battery   switch

The circuit shows a battery connected to a switch and three identical lamps, L_1, L_2 and L_3.

a) Copy the diagram and add:

    (i) an arrow to show the current direction in the circuit when the switch is closed; [1]

    (ii) a voltmeter V , to measure the voltage across L_1; [1]

    (iii) a switch, labelled S, that controls L_3 only. [1]

b) State and explain what effect adding another cell to the battery would have on the lamps in the circuit. [2]

WJEC

4 The circuit diagram shows a battery connected to five lamps. The currents through lamps **A** and **B** are shown.

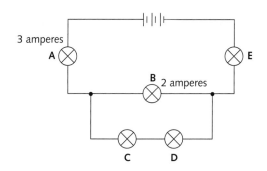

Write down the current flowing through

a) lamp **C**, [1]

b) lamp **E**. [1]

WJEC

5 (i) How much energy is transferred by a battery of EMF 4.5 V when 1.0 C of charge passes through it? [1]

    (ii) How much power is developed in a battery of EMF 4.5 V when a current of 1.0 A is passing through it? [1]

UCLES (O)

6 The diagram shows a circuit which contains two resistors.

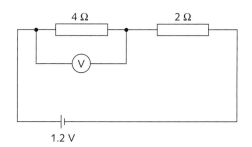

Calculate

a) the total resistance of the two resistors in series, (Ω) [1]

b) the current flowing through the cell, (A) [1]

c) the current flowing through the 4 Ω resistor, (A) [1]

d) the reading of the voltmeter, (V) [1]

e) the power produced in the 4 Ω resistor. (W) [1]

UCLES (I)

7 The figure below shows an electric kettle and the label which is on the bottom of the kettle.

heating element

a) Explain the meaning of the terms
  (i) **AC only**
  (ii) **50 Hz** [2]
b) (i) What is the power rating of the kettle in **kilowatts**?
  (ii) A kilowatt-hour is one Unit of electricity. How many Units of electricity would the kettle use in **three** hours?
  (iii) The cost of one Unit of electricity is 8p. How much would it cost to use the kettle for **three** hours? [5]
c) The plug of the kettle is fitted with a 13 A fuse.
  (i) What is the purpose of a fuse?
  (ii) How does a fuse work? [3]

NEAB

8 A small generator is labelled as having an output of 5 kW, 240 V AC (at constant frequency). It is used to provide emergency lighting for a large building in the event of a breakdown of the mains supply. The circuit is shown below.

There are 35 light fittings on the circuit, each with a 240 V, 60 W lamp.
a) Calculate the maximum current which the generator is designed to supply [2]
b) (i) Calculate the power needed when all the lamps are turned on at the same time.
  (ii) Explain why this generator is suitable for supplying the power required but would not be suitable if all the 60 W lamps were exchanged for 150 W lamps. [4]
c) Write down two reasons why all the lamps are connected in parallel rather than in series. In each answer, you should refer to both types of circuit. [4]
d) Calculate the resistance of the filament of each 60 W lamp. [4]
e) The figure below shows the current output of the generator when it is supplying all 35 of the 60 W lamps.

  (i) Calculate the frequency of the supply from the generator.
  (ii) Copy the diagram and sketch another graph to show the approximate current output of the generator when 17 lamps are removed from their fittings. [4]

UCLES (I)

9 The table shows the power rating of appliances used in the home.

appliance	power rating
fire	2000 W
television	250 W
kettle	2.5 kW
hairdrier	1200 W
vacuum cleaner	800 W

a) If all the appliances were used for the same length of time, state which one would
  (i) use the least amount of electricity, [1]
  (ii) cost the most to run. [1]
b) Calculate
  (i) the power of the fire in kW, [1]
  (ii) the cost of using the fire for 2 h if one unit of energy (kWh) costs 8p.
  You may use the following equations
  Energy used (kWh) = *power* (kW) × *time* (h)
  Cost = *number of units* × *cost per unit* [2]

WJEC

10 The information plate on a hairdrier is shown.

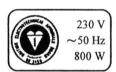

230 V
~50 Hz
800 W

a) What is the power rating of the hairdrier? [1]
b) (i) Write down the equation which links current, power and voltage. [1]
  (ii) Calculate the current in amperes, when the hairdrier is being used. Show clearly how you work out your answer. [2]
  (iii) Which **one** of the following fuses, 3A, 5A or 13A should you use with this hairdrier? [1]
c) The hairdrier transfers electrical energy to heat energy and kinetic energy.

Use the following equation to calculate the efficiency of the hairdrier in transferring electrical energy into heat energy.

efficiency = $\dfrac{\text{useful energy output}}{\text{total energy input}}$ [2]

d) One kilowatt-hour of electricity costs 6p. Use the following equation to calculate how much it will cost to use the hairdrier for 10 minutes.
cost of electricity = energy transferred × price per unit. [2]

SEG

209

Photocopy the list of topics below and tick the boxes of the ones that are included in your examination syllabus. (Your teacher should be able to tell you which they are.) Use your list when you revise. The spread number in brackets tells you where to find more information.

❏ 1 The two types of electric charge. (8.01)

❏ 2 Direction of the force between charges. (8.01)

❏ 3 How charges come from the atom. (8.01)

❏ 4 Electrical conductors and insulators. (8.01)

❏ 5 Why charged objects attract uncharged ones. (8.02)

❏ 6 Detecting charge. (8.02)

❏ 7 Induced charges. (8.02)

❏ 8 The SI unit of charge: the coulomb. (8.02)

❏ 9 Using electrostatic charge. (8.02)

❏ 10 Basic principles of a simple circuit. (8.03)

❏ 11 Measuring current. (8.03)

❏ 12 The SI unit of current: the ampere. (8.03)

❏ 13 The equation linking charge and current. (8.03)

❏ 14 The conventional current direction. (8.03)

❏ 15 Measuring PD (voltage). (8.04)

❏ 16 The meaning of EMF. (8.04)

❏ 17 The SI unit of PD (voltage): the volt. (8.04)

❏ 18 Rule linking the PDs round a circuit. (8.04)

❏ 19 The equation linking resistance, PD, and current. (8.05)

❏ 20 The SI unit of resistance: the ohm. (8.05)

❏ 21 Factors affecting the resistance of a wire. (8.05)

❏ 22 Using the heating effect of a current. (8.05)

❏ 23 Resistors and other components. (8.05)

❏ 24 Using the equation linking V, I, and R. (8.06)

❏ 25 Ohm's law. (8.06)

❏ 26 Interpreting current-PD graphs. (8.06)

❏ 27 The properties of circuits with components in series and in parallel. (8.07)

❏ 28 Equation for combined resistance of
- resistors in series
- resistors in parallel. (8.08)

❏ 29 How to solve circuit problems. (8.08)

❏ 30 Ions and their properties. (8.09)

❏ 31 How an ionized gas (air) conducts. (8.09)

❏ 32 The chemical effect of an electric current: electrolysis. (8.09)

❏ 33 Calculating electrical power. (8.10)

❏ 34 The equation linking power, PD (voltage), and current. (8.10)

❏ 35 Calculating the power dissipated in a resistor (lost because of the heating effect). (8.10)

❏ 36 The difference between AC and DC. (8.11)

❏ 37 The features of a mains circuit. (8.11)

❏ 38 The function of the fuse and earth wire in a mains circuit. (8.11)

❏ 39 How to wire a mains plug safely. (8.11)

❏ 40 Choosing the correct fuse value. (8.11)

❏ 41 Household mains circuits. (8.12)

❏ 42 The hazards of mains electricity. (8.12)

❏ 43 Calculating electrical energy. (8.13)

❏ 44 Measuring energy in kilowatt hours. (8.13)

❏ 45 Calculating the cost of electricity. (8.13)

❏ 46 Electric fields and their features. (8.14)

❏ 47 The use of lightning conductors. (8.14)

❏ 48 The simple cell and the dry cell. (8.15)

❏ 49 Primary and secondary cells. (8.15)

Magnets and Currents

- MAGNETS - MAGNETIC FIELDS - MAGNETIC EFFECT OF A CURRENT - ELECTROMAGNETS
- MAGNETIC FORCE ON A CURRENT - ELECTRIC MOTORS - ELECTROMAGNETIC INDUCTION
- GENERATORS - TRANSFORMERS - POWER TRANSMISSION AND DISTRIBUTION

Computer model of the magnetic field inside the doughnut-shaped chamber of a nuclear fusion reactor. Like the Sun, fusion reactors release energy by smashing hydrogen atoms together to form helium. One day, they may provide the energy to run power stations on Earth. In the reactor, the magnetic field is used to trap charged particles from hydrogen at a temperature of over 100 million °C.

9.01 Magnets

North Pole

Magnetic poles

If a small bar magnet is dipped into iron filings, the filings are attracted to its ends, as shown in the photograph on the opposite page. The magnetic force seems to come from two points, called the **poles** of the magnet.

The Earth exerts forces on the poles of a magnet. If a bar magnet is suspended as on the left, it swings round until it lies roughly north–south. This effect is used to name the two poles of a magnet. These are called:

● the **north-seeking pole** (or **N pole** for short)
● the **south-seeking pole** (or **S pole** for short).

If you bring the ends of two similar bar magnets together, there is a force between the poles as shown below:

Like poles repel; unlike poles attract.
The closer the poles, the greater the force between them.

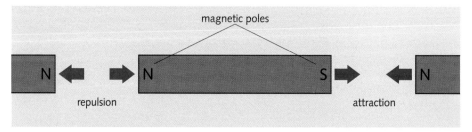

magnetic poles

repulsion   attraction

Induced magnetism

Materials such as iron and steel are attracted to magnets because they themselves become magnetized when there is a magnet nearby. The magnet **induces** magnetism in them, as shown below. In each case, the induced pole nearest the magnet is the *opposite* of the pole at the end of the magnet. The attraction between unlike poles holds each piece of metal to the magnet.

The steel and the iron behave differently when pulled right away from the magnet. The steel keeps some of its induced magnetism and becomes a **permanent magnet**. However, the iron loses virtually all of its induced magnetism. It was only a **temporary magnet**.

magnet

iron   steel

poles induced
in iron and steel

iron loses
magnetism

steel permanently
magnetized

DC   AC   Hz

Making a magnet

A piece of steel becomes permanently magnetized when placed near a magnet, but its magnetism is usually weak. It can be magnetized more strongly by stroking it with one end of a magnet, as on the right. However, the most effective method of magnetizing it is to place it in a long coil of wire and pass a large, direct (one-way) current through the coil. The current has a magnetic effect which magnetizes the steel.

Magnetic and non-magnetic materials

A **magnetic material** is one which which can be magnetized and is attracted to magnets. All strongly magnetic materials contain iron, nickel, or cobalt. For example, steel is mainly iron. Strongly magnetic metals like this are called **ferromagnetics**. They are described as *hard* or *soft* depending on how well they keep their magnetism when magnetized:

Hard magnetic materials such as steel, and alloys called Alcomax and Magnadur are difficult to magnetize but do not readily lose their magnetism. They are used for permanent magnets.

Soft magnetic materials such as iron and Mumetal are relatively easy to magnetize, but their magnetism is only temporary. They are used in the cores of electromagnets and transformers because their magnetic effect can be 'switched' on or off or reversed easily.

Non-magnetic materials include metals such as brass, copper, zinc, tin, and aluminium, as well as non-metals.

Where magnetism comes from

In an atom, tiny electrical particles called electrons move around a central nucleus. Each electron has a magnetic effect as it spins and orbits the nucleus. In many types of atom, the magnetic effects of the electrons cancel, but in some they do not, so each atom acts as a tiny magnet. In an unmagnetized material, the atomic magnets point in random directions. But as the material becomes magnetized, more and more of its atomic magnets line up with each other. Together, billions of tiny atomic magnets act as one big magnet.

If a magnet is hammered, its atomic magnets are thrown out of line: it becomes **demagnetized**. Heating it to a high temperature has the same effect.

Magnetizing a piece of steel by stroking it with a magnet.

Magnetic materials are attracted to magnets and can be made into magnets.

Q

1 What is meant by the *N pole* of a magnet?
2 Magnetic materials are sometimes described as *hard* or *soft*.
   a) What is the difference between the two types?
   b) Give one example of each type.
3 Name *three* ferromagnetic metals.
4 Name *three* non-magnetic metals.
5 The diagram on the right shows three metal bars. When different ends are brought together, it is found that A and B attract, A and C attract, but A and D repel. Decide whether each of the bars is a permanent magnet or not.

bar 1

bar 2

bar 3

Related topics: atoms and electrons **8.01**; the Earth's magnetism **9.02**; electromagnets **9.04**; transformers **9.09–9.10**

9.02 Magnetic fields

In the photograph below, iron filings have been sprinkled on paper over a bar magnet. The filings have become tiny magnets, pulled into position by forces from the poles of the magnet. Scientifically speaking, there is a **magnetic field** around the magnet, and this exerts forces on magnetic materials in it.

Magnetic field patterns

Magnetic fields can be investigated using a small **compass**. The 'needle' is a tiny magnet which is free to turn on its spindle. When near a magnet, the needle is turned by forces between its poles and the poles of the magnet. The needle comes to rest so that the turning effect is zero.

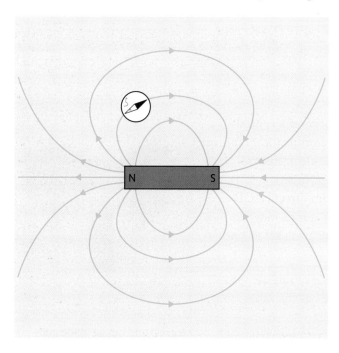

dots on paper
plotting compass
field line
N   S

The diagram on the left shows how a small compass can be used to plot the field around a bar magnet. Starting with the compass near one end of the magnet, the needle position is marked using two dots. Then the compass is moved so that the needle lines up with the previous dot... and so on. When the dots are joined up, the result is a magnetic **field line**. More lines can be drawn by starting with the compass in different positions.

In the diagram above, a selection of field lines has been used to show the magnetic field around a bar magnet:

- The field lines run from the N pole to the S pole of the magnet. The field direction, shown by an arrowhead, is defined as the direction in which the force on a N pole would act. It is the direction in which the N end of a compass needle would point.
- The magnetic field is strongest where the field lines are closest together.

If two magnets are placed near each other, their magnetic fields combine to produce a single field. Two examples are shown at the top of the next page. At the **neutral point**, the field from one magnet exactly cancels the field from the other, so the magnetic force on anything at this point is zero.

Magnet essentials

A magnet has a north-seeking (N) pole at one end and a south-seeking (S) pole at the other. When two magnets are brought together:

like poles repel, unlike poles attract.

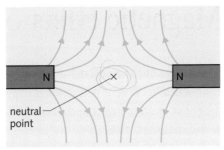

◀ At the neutral point, the fields from the two magnets cancel, so the combined field is of zero strength.

The Earth's magnetic field

The Earth has a magnetic field. No one is sure of its cause, although it is thought to come from electric currents generated in the Earth's core. The field is rather like that around a large, but very weak bar magnet.

With no other magnets near it, a compass needle lines up with the Earth's magnetic field. The N end of the needle points north. But an N pole is always attracted to an S pole. So it follows that the Earth's magnetic S pole must be in the north! It lies under a point in Canada called **magnetic north**.

Magnetic north is over 1200 km away from the Earth's geographic North Pole. This is because the Earth's magnetic axis is not quite in line with its north-south axis of rotation.

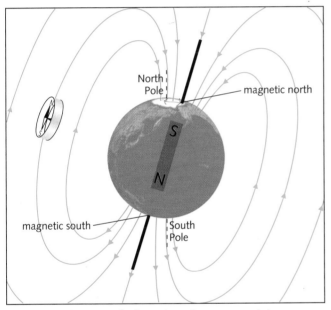

The Earth behaves as if it has a large but very weak bar magnet inside it.

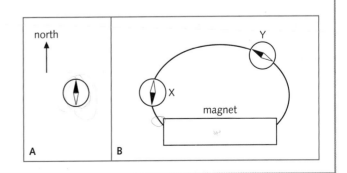

A compass is of no use in polar regions because the Earth's magnetic field lines are vertical.

1 In the diagrams on the right, the same compass is being used in both cases.
a) Copy diagram A. Label the N and S ends of the compass needle.
b) Copy diagram B. Mark in the poles of the magnet to show which is N and which is S. Then draw an arrowhead on the field line to show its direction.
c) In diagram B, at which position, X or Y, would you expect the magnetic field to be the stronger?

9.03 Magnetic effect of a current

Magnet essentials

Like poles repel; unlike poles attract. Magnetic field lines show the direction of the force on a N pole.

Magnetic field around a wire

If an electric current is passed through a wire, as shown below left, a weak magnetic field is produced. The field has these features:

- the magnetic field lines are circles
- the field is strongest close to the wire
- increasing the current increases the strength of the field.

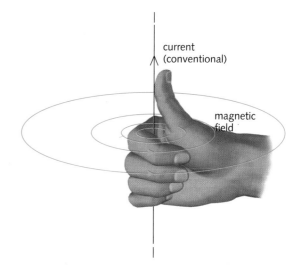

A rule for field direction The direction of the magnetic field produced by a current is given by the **right-hand grip rule** shown above right. Imagine gripping the wire with your right hand so that your thumb points in the conventional current direction. Your fingers then point in the same direction as the field lines.

Current essentials

In a circuit the current is a flow of electrons: tiny particles which come from atoms.

The current arrows shown on circuit diagrams run from + to -. This is the **conventional current direction**. Electrons, being negatively charged, flow the other way.

Magnetic fields from coils

A current produces a stronger magnetic field if the wire it flows through is wound into a coil. The diagrams below show the magnetic field patterns produced by two current-carrying coils. One is just a single turn of wire. The other is a long coil with many turns. A long coil is called a **solenoid**.

The magnetic field produced by a current-carrying coil has these features:

● the field is similar to that from a bar magnet, and there are magnetic poles at the ends of the coil
● increasing the current increases the strength of the field
● increasing the number of turns on the coil increases the strength of the field.

A rule for poles To work out which way round the poles are, you can use another **right-hand grip rule**, as shown on the right. Imagine gripping the coil with your right hand so that your fingers point in the conventional current direction. Your thumb then points towards the N pole of the coil.

Magnets are made – and demagnetized – using coils, as shown below. In audio and video cassette recorders, tiny coils are used to put magnetic patterns on tape. The patterns store sound and picture information.

Right-hand grip rule for poles

Making a magnet

Above, a steel bar has been placed in a solenoid. When a current is passed through the solenoid, the steel becomes magnetized and makes the magnetic field much stronger than before. And when the current is switched off, the steel stays magnetized. Nearly all permanent magnets are made in this way.

Demagnetizing a magnet

Above, a magnet is slowly being pulled out of a solenoid through which an alternating current is passing. Alternating current (AC) flows backwards, forwards, backwards, forwards... and so on. It produces a magnetic field which changes direction very rapidly and throws the atoms in the magnet out of line.

1 The coil in diagram A is producing a magnetic field.
   a) Give *two* ways in which the strength of the field could be increased.
   b) How could the direction of the field be reversed?
   c) Copy the diagram. Show the conventional current direction and the N and S poles of the coil.
2 Redraw diagram B to show which way the compass needles point when a current flows through the wire. (Assume that the black end of each compass needle is a N pole, the conventional current direction is away from you, into the paper, and that the only magnetic field is that due to the current.)

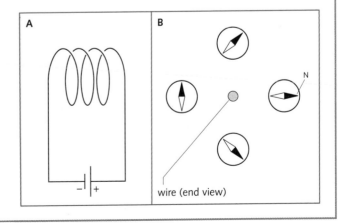

wire (end view)

Related topics: current in a circuit **8.03**; magnetic poles **9.01**; magnetic fields **9.02**; alternating current **8.11**

217

Electromagnets

A simple electromagnet

Unlike an ordinary magnet, an **electromagnet** can be switched on and off. In a simple electromagnet, a **coil**, consisting of several hundred turns of insulated copper wire, is wound round a **core**, usually of iron or Mumetal. When a current flows through the coil, it produces a magnetic field. This magnetizes the core, creating a magnetic field about a thousand times stronger than the coil by itself. With an iron or Mumetal core, the magnetism is only temporary, and is lost as soon as the current through the coil is switched off. Steel would not be suitable as a core because it would become permanently magnetized.

The strength of the magnetic field is increased by:
- increasing the current
- increasing the number of turns in the coil.

Reversing the current reverses the direction of the magnetic field.

The following devices all contain electromagnets.

The magnetic relay

A magnetic relay is a switch operated by an electromagnet. With a relay, a small switch with thin wires can be used to turn on the current in a much more powerful circuit – for example, one with a large electric motor in it:

When the switch S in the input circuit is closed, a current flows through the electromagnet. This pulls the iron armature towards it, which closes the contacts C. As a result, a current flows through the motor.

The relay above is of the 'normally open' type: when the input switch is OFF, the output circuit is also OFF. A 'normally closed' relay works the opposite way: when the input switch is OFF, the output circuit is ON. In practice, most relays are made so that they can be connected either way.

With a relay, a small switch can be used to turn on a powerful starter motor.

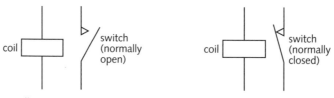

Normally-open relay (symbol)   Normally-closed relay (symbol)

The moving-coil loudspeaker

Most loudspeakers are of the moving-coil type shown on the right. The cylindrical magnet produces a strong radial ('spoke-like') magnetic field at right angles to the wire in the coil. The coil is free to move backwards and forwards and is attached to a stiff paper or plastic cone.

The loudspeaker is connected to an amplifier which gives out alternating current. This flows backwards, forwards, backwards... and so on, causing a force on the coil which is also backwards, forwards, backwards.... As a result, the cone vibrates and gives out sound waves. The sound you hear depends on how the amplifier makes the current alternate.

Moving-coil loudspeaker

Turning effect on a coil

The coil below lies between the poles of a magnet. The current flows in opposite directions along the two sides of the coil. So, according to Fleming's left-hand rule, one side is pushed *up* and the other side is pushed *down*. In other words, there is a turning effect on the coil. With more turns on the coil, the turning effect is increased.

The meter in the photograph uses the above principle. Its pointer is attached to a coil in the field of a magnet. The higher the current through the meter, the further the coil turns against the springs holding it, and the further the pointer moves along the scale.

Moving-coil meter

Q

1 There is a force on the wire in the diagram on the right.
  a) Give *two* ways in which the force could be increased.
  b) Use Fleming's left-hand rule to work out the direction of the force.
  c) Give *two* ways in which the direction of the force could be reversed.
2 Explain why the cone of a loudspeaker vibrates when alternating current passes through its coil.
3 The diagram above shows a current-carrying coil in a magnetic field. What difference would it make if
  a) there were more turns of wire in the coil
  b) the direction of the current were reversed?

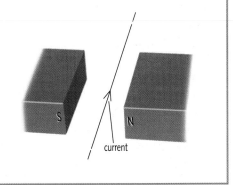

Related topics: sound waves **6.03**; current in a circuit **8.03**; magnetic fields **9.02**; field around a wire **9.03**; using a loudspeaker **10.01**

Electric motors

Turning effect on a coil

When a current flows through this coil, there is an upward force on one side and a downward force on the other. The direction of each force is given by Fleming's left-hand rule, explained on the previous spread.

If a coil is carrying a current in a magnetic field, as on the left, the forces on it produce a turning effect. Many electric motors use this principle.

A simple DC motor

magnet

coil

N

S

commutator (split ring)

battery

brushes

The action of the commutator

When the coil is nearly vertical, the forces cannot turn it much further...

...but when the coil overshoots the vertical, the commutator changes the direction of the current through it, so the forces change direction and keep the coil turning.

The diagram above shows a simple electric motor. It runs on direct current (DC), the 'one-way' current that flows from a battery.

The coil is made of insulated copper wire. It is free to rotate between the poles of the magnet. The **commutator**, or split-ring, is fixed to the coil and rotates with it. Its action is explained below and in the diagrams on the left. The **brushes** are two contacts which rub against the commutator and keep the coil connected to the battery. They are usually made of carbon.

When the coil is horizontal, the forces are furthest apart and have their maximum turning effect (leverage) on the coil. With no change to the forces, the coil would eventually come to rest in the vertical position. However, as the coil overshoots the vertical, the commutator changes the direction of the current through it. So the forces change direction and push the coil further round until it is again vertical... and so on. In this way, the coil keeps rotating clockwise, half a turn at a time. If either the battery or the poles of the magnet were the other way round, the coil would rotate anticlockwise.

The turning effect on the coil can be increased by:
● increasing the current
● using a stronger magnet
● increasing the number of turns on the coil
● increasing the area of the coil. (A longer coil means higher forces because there is a greater length of wire in the magnetic field; a wider coil gives the forces more leverage.)

Practical motors

The simple motor on the opposite page produces a low turning effect and is jerky in action, especially at low speeds. Practical motors give a much better performance for these reasons:

- Several coils are used, each set at a different angle and each with its own pair of commutator segments (pieces), as shown on the right. The result is a greater turning effect and smoother running.
- The coils contain hundreds of turns of wire and are wound on a core called an **armature**, which contains iron. The armature becomes magnetized and increases the strength of the magnetic field.
- The pole pieces are curved to create a radial ('spoke-like') magnetic field. This keeps the turning effect at a maximum for most of the coil's rotation.

In some motors, the field is provided by an electromagnet rather than a permanent magnet. One advantage is that the motor can be run from an alternating current (AC) supply. As the current flows backwards and forwards in the coil, the field from the electromagnet changes direction to match it, so the turning effect is always the same way and the motor rotates normally. The mains motors in drills and food mixers work like this.

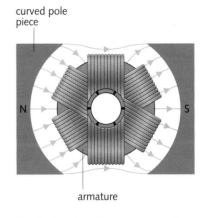

curved pole piece

armature

Practical motors have curved pole pieces, and several coils wound on an iron armature.

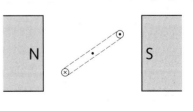

◄ In this electric drill, the motor is at the right-hand end. Note the commutator segments and the coil of the electromagnet.

Q

1 Which part(s) of an electric motor
   a) connect the power supply to the split-ring and coil
   b) changes the current direction every half-turn?
2 On the right, there is an end view of the coil in a simple electric motor.
   a) Redraw the diagram to show the position of the coil when the turning effect on it is i) maximum ii) zero.
   b) Give *three* ways in which the maximum turning effect on the coil could be increased.
   c) Use Fleming's left-hand rule to work out which way the coil will turn.
3 What is the advantage of using an electromagnet in an electric motor, rather than a permanent magnet?

N   S

⊗ = current into paper
⊙ = current out of paper

9.07 Electromagnetic induction

A current produces a magnetic field. However, the reverse is also possible: a magnetic field can be used to produce a current.

Induced EMF and current in a moving wire

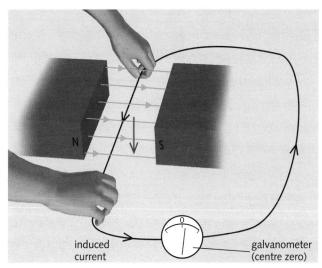

induced current — galvanometer (centre zero)

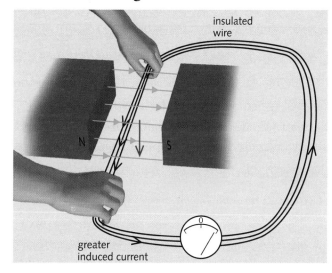

insulated wire

greater induced current

Circuit essentials

For a current to flow in a circuit, the circuit must be complete, with no breaks in it. Also, there must a source of EMF (voltage) to provide the energy. A battery is one such source. Others include a wire moving through a magnetic field, as explained on the right.

EMF stands for electromotive force. It is measured in volts.

Magnet essentials

The N and S poles of one magnet exert forces on those of another:

like poles repel, unlike poles attract.

The magnetic field around a magnet can be represented by field lines. These show the direction in which the force on an N pole would act.

When a wire is moved across a magnetic field, as shown above left, a small EMF (voltage) is generated in the wire. The effect is called **electromagnetic induction**. Scientifically speaking, an EMF is **induced** in the wire. If the wire forms part of a complete circuit, the EMF makes a current flow. This can be detected by a meter called a **galvanometer**, which is sensitive to very small currents. The one shown in the diagram is a centre-zero type. Its pointer moves to the left or right of the zero, depending on the current direction.

The induced EMF (and current) can be increased by:
● moving the wire faster
● using a stronger magnet
● increasing the length of wire in the magnetic field – for example, by looping the wire through the field several times, as shown above right.

The above results are summed up by **Faraday's law of electromagnetic induction**. In simplified form, this can be stated as follows:

> The EMF induced in a conductor is proportional to the rate at which magnetic field lines are cut by the conductor.

In applying this law, remember that field lines are used to represent the strength of a magnetic field as well as its direction. The closer together the lines, the stronger the field.

Either of the following will reverse the direction of the induced EMF and current:
● moving the wire in the opposite direction
● turning the magnet round so that the field direction is reversed.

If the wire is not moving, or is moving parallel to the field lines, there is no induced EMF or current.

Induced EMF and current in a coil

induced current

induced current
in opposite direction

If a bar magnet is pushed into a coil, as shown above left, an EMF is induced in the coil. In this case, it is the magnetic field that is moving rather than the wire, but the result is the same: field lines are being cut. As the coil is part of a complete circuit, the induced EMF makes a current flow.

The induced EMF (and current) can be increased by:
- moving the magnet faster
- using a stronger magnet
- increasing the number of turns on the coil (as this increases the length of wire cutting through the magnetic field).

Experiments with the magnet and coil also give the following results.

- If the magnet is pulled *out of* the coil, as shown above right, the direction of the induced EMF (and current) is reversed.
- If the S pole of the magnet, rather than the N pole, is pushed into the coil, this also reverses the current direction.
- If the magnet is held still, no field lines are cut, so there is no induced EMF or current.

The playback heads in audio and video cassette recorders contain tiny coils. A tiny, varying EMF is induced in the coil as the magnetized tape passes over it and field lines are cut by the coil. In this way, the magnetized patterns on the tape are changed into electrical signals which can be used to recreate the original sound or picture.

The pick-ups under the strings of this guitar are tiny coils with magnets inside them. The steel strings become magnetized. When they vibrate, current is induced in the coils, boosted by an amplifier, and used to produce sound.

1 The wire on the right forms part of a circuit. When the wire is moved downwards, a current is induced in it. What would be the effect of
   a) moving the wire upwards through the magnetic field
   b) holding the wire still in the magnetic field
   c) moving the wire parallel to the magnetic field lines?
2 In the experiment at the top of the page, what would be the effect of
   a) moving the magnet faster
   b) turning the magnet round, so that the S pole is pushed into the coil
   c) having more turns on the coil?

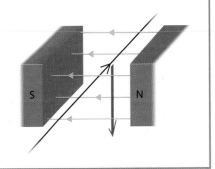

Related topics: current 8.03; EMF 8.04; magnetic fields 9.02; direction of induced current (Lenz's law) 9.12; recording signals 10.07

9.08 Generators

Most of our electricity comes from huge **generators** in power stations. There are smaller generators in cars and on some bicycles. These generators, or dynamos, all use electromagnetic induction. When turned, they induce an EMF (voltage) which can make a current flow. Most generators give out alternating current (AC). AC generators are also called **alternators**.

A simple AC generator

The diagram below shows a simple AC generator. It is providing the current for a small bulb. The coil is made of insulated copper wire and is rotated by turning the shaft. The **slip rings** are fixed to the coil and rotate with it. The **brushes** are two contacts which rub against the slip rings and keep the coil connected to the outside part of the circuit. They are usually made of carbon.

When the coil is rotated, it cuts magnetic field lines, so an EMF is generated. This makes a current flow. As the coil rotates, each side travels upwards, downwards, upwards, downwards... and so on, through the magnetic field. So the current flows backwards, forwards... and so on. In other words, it is AC. The graph shows how the current varies through one cycle (rotation). It is a maximum when the coil is horizontal and cutting field lines at the fastest rate. It is zero when the coil is vertical and cutting no field lines.

The following all increase the maximum EMF (and the current):
● increasing the number of turns on the coil
● increasing the area of the coil
● using a stronger magnet
● rotating the coil faster.

Faster rotation also increases the frequency of the AC. Mains generators must keep a steady frequency – for example, 50 Hz (cycles per second) in the UK.

Simple AC generator, connected to a bulb

Graph showing the generator's AC output

Practical generators

◀ One of the alternators (AC generators) in a large power station. It is turned by a turbine, blown round by the force of high-pressure steam. It generates an EMF of over 30 000 volts, although consumers get their supply at a much lower voltage than this.

Unlike the simple generator on the opposite page, most AC generators have a fixed set of coils arranged around a rotating electromagnet. The various coils are made from many hundreds of turns of wire. To create the strongest possible magnetic field, they are wound on specially-shaped cores containing iron. Slip rings and brushes are still used, but only to carry current to the spinning electromagnet. As the other coils are fixed, the current delivered by the generator does not have to flow through sliding contacts. (Sliding contacts can overheat if the current is very high.)

Direct current (DC) is 'one-way' current like that from a battery. DC generators are similar in construction to DC motors, with a fixed magnet, rotating coil, brushes, and a commutator to reverse the connections to the outside circuit every half-turn. When the coil is rotated, alternating current is generated. However, the action of the commutator means that the current in the outside circuit always flows the same way – in other words, it is DC.

Cars need DC for recharging the battery and running other circuits. To produce current, the engine turns a generator. However, an alternator is used, rather than a DC generator, because it can deliver more current. A device called a **rectifier** changes its AC output to DC.

Alternator from a car

Q

1 The diagram on the right shows the end view of the coil in a simple generator. The coil is being rotated. It is connected through brushes and slip rings to an outside circuit.
   a) What type of current is generated in the coil, AC or DC? Explain why it is this type of current being generated.
   b) Give *three* ways in which the current could be increased.
   c) The current varies as the coil rotates. What is the position of the coil when the current is a maximum? Why is the current a maximum in this position?
   d) What is the position of the coil when the current is zero? Why is the current zero in this position?
2 Give *three* differences between the simple AC generator on the opposite page and most practical AC generators.

9.09 Coils and transformers (1)

A *moving* magnetic field can induce an EMF (voltage) in a conductor, as on the left. A *changing* magnetic field can have the same effect.

Mutual induction

As the electromagnet above is switched on, an EMF is induced in the other coil, but only for a fraction of a second. The effect is equivalent to pushing a magnet towards the coil very fast. With a steady current through the electromagnet, no EMF is induced because the magnetic field is not changing. As the electromagnet is switched off, an EMF is induced in the opposite direction. The effect is equivalent to pulling a magnet away from the coil very fast.

The induced EMF at switch-on or switch-off is increased if:
- the core of the electromagnet goes right through the second coil
- the number of turns on the second coil is increased.

When coils are magnetically linked, as above, so that a changing current in one causes an induced EMF in the other, this is called **mutual induction**.

Using mutual induction, 10 000 volts for spark plugs is produced from a 12 volt supply. The high voltage is induced in a coil by switching an electromagnet on and off electronically.

A heart pacemaker uses mutual induction. Pulses of current through a coil in the pacemaker unit induce pulses in a coil fitted in the patient's chest. These trigger heartbeats.

A simple transformer

primary (input)
coil: 500 turns

secondary (output)
coil: 1000 turns

~
AC input 12 V
voltage

24 V AC output
voltage

core: iron or mumetal

Symbol for a transformer

AC voltages can be increased or decreased using a **transformer**. A simple transformer is shown in the diagram above. It works by mutual induction.

When alternating current flows through the **primary** (input) coil, it sets up an alternating magnetic field in the core and, therefore, in the **secondary** (output) coil. This changing field induces an alternating voltage in the output coil. Provided all the field lines pass through both coils, and the coils waste no energy because of heating effects, the following equation applies:

$$\frac{\text{output voltage}}{\text{input voltage}} = \frac{\text{turns on output coil}}{\text{turns on input coil}}$$

In symbols:
$$\frac{V_2}{V_1} = \frac{n_2}{n_1}$$

For the transformer above, $n_2/n_1 = 1000/500 = 2$. The transformer has a **turns ratio** of 2. The same ratio links the voltages: $V_2/V_1 = 24/12 = 2$. Put in words, the output coil has twice the number of turns of the input coil, so the output voltage is twice the input voltage.

A transformer does not give you something for nothing. If it increases voltage, it reduces current. This is explained in the next spread.

DC and AC

Direct current (DC) flows one way only.

Alternating current (AC) flows alternately backwards and forwards.

PD, EMF, and voltage

PD (potential difference) is the scientific name for voltage. The PD produced within a battery or other source is called the EMF (electromotive force).

For convenience, engineers often use the word voltage rather than PD or EMF, especially when dealing with AC.

Voltages in AC circuits are commonly called AC voltages, although, strictly speaking, an 'alternating current voltage' doesn't make much sense!

Q

1   In the experiment on the right, what happens when
    a) the switch is closed (turned ON)
    b) the switch is left in the closed (ON) position
    c) the switch is then opened (turned OFF)?
2   In the experiment on the right, what would be the effect of
    a) extending the iron core so that it goes through both coils
    b) replacing the battery and switch by an AC supply?
3   A transformer has a turns ratio of 1/4. Its input coil is connected to a 12 volt AC supply. Assuming there are no energy or field line losses.
    a) What is the output voltage?
    b) What turns ratio would be required for an output voltage of 36 volts?

iron core

galvanometer
(centre zero)

Related topics: PD and EMF **8.04**; magnetic field lines **9.02**; electromagnets **9.04**; electromagnetic induction **9.07**; DC and AC **9.08**

9.10 Coils and transformers (2)

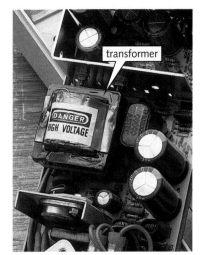

A small transformer with other components from inside a TV

Step-up and step-down transformers

Depending on its turns ratio, a transformer can increase or decrease an AC voltage.

Step-up transformers have more turns on the output coil than on the input coil, so their output voltage is *more* than the input voltage. The transformer in the diagram below is a step-up transformer. Large step-up transformers are used in power stations to increase the voltage to the levels needed for overhead power lines. The next spread explains why.

Step-down transformers have fewer turns on the output coil than on the input coil, so the output voltage is *less* than the input voltage. In battery chargers, computers, and other electronic equipment, they reduce the voltage of the AC mains to the much lower levels needed for other circuits.

Both types of transformer work on AC, but not on DC. Unless there is a *changing* current in the input coil, no voltage is induced in the output coil. Connecting a transformer to a DC supply can damage it. A high current flows through the input coil which can make it overheat.

Power through a transformer

If no energy is wasted in a transformer, the power (energy per second) delivered by the output coil will be the same as the power supplied to the input coil. So:

input voltage × input current = output voltage × output current

In symbols:

$$V_1 I_1 = V_2 I_2$$

As voltage × current is the same on both sides of a transformer, it follows that a transformer which *increases* the voltage will *reduce* the current in the same proportion, and vice versa. The figures in the diagram below illustrate this.

Power essentials

Energy is measured in joules (J).

Power is measured in watts (W).

An appliance with a power output of 1000 W delivers energy at the rate of 1000 joules per second.

In circuits, power can be calculated using this equation:

power = voltage × current
(watts)   (volts)   (amperes)
 (W)   (V)   (A)

500 turns   1000 turns

~ AC input 12 V

24 V AC output voltage ~

current: 2 A

current: 1 A

power input
= $V_1 I_1$
= 12 V x 2 A
= 24 W

core: iron or mumetal

power output
= $V_2 I_2$
= 24 V x 1 A
= 24 W

Practical transformers

The diagram on the right shows two ways of arranging the coils and core in a practical transformer. Both methods are designed to trap the magnetic field in the core so that all the field lines from one coil pass through the other.

input coil · output coil

laminated core: iron or mumetal

All transformers waste some energy because of heating effects in the core and coils. Here are two of the causes:

- The coils are not perfect electrical conductors and heat up because of their resistance. To keep the resistance low, thick copper wire is used where possible.
- The core is itself a conductor, so the changing magnetic field induces currents in it. These circulating **eddy currents** have a heating effect. To reduce them, the core is laminated (layered): it is made from thin, insulated sheets of iron or Mumetal, rather than a solid block.

output coil wound over input coil

Practical transformers

Large, well-designed transformers can have efficiencies as high as 99%. In other words, their useful power output is 99% of their power input.

Solving problems

Example Assuming that the transformer on the right has an efficiency of 100%, calculate **a)** the supply voltage **b)** the current through the input coil.

input coil: 2000 turns · output coil: 100 turns

10 V

AC supply

bulb: power 40 W

a) This is solved using the transformer equation: $\dfrac{V_2}{V_1} = \dfrac{n_2}{n_1}$

where V_1 is the supply voltage to be calculated.

Substituting values: $\dfrac{10\,\text{V}}{\text{supply voltage}} = \dfrac{100}{2000}$

Rearranged, this gives: supply voltage $= 200\,\text{V}$

b) This is solved using the power equation: $V_1 I_1 = V_2 I_2$

where $V_2 I_2$ is already known to be 40 W.

Substituting values: $200\,\text{V} \times \text{input current} = 40\,\text{W}$

Rearranged, this gives: input current $= 0.2\,\text{A}$

---

1 How does a step-up transformer differ from a step-down transformer?

2 Explain each of the following:
   a) a transformer will not work on DC
   b) the core of a transformer needs to be laminated
   c) if a transformer increases voltage, it reduces current.

3 In the circuit on the right, a transformer connected to the 230 V AC mains is providing power for a low-voltage heater. Using the information in the diagram, and assuming that the efficiency is 100%, calculate
   a) the voltage across the heater
   b) the power supplied by the mains
   c) the power delivered to the heater
   d) the current through the heater.

230 V AC mains

current: 0.1 A

4600 turns

200 turns

heater

Related topics: resistance **8.05**; power calculations **8.10**; DC and AC **9.08**; power transmission **9.11**; eddy currents **9.12**

9.11 Power across the country

power station
generation

transformer
(step-up)

400 000 V

132 000 V

33 000 V

transmission

transformer substation
(step-down)

schools

farms

light
industry

heavy
industry

homes

230 V

11 000 V

33 000 V

132 000 V

offices
and
shops

transformer substation
(step-down)

transformer substation
(step-down)

transformer substation
(step-down)

distribution

Power essentials

An appliance with a power output of 1000 watts (W) delivers energy at the rate of 1000 joules per second.

In circuits

power	=	voltage	×	current
(watts)		(volts)		(amperes)
(W)		(V)		(A)

Transformer essentials

Transformers are used to increase or decrease AC voltages. If a transformer is 100% efficient, its power output and input are equal. So if it *increases* voltage, it *reduces* current in the same proportion so that 'voltage × current' stays the same.

Power for the AC mains is *generated* in power stations, *transmitted* (sent) through long-distance cables, and then *distributed* to consumers.

Typically, a large power station might contain four generators, each producing a current of 20 000 amperes at a voltage of 33 000 volts. The current from each generator is fed to a huge step-up transformer which transfers power to overhead cables at a greatly increased voltage (275 000 V or 400 000 V in the UK). The reason for doing this is explained on the next page. The cables feed power to a nationwide supply network called the **Grid**. Using the Grid, power stations in areas where the demand is low can be used to supply areas where the demand is high. Also power stations can be sited away from heavily populated areas.

Power from the Grid is distributed by a series of **substations**. These contain step-down transformers which reduce the voltage in stages to the level needed by consumers. In Europe, for example, this is 230 V for home consumers, although industry usually takes its power at a higher voltage.

Transmission issues

AC or DC? Alternating current (AC) is used for the mains. On a large scale, it can be generated more efficiently than 'one-way' direct current (DC). However, the main advantage of AC is that voltages can be stepped up or down using transformers. Transformers will not work with DC.

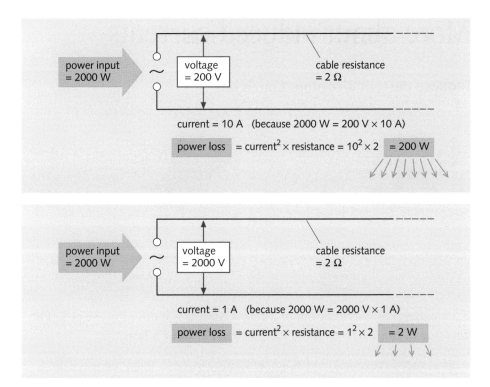

Resistance and power loss

The resistance of a conductor is measured in ohms (Ω).

When a current flows through a resistance, it has a heating effect, so power is wasted. The power loss can be calculated like this:

power loss = current^2 × resistance

◀ These calculations show the power losses in a cable when the same amount of power is sent at two different voltages (for simplicity, some units have been omitted).

High or low voltage? Transmission cables are good conductors, but they still have significant resistance – especially when they are hundreds of kilometres long. This means that energy is wasted because of the heating effect of the current. The calculations above demonstrate why less power is lost from a cable if power is transmitted through it at high voltage. By using a transformer to increase the voltage, the current is reduced, so thinner, lighter, and cheaper cables can be used.

Overhead or underground? High-voltage cables are the cheapest way of sending power over long distances. However, to prevent sparking, the only effective way of insulating the cables is to keep huge air spaces around them. That is why they have to be suspended from pylons.

Underground cables are more difficult to insulate and must therefore be used at lower voltages. To transmit the same power, they have to carry a higher current. This means that they must be thicker. They are also more expensive to lay. Despite their extra cost, underground cables are used in areas of outstanding natural beauty, where pylons would damage the environment by spoiling the landscape.

Pylons and overhead cables are not usually permitted in areas like this.

1 What is the main advantage of the Grid network?
2 What are substations for?
3 Explain each of the following.
   a) AC rather than DC is used for transmitting mains power.
   b) The voltage is stepped up before power from a generator is fed to overhead transmission cables.
4 Give an example of where underground transmission cables might be used instead of overhead ones, despite the extra cost.

5 The second paragraph on the opposite page describes the output of the four generators in a typical, large power station. Calculate the power station's total power output in MW. (1 MW = 1 000 000 W)
6 The diagram at the top of this page compares power losses from a cable at two different voltages. Calculate the power loss if the same power is sent at 20 000 V.
7 4 kW of power is fed to a transmission cable of resistance 5 Ω. Calculate the power loss in the cable if the power is transmitted at **a)** 200 V **b)** 200 000 V.

More about induced currents

Magnetic essentials

Like magnetic poles repel; unlike ones attract. Magnetic field lines run from the N pole of a magnet to the S pole.

In diagrams, the *conventional* current direction is used. This runs from the + of the supply to the -.

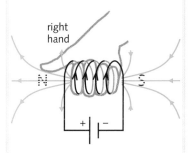

right hand

A current-carrying coil produces a magnetic field. The **right-hand grip rule** above tells you which end is the N pole. It is the end your thumb points at when your fingers point the same way as the current.

force
field
left hand
current

If a current-carrying wire is in a magnetic field as above, the direction of the force is given by **Fleming's left-hand rule**.

If a conductor is moving through a magnetic field, or in a changing field, an EMF (voltage) is induced in it.

Induced current direction: Lenz's law

coil repels magnet
induced current

coil attracts magnet
induced current in opposite direction

If a magnet is moved in or out of a coil, a current is induced in the coil. The direction of this current can be predicted using **Lenz's law**:

> An induced current always flows in a direction such that it opposes the change which produced it.

Above, for example, the induced current turns the coil into a weak electromagnet whose N pole *opposes* the approaching N pole of the magnet. When the magnet is pulled *out of* the coil, the induced current alters direction and the poles of the coil are reversed. This time, the coil attracts the magnet as it is pulled away. So, once again, the change is opposed.

Lenz's law is an example of the law of conservation of energy. Energy is spent when a current flows round a circuit, so energy must be spent to induce the current in the first place. In the example above, you have to spend energy to move the magnet against the opposing force.

Induced current direction: Fleming's right-hand rule

If a straight wire (in a complete circuit) is moving at right angles to a magnetic field, the direction of the induced current can be found using **Fleming's right-hand rule**, as shown below:

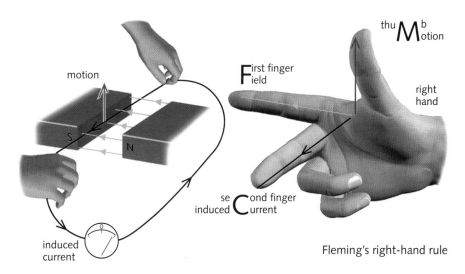

motion
induced current

thu**M**b otion
First finger ield
right hand
se**C**ond finger induced urrent

Fleming's right-hand rule

+++

On the opposite page, there is information about Fleming's right-hand and left-hand rules. The two rules apply to different situations:
- when a *current* causes *motion*, the *left*-hand rule applies
- when *motion* causes a *current*, the *right*-hand rule applies.

Fleming's right-hand rule follows from the left-hand rule and Lenz's law. The diagram on the right illustrates this. Here, the upward motion induces a current in the wire. The induced current is in the magnetic field, so there is a force on it whose direction is given by the *left*-hand rule. The force must be downwards to *oppose* the motion, so you can use this fact and the left-hand rule to work out which way the current must flow. However, the *right*-hand rule gives the same result – without you having to reason out all the steps!

motion

force on induced current opposes motion

Eddy currents

spinning aluminium disc

magnetic field stops disc spinning

magnet

If the aluminium disc above is set spinning, it may be many seconds before frictional force finally brings it to rest. However, if it spinning between the poles of a magnet, it stops almost immediately. This is because the disc is a good conductor and currents are induced in it as it moves through the magnetic field. These are called **eddy currents**. They produce a magnetic field which, by Lenz's law, opposes the motion of the disc. Eddy currents occur wherever pieces of metal are in a changing magnetic field – for example, in the core of a transformer.

Metal detectors rely on eddy currents. Typically, a pulse of current through a flat coil produces a changing magnetic field. This induces eddy currents in any metal object underneath. The eddy currents give off their own changing field which induces a second pulse in the coil. This is detected electronically.

A metal detector creates eddy currents in metal objects and then detects the magnetic fields produced.

Q

1 Look at the diagrams on the opposite page, illustrating Fleming's right-hand rule. If the directions of the magnetic field and the motion were both reversed, how would this affect the direction of the induced current?

2 On the right, a magnet is being moved towards a coil.
   a) As current is induced in the coil, what type of pole is formed at the left end of the coil? Give a reason for your answer.
   b) In which direction does the (conventional) current flow through the meter, AB or BA?

3 Aluminium is non-magnetic. Yet a freely-spinning aluminium disc quickly stops moving if a magnet is brought close to it. Explain why.

N   S

A   B

galvanometer (centre zero)

Related topics: law of conservation of energy **4.02**; right-hand grip rule **9.03**; Fleming's left-hand rule **9.05**; induced current **9.07**

1 An electromagnet is made by winding wire around an iron core.

iron core

wire coil

The diagram shows an electromagnet connected to a circuit.

a) State **two** ways of making the strength of the electromagnet weaker.   [2]

b) Explain why the core is made of iron instead of steel.   [1]

WJEC

2 **A**, **B**, **C** and **D** are small blocks of different materials. The table below shows what happens when two of the blocks are placed near one another.

Arrangement of blocks		Effect
A	B	attraction
B	C	attraction
A	C	no effect
B	D	no effect

a magnet	a magnetic material	a non-magnetic material

Use one of the phrases in the above boxes to describe the magnetic property of each block. Each phrase may be used once, more than once or not at all.

a) Block **A** is _____

b) Block **B** is _____

c) Block **C** is _____

d) Block **D** is _____   [4]

WJEC

3 The figure below shows a circuit, that includes an electrical relay, used to switch on a motor M.

springy contacts

pivot

soft iron

M

soft iron

coil   S

Explain in detail, how closing switch S causes the motor M to start.   [4]

UCLES (O)

4 The diagram shows a long wire placed between the poles of a magnet. When current **I** flows through the wire, a force acts on the wire causing it to move.

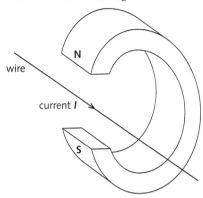

N

wire

current **I**

S

a) Use Fleming's left hand rule to find the direction of the force on the wire. Copy the diagram and show the direction of the force on your copy with an arrow labelled **F**.   [1]

b) State what happens to the force on the wire when

(i)   the size of the current through the wire is increased,   [1]

(ii) a weaker magnet is used,   [1]

(iii) the direction of the current is reversed.   [1]

c) Name **one** practical device which uses this effect.   [1]

WJEC

5 The diagram below shows a permanent magnet being moved towards a coil whose ends are connected to a sensitive ammeter. As the magnet approaches, the ammeter needle gives a **small** deflection to the **left**.

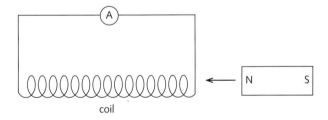

A

N   S

coil

a) State what you would expect the ammeter to show if, in turn,

(i)   the magnet was pulled away from the coil

(ii) the magnet was reversed so that the S pole was moved towards the coil

(iii) the magnet was now pulled away from the coil, at a much higher speed.   [4]

b) Give the name of the process which is illustrated by these experiments.   [1]

UCLES (O)

6 a) The chemical energy stored in a fossil fuel produces heat energy when the fuel is burned. Describe how this heat energy is then used to produce electrical energy at a power station.   [2]

b) Power stations use transformers to increase the voltage to very high values before transmitting it to all parts of the country. Explain why electricity is transmitted at very high voltages.   [1]

c) A power station produces electricity at 25 000 V which is increased by a transformer to 400 000 V. The transformer has 2000 turns on its primary coil. Use the formula

$$\frac{\text{voltage across primary coil}}{\text{voltage across secondary coil}} = \frac{\text{number of turns on primary coil}}{\text{number of turns on secondary coil}}$$

to calculate the number of turns on its secondary coil.   [2]

WJEC

7 The diagram shows a simple transformer.

primary coil (1000 turns)   secondary coil (50 turns)

The transformer is a **step-down** transformer.

a) What is a **step-down** transformer?   [1]

b) How can you tell from the diagram that this is a **step-down** transformer?   [1]

c) Calculate the output voltage of this transformer.   [3]

d) Explain why transformers are used in the National Grid.   [3]

e) What is the core of a transformer usually made of?   [2]

MEG

8 The diagram shows the main parts of one type of ammeter. There are two short iron bars inside a coil of insulated wire. One bar is fixed and cannot move and the other is on the end of a pivoted pointer. The diagram shows the ammeter in use and measuring a current of 1.5 amperes (A).

a) How much electrical charge will pass through this ammeter in one minute? Include in your answer the equation you are going to use. Show clearly how you get to your final answer and give the unit.   [3]

b) (i) Apart from heat, what will be produced by the coil of wire when the electricity passes through it?   [1]

(ii) What effect will this have on the two iron bars? What causes the effect? Draw one or more diagrams if this will help you to explain.   [4]

To answer part a), you will need information from Section 8

SEG

9 **a)** When a coil rotates in a magnetic field, an alternating voltage is produced. Explain how the voltage is produced   [2]

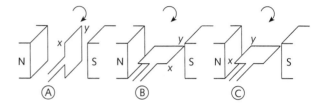

b) The diagrams A B and C show three positions of a coil as it rotates clockwise in a magnetic field produced by two poles.

The graph below shows how the voltage produced changes as the coil rotates.

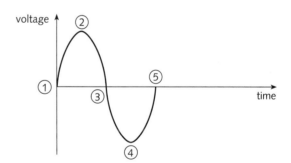

When the coil is in the position shown by diagram A, the output voltage is zero and is marked as 1 on the voltage-time graph. State which point on the voltage-time graph corresponds to the coil position shown by

(i) diagram B,   [1]

(ii) diagram C.   [1]

c) State **one** way of increasing the size of the voltage produced by **this** coil rotating in a magnetic field.   [1]

WJEC

Photocopy the list of topics below and tick the boxes of the ones that are included in your examination syllabus. (Your teacher should be able to tell you which they are.) Use your list when you revise. The spread number in brackets tells you where to find more information.

❏ 1 The two types of magnetic pole. (9.01)

❏ 2 The direction of the force between magnetic poles. (9.01)

❏ 3 Induced magnetism: permanent and temporary magnets. (9.01)

❏ 4 Methods of making a magnet. (9.01 and 9.03)

❏ 5 Magnetic and non-magnetic materials. (9.01)

❏ 6 Hard and soft magnetic materials. (9.01)

❏ 7 Demagnetizing a magnet. (9.01 and 9.03)

❏ 8 The magnetic field around a magnet. (9.02)

❏ 9 Finding field patterns with a plotting compass. (9.02)

❏ 10 The Earth's magnetic field. (9.02)

❏ 11 The magnetic field around a current-carrying wire. (9.03)

❏ 12 The magnetic field around a current-carrying coil. (9.03)

❏ 13 Factors affecting the magnetic field from a coil. (9.03)

❏ 14 The right-hand grip rule for poles. (9.03)

❏ 15 The electromagnet. (9.04)

❏ 16 Factors affecting an electromagnet's field strength. (9.04)

❏ 17 How a magnetic relay works. (9.04)

❏ 18 How a circuit breaker works. (9.04)

❏ 19 How an electric bell works. (9.04)

❏ 20 The force on a current in a magnetic field, and the factors affecting it. (9.05)

❏ 21 Fleming's left-hand rule. (9.05)

❏ 22 How a moving-coil loudspeaker works. (9.05)

❏ 23 The turning effect on a current-carrying coil in a magnetic field. (9.05)

❏ 24 How a simple DC motor works. (9.06)

❏ 25 Features of practical electric motors. (9.06)

❏ 26 Electromagnetic induction and the factors affecting it. (9.07)

❏ 27 Demonstrating an induced EMF (voltage) in a coil. (9.07)

❏ 28 Faraday's law of electromagnetic induction. (9.07)

❏ 29 How a simple AC generator works. (9.08)

❏ 30 Features of practical generators. (9.08)

❏ 31 AC voltage and current values. (9.08)

❏ 32 Demonstrating mutual induction. (9.09)

❏ 33 The action of a transformer. (9.09)

❏ 34 The equation linking a transformer's input and output voltages. (9.09)

❏ 35 The difference between a step-up and step-down transformer. (9.10)

❏ 36 The equation linking a transformer's input and output powers. (9.10)

❏ 37 Practical transformer design. (9.10)

❏ 38 The transmission and distribution of mains power across country. (9.11)

❏ 39 Why AC is used for power transmission. (9.11)

❏ 40 Why power is transmitted at high voltage. (9.11)

❏ 41 Lenz's law. (9.12)

❏ 42 Fleming's right-hand rule. (9.12)

❏ 43 Eddy currents and their effects. (9.12)

10

Electrons and Electronics

- CONTROL SYSTEMS
- TRANSDUCERS
- DIODES AND RECTIFICATION
- TRANSISTOR SWITCHES
- LOGIC GATES
- COMMUNICATIONS
- ANALOGUE AND DIGITAL SYSTEMS
- RADIO COMMUNICATION
- ELECTRON BEAMS
- OSCILLOSCOPE
- X-RAY TUBE

A grain weevil emerging from a grain of wheat. This picture, which is 50 times actual size, was produced by a scanning electron microscope. The instrument uses a narrow beam of electrons, rather than light, and the image is constructed by a computer. Unlike a light microscope, an electron microscope gives a three-dimensional image. However, the colours are false, and added by the computer.

10.01 Electronic essentials

Circuits with microchips and other semiconductor devices are called **electronic** circuits. They include the circuits in TV sets, computers, CD players, and amplifiers. Most handle very low currents, although they can control much more powerful circuits.

An electronic control system
The sound amplification system below is electronic. When you speak into the microphone, the sound waves cause tiny changes in the current through it. These changes are called **signals**. They are amplified (magnified) by the amplifier so that the loudspeaker gives out a louder version of the original sound. The extra power needed comes from the power supply.

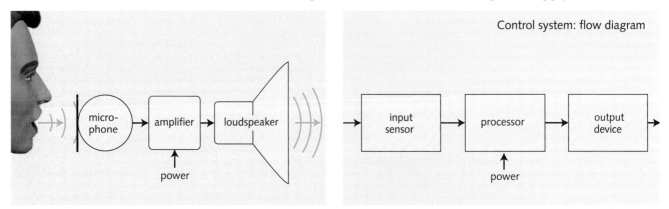

Control system: flow diagram

This is an example of a **control system**, as shown in the flow diagram above right. An **input sensor** (the microphone) sends signals to a **processor** (the amplifier) which uses them to control the flow of power to an **output device** (the loudspeaker). There are some more examples of input sensors and output devices on the opposite page.

Feedback and automatic control
Some control systems are automatic. For example, if an electric room heater has a thermostat, this switches the heater off when it gets too hot, and on again when it cools down. The thermostat is a switch controlled by a temperature sensor. It works because some of the thermal energy from the heater is fed back to the sensor. In other words, some of the output is fed back to the input. This is called **feedback**. All automatic control systems use it.

Automatic control system: flow diagram

++

Components

Here are some of the components (parts) used in electronic circuits:

Resistors keep currents and voltages at the levels needed for other components to work properly.

Capacitors store small amounts of electric charge. They are used for smoothing out current changes, passing on signals from one circuit to another, and tuning circuits so that they respond to signals of one frequency.

Capacitor

If two capacitors are connected across the same battery, the one with the higher **capacitance**, in microfarads (µF), will store most charge.

Diodes let current flow through in one direction only. Most are made from specially-treated crystals of silicon, a semiconductor.

symbol

Light-emitting diodes (LEDs) glow when a small current passes through them. They are used as indicator (on/off) lights and in some alphanumeric (letter and number) displays like those on digital clocks.

Light-emitting diode (LED)

Transistors are used for amplifying signals and for switching. Most are made from specially-treated crystals of silicon.

Integrated circuits (ICs), or 'microchips', contain many complete circuits, with resistors, transistors, other components, and connections all formed on a tiny chip of silicon only a few millimetres square.

Relays are electromagnetic switches. With a relay, a high-power circuit can be switched on (or off) by a tiny current from an electronic circuit.

Integrated circuit (IC) package with connecting pins

Input sensors *examples*	Output devices *examples*	
pressure switch (switch operated by pressing it)	LED (light-emitting diode)	relay
reed switch (switch operated by a magnet)	bulb	electric heater
variable resistor	buzzer	electric bell
thermistor (temperature-dependent resistor)	loudspeaker	electric motor
LDR (light-dependent resistor)		
microphone		

These are all **transducers** – devices that convert electrical signals into some other form, or vice versa.

1 *relay   IC   resistor   LED   capacitor*
Which of the above components
   a) stores small amounts of electric charge
   b) emits light when a small current flow through it
   c) contains many circuits, with components formed on a tiny chip of silicon
   d) uses the small current from an electronic circuit to switch a more powerful circuit?
2 Give *three* examples of transducers.

3 When a door bell is rung, what is being used as
   a) the input sensor **b)** the output device?
4 To control the temperature of an electric iron, the heating element is switched on and off automatically.
   a) What device switches the heating element on and off?
   c) Draw a flow diagram for the control system.
   b) Explain how feedback is used to control the temperature.

Related topics: thermostats 5.09; resistors 8.05; resistor colour code **page 327**; diodes 8.06 and 10.02; relay 9.04; transistors 10.03

+++

Diodes and rectification

Diodes are devices that allow current to flow through them in one direction only. Most are made from specially-treated crystals of silicon. The circuits below show what happens when a diode is connected into a circuit one way round and then the other.

When the diode is **forward biased**, it has an extremely *low* resistance, so a current flows through it and the bulb lights up. In this case, the arrowhead in the symbol points the *same* way as the *conventional* current direction.

When the diode is **reverse biased**, it has an extremely *high* resistance and the bulb does not light. In effect, the diode blocks the current.

Diodes

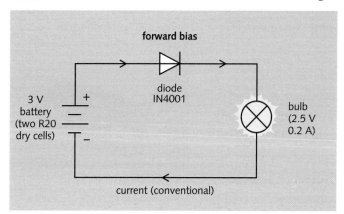

forward bias

diode
IN4001

3 V
battery
(two R20
dry cells)

bulb
(2.5 V
0.2 A)

current (conventional)

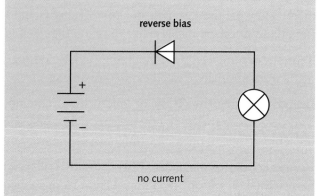

reverse bias

no current

The higher the resistance of a material (in ohms, Ω), the smaller the current for any given voltage across it.

AC flows alternately backwards and forwards. DC flows one way only. Arrows show the *conventional* current direction, from the + terminal of the battery round to the -.

Half-wave rectification

Diodes can be used to change AC to DC. This process is called **rectification**. The diodes that do it are known as **rectifiers**. A simple rectifier circuit is shown below. The diode lets the forward parts of the alternating current through, but blocks the backward parts. So the current through the resistor flows one way only. It has become a rather jerky form of DC.

A CRO (oscilloscope) can be used to show how the circuit changes the AC input. The bottom half of the output waveform is missing. The current is flowing in surges, with short periods of no current between. This is called **half-wave rectification** because of the shape of the waveform.

diode
IN4001

input

AC

connections to
oscilloscope

6 V AC
input

1 kΩ
output
resistor

output

varying DC

++

Full-wave rectification

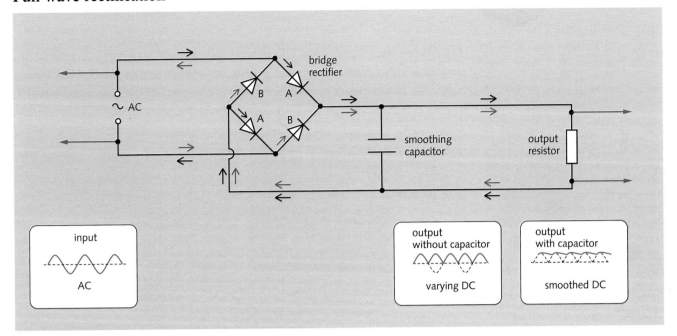

In the circuit above, four diodes have been connected to form a **bridge rectifier**. This reverses the negative (backward) parts of the AC, instead of just blocking them. So that the flow of current is always forward. The process is called **full-wave recification**. It works as follows.

When the AC is flowing forwards (black arrows), diodes A conduct but diodes B block. When the AC is flowing backwards (red arrows), diodes B conduct but diodes A block. The overall effect is that the current always flows through the resistor in the same direction.

Smoothing with a capacitor The pulsing current from a rectifier can be smoothed using a capacitor. This collects charge during the surges and releases it when the current from the rectifier falls. Smoothed in this way, the current is more like the steady DC from a battery.

DC power supplies

The electronic circuits in televisions, computers, and CD players need a low voltage DC supply (typically 9 V). However, most can be run from the AC mains (230 V in the UK, for example). This is because they are fitted with a **DC power supply**. This has a step-down transformer to reduce the voltage, a rectifier to change the AC to DC, and a capacitor to smooth the output.

This power adaptor changes the AC mains voltage to the much lower DC voltage needed by electronic games, keyboards, and similar equipment.

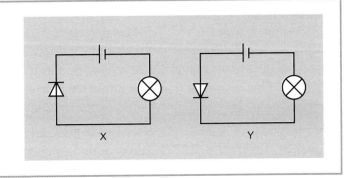

Q

1 **a)** What is the purpose of a rectifier?
   b) Why is a capacitor often included in a rectifier circuit?
2 Look at circuits X and Y on the right. In which one
   a) does the bulb light up
   b) does the diode have a high resistance
   c) is the diode forward biased?
3 How does the output from a full-wave rectifier differ from that of a half-wave rectifier?

X   Y

Related topics: current direction **8.03**; resistance **8.05**; DC and AC **9.08**; capacitors **10.01**; oscilloscope (CRO) **10.10**

243

++

 Transistors (1)

Transistors are used in TVs, CD players, and just about every other piece of electronic equipment. They can join circuits so that a small current in one controls a larger current in the next. Most form part of the integrated circuits in microchips. However, they are also manufactured as separate components.

Transistors

npn junction transistor: symbol

Type BC108 transistor

The transistor above is an **npn transistor**. It has three terminals, called the **emitter**, the **base**, and the **collector**. The circuits on this spread and the next show how it can be used as a switch.

Switching a transistor on

PD, voltage, and current

Potential difference (PD) is the scientific name for voltage. It is measured in volts (V). However, for convenience, engineers dealing with electronic circuits sometimes use the term voltage rather than PD.

Current is measured in amperes (A).

1000 mA = 1 A

In diagram A, the transistor has a blocking effect. In other words, it is switched off. No current can flow through it, so the bulb does not light.

Diagram B shows what happens when a small battery is connected between the base and the emitter. A tiny current now flows through the base and this alters the way the transistor behaves. The blocking effect vanishes, the transistor conducts, and the bulb lights up. However, the transistor will only switch on like this if the + and - connections to the batteries are the right way round. In the base and collector circuits, the conventional current direction must match the arrow direction in the transistor symbol.

You do not need an extra battery to switch a transistor on. The job can be done using a proportion of the main battery's voltage instead. The device which does it is called a **potential divider**.

++

A potential divider

A potential divider is a way of using resistors so that only a proportion of a battery's voltage is delivered.

Above, the lower resistor has *half* the total resistance of the two resistors, so its share of the battery's voltage is also a *half*.

If the one of the resistors is replaced by a variable resistor, the voltage delivered by the system can be varied. Above, it can range from zero up to 3 V.

Above, a resistor and a variable resistor are being used as a potential divider. If the variable resistor has no resistance, the voltage across it is zero and the transistor stays switched off. However, if the resistance of the variable resistor is increased, its share of the battery's voltage also increases. When it passes about 0.6 V, the transistor switches on and the bulb lights. The above principle is used in the transistor switching circuits on the next spread.

Currents and current gain

Typical values for the emitter current I_E, base current I_B, and collector current I_C through a transistor are shown below. As the current flowing out of the transistor must equal the total current flowing in: $I_E = I_B + I_C$.

Once a transistor is conducting, a small change in base current causes a much larger change in the collector current. This means that a transistor can be used to amplify signals. The **current gain** is defined as shown below right.

$$I_E = I_B + I_C$$

$$20.0 \, \text{mA} = 0.1 \, \text{mA} + 19.9 \, \text{mA}$$

$$\text{current gain} = \frac{I_C}{I_B}$$

$$= \frac{19.9 \, \text{mA}}{0.1 \, \text{mA}} = 199$$

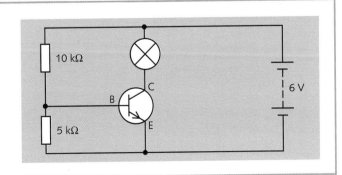

Q

1 In the circuit on the right:
  a) What do the letters E, B, and C stand for?
  b) What do the two resistors do?
  c) Is the bulb ON or OFF?
  d) What would be the effect of replacing the lower resistor with a short piece of connecting wire?
2 If, in the circuit on the right, the base current is 0.05 mA and the collector current is 4.95 mA, what is:
  a) the emitter current **b)** the current gain?

Related topics: current **8.03**; voltage (PD) **8.04**; resistors **8.05**; circuit rules **8.07**; resistors in series **8.08**

245

Transistors (2)

A light-sensitive switch

The circuit below contains a **light-dependent resistor (LDR)**, a special type of resistor whose resistance falls when light shines on it. When the LDR is put in the dark, the bulb lights up. The principle is used in lamps which come on automatically at night.

The LDR is part of a potential divider. In daylight, the LDR has a low resistance, and a low share of the battery voltage – too low to switch the transistor on. In darkness, the resistance of the LDR rises considerably, and so does its share of the battery voltage. Now, the voltage across the LDR is high enough to switch the transistor on, so the bulb lights up.

In the circuit diagrams on this spread, there is an extra resistor next to the base connection on the transistor. This is to prevent too large a base current flowing through the transistor and damaging it.

A time-delay switch

When you close the main switch in the circuit below, there is a time delay before the bulb lights up. It is caused by the capacitor in the potential divider. The capacitor charges up slowly, and it is several seconds before the voltage across it is high enough to switch the transistor on. The delay can be increased by increasing the capacitance, or increasing the resistance of the upper resistor.

+++

A temperature-sensitive switch

The circuit below contains a **thermistor**, a special type of resistor whose resistance falls considerably when its temperature rises. When the thermistor is heated, the bell rings. The principle is used in automatic fire alarms.

The thermistor is part of a potential divider. At room temperature, the thermistor has a high resistance and the major share of the battery voltage. As a result, the voltage across the lower resistor is not enough to switch the transistor on. When the thermistor is heated, its resistance falls, and the lower resistor gets a much larger share of the battery voltage. So the transistor is switched on and the bell starts to ring.

The circuit has two extra features:

● The transistor does not switch on the bell directly. Instead it switches on a relay, which switches on the bell. As the current in the bell circuit does not have to flow through the transistor, a more powerful bell can be used – or even a mains-operated bell in a completely separate circuit.

● The relay has a diode across it. This protects the transistor from the voltages generated (by electromagnetic induction) when the relay coil is switched on and off.

A relay could also be used in either of the circuits on the opposite page.

Relay

1 Give one practical use of
   a) a light-sensitive switch circuit **b)** a temperature-sensitive switch circuit.
2 Why is a relay often used with a transistor switch?
3 In the light-sensitive switch circuit on the opposite page, what would be the effect of interchanging the LDR and the 10 kΩ resistor so that the LDR is at the bottom?
4 In the temperature-sensitive switch circuit above:
   a) What would be the effect of replacing the 10 kΩ resistor with one of lower value?
   b) What change(s) would you make to the circuit so that you could vary the temperature level at which the bell sounds?

++

 10.05 # Logic gates (1)

▲ You are using logic gates when you press the buttons on a video recorder.

Video recorders, security lamps, alarm systems, and washing machines are just some of the things controlled by electronic switches called **logic gates**. The diagram below shows a simple form of gate – although this one is not electronic. It is just two ordinary switches, A and B, in a box:

Truth table

inputs		output
A	B	Q
0	0	0
0	1	0
1	0	0
1	1	1

There has to be an unbroken circuit for the bulb to light up. So, if A and B are both ON (closed), the bulb is ON. But if either A or B is OFF (open), the bulb is OFF. The **truth table** gives the results of all the possible switch settings. It uses two **logic numbers**: 0 for OFF and 1 for ON.

In practice, logic gates work electronically, using tiny transistors as switches. They are manufactured as integrated circuits (ICs), with each chip holding several gates. The chip also needs a DC power supply. Typically, this is a 5 volt supply, with one terminal marked +5 V and the other 0 V.

AND, OR, and NOT gates

There are different types of logic gate. Three of them are shown in symbol form on the opposite page. To help you remember which is which, the words AND, OR, and NOT have been written inside the symbols. However, these words are not really part of the symbols. For simplicity, the input and output connections are shown as single wires rather than complete circuits. Also, connections to the power supply have been omitted.

● Each input is made either HIGH (for example, +5 V) or LOW (0 V). As a result, the output is either HIGH or LOW, depending on the input state(s).

● In the truth tables, the output and input states are represented by the logic numbers 1 (HIGH) and 0 (LOW).

Gates can be combined so that the output of one becomes the input of another. The diagram below shows one example:

▲ A logic IC package. Twelve of the 'pins' make connections to the gates on the chip. The other two are for the power supply.

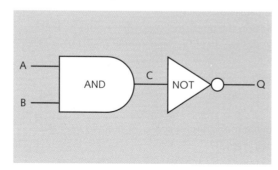

inputs			output
A	B	C	Q
0	0	0	1
0	1	0	1
1	0	0	1
1	1	1	0

++

logic 0 = LOW (OFF)   logic 1 = HIGH (ON)

AND gate

input A ——

input B ——

output Q

This has two inputs and one output.

For the output to be HIGH,
both inputs must be HIGH.
In other words...

Output Q is HIGH, if inputs A **AND** B are HIGH.

inputs		output
A	B	Q
0	0	0
0	1	0
1	0	0
1	1	1

OR gate

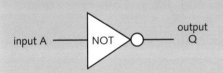

input A ——

input B ——

output Q

This has two inputs and one output.

For the output to be HIGH,
at least one of the inputs must be HIGH.
In other words...

Output Q is HIGH if input A **OR** B (or both)
is HIGH.

inputs		output
A	B	Q
0	0	0
0	1	1
1	0	1
1	1	1

NOT gate   (also called an **inverter**)

input A —— NOT

output Q

This has one input and one output.

The output is HIGH if
the input is LOW, and vice versa.
In other words...

Output Q is HIGH if input A is **NOT** HIGH.

input	output
A	Q
0	1
1	0

Using a gate

The diagram on the right shows one use for a logic
gate. The cassette recorder will only start recording if
the 'record' and 'play' buttons are pressed together.

For most practical applications, combinations of gates
are needed (see the next spread). Often, each input
sensor forms part of a potential divider, as in a
transistor switch, and the small output current switches
on lamps, motors, and other devices via a relay.

cassette recorder

Q

1 Look at the simple two-switches-in-a-box gate on the
   opposite page. Decide what type of gate it is.
2 The upper diagram on the right shows another two-
   switches-in-a-box gate. Write a truth table for this gate
   and decide what type of gate it is.
3 The lower diagram shows a combination of gates.
   a) Write a truth table for this combination, showing all
   the possible states of A, B, C, and Q.
   b) What must the states of inputs A and B be for the
   output to be HIGH?

Logic gates (2)

Using a combination of gates

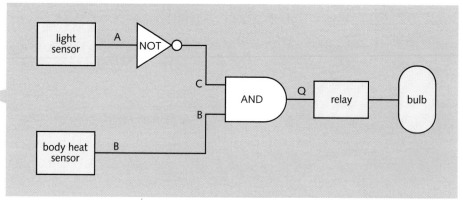

The diagram above shows how sensors and logic gates can be used to control a security lamp. The sensors and gates have been connected so that, if it is dark and someone approaches, the lamp comes on automatically. The last gate cannot provide enough power for the lamp, so it switches on a relay instead. This switches on a separate circuit with the lamp in it.

To check that the combination behaves as intended, you can write a truth table for it (see question 1). In this case, the light sensor's output is LOW (0) in the dark; the body heat sensor's output is HIGH (1) if someone approaches; the final output Q must be HIGH for the lamp to come on.

NAND and NOR gates

Two more gates are shown below. These are especially useful because all the other gates can be made by connecting or combining NAND gates (or alternatively NOR gates) in different ways. Examples are given in question 2.

logic 0 = LOW (OFF)   logic 1 = HIGH (ON)

AND gate

This has two inputs and one output.

It is equivalent to an AND gate with its output inverted by a NOT gate. In other words...

Output Q is HIGH if inputs A **AND** B are **NOT** both HIGH.

inputs		output
A	B	Q
0	0	1
0	1	1
1	0	1
1	1	0

OR gate

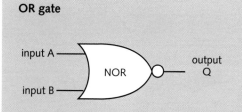

This has two inputs and one output.

It is equivalent to an OR gate with its output inverted by a NOT gate. In other words...

Output Q is HIGH if neither input A **NOR** input B is HIGH.

inputs		output
A	B	Q
0	0	1
0	1	0
1	0	0
1	1	0

+++

The bistable

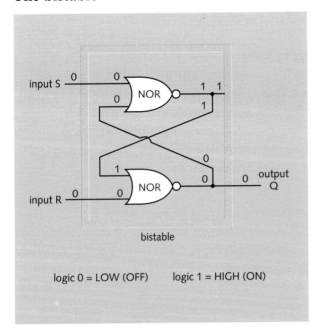

logic 0 = LOW (OFF)   logic 1 = HIGH (ON)

The arrangement above is called a **bistable**. Two NOR gates have been cross-coupled so that the output of each is fed back to one input on the other. This arrangement has a special feature. With both inputs LOW (0), there are *two* possible output states: the output can be LOW (0) as shown *or* HIGH (1).

The bistable can be made to flip from one state to the other. For example if, above, the top input is made HIGH, the bistable flips to the other output state. One brief pulse is enough to make the change: the bistable 'remembers' its new output state. This feature makes bistables very useful in computers, where data is stored in **binary code** as a series of 0's and 1's.

The two inputs are called S and R because one is used to *set* the system (change the output from LOW to HIGH), while the other is used to *reset* it.

A bistable can have two outputs, one from each gate. With only one in use, as above, it is called a **latch**. In the right-hand diagram above, an electric motor is switched on and off using a latch. Each input can be made HIGH (+5 V) by pressing a switch. One switch starts the motor, the other stops it. The touch buttons used to start and stop a video recorder work like this.

▲ In the circuit diagram above, a bistable is being used as a latch so that pressing one switch starts the motor and pressing the other switch stops it. In each case, pressing a switch changes a gate input from LOW to HIGH (+5 V)

1 Look at the security lamp system on the opposite page.
   a) Write a truth table for the system, showing all the possible states of A, B, C, and Q.
   b) From your table, work out the state of Q when it is dark and someone is approaching the sensors.
2 NAND gates can be used to make other types of gate. There are two examples on the right.
   a) Write a truth table for each arrangement, showing all the possible states of A, (B, C), and Q.
   b) Decide what type of gate each is equivalent to.
3 Redraw the diagram of the bistable (top left on this page) to show the other state of Q when both inputs are 0.

++

Communications (1)

Telephone, radio, and TV are all forms of telecommunication – ways of transmitting information over long distances. The information may be sounds, pictures, or computer data. The diagram below left shows a simple telephone system. An **encoder** (the microphone) turns the incoming information (speech) into a form which can be transmitted (electrical signals). The signals pass along the **transmission path** (wires) to a **decoder** (the earphone). This turns the signals back into useful information (speech).

Other telecommunication systems use different types of signal and transmission path. The signals may be changes in voltage, changes in the intensity of a beam of light, or changes in the strength or frequency of radio waves. They may be transmitted using wires, optical fibres, or radio waves.

▲ Like all telecommunications systems, a simple telephone system sends signals from a coder to a decoder.

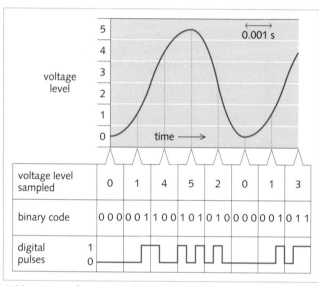

▲ How an analogue signal is converted into digital pulses. Real systems use hundreds of levels and a much faster sampling rate.

Analogue and digital transmission

The sound waves entering a microphone make the PD (voltage) across it vary – as shown in the graph above right. A continuous variation like this is called an **analogue signal**. The table shows how it can be converted into **digital signals** – signals represented by numbers. The original signal is **sampled** electronically thousands of times per second. In effect, the height of the graph is measured repeatedly, and the measurements changed into **binary codes** (numbers using only 0's and 1's). These are transmitted as a series of pulses and turned back into an analogue signal at the receiving end.

Advantages of digital transmission Signals lose power as they travel along. This is called **attenuation**. They are also spoilt by **noise** (electrical interference). To restore their power and quality, digital pulses can be 'cleaned up' and amplified at different stages by **regenerators**. Analogue signals can also be amplified, but the noise is amplified as well, so the signals are of lower quality when they reach their destination.

+++

Optical fibres

For long-distance transmission, telephone networks often use **optical fibres**. These are long, thin strands of glass which can carry digital signals in the form of pulses of light. At the transmitting end, electrical signals are encoded into light signals by an **LED** (light-emitting diode) or a **laser diode**. At the receiving end, the light signals are decoded by a **photodiode** which turns them back into electrical signals. Optical fibre cables are thinner and lighter than electric cables. They carry more signals and with less attenuation. They are not affected by electrical interference, and cannot be 'tapped'.

Optical fibres from inside a cable

Storing and retrieving information

When you listen to a recording, the music is being recreated electronically from stored information. Here are some of the methods used for storing and retrieving (getting back) information of this type:

stylus

magnification ×30

NORMAL POSITION
FI 90

magnification ×1500

Vinyl disc ('record') The information is recorded as a long, wavy-sided groove on the surface of the disc. To retrieve it, the disc is rotated so that a stylus travels along the groove. The wavy sides make the stylus vibrate and the vibrations are turned into electrical signals. They are analogue signals.

Magnetic tape This is usually on spools in a cassette. The information is recorded as a pattern of varying magnetism along the tape. To retrieve it, the tape is pulled past a tiny coil, and the motion generates electrical signals in the coil. The recording is normally analogue, though it can be digital.

Compact disc (CD) The information is recorded digitally as a sequence of microscopic bumps on a metal layer inside the disc. To retrieve it, the disc is rotated and laser light is reflected from the bumps. The reflected pulses are picked up by a photodiode and turned into electrical signals.

Q

1 The diagram on the right shows part of a telephone system.
   a) In what form do the signals travel along the fibre?
   b) What does the laser diode do?
   c) What does the photodiode do?
   d) What does the regenerator do?
   e) Give *two* advantages of sending digital signals rather than analogue ones.
   f) Give *two* advantages of using an optical fibre link rather than a cable with wires in it.
2 Give an example of information being stored
   a) in digital form **b)** in analogue form.

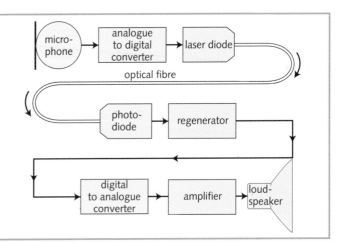

Related topics: sound waves **6.03**; optical fibres **7.04**; systems and signals **10.01**; LEDs **10.01**

++

 Communications (2)

Frequency is measured in hertz (Hz). If 1000 waves are being transmitted per second, then the frequency is 1000 Hz (10^3 Hz).

1 kilohertz (kHz)	= 10^3 Hz
1 megahertz (MHz)	= 10^6 Hz
1 gigahertz (GHz)	= 10^9 Hz

Radio communication

When an alternating current is passed through an aerial (antenna), radio waves are produced. Similarly, when radio waves reach another aerial, they generate alternating current. This principle is used in radio communication.

A simple radio system is shown below. It is designed to transmit speech. The incoming sound waves might have a frequency, typically, of around 1 kHz. This is the **audio frequency** (**AF**). The radio waves have a much higher frequency, for example 1 MHz. This is the **radio frequency** (**RF**).

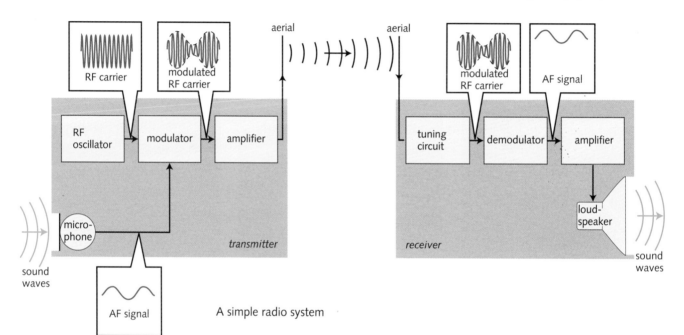

A simple radio system

Transmitter The RF oscillator produces the high frequency alternating current needed to produce the radio waves. The steady stream of waves is called the **carrier**. The AF signals from the microphone are encoded by **modulating** (varying) the carrier. As a result, when radio waves leave the aerial, they vary in a way which is a copy of the incoming sound waves.

Receiver The receiving aerial picks up a mixture of carrier frequencies from different radio stations. The tuning circuit selects the frequency required. The demodulator decodes the incoming signals by removing the RF carrier, leaving only the AF signals. These are boosted by an amplifier and sent to a loudspeaker.

AM and FM The system above uses **amplitude modulation** (**AM**): the amplitude (size) of the carrier is varied by the audio signal. In **frequency modulation** (**FM**), the frequency of the carrier is varied. One advantage of FM is that the signals are less affected by noise (electrical interference).

More uses of radio waves TV pictures are transmitted using radio waves. Microwaves are radio waves. These are used in satellite communication, mobile phones, and some cross-country telephone links. Uses of different radio frequencies are shown in the table on the left.

Typical radio frequencies

long wave	
AM radio	200 kHz
medium wave	
AM radio	1 MHz
VHF	
FM radio	100 MHz
UHF	
television	500 MHz
microwave	
satellite communication	10 GHz

How radio waves travel

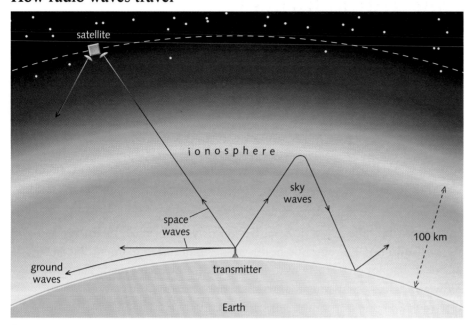

Frequencies	
ground waves	up to 3 MHz
sky waves	3–30 MHz
space waves	more than 30 MHz

The diagram above shows three ways in which radio waves can travel.

Ground (surface) waves have the lowest frequencies. They curve round the Earth's surface, but attenuation limits their range to about 1000 km.

Sky waves have higher frequencies. They are reflected by the ionosphere (a layer of charged particles in the Earth's upper atmosphere) and also by the ground. 'Bouncing' between the two, they can travel right round the Earth.

Space waves have the highest frequencies. They are not reflected by the ionosphere and can only be used for 'line of sight' (straight line) communication – although their range can be extended using satellites.

Satellite communication

Communications satellites are used to relay radio signals (microwaves) around the Earth. **Passive** satellites just reflect the signals that reach them. However, most satellites are **active**: they pick up signals from dish aerials on the ground, amplify them, and beam them back to a different area.

Most communications satellites are in **geostationary** orbits. They orbit 36 000 km above the equator, at the same rate as the Earth turns, so they always appear stationary relative to the Earth. This means that dish aerials on the ground can be fixed so that they always point in the same direction.

Dish aerials for receiving satellite TV transmissions

1 In the radio system in the diagram on the opposite page, what is the purpose of
   a) the RF oscillator **b)** the modulator
   c) the tuning circuit **d)** the demodulator?
2 **a)** What is the difference between FM and AM?
   b) Give one advantage of FM over AM.
3 Rewrite the table of typical radio frequencies on the opposite page so that all the frequencies are in megahertz.

4 Use information in the tables on this page and opposite to answer the following.
   a) Decide whether TV transmissions mainly travel as *ground waves*, *sky waves*, or *space waves*.
   b) Explain why FM radio broadcasts have a lower range than AM broadcasts.
5 **a)** What is meant by a geostationary orbit?
   b) Why are communications satellites normally put in geostationary orbits?

Related topics: satellites **2.14** and **12.04**; frequency and amplitude **6.01**; sound waves **6.03**; radio waves **7.11**

255

++

 # Electron beams (1)

Given enough energy, electrons can escape from a conductor and move through a vacuum (empty space). Beams of electrons like this are used in oscilloscopes, TV picture tubes, computer monitors, and X-ray tubes.

Thermionic emission

If a tungsten filament is heated to about 2000 °C, some of the electrons in the white hot metal gain enough energy to escape from its surface. The effect is called **thermionic emission** and it occurs in other metals and metal oxides as well. The diagram below shows an experiment to demonstrate the effect.

In the vacuum tube below, there are two electrodes, called the **anode** (+) and the **cathode** (-). The cathode in this case is a tungsten filament. Normally, electrons cannot cross the gap to the anode, so the meter reads zero. However, when the filament is switched on, a current starts to flow as electrons (-) escape from the hot surface and are attracted across to the anode (+). (With air in the tube, rather than a vacuum, the electrons would collide with gas molecules. Also, the white hot filament would burn up.)

The vacuum tube shown above right is called a **thermionic diode**. Electrons can pass from the hot cathode to the anode, but not the other way, so the tube acts as a 'one-way valve' for current.

Current and electronic charge

The electron has a negative charge of 1.6×10^{-19} C (coulombs). This is called the **electronic charge**. It is represented by the symbol e.

A flow of electrons is a flow of charge, so it is a current. The following example illustrates the link between electron flow and current:

Example If the current between a cathode and an anode is 40 mA (0.04 A), how many electrons leave the cathode every second?

In 1 s: total charge leaving cathode = current × time = 0.04 A × 1 s = 0.04 C
But: total charge = charge on one electron × number of electrons
So: 0.04 C   = 1.6×10^{-19} C   × number of electrons

Rearranged this gives: number of electrons = $\dfrac{0.04}{1.6 \times 10^{-19}} = 2.5 \times 10^{17}$

So 2.5×10^{17} electrons leave the cathode every second.

+++

Electron energy

If an electron accelerates freely from a cathode to an anode, it loses potential energy, all of which is changed into kinetic energy (energy of motion). The energy transformed can be found using the equation in the panel on the right.

For an electron (charge e) moving through a voltage V:

energy transformed = charge × voltage = eV

So: gain in kinetic energy = eV

Deflection tube

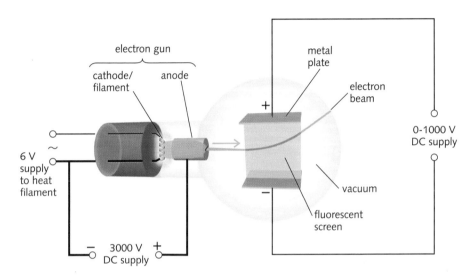

The properties of a beam of electrons can be investigated using the **deflection tube** above. The **electron gun** contains a heated filament/cathode and an anode with a hole in it. It produces a narrow beam of electrons. The screen is coated with a **fluorescent** material which glows when electrons strike it. It shows the path of the beam. Above and below the beam, there are two metal plates. When a voltage is applied across these, the beam is deflected (bent) towards the positive (+) plate.

The beam can also be deflected by a magnetic field, produced by passing a current through a pair of coils as on the right. The direction of the force is given by Fleming's left-hand rule (remembering that the conventional current direction is *opposite* to that of the electron flow).

Magnetic deflection

1 Look at the experiment with the vacuum tube (the thermionic diode) on the opposite page.
  a) What is *thermionic emission*, and where is it taking place?
  b) Why has all the air been removed from the tube?
  c) Why are electrons attracted to the anode?
  d) If the connections to the 400 V DC supply were reversed, would there still be a current in the main circuit? Give a reason for your answer.

2 In an experiment similar to the one on the opposite page, the meter reads 100 mA and the voltage between the cathode and anode is 500 V. The electronic charge is 1.6×10^{-19} C. Calculate
  a) the kinetic energy of an electron as it reaches the anode
  b) the charge (in C) reaching the anode every second
  c) the number of electrons reaching the anode every second.

Electron beams (2)

The oscilloscope

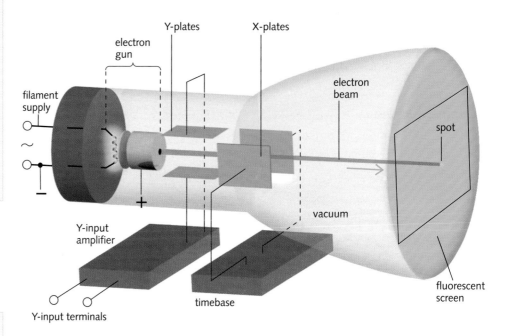

The **cathode ray oscilloscope** (**CRO**) above uses a narrow beam of electrons to trace out waveforms and other signals on a fluorescent screen. There is a bright spot on the screen where the beam strikes it. By deflecting the beam, the spot can be moved about. If it moves fast enough, it appears as a line. To deflect the beam, there are two sets of **deflection plates**:

The **Y-plates** move the beam vertically. This happens when an external source of voltage – for example, an AC supply – is connected across the Y-input terminals. The amount of vertical movement can be amplified (magnified) by turning up the **gain control**.

The **X-plates** move the beam horizontally. Normally, the movement is produced by a circuit called the **timebase** inside the oscilloscope. The timebase automatically applies a changing voltage across the plates so that the spot moves from left to right across the screen at a steady speed, flicks back to the start, moves across again... and so on, over and over again.

AC and DC essentials

Alternating current (AC) flows backwards and forwards. Direct current (DC) flows in one direction only.

Frequency essentials

Frequency is measured in hertz (Hz). If an AC supply has a frequency of 50 Hz, then the current flows backwards and forwards 50 times per second, causing 50 complete cycles of the waveform to be traced out on the screen of a CRO.

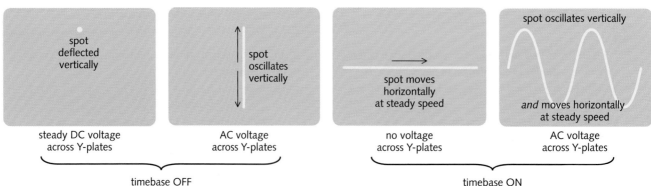

Measuring with an oscilloscope

The Y-input of the oscilloscope on the right is connected to an AC supply. From the waveform on the screen and the settings on the oscilloscope's controls, the voltage and frequency of the supply can be found as follows.

Measuring peak voltage The gain control is set at 5 V/cm. This means that the spot is deflected 1 cm vertically for every 5 volts across the Y-input terminals. The *peak* voltage is represented by the distance marked 'amplitude' on the waveform. As the amplitude is 2.0 cm:

peak voltage = 2.0 cm × 5 V/cm = 10.0 V

Measuring time and frequency The timebase control is set at 10 ms/cm. This means that the spot takes 10 milliseconds (0.01 s) to move 1 cm horizontally. As the horizontal peak-to-peak distance is 4.0 cm:

peak-to-peak time = 4.0 cm × 10 ms/cm = 40 ms = 0.04 s

This is the time taken for the spot to trace out one complete cycle of the waveform. It is known as the **period**.
So: number traced out per second = 1/0.04 = 25
So: frequency = 25 Hz

TV picture tube

Like an oscilloscope, a TV picture tube has a source of electrons at one end and a fluorescent screen at the other. In a typical tube, magnetic deflection coils pull three electron beams in a zig-zag path over the screen area. The screen is coated with fluorescent strips which glow red, green, and blue when the beams strike them. Together, the glowing strips make up a full colour picture. Desk-top computer monitors work in the same way.

X-ray tube

When very fast electrons are suddenly stopped, most of their kinetic energy is changed into thermal energy (heat). However, X-rays are also produced. This principle is used in the X-ray tube shown on the right, where X-rays are emitted from a tungsten target when electrons strike it. (Tungsten is used because of its high melting point.) The higher the accelerating voltage between cathode and anode, the shorter the wavelength of the X-rays and the more penetrating they are.

X-ray tube

Q

1 Name *three* devices that use electron beams.
2 Diagrams A, B, and C on the right represent the screen and deflection plates of an oscilloscope.
   a) Copy diagrams A and B. Label the X-plates and the Y-plates. Then indicate which plates are being used to move the spot by marking them + and -.
   b) Explain how the line in diagram C is produced.
3 The oscilloscope in the diagram on the right has an AC supply connected to its Y-input. Find
   a) the amplitude of the waveform
   b) the peak voltage of the supply
   c) the time between two peaks on the waveform
   d) the frequency of the AC supply.

Related topics: amplitude and frequency **6.01**; sounds on an oscilloscope **6.05**; TV colours **7.09**; X-rays **7.10–7.11**; AC voltage **9.08**

1 The circuit shown below allows a computer to turn an electric heater on and off. Some of the connections have been missed out.

a) (i) Copy and complete the diagram to show how the heater and fuse should be connected to the relay contacts and the mains electricity supply. [2]

(ii) The outside casing of the heater has been earthed. Explain how this increases the safety of the system.

b) The heater must come on when the voltage at C goes above 3.0 V. The relay contacts close when the current in the relay coil is 95 mA. The current gain of the transistor is 100 and its base-emitter voltage drop is 0.7 V when it is switched on.

(i) Calculate the minimum base current required for the heater to come on. [2]

(ii) State the formula linking voltage, current and resistance. [1]

(iii) Calculate a suitable value for the base resistor. [3]

MEG

2

thermistor	AND gate	pressure pad	microphone	relay switch
loudspeaker	light emitting diode	light dependent resistor	OR gate	

Select **from the above list**:
a) an input device which detects changes in light; [1]
b) an output device which produces a sound; [1]
c) a processing device which only gives an output when both inputs are high. [1]

WJEC

3 a) All electronic systems have *input sensors*, *processors* and an *output device*. Explain the function of
(i) input sensors, [1]
(ii) processors. [1]

b) The block diagram below shows an electronic system that can be used as a burglar alarm.

A, **B** and **D** are the inputs. The processor contains logic gates **X** and **Y**. The alarm is the output device. The truth table for the circuit is shown at the top of the next column.

A	B	C	D	E
0	0	0	0	0
0	1	1	0	0
1	0	1	0	0
1	1	1	0	0
0	0	0	1	0
0	1	1	1	1
1	0	1	1	1
1	1	1	1	1

(i) Use a truth table to identify the logic gates. [2]
(ii) State an input, **A**, **B** or **D** which could be connected to a sensor in order to detect a burglar. [1]
(iii) Name a suitable device which could be used as an input processor. [1]

WJEC

4 A car is fitted with a security device. To start the car, two keys are needed. The first key operates a 'hidden' switch, the second key operates the ignition switch.
If the 'hidden' switch and the ignition switch are both on, the engine will start. Turning the ignition switch without operating the 'hidden' switch will not allow the engine to start and will activate an alarm.

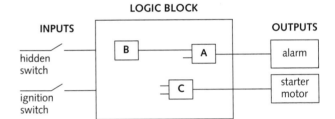

A, **B** and **C** are the three gates needed for the design of the logic block.
a) Identify gate
(i) **A** [1]
(ii) **B** [1]
(iii) **C** [1]
b) Copy the diagram and show how the **inputs** and **logic gates** are connected together. [2]
c) The logic gates used in the logic block are called digital devices. Explain what this means. [1]

WJEC

5 The block diagram below shows a burglar alarm.

The pressure sensor is under a doormat. When a person is standing on doormat **Input 1** to the processor is HIGH (**ON**).

a) A burglar steps on the doormat and the alarm bell rings.

   (i) State what happens when the burglar steps off the doormat.

   (ii) Explain your answer. [3]

b) The burglar alarm is now modified as shown in the diagram below. A bistable has been added after the pressure sensor.

   (i) What is a bistable circuit?

   (ii) Explain how a bistable circuit works. (Your answer should refer to the "SET" AND "RESET" inputs.) [3]

NEAB

6 a) The diagram shows a circuit for a temperature sensor.

The temperature of the thermistor rises.

   (i) What happens to the resistance of the thermistor? [1]

   (ii) What happens to the voltage across resistor **R**? [1]

MEG

7 A simple burglar alarm has two sensors:

● a heat source, which gives a high output when someone is nearby.

● a light sensor, which gives a high output when light shines on it.

A thermistor is used in the heat sensor.

a) What happens to the thermistor to cause a change in the sensor output? [1]

b) Suggest a suitable component for the **light sensor**. [1]

MEG

8 The diagram shows a simple electron deflection tube. Electrons are produced by the filament and accelerated through the anode down the tube.

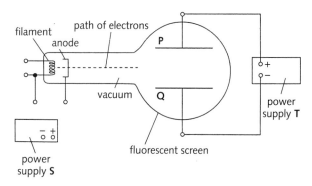

a) Explain how the filament is made to produce electrons as shown. [2]

b) What charge do electrons carry, positive, negative or zero? [1]

c) Electrons are made to accelerate towards the anode by use of the power supply **S**. Copy the diagram and show suitable connections on it. [2]

P and **Q** are two deflection plates. **P** and **Q** are connected to the terminals of a power supply **T**.

d) On your copy of the diagram, complete the path of the electrons between the plates. [2]

e) Why is a vacuum needed in the deflection tube? [1]

MEG

9 The figure below shows the structure of an X-ray tube.

a) When the cathode is heated, some electrons are released from its surface. Name this process. [1]

b) X-rays are produced when the electrons are accelerated and hit the metal target at high speed.

   (i) What causes the electrons to accelerate?

   (ii) There must be a vacuum inside the X-ray tube. Explain why. [3]

c) (i) Why is it necessary to cool the target?

   (ii) Name a suitable material for the anode.

   (iii) Give **two** reasons why this material is suitable. [5]

d) Except for the "window" there is a lead shield around the X-ray tube. Explain why. [2]

e) State **one** use for X-rays. [1]

NEAB

Photocopy the list of topics below and tick the boxes of the ones that are included in your examination syllabus. (Your teacher should be able to tell you which they are.) Use your list when you revise. The spread number in brackets tells you where to find more information.

❏ 1 The parts of an electronic control system. (10.01)

❏ 2 Input sensors and output devices. (10.01)

❏ 3 The use of feedback in automatic control systems. (10.01)

❏ 4 The function of components such as resistors, capacitors, diodes, LEDs, transistors, ICs, and relays. (10.01)

❏ 5 Transducers. (10.01)

❏ 6 Changing AC to DC: rectification. (10.02)

❏ 7 The use of diodes as rectifiers. (10.02)

❏ 8 The difference between half-wave and full-wave rectifiers and their circuits. (10.02)

❏ 9 Using a smoothing capacitor. (10.02)

❏ 10 The principle of a DC power supply. (10.02)

❏ 11 The npn junction transistor. (10.03)

❏ 12 The action of a transistor. (10.03)

❏ 13 The action of a potential divider. (10.03)

❏ 14 Using a potential divider to switch a transistor on. (10.03)

❏ 15 The meaning of current gain. (10.03)

❏ 16 Using a transistor and LDR in a light-sensitive switch. (10.04)

❏ 17 Using a transistor and capacitor in a time-delay switch. (10.04)

❏ 18 Using a transistor and thermistor in a temperature-sensitive switch. (10.04)

❏ 19 AND, OR, and NOT gates and their truth tables. (10.05)

❏ 20 Working out truth tables for combinations of gates. (10.05 – 10.06)

❏ 21 NAND and NOR gates and their truth tables. (10.06)

❏ 22 The action of a bistable. (10.06)

❏ 23 The bistable as a latch. (10.06)

❏ 24 The parts of a communication system: encoder, transmission path, and decoder. (10.07)

❏ 25 The difference between analogue and digital signals. (10.07)

❏ 26 The advantages of digital transmission. (10.07)

❏ 27 Using optical fibres in communication systems. (10.07)

❏ 28 Methods of storing information: record, magnetic tape, and CD. (10.07)

❏ 29 The principles of radio communications. (10.08)

❏ 30 The main parts of a transmitter and receiver. (10.08)

❏ 31 Modulation, and the difference between AM and FM. (10.08)

❏ 32 How radio signals travel by ground waves, sky waves, and space waves. (10.08)

❏ 33 Satellite communication. (10.08)

❏ 34 Thermionic emission. (10.09)

❏ 35 The charge on the electron. (10.09)

❏ 36 Calculating the energy gained by an electron. (10.09)

❏ 37 The deflection tube. (10.09)

❏ 38 The cathode ray oscilloscope and its parts. (10.10)

❏ 39 Measuring voltage, time, and frequency with an oscilloscope. (10.10)

❏ 40 How an X-ray tube works. (10.10)

11

Atoms and Radioactivity

- ATOMIC PARTICLES
- ISOTOPES
- IONIZATION
- ALPHA, BETA, AND GAMMA RADIATION
- RADIOACTIVE DECAY
- HALF-LIFE
- NUCLEAR FISSION
- NUCLEAR REACTORS
- MASS AND ENERGY
- THE QUANTUM THEORY AND PHOTONS
- QUARKS

The *aurora borealis* ('northern lights') in the night sky over Alaska, USA. The shimmering curtain of light is produced when atomic particles streaming from the Sun strike atoms and molecules high in the Earth's atmosphere. The Earth's magnetic field concentrates the incoming atomic particles above the north and south polar regions, so that is where aurorae are normally seen.

Inside atoms

Charge essentials

There are two types of electric charge: positive (+) and negative (-). Like charges repel; unlike charges attract.

A simple model of the atom

Everything is made of atoms. Atoms are far too small to be seen with any ordinary microscope – there are more than a billion billion of them on the surface of this full stop. However, by shooting tiny atomic particles through atoms, scientists have been able to develop **models** (descriptions) of their structure. In advanced work, scientists use a mathematical model of the atom. However, the simple model below is often used to explain the basic ideas.

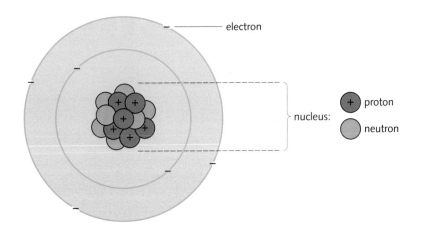

▶ A simple model of the atom. In reality, the nucleus is far too small to be shown to its correct scale. If the atom were the size of a concert hall, its nucleus would be smaller than a pea!

An atom is made up of smaller particles:
- There is a central **nucleus** made up of **protons** and **neutrons**. Around this, **electrons** orbit at high speed. The numbers of particles depends on the type of atom.
- Protons have a positive (+) charge. Electrons have an equal negative (-) charge. Normally, an atom has the same number of electrons as protons, so its total charge is zero.
- Protons and neutrons are called **nucleons**. Each is about 1800 times more massive than an electron, so virtually all of an atom's mass is in its nucleus.
- Electrons are held in orbit by the force of attraction between opposite charges. Protons and neutrons are bound tightly together in the nucleus by a different kind of force, called the **strong nuclear force**.

element	chemical symbol	atomic number (proton number)
hydrogen	H	1
helium	He	2
lithium	Li	3
beryllium	Be	4
boron	B	5
carbon	C	6
nitrogen	N	7
oxygen	O	8
radium	Ra	88
thorium	Th	90
uranium	U	92
plutonium	P	94

Elements and atomic number

All materials are made from about 100 basic substances called **elements**. An atom is the smallest 'piece' of an element you can have. Each element has a different number of protons in its atoms: it has a different **atomic number** (sometimes called the **proton number**). There are some examples on the left. The atomic number also tells you the number of electrons in the atom.

Isotopes and mass number

The atoms of any one element are not all exactly alike. Some may have more neutrons than others. These different versions of the element are called **isotopes**. They have identical chemical properties, although their atoms have different masses. Most elements are a mixture of two or more isotopes. You can see some examples in the chart on the opposite page.

The total number of protons and neutrons in the nucleus is called the **mass number** (or **nucleon number**). Isotopes have the *same* atomic number but *different* mass numbers. For example, the metal lithium (atomic number 3) is a mixture of two isotopes with mass numbers 6 and 7. Lithium-7 is the more common: over 93% of lithium atoms are of this type. On the right, you can see how to represent an atom of lithium-7 using a symbol and numbers.

mass number (nucleon number)

$^{7}_{3}Li$ —— symbol for element

atomic number (proton number)

Electron shells

Electrons orbit the nucleus at certain fixed levels only. These levels are called **shells**. Electrons normally occupy shells as near the nucleus as possible, but there is a limit to how many electrons each shell can hold – for example, no more than 2 electrons in the first shell and 8 in the second. It is an atom's outermost electrons which form the chemical bonds with other atoms, so elements with similar electron arrangements have similar chemical properties.

The **periodic table** groups all the elements according to their chemical properties. For example, all the elements in Group I are highly reactive metals – and all have a single electron in their outer shell.

For questions 4 and 5, you will need data from the table of elements on the opposite page.

1 An atoms contains *electrons*, *protons*, and *neutrons*.
   Which of these particles
   a) are outside the nucleus **b)** are uncharged
   c) have a negative charge **d)** are nucleons
   e) are much lighter than the others?

2 An aluminium atom has an atomic number of 13 and a mass number of 27. How many
   a) protons **b)** electrons **c)** neutrons does it have?

3 Chlorine is a mixture of two isotopes, with mass numbers 35 and 37. What is the difference between the two types of atom?

4 In symbol form, nitrogen-14 can be written $^{14}_{7}N$
   How can each of the following be written?
   a) carbon-12 **b)** oxygen-16 **c)** radium-226

5 Atom X has 6 electrons and a mass number of 12.
   Atom Y has 6 electrons and a mass number of 14.
   Atom Z has 7 neutrons and a mass number of 14.
   Identify the elements X, Y, and Z.

Nuclear radiation (1)

11.02

Some materials contain atoms with unstable nuclei. In time, each unstable nucleus disintegrates (breaks up). As it does so, it shoots out a tiny particle and, in some cases, a burst of wave energy as well. The particles and waves 'radiate' from the nucleus, so they are somtimes called **nuclear radiation**. Materials which emit nuclear radiation are known as **radioactive** materials. The disintegration of a nucleus is called **radioactive decay**.

Some of the materials in nuclear power stations are highly radioactive. But nuclear radiation comes from natural sources as well. Although it is convenient to talk about 'radioactive materials', it is really particular isotopes of an element that are radioactive. Here are some examples:

isotopes		
stable nuclei	*unstable nuclei, radioactive*	*found in*
carbon-12 carbon-13	carbon-14	air, plants, animals
potassium-39	potassium-40	rocks, plants, sea water
	uranium-234 uranium-235 uranium-238	rocks

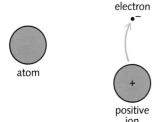

electron

atom

positive ion

If an atom loses (or gains) an electron, it becomes an ion.

Ionizing radiation

Ions are charged atoms (or groups of atoms). Atoms become ions when they lose (or gain) electrons. Nuclear radiation can remove electrons from atoms in its path, so it has an **ionizing** effect. Other forms of ionizing radiation include ultraviolet and X-rays.

If a gas becomes ionized, it will conduct an electric current. In living things, ionization can damage or destroy cells (see the next spread).

Alpha, beta, and gamma radiation

There are three main types of nuclear radiation: **alpha particles**, **beta particles**, and **gamma rays**. Gamma rays are the most penetrating and alpha particles the least, as shown below:

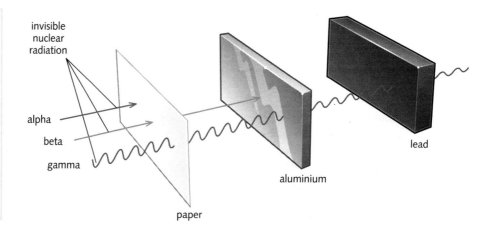

invisible nuclear radiation

alpha
beta
gamma

paper

aluminium

lead

type of radiation	alpha particles (α)	beta particles (β)	gamma rays (γ)
	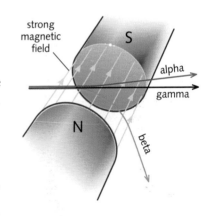 each particle is 2 protons + 2 neutrons (it is identical to a nucleus of helium-4)	each particle is an electron (created when the nucleus decays)	electromagnetic waves similar to X-rays
relative charge compared with charge on proton	+2	-1	0
mass	high, compared with betas	low	–
speed	up to 0.1 × speed of light	up to 0.9 x speed of light	speed of light
ionizing effect	strong	weak	very weak
penetrating effect	not very penetrating: stopped by a thick sheet of paper, or by skin, or by a few centimetres of air	penetrating, but stopped by a few millimetres of aluminium or other metal	very penetrating: never completely stopped, though lead and thick concrete will reduce intensity
effects of fields	deflected by magnetic and electric fields	deflected by magnetic and electric fields	not deflected by magnetic or electric fields

The nature and main properties of the three types of radiation are given in the chart above. The diagram on the right shows how the different types are affected by a magnetic field. The alpha beam is a flow of positively (+) charged particles, so it is equivalent to an electric current. It is deflected in a direction given by Fleming's left-hand rule – the rule used for working out the direction of the force on a current-carrying wire in a magnetic field. The beta particles are much lighter than the alpha particles and have a negative (-) charge, so they are deflected more, and in the opposite direction. Being uncharged, the gamma rays are not deflected by the field.

Alpha and beta particles are also affected by an electric field – in other words, there is a force on them if they pass between oppositely charged plates.

1 Name a radioactive isotope which occurs naturally in living things.
2 *alpha   beta   gamma*
   Which of these three types of radiation
   a) is a form of electromagnetic radiation
   b) carries positive charge
   c) is made up of electrons
   d) travels at the speed of light
   e) is the most ionizing
   f) can penetrate a thick sheet of lead
   g) is stopped by skin or thick paper
   h) has the same properties as X-rays
   i) is not deflected by an electric or magnetic field?
3 What is the difference between the atoms of an isotope that is radioactive and the atoms of an isotope that is not?
4 How is an ionized material different from one that is not ionized?

Related topics: electromagnetic waves **7.10–7.11**; X-rays **7.11** and **10.10**; ions **8.09**; Fleming's left-hand rule **9.05**; isotopes **11.01**

11.03 Nuclear radiation (2)

Radiation dangers

Nuclear radiation can damage or destroy living cells. It may stop vital organs in the body working properly. It can also upset the chemical instructions in cells so that the cells grow abnormally and cause cancer. The greater the intensity of the radiation, the greater the risk.

Radioactive gas and dust are especially dangerous because they can be taken into the body with air, food, or drink. Once absorbed, they are difficult to remove, and their radiation can cause damage in cells deep in the body. Alpha radiation is the most harmful because it is the most highly ionizing.

Normally, there is much less risk from radioactive sources *outside* the body. Sources in nuclear power stations and laboratories are well shielded, and the intensity of the radiation decreases as you move away from the source. Beta and gamma rays are potentially the most harmful because they can penetrate to internal organs. Alpha particles are stopped by the skin.

Background radiation

There is a small amount of radiation around us all the time because of radioactive materials in the environment. This is called **background radiation**. It mainly comes from natural sources such as soil, rocks, air, building materials, food and drink – and even space.

In some areas, over a half of the background radiation comes from radioactive radon gas (radon-222) seeping out of rocks – especially some types of granite. In high risk areas, houses may need extra underfloor ventilation to stop the gas collecting or, ideally, a sealed floor to stop it entering in the first place.

Geiger-Müller (GM) tube

This can be used to detect alpha, beta, and gamma radiation. Its structure is shown below. The 'window' at the end is thin enough for alpha particles to pass through. If an alpha particle enters the tube, it ionizes the gas inside. This sets off a high-voltage spark across the gas and a pulse of current in the circuit. A beta particle or burst of gamma radiation has the same effect.

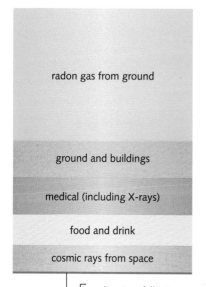

▲ Where background radiation comes from (average proportions).

▲ This nuclear laboratory worker is about to use a GM tube and ratemeter to check for any traces of radioactive dust on her clothing.

The GM tube can be connected to the following:

● **A ratemeter** This gives a reading in counts per second. For example, if 50 alpha particles were detected by the GM tube every second, the ratemeter would read 50 counts per second.

● **A scaler** This counts the *total* number of particles (or bursts of gamma radiation) detected by the tube.

● **An amplifier and loudspeaker** The loudspeaker makes a 'click' when each particle or burst of gamma radiation is detected.

When the radiation from a radioactive source is measured, the reading always *includes* any background radiation present. So an average reading for the background radiation alone must also be found and subtracted from the total.

Cloud chamber

This is useful for studying alpha particles because it makes their tracks visible. The chamber has cold alcohol vapour in the air inside it. The alpha particles make the vapour condense, so you see a trail of tiny droplets where each particle passes through. At one time, cloud chambers were widely used in nuclear research, but they have since been replaced by other devices.

Cloud chamber

Tracks of alpha particles in a cloud chamber. The colours are false and have been added to the picture. The green and yellow lines are the alpha tracks. The red line is the track of a nitrogen nucleus that has been hit by an alpha particle.

Q

1 What, on average, is the biggest single source of background radiation?

2 Radon gas seeps out of rocks underground. Why is it important to stop radon collecting in houses?

3 Which is the most dangerous type of radiation
   a) from radioactive sources outside the body
   b) from radioactive materials absorbed by the body?

4 In the experiment on the right:
   a) What is the count rate due to background radiation?
   b) What is the count rate due to the source alone?
   c) If the source emits one type of radiation only, what type is it? Give a reason for your answer.

count rate (average)...	counts per second
...with the source in place	28
...with the source and block in place	18
...with the source and block removed	2

11.04 Radioactive decay (1)

The symbol system used for representing atoms can also be used for nuclei and other particles

Nucleus *example*

mass number (nucleon number): total number of nucleons (protons + neutrons) in the nucleus

$^{4}_{2}\text{He}$ —— chemical symbol for element

atomic number (proton number): also the relative charge on the nucleus compared with +1 for a proton

Alpha particle
(helium nucleus)

4 nucleons

$^{4}_{2}\alpha$ or $^{4}_{2}\text{He}$

relative charge +2

Beta particle
(electron)

mass negligible compared with a proton or a neutron

$^{0}_{-1}\beta$ or $^{0}_{-1}\text{e}$

relative charge equal but opposite to that on a proton

If an isotope is radioactive, it has an unstable arrangement of neutrons and protons in its nuclei. The emission of an alpha or beta particle makes the nucleus more stable, but alters the numbers of protons and neutrons in it. So it becomes the nucleus of a different element. The original nucleus is called the **parent** nucleus. The nucleus formed is the **daughter** nucleus. The daughter nucleus and any emitted particles are the **decay products**.

Alpha decay

Radium-226 (atomic number 88) decays by alpha emission. The loss of the alpha particle leaves the nucleus with 2 protons and 2 neutrons less than before. So the mass number drops to 222 and the atomic number to 86. Radon has an atomic number of 86, so radon is the new element formed:

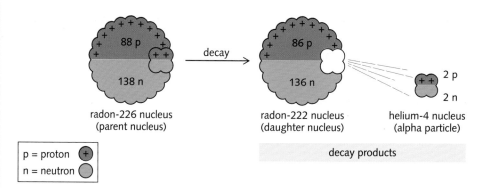

radon-226 nucleus (parent nucleus)   radon-222 nucleus (daughter nucleus)   helium-4 nucleus (alpha particle)

p = proton (+)
n = neutron ( )

decay products

Nuclear essentials

Atoms of any one element all have the same number of protons in their nucleus.

Elements exist in different versions, called isotopes. For example, lithium is a mixture of two isotopes: lithium-6 (with 3 protons and 3 neutrons in the nucleus) and lithium-7 (with 3 protons and 4 neutrons).

Any one particular type of atom, for example lithium-7, is called a **nuclide**. However the word 'isotope' is commonly used instead of nuclide.

Radioactive isotopes have unstable nuclei. In time each nucleus decays (breaks up) by emitting an alpha or beta particle and, in some cases, a burst of gamma radiation as well.

The decay process can be written as a nuclear equation:

$$^{226}_{88}\text{Ra} \rightarrow ^{226}_{88}\text{Rn} + ^{4}_{2}\alpha$$

During alpha decay:

- the top numbers balance on both sides of the equation (226 = 222 + 4), so the nucleon number is conserved (unchanged)
- the bottom numbers balance on both sides of the equation (88 = 86 + 2), so charge is conserved
- a new element is formed, with an atomic number 2 less than before. The mass number is 4 less than before.

Beta decay

Iodine-131 (atomic number 53) decays by beta emission. When this happens, a neutron changes into a proton, an electron, and an uncharged, almost massless relative of the electron called an antineutrino. The electron and antineutrino leave the nucleus at high speed. As a proton has replaced a neutron in the nucleus, the atomic number rises to 54. This means that a nucleus of xenon-131 has been formed:

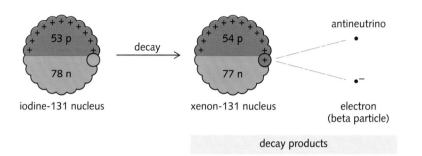

iodine-131 nucleus   xenon-131 nucleus   electron (beta particle)

antineutrino

decay products

The decay process can be written as a nuclear equation:

$$^{131}_{53}\text{I} \rightarrow\ ^{131}_{54}\text{Xe} +\ ^{0}_{-1}\beta +\ ^{0}_{0}\bar{\nu} \qquad\qquad (\bar{\nu} = \text{antineutrino})$$

During this type of beta decay:

- the top numbers balance on both sides of the equation ($131 = 131 + 0 + 0$), so the nucleon number is conserved
- the bottom numbers balance on both sides of the equation ($53 = 54 - 1 + 0$), so charge is conserved
- a new element is formed, with an atomic number 1 more than before. The mass number is unchanged.

Gamma emission

With some isotopes, the emission of an alpha or beta particle from a nucleus leaves the protons and neutrons in an 'excited' arrangement. As the protons and neutrons rearrange to become more stable, they lose energy. This is emitted as a burst of gamma radiation.

- Gamma emission by itself causes no change in mass number or atomic number.

Beta⁻ and beta⁺

There is a less common form of beta decay, in which the emitted beta particle is a **positron**. This is the **antiparticle** of the electron, with the same mass, but opposite charge (+1). During this type of decay, a proton changes into a neutron, a positron, and a neutrino. The element formed has an atomic number one *less* than before.

To distinguish the two types of beta decay, they are sometimes called beta⁻ decay (electron emitted) and beta⁺ decay (positron emitted).

1 The following equation represents the radioactive decay of thorium-232. A, Z, and X are unknown.

$$^{232}_{90}\text{Th} \rightarrow\ ^{A}_{Z}X +\ ^{4}_{2}\alpha$$

a) What type of radiation is being emitted?
b) What are the values of A and Z?
c) Use the table on page 264 to decide what new element is formed by the decay process.
d) Rewrite the above equation, replacing A, Z, and X with the numbers and symbols you have found.
e) What are the decay products?

2 When redioactive sodium-24 decays, magnesium-24 is formed. The following equation represents the decay process, but the equation is incomplete:

$$^{24}_{11}\text{Na} \rightarrow\ ^{24}_{12}\text{Mg} + \underline{\quad\quad}$$

Assuming that only one charged particle is emitted:

a) What is the mass number of this particle?
b) What is the relative charge of this particle?
c) What type of particle is it?

11.05 Radioactive decay (2)

Radioactive decay happens spontaneously (all by itself) and at random. There is no way of predicting when a particular nucleus will disintegrate, and the process is unaffected by pressure, temperature, or chemical change. However some types of nuclei are more unstable than others and decay at a faster rate.

Rate of decay and half-life

Iodine-131 is a radioactive isotope of iodine. The chart below illustrates the decay of a sample of iodine-131. On average, 1 nucleus disintegrates every second for every 1 000 000 nuclei present.

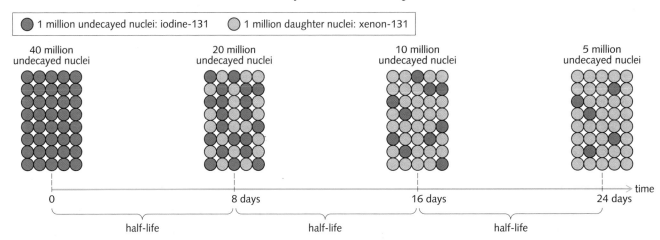

To begin with, there are 40 million undecayed nuclei. 8 days later, half of these have disintegrated. With the number of undecayed nuclei now halved, the number of distintegrations over the next 8 days is also halved. It halves again over the next 8 days... and so on. Iodine-131 has a **half-life** of 8 days.

radioactive isotope	half-life
boron-12	0.02 seconds
radon-220	52 seconds
iodine-128	25 minutes
radon-222	3.8 days
strontium-90	28 years
radium-226	1602 years
carbon-14	5730 years
plutonium-239	24 400 years
uranium-235	7.1×10^8 years
uranium-238	4.5×10^9 years

> The half-life of a radioactive isotope is the time taken for half the nuclei present in any given sample to decay.

The half-lives of some other radioactive isotopes are given on the left. It might seem strange that there should be any short-lived isotopes still remaining. However, some are radioactive daughters of long-lived parents, while others are produced artificially in nuclear reactors.

Activity and half-life

In a radioactive sample, the average number of disintegrations per second is called the **activity**. The SI unit of activity is the **becquerel** (**Bq**). An activity of, say, 100 Bq means that 100 nuclei are disintegrating per second.

The graph at the top of the next page shows how, on average, the activity of a sample of iodine-131 varies with time. As the activity is always proportional to the number of undecayed nuclei, it too halves every 8 days. So 'half-life' has another meaning as well:

> The half-life of a radioactive isotope is the time taken for the activity of any given sample to fall to half its original value.

◀ Radioactive decay of iodine-131. Iodine-131 has a half-life of 8 days. From any point on the curve, it always takes 8 (days) along the time axis for the activity to halve.

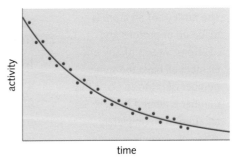

▲ Radioactive decay is a random process. So, in practice, the curve is a 'best fit' of points which vary irregularly like this.

To obtain a graph like the one above, a GM tube is used to detect the particles emitted by the sample. The number of counts per second recorded by the ratemeter is proportional to the activity – though not equal to it, because not all of the emitted particles are detected.

Stability of the nucleus

In a nucleus, some proportions of neutrons to protons are more stable than others. If the number of neutrons is plotted against the number of protons for all the different isotopes of all the elements, the general form of the graph is as shown on the right. It has these features:

- Stable isotopes lie along the stability line.
- Isotopes above the stability line have too many neutrons to be stable. They decay by beta⁻ (electron) emission because this reduces the number of neutrons.
- Isotopes below the stability line have too few neutrons to be stable. They decay by beta⁺ (positron) emission because this increases the number of neutrons.
- The heaviest isotopes (proton numbers > 83) decay by alpha emission.

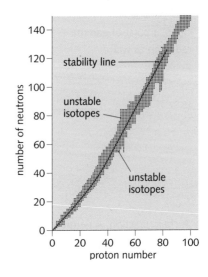

Q

To answer questions 1 and 2, you will need information from the table of half-lives on the opposite page.

1 If samples of strontium-90 and radium-226 both had the same activity today, which would have the lower activity in 10 years' time?

2 If the activity of a sample of iodine-128 is 800 Bq, what would you expect the activity to be after
a) 25 minutes **b)** 50 minutes **c)** 100 minutes?

3 The graph on the right shows how the activity of a small radioactive sample varied with time.
a) Why are the points not on a smooth curve?
b) Estimate the half-life of the sample.

Nuclear energy

When alpha or beta particles are emitted by a radioactive isotope, they collide with surrounding atoms and make them move faster. In other words, the temperature rises as nuclear energy (potential energy stored in the nucleus) is transformed into thermal energy (heat).

In radioactive decay, the energy released per atom is around a million times greater than that from a chemical change such as burning. However, the rate of decay is usually very slow. Much faster decay can happen if nuclei are made more unstable by bombarding them with neutrons. Whenever a particle penetrates and changes a nucleus, this is called a **nuclear reaction**.

Fission

Natural uranium is a dense radioactive metal consisting mainly of two isotopes: uranium-238 (over 99%) and uranium-235 (less than 1%). The diagram below shows what can happen if a neutron strikes and penetrates a nucleus of uranium-235. The nucleus becomes highly unstable and splits into two lighter nuclei, shooting out two or three neutrons as it does so. The splitting process is called **fission**, and the fragments are thrown apart as energy is released. If the emitted neutrons go on to split other nuclei... and so on, the result is a **chain reaction**, and a huge and rapid release of energy.

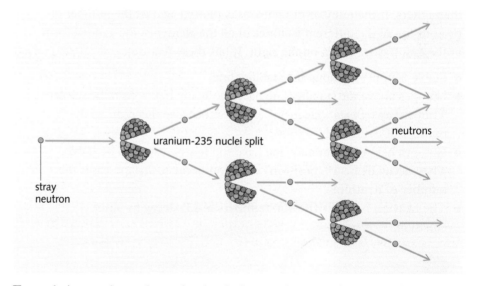

stray neutron

uranium-235 nuclei split

neutrons

▶ A chain reaction. A neutron causes a uranium-235 nucleus to split, producing more neutrons, which cause more nuclei to split... and so on.

For a chain reaction to be maintained, the uranium-235 has to be above a certain **critical mass**, otherwise too many neutrons escape. In the first atomic bombs, an uncontrolled chain reaction was started by bringing two lumps of pure uranium-235 together so that the critical mass was exceeded. In present-day nuclear weapons, plutonium-239 is used for fission.

Fission in a nuclear reactor

In a **nuclear reactor** in a nuclear power station, a controlled chain reaction takes place and thermal energy (heat) is released at a steady rate. The energy is used to make steam for the turbines, as in a conventional power station. In many reactors, the nuclear fuel is uranium dioxide, the natural uranium being enriched with extra uranium-235. The fuel is in sealed cans (or tubes).

To maintain the chain reaction in a reactor, the neutrons have to be slowed down, otherwise many of them get absorbed by the uranium-238. To slow them, a material called a **moderator** is needed. Graphite is used in some reactors, water in others. The rate of the reaction is controlled by raising or lowering **control rods**. These contain boron or cadmium, materials which absorb neutrons.

Nuclear waste

After a fuel can has been in a reactor for three of four years, it must be removed and replaced. The amount of uranium-235 in it has fallen and the fission products are building up. Many of these products are themselves radioactive, and far too dangerous to be released into the environment. They include the following isotopes, none of which occur naturally.

- Strontium-90 and iodine-131, which are easily absorbed by the body. Strontium becomes concentrated in the bones; iodine in the thyroid gland.
- Plutonium-239, which is produced when uranium-238 is bombarded by neutrons. It is itself a nuclear fuel and is used in nuclear weapons. It also highly toxic. Breathed in as dust, the smallest amount can kill.

Spent fuel cans are taken to a reprocessing plant where unused fuel and plutonium are removed. The remaining waste, now a liquid, is sealed off and stored with thick shielding around it. Some of the isotopes have long half-lives, so safe storage will be needed for thousands of years. The problem of finding acceptable sites for long-term storage has still not been solved.

A nuclear reactor (PWR, or pressurized water reactor)

control rods

hot water

cool water

steel pressure vessel

nuclear fuel in core

Energy and mass

According to Albert Einstein (1905), energy itself has mass. If an object gains energy, its mass increases; if it loses energy, its mass decreases. The mass change m (kg) is linked to the energy change E (joules) by this equation:

$$E = mc^2$$

(where c is the speed of light, 3×10^8 m/s)

The value of c^2 is so high that energy gained or lost by everyday objects has a negligible effect on their mass. However, in nuclear reactions, the energy changes per atom are much larger, and produce detectable mass changes. For example, when the fission products of uranium-235 are slowed down in a nuclear reactor, their total mass is found to be reduced by about 0.1%.

The steel flasks on this train contain waste from a nuclear reactor.

1 The high temperatures deep underground are caused by the decay of radioactive isotopes in the rocks. Why does radioactive decay cause a rise in temperature?
2 What is meant by **a)** fission **b)** a chain reaction?
3 Give one example of
   a) a controlled chain reaction
   b) an uncontrolled chain reaction.
4 **a)** Where does plutonium-239 come from?
   b) Why is plutonium-239 so dangerous?
5 In a typical fission process, uranium-235 absorbs a neutron, creating a nucleus which splits to form barium-141, krypton-92, and three neutrons.

	mass/kg
neutron	1.674×10^{-27}
uranium-235 nucleus	390.250×10^{-27}
barium-141 nucleus	233.964×10^{-27}
krypton-92 nucleus	152.628×10^{-27}

a) Using the data above, calculate the total mass of the uranium nucleus and the neutron.
b) Calculate the total mass of the barium and krypton nuclei and the three neutrons.
c) Use $E = mc^2$ to calculate the energy released per decay by the fission process.

Using radioactivity

Radioactive isotopes are called **radioisotopes** (or **radionuclides**). Some are produced artificially in a nuclear reactor when nuclei absorb neutrons or gamma radiation. For example, all natural cobalt is cobalt-59, which is stable. If cobalt-59 absorbs a neutron, it becomes cobalt-60, which is radioactive.

Here are some of the practical uses of radioisotopes.

Tracers

Radioisotopes can be detected in very small (and safe) quantities, so they can be used as **tracers** – their movements can be tracked. Examples include:

- Checking the function of body organs. For example, to check thyroid function, a patient drinks a liquid containing iodine-123, a gamma emitter. Over the next 24 hours, a detector measures the activity of the tracer to find out how quickly it becomes concentrated in the thyroid gland.
- Tracking a plant's uptake of fertilizer from roots to leaves by adding a tracer to the soil water.
- Detecting leaks in underground pipes by adding a tracer to the fluid in the pipe.

For tests like those above, artificial radioisotopes with short half-lives are used so that there is no detectable radiation after a few days.

Radiotherapy

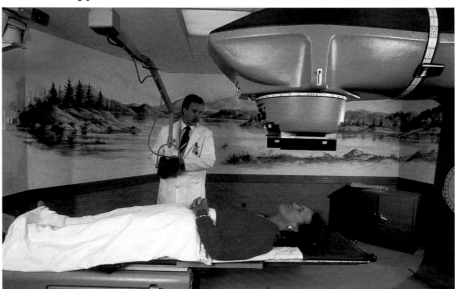

▶ A concentrated beam of gamma rays from a cobalt-60 source will be directed at one small area of this patient's body to kill the cancer cells in a tumour.

Cobalt-60 is a strong gamma emitter. Gamma rays can penetrate deep into the body and kill living cells. So a highly concentrated beam from a cobalt-60 source can be used to kill cancer cells. Treatment like this is called **radiotherapy**.

Testing for cracks

Gamma rays have the same properties as short-wavelength X-rays, so they can be used to photograph metals to reveal cracks. A cobalt-60 gamma source is compact and does not need electrical power like an X-ray tube.

Thickness monitoring

In some production processes a steady thickness of material has to be maintained. The diagram below shows one way of doing this.

◀ The moving band of tyre cord has a beta source on one side and a detector on the other. If the cord from the rollers becomes too thin, more beta radiation reaches the detector. This sends signals to the control unit, which adjusts the gap between the rollers.

Carbon dating

There is carbon in the atmosphere (in carbon dioxide) and in the bodies of animals and plants. A small proportion is radioactive carbon-14 (half-life 5730 years). Although carbon-14 decays, the amount in the atmosphere changes very little because more is continually being formed as nitrogen in the upper atmosphere is bombarded by cosmic radiation from space. While plants and animals are living, feeding, and breathing, they absorb and give out carbon, so the proportion of carbon-14 in their bodies stays constant. But when they die, no more carbon is taken in and the proportion of carbon-14 is gradually reduced by radioactive decay. By measuring the activity of a sample, the age of the remains can be estimated. This is called **carbon dating**. It can be used to find the age of organic materials such as wood and cloth. However, it assumes that the proportion of carbon-14 in the atmosphere was the same hundreds or thousands of years ago as it is today.

Human remains from a Danish peat bog. Carbon dating showed that this man died around 220–240 BC.

Dating rocks

When rocks are formed, some radioisotopes become trapped in them. For example, potassium-40 is trapped when molten material cools to form igneous rock. As the potassium-40 decays, more and more of its stable decay product, argon-40 is created. Provided none of this argon gas has escaped, the age of the rock (which may be hundreds of millions of years) can be estimated from the proportions of potassium-40 to argon-40. Igneous rock can also be dated by the proportion of uranium to lead isotopes – lead being the final, stable product of a series of decays that starts with uranium.

Q

1 **a)** What are radioisotopes?
   b) How are artificial radioisotopes produced?
   c) Give *two* medical uses of radioisotopes.
2 Give *two* uses of gamma radiation.
3 In the thickness monitoring system shown above:
   a) Why is a beta source used, rather than alpha or gamma source?
   b) What is the effect on the detector if the thickness of the tyre cord increases?

4 **a)** Give *two* uses of radioactive tracers.
   b) Why is it important to use radioactive tracers with short half-lives?
5 Carbon-14 is a radioactive isotope of carbon.
   a) What happens to the proportion of carbon-14 in the body of a plant or animal while it is alive?
   b) Why does the proportion of carbon-14 in the remains of dead plant and animals give clues about their age?

Related topics: alpha, beta, and gamma radiation **11.02–11.03**; radioactive decay **11.04–11.05**; half-life **11.05**

11.08 Atoms and particles (1)

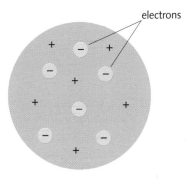

electrons

Thomson's 'plum pudding' model
of the atom

Atoms are made up of even smaller particles. From experimental evidence collected over the past hundred years, scientists have been able to develop and improve their models (descriptions) of atoms and the particles in them.

Thomson's 'plum pudding' model

The **electron** was the first atomic particle to be discovered. It was identified by J. J. Thomson in 1897. The electron has a negative (-) electric charge, so an atom with electrons in it must also contain positive (+) charge to make it electrically neutral. Thomson suggested that an atom might be a sphere of positive charge with electrons dotted about inside it rather like raisins in a pudding. This became knows as the 'plum pudding' model.

Rutherford's nuclear model

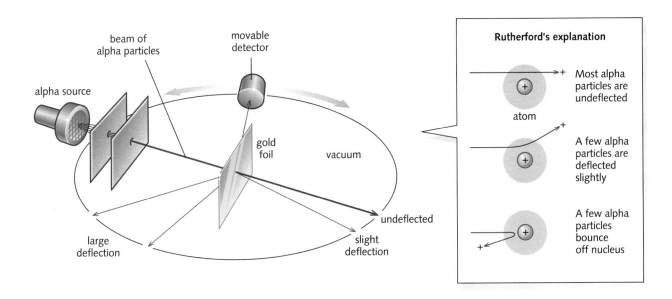

The above experiment was carried out in 1911 by Geiger and Marsden under the supervision of Ernest Rutherford. It produced results which could not be explained by the plum pudding model. Thin gold foil was bombarded with alpha particles, which are positively charged. Most passed straight through the gold atoms, but a few were repelled so strongly that they bounced back or were deflected through large angles. Rutherford concluded that the atom must be largely empty space, with its positive charge and most of its mass concentrated in a tiny **nucleus** at the centre. In his model, the much lighter electrons orbited the nucleus rather like the planets around the Sun.

Discovering particles in the nucleus

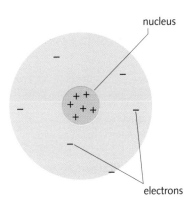

Rutherford's model of the atom: electrons orbit a central nucleus. (If the nucleus were correctly drawn to scale, it would be too small to see.)

Rutherford's model said nothing about what was inside the nucleus. However, in 1919, Rutherford bombarded nitrogen gas with fast alpha particles and found that positively charged particles were being knocked out. These were **protons**. In 1932, James Chadwick discovered that the nucleus also contained uncharged particles with a similar mass to protons. He called these **neutrons**.

++

The problem of spectral lines

Light comes from atoms. The spectrum of white light is a continuous range of colour from red (the longest wavelength) to violet (the shortest). However, not all spectra are like this. For example, if there is an electric discharge through hydrogen, the glowing gas emits particular wavelengths only, so the spectrum is made up of lines, as shown below. As it stood, Rutherford's model could not explain why spectra like this occurred. To solve this problem, the model had to be modified.

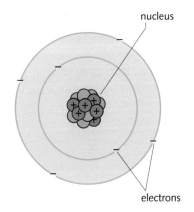

Light essentials
Light is one type of electromagnetic radiation (electromagnetic waves). The colour seen depends on the wavelength of the light.

◀ Part of the line spectrum of hydrogen. Each line represents light of a particular wavelength.

shorter...................................wavelength...................................longer

The Rutherford-Bohr model

In 1913, Neils Bohr modified Rutherford's model by applying the **quantum theory** devised by Max Planck in 1900. According to this theory, energy cannot be divided into ever smaller amounts. It is only emitted (or absorbed) in tiny 'packets', each called a **quantum**. Bohr reasoned that electrons in higher orbits have more energy than those in lower ones. So, if only quantum energy changes are possible, only certain electron orbits are allowed. This modified model is known as the **Rutherford-Bohr model**.

Using the model, Bohr was able to explain why atoms emit light of particular wavelengths only (see the next spread). He even predicted the positions of the lines in the spectrum of hydrogen. However, his calculations did not work for substances with a more complicated electron structure. To deal with this problem, scientists have developed a **wave mechanics** model in which allowed orbits are replaced by allowed **energy levels**. However, this is an entirely mathematical approach, and the Rutherford-Bohr model is still used as a way of representing atoms in pictures.

nucleus

electrons

The Rutherford-Bohr model of the atom (with nuclear particles included). In this model, only certain electron orbits are allowed.

1 What is the difference between Rutherford's model of the atom and Thomson's 'plum pudding' model?

2 What is the difference between the Rutherford-Bohr model of the atom and Rutherford's model?

3 On the right, a beam of alpha particles is being directed at a thin piece of gold foil. How does the Rutherford model of the atom explain why
  a) most of the alpha particles go straight through the foil
  b) some alpha particles are deflected at large angles?

4 Why do the results of the experiment on the right suggest that the nucleus has a positive charge?

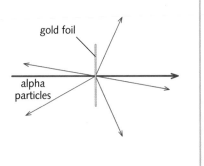

gold foil

alpha particles

+++

Atoms and particles (2)

If an electron gains energy...

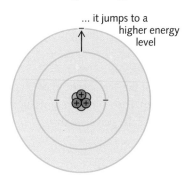

... it jumps to a higher energy level

When the electron drops back to a lower level...

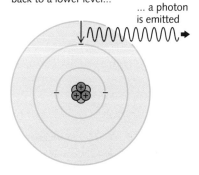

... a photon is emitted

▲ How an atom gives off light

How an atom gives off light

Bohr's explanation of how an atom gives off light was like this.

If an electron gains energy in some way – for example, because its atom collides with another one – it may jump to a higher energy level. But the atom does not stay in this **excited state** for long. Soon, the electron loses energy by dropping back to a lower level. According to the quantum theory, the energy is radiated as a pulse of light called a **photon**. The greater the energy change, the shorter the wavelength of the light.

As a line spectrum contains particular wavelengths only, it provides evidence that only certain energy changes are occurring within the atom – and therefore that only certain energy levels are allowed.

Fundamental particles

A **fundamental particle** is one which is *not* made up of other particles. An atom is not fundamental because it is made up of electrons, protons, and neutrons. But are these fundamental? To answer this and other questions, scientists carry out experiments with **particle accelerators**. They shoot beams of high-energy particles (such as protons) at nuclei, or at other beams, and detect the particles emerging from the collisions. In collider experiments, new particles are created as energy is converted into mass. However, most of these particles do not exist in the atoms of ordinary matter.

▶ Part of the proton-antiproton collider at the Fermilab research centre, Illinois, USA. Electromagnets are used to accelerate the particles round a circular path over 8 km long.

The present theory of particles is called the **standard model**. According to this model, electrons are fundamental particles. However, neutrons and protons are made up of other particles called **quarks**, as shown in the chart on the next page. In ordinary matter, there are two types of quark, called the **up quark** and the **down quark** for convenience. Each proton or neutron is made up of three quarks. The quarks have fractional charges compared with the charge on an electron.

++

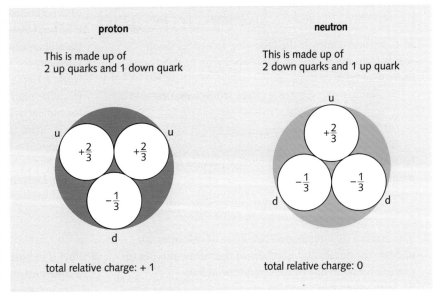

total relative charge: + 1   total relative charge: 0

Individual quarks have never been detected. The existence of quarks has only been deduced from the patterns seen in the properties of other particles – for example, how high-energy particles are scattered.

Quark changes in beta decay

In the most common form of beta decay, a neutron decays to form a proton, an electron (the beta particle), and an antineutrino:

neutron → proton + electron + antineutrino

If this is rewritten to show the quarks:

up quark   up quark
down quark   →   up quark   + electron + antineutrino
down quark   down quark

From the above, you can see that this type of beta decay occurs when a down quark changes into an up quark, as follows:

down quark → up quark + electron + antineutrino
$(-1/3)$ $(+2/3)$ (-1) (0)

The relative charges underneath the equation show that there is no change in total charge. In other words, charge is conserved.

In the less common form of beta decay, a proton decays to form a neutron, a positron (the beta particle), and a neutrino. This happens when an up quark in the proton changes into a down quark.

> **Decay essentials**
>
> The break-up of an unstable nucleus is called radioactive decay. During beta decay, a beta particle is shot out. In most cases, this particle is an electron (-). However, more rarely, it a positron (+), an antiparticle with the same mass as an electron, but opposite charge.

1 When an electron drops back to a lower energy in an atom, it loses energy.
  a) What happens to this energy?
  b) If the difference between the two energy levels was greater, how would this affect the wavelength of the light emitted?
  c) Why do atoms emit certain wavelengths only?
2 What is meant by a fundamental particle?

3 Which of the following are thought to be fundamental particles?
  electrons   protons   neutrons   quarks
4 Quarks have a fractional charge. Explain why, if a neutron is made up of three quarks, it is uncharged.
5 In one form of beta decay, an up quark changes into a down quark. Explain why, in this case, the beta particle emitted must be a positron and not an electron.

1

electrons	nuclei	protons	wave

a) Copy and complete the following sentences using words from the above list. Each word may be used once, more than once or not at all.

(i) Radioactive substances have atoms with unstable

_____ . [1]

(ii) Beta particles are _____ . [1]

(iii) Gamma rays are _____ . [1]

b) Name another type of radioactive particle not mentioned in part (**a**). [1]

WJEC

2 The symbol $^{35}_{17}Cl$ represents one atom of chlorine.

a) State the names and numbers of the different types of particle found in one of these chlorine atoms. [3]

b) State where these particles are to be found in the atom. [2]

UCLES (O)

3

proton number	26
mass number	59
radiation emitted	beta and gamma

The table above shows information about a radioisotope of iron called iron 59.

a) Calculate:

(i) the number of neutrons in the nucleus; [1]

(ii) the total number of charged particles in a single atom of iron 59. [1]

b) Iron 59 and iron 56 are both isotopes of iron. What are isotopes? [1]

c) Iron 59 emits two types of radiation. Briefly explain how the gamma radiation could be separated from the beta radiation emitted. [1]

WJEC

4 Phosphorus-32 is a radioactive isotope. It can be used to prove that plants absorb phosphorus from the soil around them.

a) (i) The stable isotope of phosphorus has a mass number of 31. State the structural different between atoms of phosphorus-31 and phosphorus-32. [2]

(ii) Explain why both isotopes of phosphorus have identical chemical properties. [1]

b) Phosphorus-32 is a **beta-emitter** with a **half-life** of 14 days.

(i) What is a beta particle? [1]

(ii) The atomic number of phosphorus-32 atom is 15. State the new values of the atomic and mass numbers of the atom just after it has emitted a beta particle. [2]

(iii) Explain what is meant by the term **half-life**. [1]

c) A solution of the isotope is watered onto the soil around the plant. Each day for the next week, a leaf is removed from the plan and tested for radioactivity.

(i) State **three** safety precautions which should be adopted when doing experiments with phosphorus-32. [3]

(ii) Describe **two** methods which could be used to measure the activity of a leaf. [2]

MEG

5 Phyl is in hospital. She is injected with the radioisotope technetium-99m.

This isotope is absorbed by the thyroid gland in her throat. A radiation detector placed outside her body and above her throat detects the radiation.

Technetium-99m has a half-life of 6 hours. It emits gamma radiation.

a) Why is an emitter of alpha radiation unsuitable? [1]

b) (i) How long will it take for the activity of the technetium-99m to fall to a quarter of its original value? [2]

(ii) After 24 hours, how will the activity of the technetium-99m compare with its original value? [2]

c) Eventually the level of radiation from the technetium-99m will fall to less than the level of the background radiation. State **two** naturally occurring sources of background radiation. [2]

MEG

6 The radioactive isotopes in the Chernobyl fallout which caused most concern were iodine 131 and caesium 137. Both are beta and gamma emitters. Iodine 131, in rainfall, found its way into milk but caesium 137, with a half-life of 30 years may cause more long term problems.

a) From which part of the atom do the beta and gamma rays come? [1]

b) Explain what the number 131 tells you about the iodine atom. [2]

c) After the Chernobyl accident, a milk sample containing iodine 131, was found to have an activity of 1600 units per litre. The activity of the sample was measured every 7 days and the results are shown in the table below.

time (days)	0	7	14	21	28	35
activity (units per litre)	1600	875	470	260	140	77

(i) Draw a graph of activity against time, using the grid on the next page as a guide. [2]

(ii) Estimate the half-life of iodine 131 and show on the graph how you arrived at your answer. [2]

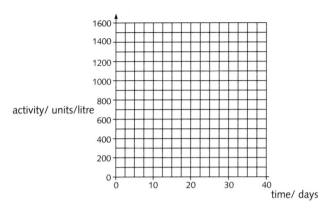

d) Give a reason why caesium 137 could cause longer term problems than iodine 131. [2]

WJEC

7 a) (i) Explain why some substances are radioactive and some are not. [2]
(ii) State the cause of background radiation. [1]
(iii) Explain what you understand by the meaning of the *half-life* of a radioactive element. [2]
b) Technetium-99m is a radioactive material with a half-life of 6 hours. It is used to study blood flow around the body. A sample of technetium-99m has an activity of 96 counts per minute when injected into a patient's blood stream. Estimate
(i) its activity after 12 hours, [1]
(ii) how long it will take for the radioactivity from the injection to become undetectable. [1]
c) Technetium-99m is a gamma (γ) emitter and does not produce alpha (α) or beta (β) radiations. Explain why it is safe to inject technetium-99m into the body. [2]
d) Radioactive salt (sodium chloride) is also used in medicine. The radioactive sodium (Na) in the salt decays, according to the equation shown below, to form magnesium (Mg).

$$^{24}_{11}\text{Na} \longrightarrow\ ^{24}_{12}\text{Mg} + \textbf{X} + \gamma \text{ radiation}$$

(i) Name the particle **X**. [1]
(ii) Use the information given in the equation above to find the
I. total number of charged particles in each sodium atom, [1]
II. number of neutrons in the nucleus of a sodium 24 atom. [1]

WJEC

8 This question is about information given in a leaflet about radon.
a) Extract 1 "Radon is a naturally occurring radioactive gas. It comes from uranium which occurs in rocks and soils."
(i) Explain the meaning of the word **radioactive**.
(ii) Explain, in detail, the danger of breathing radon gas into the lungs. [4]

Extract 2 is a diagram showing how radon decays

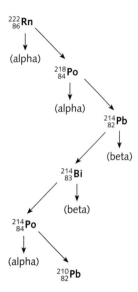

Two of the nuclei shown in the diagram are isotopes of polonium.
b) Explain the meaning of the word **isotope**. [1]
c) In the diagram, radon is shown as $^{222}_{86}\text{Rn}$. In a neutral radon atom, what is the number of
(i) protons,
(ii) electrons,
(iii) neutrons [3]

NEAB

9 A radioactive isotope of gold has the symbol $^{196}_{79}\text{Au}$. If this isotope is injected into the bloodstream of a patient, it can be used by doctors as a tracer to monitor the way the patient's heart works. The isotope emits gamma radiation that is detected outside the patient's body.
a) Why would an isotope that emits alpha radiation be unsuitable as a tracer to monitor the working of the heart? [1]
b) Give one non-medical use for a radioactive tracer. [1]

SEG

10 Isotopes of the radioactive element uranium occur naturally in small proportions in some rocks. The table gives information about **one** uranium isotope.

nucleon (mass) number	238
proton (atomic) number	92
radiation emitted	alpha particle

a) How many neutrons are there in an atom of this uranium isotope? [1]
b) From which part of the uranium atom does the alpha particle come? [1]

SEG

Photocopy the list of topics below and tick the boxes of the ones that are included in your examination syllabus. (Your teacher should be able to tell you which they are.) Use your list when you revise. The spread number in brackets tells you where to find more information.

❏ **1** The particles in an atom. (11.01)

❏ **2** The particles in the nucleus of an atom. (11.01)

❏ **3** The forces binding the particles in an atom together. (11.01)

❏ **4** The meaning of atomic number (proton number). (11.01)

❏ **5** The meaning of mass number (nucleon number). (11.01)

❏ **6** Isotopes. (11.01)

❏ **7** Electron shells. (11.01)

❏ **8** Radioactive materials and the radiation they produce. (11.02)

❏ **9** Ionizing radiation. (11.02)

❏ **10** Alpha particles and their properties. (11.02)

❏ **11** Beta particles and their properties. (11.02)

❏ **12** Gamma rays and their properties. (11.02)

❏ **13** The dangers of nuclear radiation. (11.03)

❏ **14** The main sources of background radiation. (11.03)

❏ **15** Detecting radiation with a Geiger-Müller tube. (11.03)

❏ **16** Using a cloud chamber to show the tracks of alpha particles. (11.03)

❏ **17** The changes in the nucleus that occur during alpha decay. (11.04)

❏ **18** The changes in the nucleus that occur during beta decay. (11.04)

❏ **19** Writing nuclear equations. (11.04)

❏ **20** How the rate of radioactive decay changes with time. (11.05)

❏ **21** The meaning of half-life. (11.05)

❏ **22** Measuring the activity of a radioactive sample. (11.05)

❏ **23** Working out a half-life from a radioactive decay curve. (11.05)

❏ **24** Why some isotopes have more stable nuclei than others. (11.05)

❏ **25** The release of energy by radioactive decay. (11.06)

❏ **26** What a nuclear reaction is. (11.06)

❏ **27** What happens during fission. (11.06)

❏ **28** What a chain reaction is. (11.06)

❏ **29** How a controlled chain reaction is used in a nuclear reactor. (11.06)

❏ **30** The parts of a nuclear reactor. (11.06)

❏ **31** The problems of nuclear waste. (11.06)

❏ **32** The link between energy and mass. (11.06)

❏ **33** What radioisotopes are. (11.07)

❏ **34** Using radioisotopes
- as tracers
- in radiotherapy
- to find cracks in metals
- for thickness monitoring
- for dating old materials. (11.07)

❏ **35** Evidence for the nucleus. (11.08)

❏ **36** The Rutherford-Bohr model of the atom. (11.08)

❏ **37** The quantum theory explanation of how an atom gives off light. (11.09)

❏ **38** Quarks. (11.09)

❏ **39** Quark changes in beta decay. (11.09)

The Earth in Space

Part of the Eagle Nebula, as seen by the Hubble Space Telescope from its orbit around the Earth. This vast pillar of gas and dust is billions of kilometres across. Within it, new stars are forming as matter is clumped together by the pull of gravity. The picture is also a view back in time. The nebula is so far away that its light has taken 7000 years to reach the Earth.

Sun, Earth, and Moon

Diameters

Sun	1 390 000 km
Earth	12 800 km
Moon	3500 km

Distances (average)

Earth to Sun	149 600 000 km
Earth to Moon	384 000 km

The Sun

The Sun is a huge, hot, brightly glowing ball of gas, called a **star**. Its diameter is more than a hundred times that of the Earth. The Sun is extremely hot, with a temperature of 6000 °C on the surface, rising to 15 000 000 °C in the centre. Its energy comes from nuclear reactions deep in its core.

The Earth: day, night, and seasons

Earth turns slowly on its axis once a day. Half of the Earth is in sunlight, and half in shadow (in darkness). As each place moves from sunlight into shadow, it passes from daytime into night.

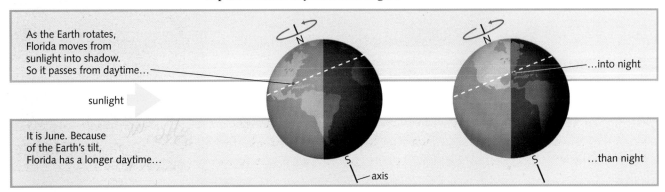

As the Earth rotates, Florida moves from sunlight into shadow. So it passes from daytime...

sunlight

It is June. Because of the Earth's tilt, Florida has a longer daytime...

...into night

...than night

axis

Solar heating

radiant energy from Sun

Earth

The Earth is heated by radiant energy from the Sun. Zones A and B receive equal amounts of energy per second. But zone A has a larger surface area, so the energy is more spread out. This is one reason why zone A is colder than zone B.

The Earth moves round the Sun in a near-circular path. The path is called an **orbit**. Each orbit takes just over 365 days, or one year. The Earth's axis is tilted by 23.5° as shown in the diagrams. Because of this, most regions get varying hours of daylight through the year and varying climatic conditions. In other words, they have different seasons. When it is summer, there are two reasons for the higher temperatures. First, because of the tilt, the surface is more 'square on' to the Sun, so the Sun's radiation is less spread out, as explained in the panel on the left. Second, there are more hours of sunlight.

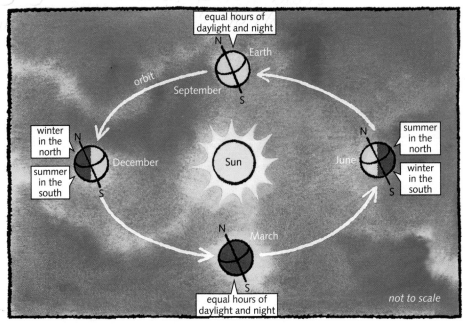

equal hours of daylight and night

Earth

orbit

September

winter in the north

summer in the south

December

Sun

June

summer in the north

winter in the south

March

equal hours of daylight and night

not to scale

▶ Many parts of the world get four seasons: spring, summer, autumn, and winter. However in equatorial regions other seasons apply.

The Moon

The Moon moves around the Earth in a near-circular orbit. Each orbit takes about a month – or, more accurately, 27.3 days. The Moon also takes 27.3 days to turn once on its axis, which is why it always keeps the same face toward us.

The Moon is smaller than the Earth and has a rocky, cratered surface. The craters were mainly caused by the impact of large meteorites over a billion years ago. The 'seas' are not seas at all, but fairly flat areas of basalt rock.

We see the Moon because its surface reflects sunlight. Once a month, when there is a 'full Moon', the whole of the sunlit side is facing us. But most of the time, we can only see part of the sunlit side. The rest is in shadow.

When we look at the Moon, only the sunlit part is visible.

Eclipses

The Moon is much smaller and closer than the Sun. By chance, its distance is such that it *appears* almost exactly the same size to us. As the Moon orbits the Earth, it sometimes passes between us and the Sun. Then, the Sun's disc appears to be covered by the Moon: there is a **solar eclipse**.

If the Moon's orbit and the Earth's orbit were in the same plane, then there would be a solar eclipse every month. However, the Moon's orbit is slightly tilted, so solar eclipses do not happen that frequently. Sometimes, the Moon's orbit takes it into the Earth's shadow. Then the Moon dims: there is a **lunar eclipse**. (Some sunlight still gets through to the Moon because it is refracted (bent) by the Earth's atmosphere.)

Solar eclipse (eclipse of the Sun)

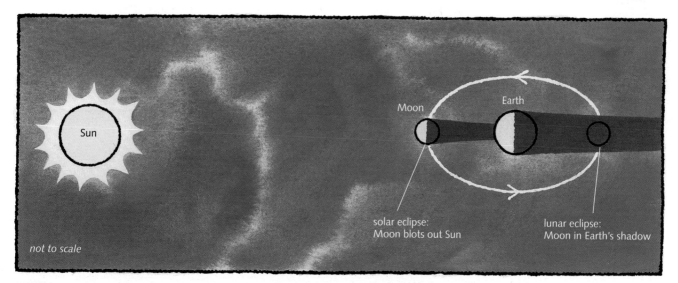
not to scale

solar eclipse: Moon blots out Sun

lunar eclipse: Moon in Earth's shadow

1 Give the time taken (to the nearest day) for
   a) one rotation of the Earth on its axis
   b) one rotation of the Moon on its axis
   c) one orbit of the Earth about the Sun
   d) one orbit of the Moon about the Earth.
2 Explain the following.
   a) From the Earth, we always see the same side of the Moon.
   b) The Moon sometimes appears as a crescent.

c) Well north of the equator, there are more hours of daylight in June than in December.
d) Well north of the equator, average temperatures are higher in June than in December.
3 Describe the relative positions of the Sun, Earth, and Moon
   a) during a solar eclipse (eclipse of the Sun)
   b) during a lunar eclipse (eclipse of the Moon).

The Solar System (1)

Orbits

ellipse

circle

Sun

moon

planet

not to scale

The Earth is one of many **planets** in orbit around the Sun. The Sun, planets, and other objects in orbit, are together known as the **Solar System**. The Solar System is so large that it is almost impossible to show the planets' sizes and their distances from the Sun on the same scale diagram. That is why *two* diagrams have been used here – one below and one on the next page.

Planets are not hot enough to give off their own light. We can only see them because they reflect light from the Sun. From Earth, they look like tiny dots in the night sky. Without a telescope, it is difficult to tell whether you are looking at a star or a planet.

The planets are kept in orbit by the gravitational pull of the Sun. Most are in an almost circular orbit with the Sun at the centre. However, for Mercury, Mars, and Pluto, the orbit is more of an **ellipse** ('stretched out circle'). The planets all travel round the Sun in the same direction. They also travel in approximately the same plane, apart from Pluto, whose orbit is tilted relative to the others. Most of the planets have smaller **moons** in orbit around them.

The table at the top of the next page gives some data about the planets. Here are two features shown by the data:

- The further a planet is from the Sun, the slower it travels, and the more time it takes to complete an orbit.
- In general, the further the planet is from the Sun, the lower its average surface temperature. This is because the intensity of the Sun's radiation weakens with distance. (Doubling the distance means that the energy per second reaching each square metre of a surface is reduced to a quarter.)

On the next spread, there is more information about the planets, and about other objects orbiting the Sun.

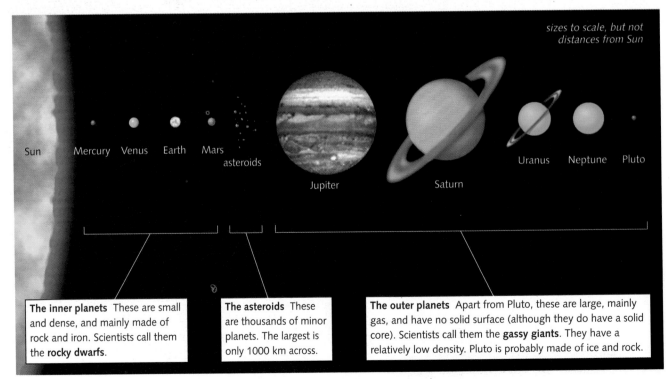

sizes to scale, but not distances from Sun

Sun   Mercury   Venus   Earth   Mars   asteroids   Jupiter   Saturn   Uranus   Neptune   Pluto

The inner planets These are small and dense, and mainly made of rock and iron. Scientists call them the **rocky dwarfs**.

The asteroids These are thousands of minor planets. The largest is only 1000 km across.

The outer planets Apart from Pluto, these are large, mainly gas, and have no solid surface (although they do have a solid core). Scientists call them the **gassy giants**. They have a relatively low density. Pluto is probably made of ice and rock.

	Mercury	Venus	Earth	Mars	Jupiter	Saturn	Uranus	Neptune	Pluto
average distance from Sun/ million km	58	108	150	228	778	1420	2870	4490	5900
time for one orbit/ years	0.24	0.62	1.00	1.88	11.86	29.46	84.01	164.8	247
diameter (at equator)/ km	4880	12 100	12 800	6790	142 980	120 540	51 120	49 530	2300
mass compared with Earth (Earth = 1)	0.06	0.82	1.00	0.11	318	95.2	14.5	17.2	0.002
average density/ g/cm³ *	5.4	5.2	5.5	3.9	1.3	0.7	1.3	1.8	1.1
average surface temperature	350 °C	480 °C	22 °C	-23 °C	-150 °C	-180 °C	-210 °C	-220 °C	-230 °C
number of moons	0	0	1	2	16	23	15	8	1

* For comparison: water has a density of $1.0 \, g/cm^3$ (1 cubic centimetre has a mass of 1 gram); iron has a density of $7.9 \, g/cm^3$

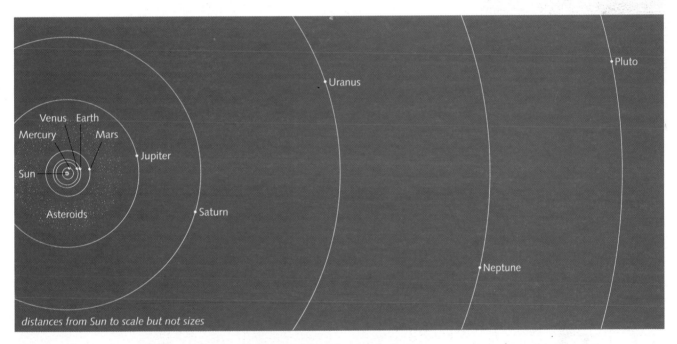

distances from Sun to scale but not sizes

The Sun is just one of billions of stars. Scientists have detected planets around other stars, although other 'solar systems' are far too distant for their planets to be viewed through a telescope. To fit the nearest star on the diagram above, the page would have to be more than a kilometre wide!

To answer the following, you will need to refer to data in the table at the top of the page.

1 Which is the largest of the rocky dwarfs?
2 Which is the largest of the gassy giants?
3 Which planet travels round the Sun at the highest speed?
4 A tiny planet called Ceres takes 4.60 years to orbit the Sun. Between the orbits of which other planets does Ceres lie? Give a reason for your answer.

5 a) Which planet receives the most radiant energy per square metre from the Sun? Explain your answer.
   b) Why does Mars have a lower average surface temperature than Earth?
   c) One of the planets has a much higher average surface temperature than might be expected, because its atmosphere causes a severe greenhouse effect. Which planet do you think this is? Give a reason for your answer.

The Solar System (2)

The inner planets

Mercury is the closest planet to the Sun. In many ways, it is a larger version of our own Moon. It has a cratered surface and no atmosphere.

Venus is the brightest object in the night sky (apart from the Moon). It is almost the same size as the Earth, but conditions there are very different. The planet is covered by thick clouds of sulphuric acid, and its atmosphere (97% carbon dioxide) causes a severe greenhouse effect. Down on the surface, the temperature can reach nearly 500 °C.

Earth is the only planet in the Solar System known to support life.

Mars is sometimes called the red planet because of its surface colour. It has a thin atmosphere (mainly carbon dioxide), a dusty surface, and polar caps. From the shapes of some of its valleys, scientists think that water may once have flowed there. It also has volcanoes, although none are active.

The asteroids

The asteroids have diameters ranging from a few kilometres up to 1000 km. Most have orbits between those of Mars and Jupiter. But some have much more elliptical orbits that cross the paths of other planets. There is some evidence that, around 65 million years ago, an asteroid about 10 km across struck the Earth. The effects of this may have caused the extinction of the dinosaurs.

The outer planets

Jupiter is more massive than all the other planets put together. It is mainly gas (its atmosphere is 90% hydrogen) and has no solid surface. The **Great Red Spot** is a huge storm that has raged for centuries. One of Jupiter's moons, Io, has active volcanoes on it – the first to be found beyond the Earth.

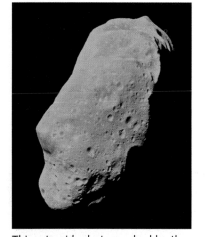

This asteroid, photographed by the *Galileo* spacecraft, is nearly 60 km long.

Great Red Spot

Earth

Jupiter's Great Red Spot is a storm so big that the Earth would fit inside it!

Saturn's rings are millions of pieces of ice and rock, each in its own orbit about the planet.

Saturn too is mainly gas. It is surrounded by rings. These are not a solid mass, but millions of pieces of ice and rock ranging in size from microscopic grains to boulders. Each is a tiny 'moonlet' in its own orbit.

Uranus is another gassy giant. It is unusual in that its axis of rotation is tilted at more than 90°. It too has rings, but much fainter ones than Saturn's.

Neptune is the outermost of the gassy giants. It also has a faint ring system.

Pluto is small and icy. Its orbit, which takes nearly 250 years, is elliptical, so its distance from the Sun varies considerably. Although called the 'outermost planet', it is actually inside the orbit of Neptune at present.

Comets, meteors, and meteorites

Comets have highly elliptical orbits which, in some cases, can take them out beyond Pluto and then close in to the Sun. In the 'head' of a comet, there is an icy lump, typically several kilometres across. Heated by the Sun, particles of dust and gas stream off it into space, forming a huge 'tail' millions of kilometres long. This is visible because it reflects the sunlight.

As the Earth moves through space, it runs into tiny grains of material which hit the atmosphere so fast that they burn up. Each one causes a streak of light called a **meteor**. Rarely, a larger chunk of material reaches the ground without completely burning up. The chunk is called a **meteorite**.

> **Ice in space**
>
> To astronomers, 'ice' does not necessarily mean frozen water. It can also mean frozen carbon dioxide, methane, or ammonia.

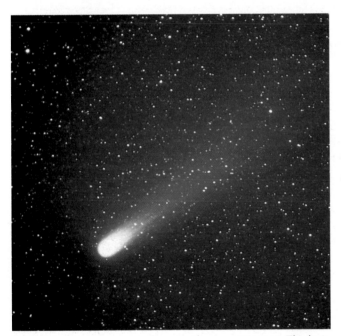

Halley's comet can be seen from Earth every 76 years. The last time was in 1986.

A large meteorite caused this impact crater in Arizona, USA, around 50 000 years ago. The crater is 800 metres across.

---

1 **a)** Which planet is most easily visible from Earth?
   b) What is the Great Red Spot, and which planet is it on?
2 **a)** Apart from Saturn, which other planets have ring systems?
   b) What are the rings?
3 How is the 'tail' of a comet formed?

4 What is the difference between a meteor and a meteorite?
5 If Pluto is now closer to the Sun than Neptune is, why is Pluto called the 'outermost planet'?
6 Explain why it would be very difficult for astronauts to land on **a)** Venus **b)** Jupiter.

Related topics: planetary data **12.02**; comets in orbit **12.04**; formation of the Solar System **12.05**

Objects in orbit

Gravity and orbits

With no force acting on it, a planet, a moon, or any other object, would travel through space in a straight line. To move in the curved path of an orbit, there must be an inward force acting on it. That force is provided by gravity.

There is gravitational attraction between *all* masses. The force between everyday objects is far too weak to detect, but with objects as massive as moons and planets, the force is considerable, and controls their motion.

Gravitational force weakens with distance. Isaac Newton found that the force obeys an inverse square law: *doubling* the distance between two masses reduces the gravitational force between them to a *quarter*... and so on.

Comets in orbit

Comets have highly elliptical orbits. Here is an example:

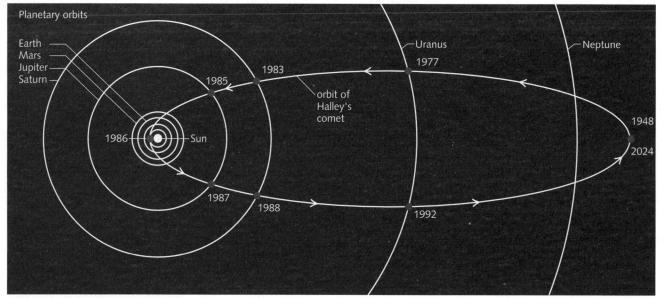

▲ The orbit of Halley's comet. From the positions and dates, you can see that the comet speeds up as it approaches the Sun and slows down as it moves away from it.

A comet has least speed when it is furthest from the Sun. That is also when the gravitational pull on it is weakest. As the comet moves closer to the Sun, the force of gravity increases. Also, the comet speeds up as it 'falls' towards the Sun – in other words, as its potential energy is changed into kinetic energy.

Satellites in orbit

Any object in orbit around a more massive one is called a **satellite**. So the Moon is a natural satellite of the Earth. However, when people talk about 'satellites', they usually mean artificial satellites launched from Earth.

There are hundreds of artificial satellites in orbit around the Earth. Most are in circular orbits. A satellite in a low orbit needs the highest speed. For example, a satellite at a height of 300 km, just above the Earth's atmosphere, must travel at 29 100 km/hour to maintain a circular orbit. At this speed, it takes 86 minutes to orbit the Earth. This is the **period** of its orbit. A higher orbit requires a lower speed, and the period is longer.

A satellite in a geostationary orbit always appears in the same position relative to the ground because the period of its orbit, 24 hours, matches the period of the Earth's rotation.

To be geostationary, a satellite must be put in a circular orbit 35 900 km above the equator. The required speed is 11 100 km/hour.

Communications satellites beam radio, TV, and other signals from one part of the Earth to another. Satellites like this are normally put into a **geostationary orbit**: their motion exactly matches the Earth's rotation so that they appear stationary relative to the ground. As a result, dish aerials on the ground do not have to track them, but can point in a fixed direction.

Navigation satellites are used by boats and other craft to locate their position. The **Global Positioning System** (**GPS**) has a network of satellites transmitting synchronized time signals. Down on the ground, a receiver picks up signals from different satellites, compares their arrival times, and uses the data to calculate its position to within a few metres.

Monitoring satellites, such as weather satellites, contain cameras or other detectors for scanning and surveying the Earth. Some are in low orbits which pass over the North and South Poles. As the Earth rotates beneath them, they can scan the whole of its surface.

Astronomical satellites, such as the Hubble Space Telescope, contain equipment for observing distant stars and galaxies. Unlike observatories on Earth, the light or other radiation they receive is not disrupted and weakened by the presence of the atmosphere.

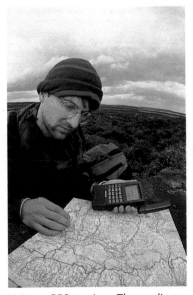

Using a GPS receiver. The readings on the display give the position.

1 The diagram on the right shows the orbit of a comet. At which point
   a) is the Sun's gravitational pull on the comet greatest
   b) is the Sun's gravitational pull on the comet least
   c) does the comet have the greatest speed
   d) does the comet have the least speed?
2 a) What is a *geostationary* orbit?
   b) What is the period (orbit time) of a satellite in a geostationary orbit?
   c) Why are communications satellites normally put into a geostationary orbit?

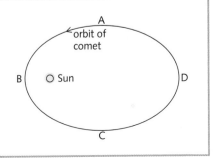

Related topics: force, motion, and gravity **2.07–2.09**; circular motion and orbits **2.14**; satellite communications **10.08**

Sun, stars, and galaxies (1)

The Sun is a star. As stars go, it is rather average. There are much bigger and much brighter stars. However all other stars look like tiny dots to us because they are much further away.

Light year

Distances between stars are so vast that astronomers have special units for measuring them. For example:

One **light year** (**ly**) is the distance travelled by light in one year. The speed of light is nearly 300 000 kilometres per second, so light travels more than 9 million million kilometres in one year. Expressed more accurately:

$$1 \text{ light year} = 9.5 \times 10^{12} \text{ km}$$

The nearest star to the Sun, *Proxima Centauri*, is 4.2 light years away. In other words, its light takes 4.2 years to reach us: we see it as it was 4.2 years ago. For comparison, light from the Sun takes 8 minutes to reach us.

Galaxies

The Sun is a member of a huge star system called a **galaxy**. This contains over 100 billion (10^{11}) stars, and is nearly 100 000 light years across. Between the stars, there is thinly spread gas and dust called **interstellar matter**. The gas is mainly hydrogen. The galaxy is slowly rotating, and is held together by gravitational attraction.

Our galaxy is called the **Milky Way**. You can see the edge of its disc as a bright band of stars across the night sky. It is just one of many billions of galaxies in the known **Universe**.

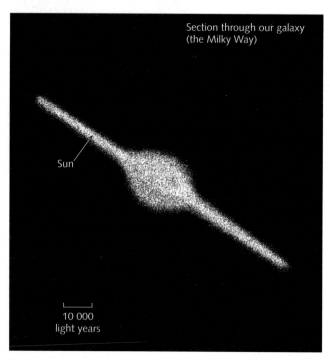

Section through our galaxy (the Milky Way)

Sun

10 000 light years

Our own Sun is about halfway out from the centre of our galaxy.

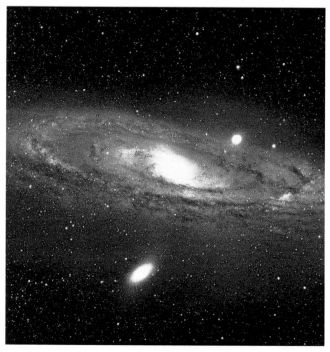

The Andromeda Galaxy is 2 million light years away. It is very similar in structure to our own galaxy.

The birth of a star

nebula of gas and dust

nuclear fusion starts in Sun

not to scale

blob of matter begins to collect at centre

matter becomes more dense and hot

The formation of the Solar System

Scientists think that the Sun and the rest of the Solar System formed about 4500 million years ago in a huge cloud of gas and dust called a **nebula**. Gravity slowly pulled the the material into blobs. One blob in the centre grew especially large as more and more material crashed into it. It also heated up as the gravitational potential energy of the incoming material was converted into thermal energy. Around it, smaller blobs orbited, growing bigger as they swept up most of the outer material in the cloud. Later, these smaller blobs would contract and cool to form planets and moons.

The Sun formed from the large blob at the centre of the cloud. In time, it became massive enough to collect most of the hydrogen gas from around it. Deep inside the blob, the gas became hotter and more compressed. Eventually, its temperature and pressure were high enough to trigger the start of a process called **nuclear fusion**, explained on the next page. Fusion releases a huge amount of energy. Once it had started, the blob 'lit up' to become a star: the Sun. Other stars formed – and are being formed – in the same way.

During the type of fusion that happens in the Sun, nuclear reactions convert hydrogen into helium. Scientists think that the Sun has enough hydrogen left in its core to keep it shining for another 6000 million years.

The Great Nebula in the constellation of Orion. Stars are forming in this huge cloud of gas and dust.

1 Explain what is meant by the terms
  a) nebula b) galaxy c) Milky Way d) Universe.
2 The Sun mainly uses hydrogen as its nuclear fuel.
  a) About how long ago did the Sun start to shine?
  b) What is the name of the process that supplies the Sun with its energy?
  c) About how long will it be before the Sun's core runs out of hydrogen?

  d) What will have happened to all the hydrogen in the core?
3 *Proxima Centauri*, a star, is 4.2 light years away.
  a) What is meant by a light year?
  b) How far away is *Proxima Centauri* in km?
  c) Today, the fastest rockets can reach speeds of up to 50 000 km/hour. If a spacecraft travelled to *Proxima Centauri* at this average speed, about how long would its journey take?

Related topics: potential and thermal energy **4.01**; Solar System **12.02–12.03**; gravity **12.04**; stars and constellations **12.08**

295

Sun, stars, and galaxies (2)

Atomic essentials

Everything is made from about a hundred basic substances called elements. The smallest bit of an element is an atom. The nucleus of an atom is made up of protons and (in most cases) neutrons. Each element has a different number of protons in the nucleus.

hydrogen atom
(1 proton)

helium atom
(2 protons)

carbon atom
(6 protons)

electron

nucleus:
⊕ proton
◯ neutron

Fusion power... in the Sun

If hydrogen nuclei can be made to fuse (join) together to form helium nuclei, energy is released. But nuclei do not readily join because they are electrically charged, and repel each other. To make them fuse, they have to collide at extremely high speeds. In practice, this means maintaining a gas at an extremely high temperature: for example, 15 000 000 °C in the Sun's core.

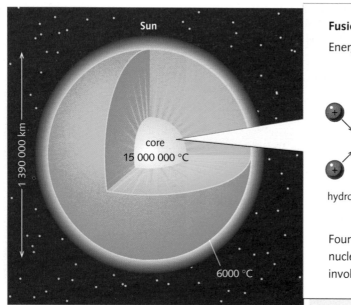

Sun

1 390 000 km

core
15 000 000 °C

6000 °C

Fusion in the Sun's core

Energy is released as hydrogen is converted into helium.

hydrogen nuclei

fusion
+ other changes

helium nucleus
+ other particles

Four hydrogen nuclei fuse together for each helium nucleus formed. This is a multi-stage process which also involves the creation of two neutrons from two protons.

... and on Earth

One day, fusion reactors may be used in power stations, but not for many years yet. The Sun's huge size and gravitational pull can maintain the conditions necessary for fusion. But on Earth, no ordinary container can hold hydrogen at such a high temperature and keep it compressed. To overcome these problems, scientists are trying to develop a fusion reactor that uses magnetic fields to trap the nuclei.

Potentially, the advantages of fusion reactors are considerable. They will produce more energy per kilogram of fuel than any conventional nuclear reactor. Their hydrogen fuel can be extracted from sea water. Their main waste product, helium, is not radioactive. And they have built-in safety: if the system fails, fusion stops.

Magnetic containment chamber for fusion experiments

Death of a star

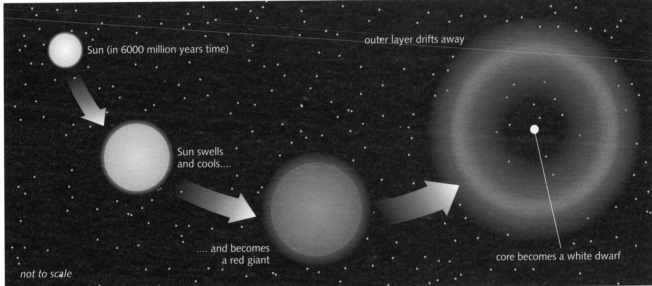

Sun (in 6000 million years time)

outer layer drifts away

Sun swells and cools....

.... and becomes a red giant

core becomes a white dwarf

not to scale

In the Sun's core, thermal activity prevents gravity from pulling the material further inwards. However, in about 6000 million years time, all of the hydrogen in the core will have been converted into helium, hydrogen fusion will cease, and the core will collapse. At the same time, the Sun's outer layer will expand to about 100 times its present diameter and cool to a red glow. The Sun will then be a **red giant**. Eventually, its outer layer will drift into space, exposing a hot, extremely dense core called a **white dwarf**. This tiny star will use helium as its nuclear fuel, converting it into carbon by fusion. When the helium runs out, the star will cool and fade for ever.

▲ In about 6000 million years time, the Sun will become a red giant. Later, its core will become a white dwarf, before it cools and fades for ever.

Supernovae and stardust

In every galaxy, new stars are forming and old ones are dying. The most massive stars have a different fate from that of our Sun. Eventually, their outer layers blow up in a gigantic nuclear explosion called a **supernova**. This leaves a core in which matter is so compressed that electrons and protons react to form neutrons. The result is a **neutron star**.

In stars, fusion reactions change lighter elements into heavier ones. However, to make very heavy elements (gold and uranium for example), the extreme conditions that create a supernova are needed. That is because, to make elements heavier than iron, energy must be *supplied* for fusion, and is not released by it. The Sun and inner planets contain very heavy elements. This suggests that the nebula in which they formed included 'stardust' from an earlier supernova. In other words, the Sun is a **second-generation star**.

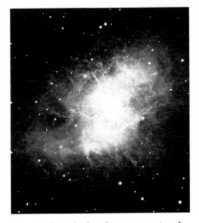

The Crab Nebula: the remnants of a supernova

1 What element will the Sun use as its nuclear fuel when its core runs out of hydrogen?

2 Describe in stages what will happen to the Sun when its core runs out of hydrogen.

3 Stars and planets contain many elements, but the nebulae in which they form are mainly hydrogen. What process produces all the other elements?

4 What is a supernova?

5 What is a neutron star, and where is it formed?

6 What evidence is there that the nebula in which the Solar System formed contained remnants from an earlier supernova?

7 Why is nuclear fusion much more difficult to achieve in experiments on Earth than it is in the Sun?

Related topics: atoms and elements **11.01**; nuclear reactors **11.06**; proton-neutron conversion **11.09**; gravity **12.04**

The expanding Universe

There are billions of galaxies in the Universe. Neighbouring galaxies are, typically, a few million light years apart. The most distant galaxies observed from Earth may be 15 billion light years away – their light has taken 15 billion (15×10^9) years to reach us.

The expanding Universe

When objects move away from Earth at high speed, the light waves from them become 'stretched out'. This is knows as the **Doppler effect**. It means that the wavelengths are shifted towards the red end (the longer wavelength end) of the visible spectrum. This is called **red shift**.

In the 1920s, Edwin Hubble observed that light from distant galaxies is red shifted, and that, in general, the red shift increases with the distance of the galaxy. This implies that the more distant galaxies are receding (moving away) from us at higher speed. We seem to be living in an expanding Universe.

The Big Bang theory

According to this theory, the Universe (and time) began about 10-20 billion years ago when a single, hot 'superatom' erupted in a burst of energy called the **Big Bang**. All the matter in the Universe came from this. Here are two pieces of evidence to support the theory:

- As the galaxies appear to be moving apart, they may once have been together in the same space.
- Radio telescopes have picked up background microwave radiation from every direction in space. This may be the heavily red-shifted remnants of radiation from the Big Bang.

The Big Bang was not an explosion into existing space. Space itself started to expand: the galaxies are separating because the space between them is increasing. To think about this, it helps to use a simplified model of an expanding Universe, such as the one shown on the next page.

Stars, galaxies, and gravity

The Sun is one star in a huge star system called a galaxy. This contains over 100 billion stars.

Stars and galaxies are shaped by gravity. There is gravitational attraction between *all* masses: the greater the masses and the closer they are, the stronger the force.

The light year

One light year is the distance travelled by light in one year. It is equal to 9.5×10^{12} km.

Typically, neighbouring stars are a few light years apart.

Electromagnetic waves

These include light and microwaves. Here are some typical wavelengths:

Visible spectrum
from 0.000 4 mm (violet light)
to 0.000 7 mm (red light)

Microwaves
from 0.001 mm to 300 mm

wavelength

▶ With radio telescope arrays like this, scientists have been able to detect radio waves from the most distant parts of the Universe, including microwaves which may be the remnants of radiation from the Big Bang.

A model of a two-dimensional expanding Universe

The observable Universe exists in three dimensions because objects can have length, width, and depth. But in the simple model above, space is represented by a two-dimensional surface: the elastic surface of an inflating balloon.

Imagine that you are on one of the galaxies as the balloon inflates. All the other galaxies appear to be moving away from you. The more distant they are, the faster they recede – just as Hubble observed. This applies whichever galaxy you are on. No single galaxy is at the centre of the expansion.

The fate of the Universe

Until recently, it was thought that gravitational attraction might be slowing the expansion of the Universe. According to this model, the fate of the Universe will depend on its total mass – which is not accurately known. If the mass is *less* than a certain critical value the Universe will keep expanding for ever. But if it is *more* than the critical value, the expansion will eventually stop and be followed by a contraction. Ultimately, there will be a Big Crunch.

The above model has now been thrown into question by evidence which suggests that the Universe's rate of expansion may actually be *increasing*. However, the reason for the increase is not yet clear.

Estimating the age of the Universe

Scientists have estimated the rate at which the galaxies appear to be moving apart. The value has not been agreed, but it may be about $1/15\,000$ km per year per million km of separation. This is called the **Hubble constant**. Assuming a constant rate of expansion, it is possible to work out that the galaxies must have started to separate about 15 000 million years ago. If so, that is when the Big Bang occurred.

1   5   5 million   5 billion   15 billion
            (5×10^6) (5×10^9) (1.5×10^{10})

Which of the above numbers could represent
a) the separation between two neighbouring galaxies, in light years
b) the separation between two neighbouring stars, in light years
c) the distance from Earth to the most distant galaxies observed, in light years
d) the age of the Universe, in years.

2 Light from distant galaxies shows red shift.
a) What is meant by red shift?
b) What is thought to be the cause of the red shift?

3 What evidence is there that the Universe may have started with a Big Bang?

4 If the expansion of the Universe is slowing down, what force is causing this to happen?

5 The value of the Hubble constant is uncertain. If its value is $1/10\,000$ km per year per million km separation, how old is the Universe?

Related topics: light, radio waves, microwaves **7.10–7.11**; gravitational attraction **12.04**; estimating distances in space **12.08**

299

Patterns and positions

Constellations

For thousands of years, people have been looking at the sky and seeing patterns in the positions of the brightest stars. The different groups of stars are called **constellations**. They have been named after animals, objects, and figures from mythology. For example: the Great Bear, the Cross, and Orion (the Hunter). In reality, the stars in each constellation are vast distances apart and not grouped together. For example, one star may be much further away than another, but look just as bright because it is hotter or bigger.

For practical reasons, astronomers still divide up the sky into constellations. It helps them locate and identify stars and other objects in space.

Apparent motion

We view the stars from from a slowly rotating roundabout called the Earth. So, like the Moon, the stars appear to move during the course of the night. In the northern hemisphere, the whole night sky appears to revolve about *Polaris*, the Pole Star, as shown below. The Pole Star stays in the same position because it is almost exactly in line with the Earth's north–south axis of rotation. In the southern hemisphere, the sky also appear to revolve, but there is no equivalent bright star in line with the axis.

The stars are so far away from us that, from day to day, their relative positions in the sky do not noticeably change. However, five dots in the sky *do* change position. These are the five 'naked eye' planets, the ones visible without a telescope: Mercury, Venus, Mars, Jupiter, and Saturn. Being very much closer to us than the stars, their motion is more apparent. In fact, the word 'planet' comes from a Greek word meaning 'wanderer'.

Sun, stars, and planets

The Sun is a star. Other stars look like tiny dots because they are so much further away.

The Sun has planets in orbit around it. The nearest star is almost 7000 times further away from us than the most distant planet.

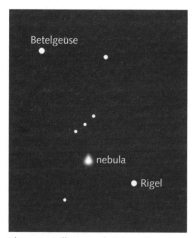

The Cross is visible from the Earth's southern hemisphere. It is is one of the few constellations that looks anything like its name!

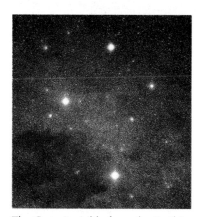

Betelgeuse

nebula

Rigel

The constellation of Orion. Its stars may appear to form a group, but are not related. Rigel is nearly twice as far away as Betelgeuse.

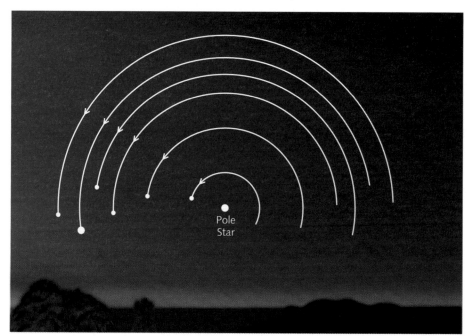

Pole Star

In the northern hemisphere, the stars appear to move in circles about the Pole Star. This diagram shows the tracks of a few of them over a twelve-hour period. In reality, it is the Earth that is rotating.

One month later

How the apparent position of a planet (Mars) can change relative to the stars.

Estimating distances in space

Over the years, astronomers have developed a range of methods for estimating the distances to planets, stars, and galaxies.

Planets The mathematical laws governing orbital motion are well understood. So, if the time taken for a planet to orbit the Sun is measured, its distance from the Sun can be calculated.

Nearby stars As the Earth orbits the Sun, our viewpoint in space changes, so nearby stars appear to move slightly against the background of very distant ones, as shown on the right. This apparent movement is called **parallax**: the closer the star, the greater the parallax. If the angle of parallax is measured, the distance can be calculated using trigonometry.

Distant stars If one star is further away than an identical but closer star, it *appears* less bright because of its greater distance. This principle can be used to estimate distance. But first, the light from the stars must be analysed to identify a matching pair, and the position of the closer star found by parallax. This method also works for stars that can be identified in neighbouring galaxies.

Distant galaxies Galaxies are rushing away from us because the Universe is expanding. The further away a galaxy is, the faster it recedes, and the more its light is red shifted (moved towards the red end of the spectrum). This principle, established by Edwin Hubble, can be used to estimate distances.

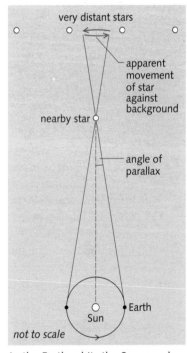

As the Earth orbits the Sun, nearby stars appear to move slightly against the background of very distant stars.

---

1 Stars and planets look like tiny dots in the night sky. How is it possible, without a telescope, to tell which is a planet and which is a star?
2 **a)** Why do nearly all the stars in the night sky appear to move round in circles?
  b) Why does the Pole Star not appear to move?
3 During the course of a year, the star on the right appears to move from side to side.
  a) Why does the effect occur?
  b) What use can be made of the effect?

1

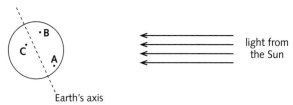

Earth's axis

The diagram shows the Earth and three cities **A**, **B**, **C** on the Earth's surface.

a) State:
 (i)   which cities are in daylight;   [1]
 (ii) which city receives the most amount of light during the day.   [1]
b) State how long it would take city **C** to return to the same place again as the Earth spins on its axis.   [1]

WJEC

2 The diagram shows the Earth in four different positions in its orbit around the Sun. Assume that the Earth is always the same distance from the Sun.

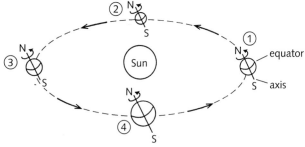

a) (i)   When the Earth is in position 1, it is summer in the northern hemisphere. Why is this?   [2]
 (ii) What is the season in the northern hemisphere when the Earth is in
       position 2?   position 3?   [2]
 (iii) What is the season in the southern hemisphere when the Earth is in position 3?   [1]

b) The order of some planets outwards from the Sun is as follows:

Mercury   Venus   Earth   Mars   Jupiter   Saturn   Uranus

How would you expect the average day-time temperature on Uranus to compare with that on Mars? Explain your answer.   [2]

MEG

3 a)

Earth	Sun	Moon

Copy the sentences below and select **one or two** words from the boxes above to complete the sentences. Each word can be used once, more than once or not at all.
 (i)   The _____ takes 24 hours to spin on its own axis.   [1]
 (ii) The _____ takes 365 days to orbit the
       _____   [1]
 (iii) The _____ takes 27 days to orbit the
       _____   [1]

 (iv) An eclipse of the Moon occurs when the _____ moves into the shadow of the _____ .   [1]
 (v) An eclipse of the Sun occurs when a shadow of the _____ falls on part of the _____ .   [1]
b) Explain why
 (i)   in summer, daytime lasts longer than night,   [1]
 (ii) we can see the moon,   [1]
 (iii) the shape of the moon appears to change over a four week period.   [1]

WJEC

4 a) The box contains the names of eight of the nine planets in the Solar System.

Earth   Jupiter   Mars   Mercury   Neptune   Pluto   Saturn   Uranus

 (i)   Name the planet which has **not** got its name in the box.   [1]
 (ii) Which planet takes about 365 days to complete its orbit?   [1]
 (iii) Which planet has the shortest orbit?   [1]
 (iv) Which star do **all** the planets orbit?   [1]
 (v) Which planet has the longest orbit?   [1]
 (vi) What is the shape of each orbit?   [1]
b) (i)   We can see the Moon. Explain why.   [2]
 (ii) We can see stars. Explain why.   [2]
 (iii) On some nights we cannot see any stars. Explain why.   [2]
c) Copy and complete each sentence by choosing the correct words from the box. You may use the words once, more than once or not at all.

Big Bang   black hole   galaxy   Milky Way   Solar System   star   Universe

The Sun is at the centre of the _____ which is part of a _____ called the _____ .
This is all part of a much larger system called the
_____ .   [4]

SEG

5

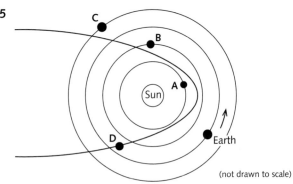

(not drawn to scale)

The diagram shows the orbits of some bodies around the Sun. The arrow shows the direction of the Earth's orbit.
a) Choosing from **A**, **B**, **C** and **D**, state which body is
 (i)   a comet   [1]
 (ii) Venus.   [1]

b) Copy the diagram and **mark on the orbit of A** an arrow to show the direction in which it moves. [1]

c) (i) Describe the shape of the orbit of **D**. [1]

(ii) Name the force which keeps **D** in its orbit. [1]

WJEC

6 a) Astronomers use telescopes to observe stars and galaxies.

(i) What is a galaxy?

(ii) Briefly explain how stars are formed. [3]

b) The Hubble Space Telescope is in orbit around the Earth.

(i) Name the force which keeps the Hubble Telescope in orbit.

(ii) Astronomers can obtain better photographs using the Hubble Telescope than with telescopes on the ground. Explain why. [3]

NEAB

7 a) Explain how the Sun and planets within the Solar system were formed. [1]

b) Describe what you understand by:

(i) a galaxy; [1]

(ii) the Universe. [1]

c) The Sun in our solar system is in the part of its life cycle called the **stable period**. Explain why the Sun is stable. [3]

WJEC

8 a) Nuclear fusion in the Sun releases large amounts of energy.

Explain what is meant by nuclear fusion. [3]

b) Astronomers believe that the Universe is expanding.

(i) State **one** piece of evidence which scientists may use to support this belief.

(ii) How might the Universe have started? [2]

NEAB

9 It is a very clear night. Luke is looking up and sees the Milky Way, a hazy band of light across the night sky.

a) What in the Milky Way produces this hazy band of light? [1]

b) The planet Venus is also seen as a bright speck of light. Explain why Venus shines brightly. [2]

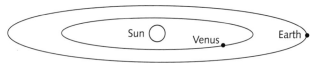

not to scale

c) The diagram shows the orbits of Venus and the Earth about the Sun.

(i) What causes these planets to orbit the Sun? [1]

(ii) Suggest why the orbit time for Venus is less than for the Earth. [2]

d) A year later Luke looks up into the sky from the same place and at the same time of night.

(i) Copy the table and put ticks in the boxes that would fit in with his observations. [1]

	in the same position	in a new position
Venus		
Milky Way		

(ii) Explain Luke's observations. [2]

MEG

10 Read the following passage carefully and then answer the questions which follow it.

*Astronomers believe that the Universe is expanding. Everywhere they look they see that galaxies are moving away from us and away from each other. Edwin Hubble discovered that the greater the distance of the galaxy from us the faster its velocity away from us. In fact the **distance and velocity are directly proportional to one another**, a result known as **Hubble's law**.*

There are great difficulties in making the measurements of distance which are needed to check Hubble's law. One method of measuring this distance relies on looking in the galaxies for stars whose real brightness is known. To understand the idea imagine a town in which all the street lamps are identical. The ones which are furthest away look faintest. One problem is that there are clouds of dust in space which make some stars look fainter than they should be.

Not all the answers to these questions will be found in the passage. Your knowledge of Physics is needed as well.

a) What is a galaxy? [1]

b) The Ursa Major galaxy is 1×10^9 light years away from us and is receding at a velocity of 15 Mm/s. The Hydra galaxy is receding with a velocity of 60 Mm/s. Use Hubble's law to predict the distance of the Hydra galaxy away from us. (The first paragraph of the passage may help you.) [3]

c) Explain **two** problems astronomers have in estimating the distances of galaxies. (The second paragraph of the passage may help you.) [4]

d) How can particular chemical elements be identified in a galaxy? [2]

MEG

Photocopy the list of topics below and tick the boxes of the ones that are included in your examination syllabus. (Your teacher should be able to tell you which they are.) Use your list when you revise. The spread number in brackets tells you where to find more information.

❑ **1** The Sun is a star. (12.01)

❑ **2** The relative sizes and distances apart of the Sun, Earth, and Moon. (12.01)

❑ **3** The Earth's orbit around the Sun. (12.01)

❑ **4** How the Earth's rotation causes day and night. (12.01)

❑ **5** Why a year has different seasons. (12.01)

❑ **6** The Moon's orbit around the Earth. (12.01)

❑ **7** Why we always see the same face of the Moon. (12.01)

❑ **8** Solar eclipses and their cause. (12.01)

❑ **9** Lunar eclipses and their cause. (12.01)

❑ **10** Circular and elliptical orbits. (12.02)

❑ **11** What the Solar System is. (12.02)

❑ **12** The order of the planets in the Solar System. (12.02)

❑ **13** The relative sizes and distances apart of the Sun and planets. (12.02)

❑ **14** The link between a planet's distance from the Sun and the period (time) of its orbit. (12.02)

❑ **15** The link between a planet's distance from the Sun and its surface temperature. (12.02)

❑ **16** The inner planets. (12.02 and 12.03)

❑ **17** The outer planets. (12.02 and 12.03)

❑ **18** The asteroids (minor planets). (12.02 and 12.03)

❑ **19** Comets and their orbits. (12.03 and 12.04)

❑ **20** Meteors and meteorites. (12.03)

❑ **21** Gravity and orbits. (12.04)

❑ **22** Satellites and their uses. (12.04)

❑ **23** The meaning of geostationary orbit. (12.04)

❑ **24** The light year as a unit of length. (12.05)

❑ **25** The distance to the nearest star. (12.05)

❑ **26** The Milky Way. (12.05)

❑ **27** Galaxies. (12.05)

❑ **28** The Universe. (12.05 and 12.07)

❑ **29** Nebulae. (12.05)

❑ **30** The formation of the Sun: the birth of the Solar System. (12.05)

❑ **31** The age of the Sun. (12.05)

❑ **32** Nuclear fusion as the Sun's energy source. (12.06)

❑ **33** Producing nuclear fusion on Earth. (12.06)

❑ **34** The death of a star. (12.06)

❑ **35** Red giants and white dwarfs. (12.06)

❑ **36** Supernovae and the formation of new elements. (12.06)

❑ **37** Neutron stars. (12.06)

❑ **38** The expanding Universe. (12.07)

❑ **39** Red shift and the Doppler effect. (12.07)

❑ **40** The Big Bang theory and the evidence for it. (12.07)

❑ **41** The age of the Universe. (12.07)

❑ **42** The Hubble constant. (12.07)

❑ **43** The fate of the Universe. (12.07)

❑ **44** Constellations. (12.08)

❑ **45** The apparent motion of planets and stars. (12.08)

❑ **46** Estimating the distances to planets, stars, and galaxies. (12.08)

13

History of Key Ideas

- ● CHANGING IDEAS ON FORCE, MOTION, ENERGY, AND HEAT
- ● CHANGING IDEAS ON LIGHT, RADIATION, AND ATOMS
- ● CHANGING IDEAS ON THE EARTH, SUN, PLANETS, STARS, AND UNIVERSE

This ancient stone circle at Stonehenge in Wiltshire, England, was built in about 1500 BC. Its builders left no written records to explain its purpose, although archaelogists think that it was probably used to observe the movements of the Sun and Moon. On Midsummer's Day, the Sun rises over the Heel stone (seen in the foreground), so Stonehenge may have been a gigantic calendar.

Force, motion, and energy

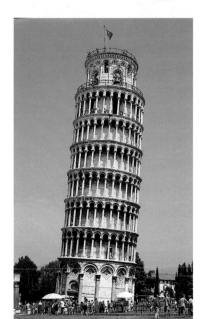

▲ It is said that Galileo investigated the laws of motion by dropping cannon balls from the top of Pisa's famous tower. There is no evidence to support this story. However, Galileo was born in Pisa, Italy (in 1564), and studied and lectured there.

Forces and motion

On Earth, unless there is a force to overcome friction, moving things eventually come to rest. Over 2300 years ago, this led Aristotle and other Greek philosophers to believe that a force was always needed for motion. The more speed something had, the more force it needed. But in the heavens, the Sun, Moon, and stars obeyed different rules. They moved in circles for ever and ever. These ideas were generally accepted until the early 1600s, when Galileo Galilei started to come up with new ideas about motion. From his observations, Galileo deduced that, without friction, sliding objects would keep their speed. Also, all falling objects, light or heavy, would gain speed at the same steady rate.

Our present-day ideas about forces and motion mainly come from Isaac Newton, who put forward his three **laws of motion** in 1687. Our definition of force is based on his second law: force = mass × acceleration. Newton also realized that 'heavenly bodies' did not obey different rules from everything else. The motion of the Moon around the Earth was controlled by the same force – gravity – that made objects fall downwards on Earth. Newton is supposed to have had this idea while watching an apple fall from a tree, although his mathematical treatment of gravity was much more complicated than this simple experience suggests.

In 1905, Albert Einstein put forward his **special theory of relativity**. From this, we now know that, near the speed of light, Newton's second law is no longer valid. However, at the speeds we normally measure on Earth, the law is quite accurate enough.

Energy and heat

The modern, scientific meaning of energy arose in the early 1800s when scientists and engineers were developing ways of measuring the performance of steam engines. Steam engines used forces to move things. They did **work**. To do this, they had to spend **energy**. So it made sense to measure energy and work in the same units (we now use the joule).

▶ A modern replica of Stephenson's *Locomotion*. The original, built in 1825, was used on the world's first public steam railway. The development of steam engines like this led to advances in scientists' understanding of the relationship between work, energy, and heat.

With the idea of energy established, people soon realized that energy could exist in different forms – electrical, potential, kinetic, and so on. However, the law of conservation of energy was not developed until 1847.

Today, we link heat with energy. However, scientists once thought that heat was an invisible, weightless fluid called 'caloric' which flowed out of hot things and was squeezed from solids when they were rubbed. In the 1790s, Count Rumford did some experiments which suggested that the caloric theory was wrong. While boring cannon barrels, he found that he could get an endless supply of heat by keeping the borer turning. If heat was a fluid, then the supply should run out. Instead, the amount of heat seemed to be directly linked with the amount of work being done. The link between work and heat was firmly established in 1849 by James Joule. He found that it always took 4.2 joules of work to produce 1 calorie of heat (an old unit, equivalent to the heat required to increase the temperature of 1 gram of water by 1 °C). However, Joule's work did not explain what heat *was*.

We now know that materials are made up of particles (atoms or molecules) which are in a state of random motion, and that heat is associated with that motion. In a solid or liquid, the particles vibrate. In a gas they move about freely at high speed. The higher the temperature, the faster the particles move. The random motion of the particles is called **thermal activity**, and the energy which an object has because of it is called **internal energy** (the sum of the kinetic and potential energies of all the particles.)

▲ Boring out cannon barrels made them hot. Count Rumford discovered that the amount of heat produced was related to the amount of work done during the boring process.

higher temperature | thermal energy (heat) | lower temperature

If a hot object is put in contact with a colder one, as above, energy is transferred from one to the other because of the temperature difference. This energy is called **heat**. So internal energy is the *total* amount of energy due to thermal activity, while heat represents an amount of energy *transferred*. However, for simplicity, both can be called **thermal energy**.

◄ In engines, releasing thermal energy by burning fuel is one stage in the process of producing motion.

Rays, waves, and particles

Light and radiation

Over 2300 years ago, the Ancient Greeks knew that light travelled in straight lines. The Romans used water-filled glass spheres to magnify things. But it was not until the 1200s that glass lenses were first made, for spectacles. The telescope was invented in the early 1600s. In the same century, Snell discovered the law of refraction, Huyghens suggested that light was a form of wave motion, and Newton demonstrated that white light was a mixture of colours. Newton also tried to explain the nature of light. He thought that light was made up of millions of tiny 'corpuscles' (particles).

▶ One of Newton's experiments. Newton passed white sunlight into a glass prism, and produced a spectrum. When he recombined the colours with a second prism, he obtained white light again. He concluded that the colours must be from the white light and not produced by the glass.

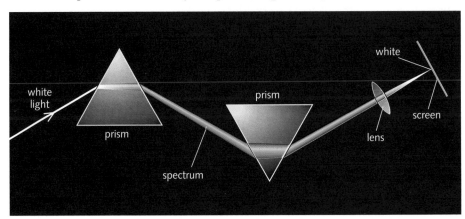

In the early 1800s, Thomas Young investigated the interference and diffraction of light and successfully used the wave theory to explain these effects. From his results, he was also able to calculate a value for the wavelength of light. Young's work seemed to put an end to Newton's 'corpuscles', but these were to appear later in another form. Some materials give off electrons when they absorb light. This is called the **photoelectric effect**. In 1905, Einstein was able to explain it by assuming that light consisted of particle-like bursts of wave energy, called **photons**. Light, it seemed, could behave like waves *and* particles.

James Clerk Maxwell was the first to put forward the idea that light was a type of **electromagnetic radiation**. He did this in 1864. From his theoretical work on electric and magnetic fields, he predicted the existence of electromagnetic waves, calculated what their speed should be, and found that it matched the speed of light. His equations also predicted the existence of radio waves, although 'real' radio waves were not detected until the 1880s. X-rays were discovered by Wilhelm Röntgen in 1895, but their electromagnetic nature was not established until 1912.

In 1896, Henri Becquerel detected a penetrating radiation coming from uranium salts. He had discovered **radioactivity**. Later, Marie Curie showed that the radiation came from within the atom and was not due to reactions with other materials. In 1899, Ernest Rutherford investigated radioactivity and identified two types of radiation, which he called alpha and beta. The following year, he discovered gamma rays. Today, we know that waves, such as gamma radiation, can behave like particles, and that particles can also behave like waves. Scientists call this **wave-particle duality**.

Marie Curie in her laboratory

Atoms and electrons

The word 'atom' comes from the Greek *atomos*, meaning indivisible. The first modern use of the word was by John Dalton, who put forward his atomic theory in 1803, in order to explain the rules governing the proportions in which different elements combined chemically. Dalton suggested that all matter consisted of tiny particles called atoms. Each element had its own type of atom, and atoms of the same element were identical. Atoms could not be created or destroyed, nor could they be broken into smaller bits.

But what were atoms made of? The first clues came in the 1890s, when scientists were studying the conduction of electricity through gases. They found that atoms could give out invisible, negatively charged rays. J. J. Thomson investigated the rays and deduced that they were particles much lighter than atoms. This was in 1897. Thomson had discovered the **electron**.

If an atom contained electrons, it must also contain positive charge to make it electrically neutral. But where was this charge? In 1911, a team led by Ernest Rutherford directed alpha particles at thin gold foil. They found that most passed straight through but a few were deflected at huge angles. To explain this, Rutherford suggested that each atom must be largely empty space, with its positive charge and most of its mass concentrated in a tiny **nucleus**.

Ernest Rutherford (right) and his assistant Hans Geiger, in 1912. They are standing next to the apparatus which they used for detecting alpha particles.

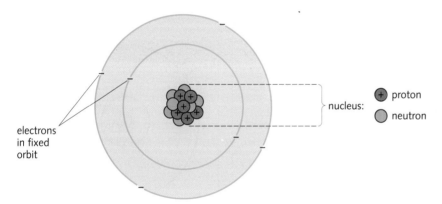

electrons in fixed orbit

nucleus: (+) proton ( ) neutron

◀ The Rutherford-Bohr model of the atom (with nuclear particles included). The picture is not to scale. With an atom of the size shown, the nucleus would be far too small to see.

In Rutherford's model (picture) of the atom, electrons orbited the nucleus like planets around the Sun. Unfortunately, the model had a serious flaw: according to classical theory, an orbiting electron ought to radiate energy continuously and spiral into the nucleus, so its orbit could not be stable. In 1913, Neils Bohr used the **quantum theory** to solve this problem. According to Bohr, electrons were in fixed orbits and could not radiate continuously. They could only lose energy by jumping to a lower orbit and emitting a quantum ('packet') of electromagnetic energy – in other words, a photon. Using this model, Bohr was able to predict the positions of the lines in the hydrogen spectrum. However, his calculations did not work for elements with a more complicated electron structure. To deal with this problem, scientists later developed a mathematical, **wave-mechanics** model of the atom.

The Rutherford-Bohr model of the atom said nothing about what was inside the nucleus. However, in 1919, Rutherford used alpha particles to knock positively charged particles out of the nucleus. These were **protons**. In 1932, James Chadwick discovered that the nucleus also contained **neutrons**. In recent years, experiments with particle accelerators have suggested that protons and neutrons are made from particles called **quarks**.

Richard Feynmann giving a lecture at the California Institute of Technology. Advances made by Professor Feynmann in quantum electrodynamics won him the 1965 Nobel Prize for Physics.

309

13.03 The Earth and beyond

The centre of the Universe?

The ancient view of the Earth was that it was flat. However, by about 600 BC, Greek mariners had observed how the positions the stars altered as they sailed north or south, and realized that the Earth's surface must be curved. Around 350 BC, Aristotle believed that the Earth was a stationary sphere at the centre of the Universe. The Sun, Moon, planets, and stars lay on transparent, crystal spheres which rotated about the Earth, so they moved in perfect circles.

The idea that the 'heavenly bodies' must move in perfect circles around the Earth was to cause difficulties for many centuries. When viewed from Earth, the planets do not move across the sky at a steady rate, and sometimes appear to move backwards and forwards. Around 150 AD, Ptolemy came up with an elaborate explanation for this. The planets *did* move in perfect circles, but sometimes they followed small circles superimposed on a larger one.

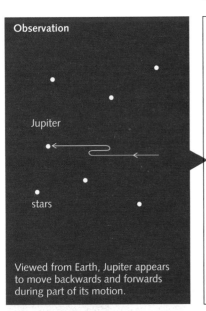

Observation

Jupiter

stars

Viewed from Earth, Jupiter appears to move backwards and forwards during part of its motion.

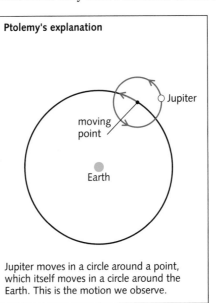

Ptolemy's explanation

Jupiter

moving point

Earth

Jupiter moves in a circle around a point, which itself moves in a circle around the Earth. This is the motion we observe.

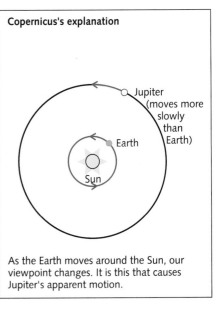

Copernicus's explanation

Jupiter (moves more slowly than Earth)

Earth

Sun

As the Earth moves around the Sun, our viewpoint changes. It is this that causes Jupiter's apparent motion.

▲ Galileo using a telescope he designed and built himself.

It was not until the 1500s that the views of Aristotle and Ptolemy were seriously questioned. The person responsible was Nicolaus Copernicus, who decided to take a fresh look at the problem of the observed motion of the planets. In 1543, he published his theory that the Sun must be at the centre of the Universe, with the Earth and planets moving around it. Over the following years, this idea was strongly opposed by the Church, which insisted that the Earth must be central. Later, Galileo supported Copernicus's ideas, but was forced to renounce them or risk torture and execution. In 1610, he had observed tiny moons moving around Jupiter – evidence that the Earth was not central to all objects in the heavens.

During the late 1500s, observations made by Tycho Brahe greatly increased the amount of accurate data on the positions of the planets. During the 1600s, the evidence for the Copernican model became overwhelming. Kepler established the laws of planetary orbits, Newton published his theory of gravitation, and put Kepler's laws on a firm mathematical basis.

◀ When William Herschel built this reflecting telescope in 1789, it was the largest in the world. It could be raised or lowered by pulleys, and there were rollers under the platform so that it could be turned.

Caroline Herschel, William's sister, was also an expert astronomer. She discovered comets and nebulae, and made a huge catalogue of her brother's observations.

Sun, stars, and galaxies

By the late 1600s, it was clear that the stars were similar to the Sun, but much further away. In the late 1700s, William Herschel used a large telescope to study how the stars were distributed. He concluded that the Sun was near the centre of a huge, lens-shaped system of stars, which he called the **Galaxy**.

By the early 1800s, astronomers were making increasingly accurate estimates of the distances to the stars. These were based on the following principle. During the course of a year, as the Earth moves round the Sun, our viewpoint in space changes, so nearby stars appear to move against the background of very distant stars. This apparent movement is called **parallax**. By measuring it, the distance to nearby stars can be calculated using trigonometry.

In 1918, Harlow Shapley mapped the relative distances of star clusters and found that the Sun was not at the centre of our Galaxy after all. And in the 1920s, Edwin Hubble discovered that our Galaxy was not alone. There were millions of other galaxies in the Universe. Hubble also made another significant discovery about galaxies. From the altered wavelengths of their light, he concluded that they must be rushing away from each other. This discovery led to the development of the **Big Bang theory** – the idea that, billions of years ago, the whole of space and everything in it started to expand from a single, atom-sized concentration of matter and energy.

The Hubble Space Telescope is in orbit around the Earth. It transmits pictures back to the ground which enable astronomers to see distant stars and galaxies without the distorting effects of the Earth's atmosphere.

13.04 Key developments in physics

c. 400 BC	Democritus suggests that there might be a limit to the divisibility of matter. (*Atomos* is the Greek word for indivisible.)
c. 350 BC	Aristotle suggests that the Earth is at the centre of the Universe, with the Sun, Moon, and planets on crystal spheres around it.
c. 240 BC	Eratosthenes estimates the diameter of the Earth by comparing shadow angles in different places.
AD	
c. 60	Hero makes a small turbine driven by jets of steam.
c. 150	Ptolemy suggests that the Earth is at the centre of the Universe, and that the Sun, Moon, and planets are moving in perfect circles.
c. 1000	Magnetic compass used in China.
1543	Copernicus suggests that the Sun is at the centre of the Universe, with the Earth and planets moving around it.
1600	Gilbert suggests that the Earth acts like a giant bar magnet.
1604	Galileo shows that all falling objects should have the same, steady acceleration.
1621	Snell states his law of refraction.
1644	Torricelli makes the first mercury barometer.
1654	Guericke demonstrates atmospheric pressure.
1662	Boyle states his law for gases.
1678	Huyghens puts forward his wave theory of light.
1679	Hooke states his law for elastic materials.
1687	Newton publishes his theory of gravity and laws of motion.
1714	Fahrenheit makes the first mercury thermometer.
1752	Franklin performs a hazardous experiment with a kite to show that lightning is electricity.
c. 1790	Herschel discovers the shape of our galaxy.
1800	Volta makes the first battery.
1803	Dalton suggests that matter is made up of atoms.
	Young demonstrates the wave nature of light.
1821	Faraday makes a simple form of electric motor.
1825	Ampère works out a law for the force between current-carrying conductors.
1827	Ohm states his law for metal conductors.
1832	Faraday demonstrates electromagnetic induction.
1832	Sturgeon makes the first moving-coil meter.
1840	First use of the words 'physicist' and 'scientist'.
1849	Fizeau measures the speed of light.
	Joule establishes the link between heat and work.

1852	Kelvin states the law of conservation of energy.
1864	Maxwell predicts the existence of radio waves and other electromagnetic waves.
1877	Cailletet liquefies oxygen.
1879	Swan and Edison make the first electric light bulbs.
1888	Hertz demonstrates the existence of radio waves.
1894	Marconi transmits the first radio signals.
1895	Röntgen discovers X-rays.
1896	Becquerel discovers radioactivity.
1897	Thomson discovers the electron.
1898	M. Curie discovers radium and polonium.
1899	Rutherford identifies alpha and beta rays.
1900	Planck proposes the quantum theory.
1905	Einstein uses the quantum theory to explain the photoelectric effect, and publishes his special theory of relativity.
1911	Rutherford proposes a nuclear model of the atom.
1913	Bohr uses the quantum theory to modify Rutherford's model of the atom.
1916	Einstein publishes his general theory of relativity.
1919	Rutherford splits the atom and discovers the proton.
1924	De Broglie suggests that particles can behave as waves.
1925	Schrödinger develops a wave-mechanics model of the atom.
1927	Lemaitre suggests the possibility of the Big Bang.
1928	Geiger and Müller invent their radiation detector.
1929	Hubble discovers that the Universe is expanding.
1932	Chadwick discovers the neutron.
	Cockroft and Walton produce the first nuclear change using a particle accelerator.
1938	Hahn discovers nuclear fission.
1942	Fermi builds the first nuclear reactor.
1947	Bardeen, Brattain, and Shockley make the first transistor.
1957	First artificial satellite, Sputnik I, put into orbit.
1958	St Clair Kilby makes the first integrated circuit.
1960	Maiman builds the first laser.
1963	First geostationary communications satellite.
1969	First manned landing on the Moon.
1971	Intel Corporation makes the first microprocessor.
1977	First experimental evidence of quarks.
1990	Hubble Space Telescope launched.

Source: *the Biographical Encyclopedia of Scientists*, published by the Institute of Physics   *c.* = *circa* (about)

14

Experimental Physics

- SAFETY IN THE LABORATORY   ● PREPARING FOR AN EXPERIMENTAL ENQUIRY
- GETTING EVIDENCE   ● DEALING WITH EVIDENCE   ● EVALUATING EVIDENCE
- SUGGESTIONS FOR EXPERIMENTAL ENQUIRIES   ● KEY EXPERIMENTAL SKILLS CHECKLIST

The worker inside the cage is quite safe, despite the 2.5 million volt sparks from the huge Van de Graaff generator. The electric discharges strike the metal bars, rather than pass between them, so the cage has a shielding effect. In fact, if safety procedures were ignored, some of the experiments done in a school laboratory would be much more dangerous than this one.

Safety in the laboratory

When doing any experimental work, the most important thing of all is safety. Here are some dos and don'ts:

General

● When moving around the laboratory, always walk. Don't run.

● Keep bags and coats away from the work area, so that they can't catch fire or be pushed against equipment.

● Keep bags and coats off the floor so that people can't trip over them.

● Never take food or drink into the laboratory.

Bunsens and tripods

● If a bunsen burner is alight, but not in use, always leave it on the yellow flame setting so that the flame can be seen.

● Make sure that bunsens and tripods have a heatproof mat underneath.

● Give a hot tripod plenty of time to cool down before attempting to move it.

● Don't attempt to move a tripod when there is a beaker resting on it.

Glass thermometers

● Don't put glass thermometers where they can roll off the bench.

● Keep glass thermometers away from bunsen flames.

● Support thermometers safely: see **Safe support** below.

● Mercury, used in some thermometers, is toxic. If a thermometer breaks and mercury runs out, don't handle it.

Glass tubing

● Never attempt to push glass tubing (or glass thermometers) through a hole in a bung. The laboratory technician has a special tool for doing this.

● Always handle hot glass tubing with tongs. Rest it in on a heatproof mat; don't put it straight on the bench.

● Hot glass tubing can stay hot for a long time. Give it plenty of time to cool down before you attempt to pick it up.

Safe support

● When clamping a test-tube, don't overtighten the clamp. And make sure that the clamp has soft pads to touch against the glass. This also applies when clamping a glass thermometer.

● In experiments where you have to suspend a load, make sure that the supporting clampstand is stable enough to take the heaviest load you will be using. You may need to weigh it down for this.

A yellow bunsen flame is easier to see than a blue one.

In experiments like this, make sure that the apparatus is stable enough to support the heaviest load.

Electricity

- Before making any changes to the wiring in your circuits, always switch off the power or disconnect the battery.

- Remember: low voltage circuits may not give you a shock, but they can cause burns if the current is too high and a wire overheats.

- Never make a direct connection across the terminals of a battery. Don't put wires or tools where they might connect across the terminals.

- If a mains appliance is faulty, switch off the power and pull out the plug. Don't change the fuse. Ask the laboratory technician to deal with the fault.

- Electrical fires: see **Fire** below.

In many modern laboratories, the mains circuits are protected by RCDs (residual current devices), so the risk of shocks is reduced. But...

- If someone has been electrocuted, and is still touching the faulty appliance, don't touch the person. Switch off the power and pull out the plug.

Emergency! But the first job is to switch off the power and pull out the plug.

Eye protection

- Always wear eye protection (e.g. safety goggles) when:
  - stretching metal wires or plastic cords
  - breaking or grinding solids (e.g. rock samples)
  - heating liquids
  - dealing with acids, alkalis, or any other liquid chemicals that might splash.

Light

- Don't look directly into a laser beam or other source of bright light. Don't stand where laser light might be reflected into your eyes.

- If you need to study the Sun's image, project it onto a card. Never look through a telescope or binoculars pointing straight at the Sun – even if there is a filter in front.

Radioactive sources

- The radioactive sources used in school laboratories should always be sealed.

- Radioactive sources should be kept well away from the body, and never place where they are pointing at people.

Fire

- Don't heat flammable liquids (e.g. methylated spirits) over a bunsen. If heating is required, a water bath should be used – with hot water heated well away from the experiment.

- Don't throw water on burning liquids (e.g. methylated spirits). Smother the fire with a fire blanket or use a carbon dioxide extinguisher.

- Don't throw water on electrical fires. Switch off the supply and use a carbon dioxide extinguisher.

flammable liquid

hot water

The only safe way to heat a flammable liquid is to use a water bath.

Experimental enquiry (1) – preparing

This spread should help you plan an experimental enquiry. The handwritten notes show part of one student's commentary on her enquiry.

Presenting the problem
Start by describing the problem you are going to investigate, and the main features of the method you will use to tackle it.

> I am going to investigate how the resistance of nichrome wire depends on its length.
>
> I know that resistance can be calculated with this equation:
>
> $$\text{resistance (in } \Omega) = \frac{\text{voltage (in V)}}{\text{current (in A)}}$$
>
> So to find the resistance of a length of nichrome wire, I need to put the wire in a circuit, then measure the voltage across it and the current through it. I will do this for different lengths of nichrome.

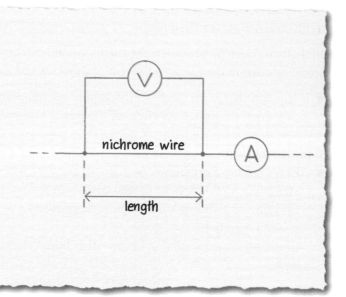

> I think I can predict how the resistance will vary with length. If the length of wire is doubled, the current (flow of electrons) has to be pushed between twice as many atoms. So I would expect the resistance to double as well.

Making a prediction
You may have an idea of what you expect to happen in your enquiry. This prediction is called your **hypothesis**. You should write it down. It may not be right! It is just an idea. The aim of your enquiry is to test it.

Dealing with variables
Quantities like length, current, and voltage are called **variables**. They can *change* from one situation to another.

Key variables These are the variables that can affect what happens in an experiment. You must decide what they are. For example, in the nichrome wire experiment, length is one of the key variables because changing the length of wire changes the resistance.

> In my experiment, three of the key variables are:
>
> <u>length</u> of nichrome wire – to be measured with a ruler marked in mm
>
> <u>voltage</u> – to be measured with a voltmeter
>
> <u>current</u> – to be measured with an ammeter
>
> I shall start with 50cm of thin nichrome wire, put a voltage of 6V across it, and measure the current through it. From the voltmeter and ammeter readings, I can calculate the resistance.
>
> I will take more sets of readings, shortening the wire by 5cm each time until it is only 10cm long.
>
> For convenience, I will probably keep the voltage fixed at 6V throughout the experiment.

You must also decide how to measure the variables, and over what range. For example, in planning the nichrome wire experiment, you would have to:

- decide what the highest voltage and current values should be (safety must be considered here)
- decide what lengths of wire to use.

Controlling variables Some variables don't have to be measured, but they do need to be controlled. For example, in the nichrome wire experiment, you might want to keep the wire at a steady temperature, in case the temperature affects the resistance.

Some variables can be difficult to control. In your experiment, you may want to use the same thickness of nichrome wire each time, but this depends on how accurately the wire was manufactured. You must take factors like this into account when deciding how reliable your results are.

A fair test When doing an experiment, you should change just one variable at a time and find out how it affects one other. If lots of variables change at once, it will not be a fair test. For example, if you want to find out how the length of a wire affects its resistance, it wouldn't be fair to compare a long, thick wire with short, thin one.

Final preparations

Decide what equipment you need, how you will arrange it, and how you will use it.

To help your planning, you may need to carry out a trial run of the experiment. Before you do this, make sure that all your procedures are safe.

Prepare tables for your readings *before* you start your experiments. Look at the next spread on **getting the evidence** before doing this.

> Equipment needed:
>
> voltmeter (0–6V), ammeter (0–3A), 50cm of 0.28mm diameter nichrome wire, ...

nichrome: length cm	voltage V	current A	resistance Ω
50			
45			
40			
35			
30			
25			
20			

> There are two more variables I need to control:
>
> temperature – I know from reference books that the resistance of nichrome changes with temperature. So I will use a large beaker of cold water to keep the temperature of the nichrome steady.
>
> diameter (thickness) of nichrome wire – this could affect the resistance. To make sure that I have the same diameter all the time, I will use lengths of wire taken from the same reel, and check each piece with a gauge before using it.

> I will set up this circuit:

> I am not sure how big the maximum current will be, so I will do a trial run of the experiment first. I will start with an ammeter that can measure several amperes, but may be able to change to a more sensitive meter for the main experiment.
>
> Safety:
> I must make sure that the power supply is switched off before I remove the nichrome wire to change its length.

Experimental enquiry (2) – getting the evidence

voltage	
V	
2.3	
2.1	

Remember to include a unit in the heading at the top of each column.

You can only read this voltmeter to the nearest 0.1 V.

This spread should help you take and record measurements correctly.

Units

When you write down a measurement, remember to include the unit. For example:

voltage = 2.3 V

If you just write down '2.3', you may not be able to remember whether this was supposed to be a voltage of 2.3 V or 2.3 mV.

When writing measurements in a table, you don't need to put the unit after each number. But be sure to include the unit in the heading at the top of each column. You can see an example on the left.

Uncertainties

No measurement is exact. There is always some **uncertainty** about it. For example, you may only be able to read a voltmeter to the nearest 0.1 V.

Say that you measure a voltage of 2.3 V and a current of 1.2 A. To work out the resistance in ohms (Ω), you divide the voltage by the current on a calculator and get...

1.916 666 7

This should be recorded as 1.9 Ω. Uncertainties in your voltage and current readings mean that you cannot justify including any more figures. In this case, you are giving the result to two **significant figures**.

Taking enough readings

For a graph, you should have at least five sets of readings.

Not all experiments give you readings for a graph. Sometimes, you have to measure quantities that don't change – the diameter of a wire for example. In cases like this, you should repeat the measurement at least three times and find an average. Repeating a measurement helps you spot mistakes. It also gives you some idea of the uncertainty. Look at this example.

The diameter of a wire was measured four times:

1.41 mm   1.34 mm   1.19 mm   1.30 mm

You can work out the average like this:

$$\text{average} = \frac{(1.41 + 1.34 + 1.19 + 1.30)}{4} = 1.31 \text{ mm}$$

The original four numbers ranged from less than 1.2 to more than 1.4. So, the last figure, 1, in the average of 1.31, is completely uncertain. Therefore, you should write down the average diameter as 1.3 mm.

Reading scales

On many instruments, you have to judge the position of a pointer or level on a scale and work out the measurement from that. Here are some ways of making sure that you take the correct reading:

A Using a glass thermometer to measure the temperature of a liquid: keep the liquid well stirred, give the thermometer time to reach the temperature, and keep the bulb of the thermometer in the liquid while you take the reading.

B Using a ruler: be sure that the scale is right alongside the point you are trying to measure.

C Measuring a liquid level on a scale: look at the level of the liquid's flat surface, not its curved meniscus.

D Reading a meter: look at the pointer and scale 'square on'. (The pointer may have a flat end like that shown here, so that you can look at it edge on.)

A

B

C

D

Can you read the instruments below correctly? The answers are on page 333.

14.04 Experimental enquiry (3) – handling the evidence

I have used my voltage and current readings to calculate the resistance of each length of nichrome wire. Now I shall use these values to plot a graph of resistance against length.

Length is the <u>independent</u> variable (the one I chose to change), so it goes along the bottom axis. Resistance goes up the side.

The points on my graph are a little scattered, but I think that the line of best fit is a straight line.

This line ought to go through the origin. If the wire has zero length, there is no metal to resist the current, so the resistance should also be zero.

I have rejected one point on my graph. In my table, the current reading for that point seems far too low. I probably misread the ammeter.

As the graph is a straight line through the origin, the resistance of the nichrome wire is in direct proportion to its length. This agrees with my original hypothesis that doubling the length of wire ought to make it twice as difficult to push electrons through.

This page should help you to analyse your data and draw conclusions from it. The handwritten notes show part of one student's commentary on her enquiry.

Drawing a graph

A graph can help you see trends in your data.

Choosing axes Decide which variable to put along the bottom axis. Usually, it is the one you chose to vary by set amounts – the length of nichrome wire, for example. This is the **independent variable**. The resistance would be the **dependent variable** because its value depends on the length you chose. It goes up the side axis.

Choosing scales Check your highest readings, then choose the largest scales you can for your axes.

Labelling axes Along each axis, write in what is being measured and the units being used.

Drawing the best line Because of uncertainties, the points on a graph will be uneven. So don't join up the points! Instead, draw the straight line or smooth curve that goes closest to most of them. This is called a **line of best fit**. Before you draw it:

- Decide whether the line should go through the origin.
- Decide whether any readings should be rejected. Some may be so far out that they are probably due to mistakes rather than uncertainties. See if you can find out why they occurred.

From the way points scatter about a line of best fit, you can see how reliable your readings are. But for this, you need plenty of points.

Trends and conclusions

From the shape of your graph, you can draw conclusions about the data.

The simplest form of graph is a straight line through the origin. A graph of resistance against length of wire might be like this. If so, it means that if the length doubles, the resistance doubles... and so on. in this case, resistance and length are in **direct proportion**.

If you think that your graph supports your original prediction, then say so and explain your reasons.

Experimental enquiry (4) – evaluating the evidence

This page should help you decide how reliable your conclusions are, and how your enquiry could be improved or extended.

> The points on the graph are uneven. But as they zig–zag at random, I am fairly sure that, without uncertainties, they would lie on a straight line.
>
> There are several reasons why the points may have been so scattered...

> To get a more reliable graph, I need to find a more accurate method of measuring resistance...

> To extend my enquiry, I could find out how the resistance of the nichrome wire depends on the diameter...

Reliability

In reaching your conclusions, remember that there are uncertainties in your measurements, and variables that you may not have allowed for. So your results can never *prove* your original prediction. You must decide how far they *support* it.

If you think that your results are unreliable in any way, see if you can explain why.

You may have some results which do not agree with the others and look like mistakes. These are called **anomalous results**. Try to explain what caused them.

Suggesting improvements

Having completed your enquiry, suggest ways of improving it so that your conclusions are more reliable.

Looking further

Suggest some further work which might produce extra evidence or take your enquiry further.

Writing your report

The student's commentary was designed to help you understand the different stages of an enquiry. It includes far more detail than you would normally put in a report.

When producing your own report, these are the things you *should* include:

Planning   1
- A description of what the enquiry is about.
- A prediction of what you think will happen, and why.
- A list of key variables, and a description of how you will measure or control each one.
- A list of the equipment needed.
- Diagrams showing how the equipment will be set up.
- A description of what you plan to do.

Getting evidence   2
- A description of what you did, including comments about any difficulties and how you overcame them.
- Tables showing all measurements, including units.

Analysing and concluding   3
- Graphs and charts.
- Calculations based on your data.
- A conclusion, including details of:
    – what you found out.
    – whether your findings matched your prediction.

Evaluating   4
- Comments about:
    – how reliable you think your results were
    – any anomalous results, and their possible causes
    – how your enquiry could be improved
    – further work that could be done.

14.06 Some experimental enquiries

Here are some suggestions for practical work. Some are full enquiries. Others are shorter exercises to help you develop your experimental skills.

Measuring newspaper

Plan and carry out experiments to measure:
a) the thickness of one sheet of newspaper **b)** the mass of one sheet of newspaper **c)** the density of the paper used.

Start by thinking about the following:
If a single sheet is too thin to measure accurately, how can you improve the accuracy?

Wet or dry?

The makers of a well-known brand of soft tissue paper claim that their tissues are just as strong wet as dry. Are they right? Plan and carry out an enquiry to test their claim.

Start by thinking about the following:
What is meant by the 'strength' of a tissue? Do you need use a whole tissue? When comparing tissues, how can you make sure that your test is fair?

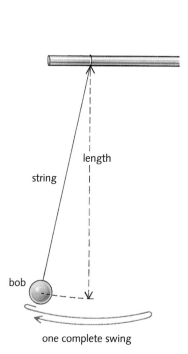

Fine or coarse?

Coarse glasspaper ('sandpaper') rubs through a wooden surface more quickly than fine glasspaper. But does it produce more friction? Plan and carry out experiments to find out.

Start by thinking about the following:
How can you measure the frictional force when glasspaper is rubbed on wood? How can you keep the glasspaper pressed against the wood? Will the force used to press the glasspaper against the wood affect the result? How can you make sure that your test is fair?

string

length

bob

one complete swing

Pendulum

The time of one complete swing of a pendulum is called its period.
The period of swing *might* be affected by these factors: the mass of the bob, the amplitude (size) of the swing, the length of the pendulum.

Plan and carry out an enquiry to find out which factors affect the period.

Start by thinking about the following:
The period of your pendulum will probably be a couple of seconds at most. How are you going to find the time of one swing accurately? How are you going to measure the size of the swing?

Note: make sure that the top of the pendulum string is firmly held so that there is no movement at that point.

Further work:
Find out how the period of one pendulum compares with another of four times the length. Is there a simple connection between the length and the period? Does the connection work for other lengths as well?

Stretching rubber

A company wants to market a cheap spring balance for weighing letters. Their designer suggests that, to save money, they could use a rubber band instead of a spring. Their technician says that this would be unsatisfactory because rubber bands change length and 'springiness' once they have been stretched. Who is correct? Plan and carry out an enquiry to find out.

Find the mass

Plan and carry out an experiment to find the mass of a lump of Plasticine (or some other solid). You are not allowed to use a balance with a mass scale already marked on it. And you are not allowed to use slotted masses of less than 50 g.

Further work:

Take the problem a stage further. Plan and carry out experiments to measure a much smaller mass – such as the mass of a pen or pencil.

This time, you can use a selection of standard masses down to 5 g.

Start by thinking about the following:

Your original design will probably not be sensitive enough to measure a small mass. Can it be modified in some way to make it more sensitive?

Bouncing ball

Some table tennis balls have more 'bounce' than others. Plan and carry out an enquiry to compare the bounce of two table tennis balls.

Start by thinking about the following:

What is meant by 'bounce'? What do you need to measure? When comparing the balls, how can you make sure that your test is fair?

Parachute design

The diagram on the right shows a simple model parachute. Plan and carry out an enquiry to find out if there is a link between the design of the parachute and the speed at which it falls.

Start by thinking about the following:

Shape and area are two possible features of the design. Will you investigate both? How will you make sure that your tests are fair? How will you work out the speed of fall?

Double-glazing

In cooler countries, people fit double-glazing in their houses because two layers of glass, with air between, are supposed to lose thermal energy (heat) more slowly than a single layer. But does double-glazing cut down thermal energy loss? Plan and carry out an enquiry to find out.

Start by thinking about the following:

How are you going to set up a double layer of glass with air between? What will you use as a source of thermal energy? How will you tell whether the flow of thermal energy is reduced when the extra layer of glass is added? Will your test be fair?

glass

glass

air

Salt on ice

During winter, salt is often sprayed on the roads to melt the ice. Pure ice has a melting point of 0°C. Adding salt to ice affects the melting point.

Plan and carry out experiments to find out how the melting point of ice changes when salt is mixed in. Find out if there is a connection between the melting point and the concentration of salt in the ice. (The concentration can be measured in grams of salt per cm^3 of ice.)

Start by thinking about the following:
How will you make sure that the salt and ice are properly mixed? How are you going to measure the melting point?

The speed of sound

length of air column

In the diagram on the left, someone is holding a vibrating tuning fork above a measuring cylinder. Sound waves travel down the cylinder and back, and make the air inside vibrate. If the length of the air column is exactly a quarter of the wavelength of the sound, the air vibrations are strongest and the air gives out its loudest note. The effect is called resonance.

The speed of sound is linked to its frequency and wavelength by this equation:

$$\text{speed (m/s)} = \text{frequency (Hz)} \times \text{wavelength (m)}$$

Using the information above, plan and carry out an enquiry to find the speed of sound in air.

Start by thinking about the following:
As a measuring cylinder has a fixed length, how will you vary the length of the air column inside?

Apparent depth

The person in the diagram on the left is looking at a pin on the bottom of a beaker of water. Light from the pin is refracted (bent) when it leaves the water. As a result, the water looks less deep than it really is and the pin appears closer to the surface than it really is.

Plan and carry out an experiment to find the apparent depth of some water in a beaker.

Start by thinking about the following:
If you look at a pin in some water, it is an image of the pin which you are seeing. How can you locate the position of this image? Could you use a similar method to that used to find the position of an image in a mirror?

Two pairs or one?

People claim that two pairs of socks are warmer than one. But does an extra pair cut down the loss of thermal energy (heat)? Plan and carry out an enquiry to find out. (You do not have to use warm feet as your source of thermal energy!)

Start by thinking about the following:
How are you going to tell that one object is losing heat more rapidly than another? How will you make sure that your test is fair?

Image size and distance

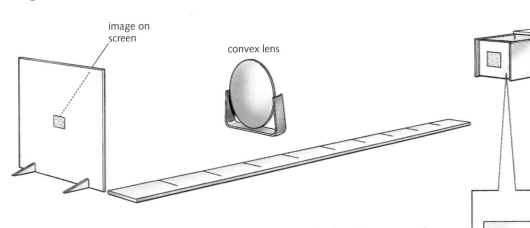

Place a bright object well away from a convex lens as in the diagram, and you can get a clear image on a screen. If you move the object closer, the size and the position of the image both change, and you need to move the screen to get a clear image again.

Is there a connection between the size of the image and its distance from the lens? Plan and carry out an enquiry to find out.

Current–voltage investigations

Plan and carry out experiments to find out how the current through each of the following depends on the voltage across it:

1) nichrome wire, kept at constant temperature
2) the filament of a bulb
3) a semiconductor diode.

Start by thinking about the following:
How will you vary the voltage across each component and measure the current through it? What checks must you do to make sure that the current through each component is safe, and does not cause damage?

Making a resistor

Resistors are used for keeping voltages and currents at correct levels in electronic circuits.

Using nichrome wire, make a resistor with a resistance of $5\,\Omega$.

Start by thinking about the following:
How does the length of wire affect its resistance? How is resistance calculated? What circuit will you use to test the nichrome? From your measurements, how can you work out how much wire you need?

Thermistor investigation

Thermistors have a resistance that varies considerably with temperature. They can be used as temperature sensors. Plan and carry out an experiment to find out how the resistance of a thermistor varies between $0\,°C$ and $100\,°C$.

Start by thinking about the following:
How will you change and control the temperature of the thermistor? How will you measure the resistance of the thermistor? How will you make sure that your circuit doesn't heat up the thermistor?

14.07 # Key experimental skills checklist

Planning

In planning an experimental enquiry, you should be able to:

a turn an idea into a form that can be investigated. .... ☐

b carry out trial runs if necessary. .... ☐

c make predictions, where appropriate. .... ☐

d decide what the key factors (e.g. key variables) are. .... ☐

e plan how to vary or control the key variables. .... ☐

f decide on the range and number of measurements needed. .... ☐

g decide how much evidence you will need, and recognize which
variables may be difficult to control. .... ☐

h select equipment, and plan how to use it – safely. .... ☐

Getting evidence

In getting your evidence, you should be able to:

a use the equipment safely, and with skill. .... ☐

b make accurate measurements. .... ☐

c make enough measurements to produce reliable evidence. .... ☐

d consider what uncertainties there are. .... ☐

e repeat measurements as necessary. .... ☐

f record measurements clearly. .... ☐

Analysing and concluding

In analysing your evidence and reaching conclusions, you should be able to:

a present data clearly. .... ☐

b present data in the form of a graph using a line of best fit. .... ☐

c identify trends or patterns in your data. .... ☐

d use a graph to identify how variables are related. .... ☐

e present numerical results to an appropriate level of accuracy. ...... ☐

f check that your conclusions match the evidence. .... ☐

g explain whether or not your results match your original prediction. ... ☐

h explain your conclusions, if you can, using your knowledge of physics. ☐

Evaluating

In evaluating your enquiry, you should be able to:

a decide whether you have enough evidence to reach a firm conclusion. ☐

b decide whether any results should be rejected, and if so, why. ...... ☐

c decide, from the uncertainties, how reliable your results are. .... ☐

d suggest improvements to the methods you have used. .... ☐

e suggest further work that could produce extra evidence or take
your enquiry further. .... ☐

Electrical symbols and codes

Electrical symbols

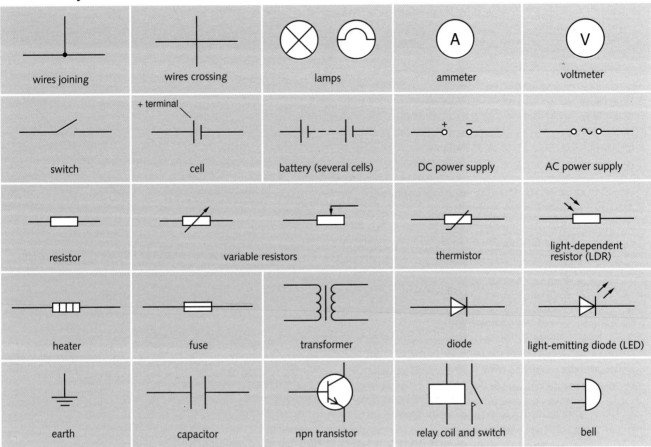

wires joining	wires crossing	lamps	ammeter	voltmeter
switch	cell (+ terminal)	battery (several cells)	DC power supply	AC power supply
resistor	variable resistors		thermistor	light-dependent resistor (LDR)
heater	fuse	transformer	diode	light-emitting diode (LED)
earth	capacitor	npn transistor	relay coil and switch	bell

Resistor codes

The resistance of a resistor in ohms (Ω) is normally marked on it using one of these codes:

The resistor is marked with coloured rings. Each colour stands for a number:

black	0
brown	1
red	2
orange	3
yellow	4
green	5
blue	6
violet	7
grey	8
white	9

You 'read' the first three rings like this:

first figure   second figure   number of noughts

red   violet   orange
2   7   000

So: resistance = 27 000 Ω
              = 27 kΩ

The fourth ring gives the **tolerance**. This tells you by how much the resistance may differ from the marked value:

gold ±5%   silver ±10%   no colour ±20%

The resistance is printed on the resistor:

R27 means 0.27 Ω
2R7 means 2.7 Ω
3K0 means 3.0 Ω
5K6 means 5.6 Ω
47K means 47 kΩ
2M2 means 2.2 MΩ

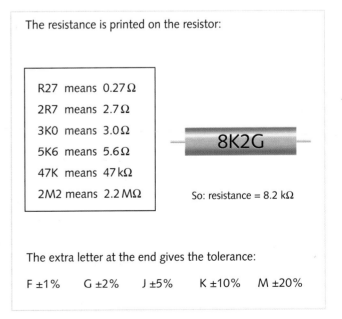

8K2G

So: resistance = 8.2 kΩ

The extra letter at the end gives the tolerance:

F ±1%   G ±2%   J ±5%   K ±10%   M ±20%

1 The diagram shows a crane lifting a load of 30 000 N through a distance of 10 metres.

How much useful work does the crane do on the load?
A 3 000 J
B 3 000 N/m
C 300 000 J
D 300 000 N   [L. EXAM.]

2 Which of these (**A**, **B**, **C** or **D**) involves most power?
A a force of 10 N moving 10 m in 10 s
B a force of 20 N moving 5 m in 10 s
C a force of 10 N moving 5 m in 5 s
D a force of 10 N moving 10 m in 5 s   [L. EXAM.]

3 A car is travelling on a level road. The driver has to stop quickly. Which of these (**A**, **B**, **C** or **D**) has the greatest effect on the stopping distance?
A the kinetic energy of the car
B the potential energy of the car
C the straightness of the road
D how far the driver can see   [L. EXAM.]

4 A skier is sliding down a slope at a steady speed. Which of the following is true?

A there are no forces on the skier
B the forces on the skier are balanced
C there is an unbalanced force downwards
D there is an unbalanced force along the slope [L. EXAM.]

5 Which of these (**A**, **B**, **C** or **D**) depends on the atmosphere exerting pressure?
A a ball falling to the ground
B drinking through a straw
C the spray from a can of cola
D bath water emptying down a plug hole   [L. EXAM.]

6 A constant force acts on an object. If there is no friction, which of these velocity (*v*) – time (*t*) graphs (**A**, **B**, **C** or **D**) shows the motion of the object? [L. EXAM.]

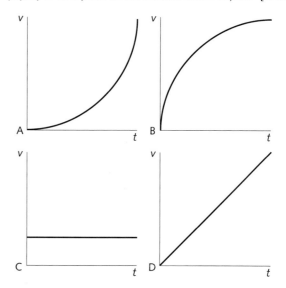

7 The four objects **A**, **B**, **C** and **D** all have the same weight. Which one produces the greatest pressure on the bench?

[L. EXAM.]

8 Here is a diagram of a wave.

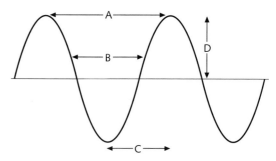

Which letter (**A**, **B**, **C** or **D**) shows the amplitude? [L. EXAM.]

9 The ray diagrams show a ray of light passing through a block of glass. The block is in air.

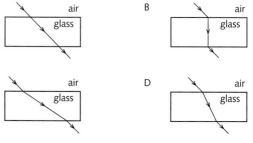

Which of these (**A**, **B**, **C** or **D**) is correct?   [L. EXAM.]

10 One of these diagrams (**A**, **B**, **C** or **D**) shows what happens when a vertical ray of light is reflected by a mirror. Which one is it? [L. EXAM.]

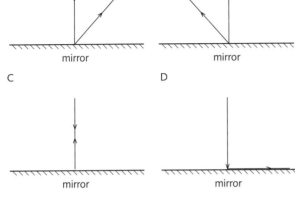

11 A coil of wire is rotated in a permanent magnetic field. Which of these (**A**, **B**, **C** or **D**) will happen?
  A the coil starts to rotate on its own
  B the magnetic field reduces to zero
  C an electric current is produced
  D the magnet starts to rotate [L. EXAM.]

12 Which of these statements (**A**, **B**, **C** or **D**) about ultraviolet light (UV) is **not** true?
  A it makes some materials fluoresce
  B it can cause tanning of the skin
  C it is emitted by the Sun
  D it travels faster than visible light [L. EXAM.]

13 The circuits shown below are made from the same batteries and lamps.

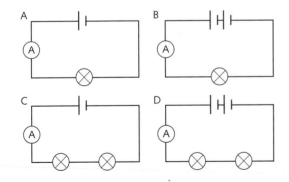

In which circuit (**A**, **B**, **C** or **D**) is the current the greatest? [L. EXAM.]

14 Jean is using an electric grass cutter which should have a 10 A (amperes) fuse fitted in its plug. It has been wrongly fitted with a 3 A fuse. The grass cutter will
  A operate normally
  B blow the fuse
  C cut more slowly
  D cut more quickly [L. EXAM.]

15 Which of these (**A**, **B**, **C** or **D**) shows two lamps in parallel with the cell (battery)? [L. EXAM.]

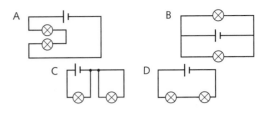

16 Which of these (**A**, **B**, **C** or **D**) shows a correctly wired ammeter and voltmeter? [L. EXAM.]

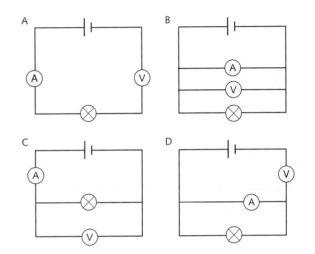

17 We measure the electricity used at home in kilowatt hours and not joules because:
  A kilowatt hours measure power
  B kilowatt hours are larger units
  C joules measure power
  D joules are larger units [L. EXAM.]

18 Giles has a 2 kW electric fire. The meter shows that there is only 3 kWh of electricity left. How long can Giles have his fire on? Is it
  A 40 minutes
  B 1 hour
  C 1 hour 30 minutes
  D 6 hours [L. EXAM.]

19 Iodine-131 has a half-life of 8 days. If a sample of iodine-131 has an activity of 600 Bq, what would you expect its activity to be 24 days later?
  A 300 Bq   **B** 200 Bq
  C 75 Bq   **D** zero

20 During a lunar eclipse, which of the following occurs?
  A The Moon is in the Earth's shadow.
  B The Moon comes between the Sun and the Earth.
  C The Moon is hidden behind the Sun.
  D The Earth is in the Moon's shadow.

SI units and prefixes

quantity	unit	symbol
mass	kilogram	kg
length	metre	m
time	second	s
area	square metre	m^2
volume	cubic metre	m^3
force	newton	N
weight	newton	N
pressure	pascal	Pa
energy	joule	J
work	joule	J
power	watt	W
frequency	hertz	Hz
PD, EMF (voltage)	volt	V
current	ampere	A
resistance	ohm	Ω
charge	coulomb	C
capacitance	farad	F
temperature	kelvin	K
	degree Celsius	°C

prefix	meaning	
G (giga)	1 000 000 000	(10^9)
M (mega)	1 000 000	(10^6)
k (kilo)	1000	(10^3)
d (deci)	$\frac{1}{10}$	(10^{-1})
c (centi)	$\frac{1}{100}$	(10^{-2})
m (milli)	$\frac{1}{1000}$	(10^{-3})
µ (micro)	$\frac{1}{1\,000\,000}$	(10^{-6})
n (nano)	$\frac{1}{1\,000\,000\,000}$	(10^{-9})
p (pico)	$\frac{1}{1\,000\,000\,000\,000}$	(10^{-12})

Examples

1 µF (microfarad) = 10^{-6} F

1 ms (millisecond) = 10^{-3} s

1 km (kilometre)   = 10^3 m

1 MW (megawatt) = 10^6 W

Note: 'micro' means 'millionth'; 'milli' means 'thousandth'.

Elements

For simplicity, many of the rarer elements have been omitted from the table below.

atomic number (proton number)	element	chemical symbol
1	hydrogen	H
2	helium	He
3	lithium	Li
4	beryllium	Be
5	boron	B
6	carbon	C
7	nitrogen	N
8	oxygen	O
9	fluorine	F
10	neon	N
11	sodium	Na
12	magnesium	Mg
13	aluminium	Al
14	silicon	Si
15	phosphorus	P
16	sulphur	S
17	chlorine	Cl
18	argon	Ar
19	potassium	K
20	calcium	Ca
22	titanium	Ti
25	manganese	Mn
26	iron	Fe
27	cobalt	Co
28	nickel	Ni
29	copper	Cu
30	zinc	Zn
35	bromine	Br
38	strontium	Sr
47	silver	Ag
48	cadmium	Cd
50	tin	Sn
53	iodine	I
55	caesium	Cs
74	tungsten	W
78	platinum	Pt
79	gold	Au
80	mercury	Hg
82	lead	Pb
86	radon	Rn
88	radium	Ra
90	thorium	Th
92	uranium	U
94	plutonium	Pu

Answers

1.01 (page 9)
1 1000 g **2** 1000 mm **3** $1 \times 10^6 \mu s$ **4** 6 m² **5** 2 km, 0.2 km, 20 km **6** 5 s, 50 s **7** 1.5×10^3 m, 1.5×10^6 m, 1.5×10^{-1} m, 1.5×10^{-2} m

1.02 (page 11)
5 a) 1.564 m **b)** 1.750 kg **c)** 26 000 kg (2.6×10^4 t) **d)** 6.2×10^{-5} s (0.000 062 s) **e)** 36.5 kg **f)** 6.16×10^{-10} m **6 a)** 5×10^{-3} kg **b)** 5000 mg

1.03 (page 13)
1 10^6 cm³ **2** 10^3 cm³ **3** 10^6 ml **4 a)** 2001 **b)** 2×10^5 cm³ **c)** 2×10^5 ml **5 a)** 2.7 g/cm³ **b)** 54 g **c)** 10 cm³ **6** Steel (stainless) **7** 39 kg **8** 4 m³ **9** 22.8×10^3 kg

1.04 (page 15)
1 Crowns: A silver, B gold, C mixture **2 a)** 70 g, 100 cm³, 0.7 g/cm³ **b)** 120 g, 48 cm³, 2.5 g/cm³

Examination questions (page 16)
1 a) 2500 m **b)** 2 m **c)** 3000 kg **d)** 2 litres **2** B and D **3** A only is true **4** D **5** B **6** 1.25 kg/m³

2.01 (page 19)
1 20 m/s **3 a)** 64 m **b)** 20 s **4** Runner 6.67 m/s, Grand Prix car 100 m/s, jet car 286 m/s, Concorde 667 m/s, Space Shuttle 10 000 m/s **6** 2.5 m/s² **7** 4 m/s² **8 a)** 12 m/s **b)** 44 m/s **9** 17 m/s

2.02 (page 21)
1 b) A and B **c)** B and C **d)** 4 m/s **e)** 60 m **f)** 3 m/s **2 a)** 30 m/s **b)** 3 m/s² **c)** 6 m/s² **d)** 150 m **e)** 525 m **f)** 25 s **g)** 21 m/s

2.03 (page 23)
1 a) 42 m/s **b)** 208 m **2 a)** 1.2 m/s **b)** 140 m **3 a)** 20 s **b)** 400 m **4 a)** 720 m **b)** 24 s

2.04 (page 25)
2 a) 0.1 s **b)** 200 mm/s **c)** 800 mm/s **d)** 600 mm/s² **3 a)** 10 mm **b)** 100 mm/s **c)** 50 mm **d)** 500 mm/s **e)** 400 mm/s **f)** 1000 mm/s²

2.05 (page 27)
1 a) 10 m/s **b)** 20 m/s **c)** 50 m/s **2 a)** 30 m/s **b)** 40 m/s **c)** 70 m/s **3 a)** 10 m/s **b)** 0 m/s **c)** 30 m/s **4 a)** Downwards **b)** B **c)** B **d)** 10 m/s² **e)** 10 m/s² **f)** 10 m/s² **g)** C

2.06 (page 29)
1 a) 3 s **b)** 30 m/s **2 a)** 4 s **b)** 80 m **3 a)** 3 s **b)** 3 s **c)** 90 m

2.07 (page 31)
3 c) Equal **d)** Less

2.08 (page 33)
1 b) 10 N, 20 N **2 a)** 1000 N **b)** 1.25 m/s² **c)** Acceleration = 0

2.09 (page 35)
1 a) 50 N, 100 N **b)** 10 m/s² (both) **c)** 10 N/kg **2 a)** 1000 N **b)** 100 kg **c)** 100 kg **d)** 37 N **e)** 3.7 m/s²

2.10 (page 37)
1 a) 500 N **b)** 500 N

2.11 (page 39)
2 a) 17 N **b)** 7 N **c)** 13 N at 23° to 12 N force **3 a)** Horizontal component 87 N, vertical component 50 N **b)** 350 N **c)** Force reduced (to 250 N)

2.12 (page 41)
3 a) 48 kg m/s **b)** 72 kg m/s **c)** 24 kg m/s **d)** 8 kg m/s² **e)** 8 N **f)** 2 m/s **g)** 0.67 m/s² (i) 8 N **4 a)** 7500 N **b)** 7500 N

2.13 (page 43)
1 a) 0 kg m/s **b)** 0 kg m/s **c)** 12 kg m/s to the left **d)** 12 kg m/s to the right **e)** 4 m/s to the right **2 a)** 80 kg m/s to the right **b)** 20 kg m/s to the left **c)** 60 kg m/s to the right **d)** 60 kg m/s to the right **e)** 3 m/s to the right

2.14 (page 45)
3 Centripetal force **a)** less **b)** less **c)** more **4 b)** Speed unchanged **c)** Speed less **d)** Centripetal force less

Examination questions (pages 46-47)
1 b) 100 m **2 a)** (i) 8 m (ii) 2.0 s **b)** 4.0 m/s **3 a)** (iii) 2.0 kg **4 a)** 25 s **b)** 1080 N **5 a)** 2000 N **b)** (i) 1200 N (iii) 1.5 m/s² **6 a)** (i) 4 m/s (ii) 4 m/s **b)** (i) 0 (ii) 5 m/s **7 a)** (i) same (ii) 0 **b)** 0.8 m/s **8 b)** (i) 60 000 kg m/s (ii) 60 000 kg m/s (iii) 3 m/s **9 b)** (i) $V_1 = V_2$ (ii) $V_1 = V_2/2$

3.01 (page 51)
3 a) 16 Nm **b)** 12 Nm **c)** No; clockwise **d)** 1 N **e)** Downwards **4 a)** 21 N **b)** 10 N, 8 N, and 3 N forces; 84 Nm **c)** 21 N force; 84 Nm **d)** Yes

3.02 (page 53)
2 b) 1 N

3.03 (page 55)
4 a) 40 mm **f)** 3.89 N **c)** 2.78 N

3.04 (page 57)
1 a) 50 Pa **b)** 100 Pa **2 a)** 200 N **b)** 400 N **4 a)** 300 N **b)** 7500 Pa **c)** 500 Pa

3.05 (page 59)
1 a) Less **b)** Same **c)** Same **d)** Less **2 a)** 24 m³ **b)** 19 200 kg **c)** 192 000 N **d)** 16 000 Pa **3** 20 000 Pa

3.06 (page 61)
1 a) 200 Pa **b)** 200 Pa **c)** 100 N **2 a)** Increased output force **b)** Increased output force

3.07 (page 63)
4 a) 100 mm of mercury **b)** 860 mm of mercury **c)** 113 000 Pa **5 a)** 96 000 Pa **b)** 0.96 atm **c)** 960 mb **6 a)** 9810 Pa **b)** 10.3 m

3.08 (page 65)
1 a) 1000 N **b)** 1000 N **2 a)** Polythene, pine **b)** Pine **4** 3000 N **5 a)** 5400 N **b)** 2000 N **c)** 2000 N **d)** 3400 N

3.09 (page 67)
1 a) Increases **b)** Increases **3 a)** Increases **b)** Decreases **c)** Less

Examination questions (pages 68-69)
2 a) 0.4 N m **b)** 1.6 N **3 a)** 2.0 N **b)** 0.32 N **c)** (i) 0.34 N
4 b) (i) 30 N m (ii) 0.38 m **5 b)** (i) 10.0 cm (ii) 14.0 cm
(iii) 2.5 N **6 a)** 100 000 Pa **7 c)** 200 N **8 a)** the same as; more
than; less than **c)** 2.5 N/cm² **9 a)** (i) 0.5 m² (ii) 2.0 m²
b) 50 000 N/m² **10 a)** 1 200 000 N **b)** (i) 1 000 000 N

4.01 (page 73)
1 60 J **2** 0.5 m **3 a)** 10 000 J **b)** 35 000 000 J **c)** 500 000 J
d) 200 J **4** 18

4.02 (page 75)
1 a) 50 J **b)** 50 J

4.03 (page 77)
1 a) 240 J **b)** 360 J **2 a)** 75 J **b)** 300 J **3** 20 m/s **4 a)** 25 J
b) 25 J **c)** 5 m **d)** 5 m

4.04 (page 79)
3 a) 18 m **b)** 87 m **c)** 105 m **4 a)** 50 000 J **b)** 200 000 J

4.05 (page 81)
1 a) 30% **2** 500 W **3 a)** 3000 W **b)** 3000 W **c)** 60 000 J
d) 75% **4 a)** 6000 J **b)** 300 J **c)** 300 W **5 a)** 6000 N
b) 4000 W **6** 50 000 W

4.06 (page 83)
3 c) X: 2000 MW, Y: 500 MW **e)** X: 36%, Y: 27%

4.07 (page 85)
2 b) B **c)** E **d)** A **e)** A

4.10 (page 91)
2 a) 50 J **b)** 50 J **c)** 50 N **3 a)** 2000 J **b)** 4000 J **c)** 40 N

4.11 (page 93)
1 a) 900 J **b)** 900 J **c)** 100 N **2 a)** 2 m **b)** 100 N

Examination questions (pages 94-95)
2 a) (i) PE (ii) PE + KE (iii) PE + KE **3 b)** 0.75 J
5 a) 225 000 J **b)** 225 000 J **c)** 1.25 m **d)** 3 m/s **6 a)** kettle
2 kW; food mixer 600 W **b)** television **c)** food mixer
9 a) wood – yes, no; uranium – no, no

5.02 (page 101)
1 a) 100 °C **b)** 373 K **c)** -273 °C **d)** 0 K **e)** 0 °C **f)** 273 K

5.07 (page 111)
2 a) 12 m³ **b)** 15 m³

5.08 (page 113)
3 6 atm

5.09 (page 115)
2 b) Right

5.10 (page 117)
2 a) 400 J **b)** 200 000 J **c)** 2 100 000 J **3 a)** 8400 J **b)** 42 000 J
c) 5 °C

5.11 (page 119)
1 b) 68 °C **3 a)** 3 300 000 J **b)** 23 000 000 J **4** 0.12 kg

Examination questions (pages 120-121)
2 e) 3.5×10^4 J/s (W) **3 b)** (i) 2 mm (ii) 200 mm
4 a) (i) liquid (ii) liquid **b)** (i) 440 °C **5 a)** unchanged
b) decreased **c)** increased **d)** increased **9 b)** 12.6 MJ
(12 600 000 J) **10 a)** 80 °C

6.01 (page 125)
1 b) 2 m **c)** 0.5 m **d)** 2 Hz **e)** 4 m/s **f)** 4 m **g)** 1 Hz

6.04 (page 131)
1 b) 1320 m **4 a)** 440 m **b)** 1.33 s **c)** 82.5 m

6.05 (page 133)
1 a) C **b)** A and D **c)** B **4 a)** 20 kHz **b)** 16.5 m **c)** 0.016 5 m

6.06 (page 135)
4 a) 40 000 Hz **b)** 21 m **c)** 0.035 m

6.07 (page 137)
3 a) B **b)** 2900 km

6.08 (page 139)
1 a) 3 **c)** Less

6.09 (page 141)
1 b) 1.2 m **c)** 275 Hz **d)** 137.5 Hz **e)** 550 Hz

6.10 (page 143)
3 a) 0.18 s **b)** 21

Examination questions (pages 144-145)
1 c) (i) 2 Hz (ii) 0.25 m **2 a)** 15 s **b)** (ii) 264 m **3 b)** (ii) 3.3 m
4 a) (i) A (ii) B **5 a)** (ii) 3 (iii) 0.05 s (iv) 20 Hz **6 c)** 680 Hz
7 a) (i) 0.48 m/s (ii) 5000 m/s **8 a)** (i) P (ii) S **b)** (i) AB

7.01 (page 149)
3 a) 1.28 s **b)** 500 s

7.02 (page 151)
2 7.5 m

7.03 (page 153)
3 226 000 km/s

7.06 (page 159)
1 a) 12 cm from lens, height 2 cm, real and inverted **b)** 15 cm
from lens, height 3 cm, real and inverted **c)** 1.5

7.07 (page 161)
2 Away from film **3 a)** Larger **b)** Closer to film **6 a)** Smaller
b) Towards screen

7.09 (page 165)
1 Red, green, blue **2** White **3** Yellow **4** Red, green, blue **5** All
6 a) Blue **b)** Red, green **7 a)** Green **b)** Red, blue **8** Black

7.10 (page 166)
4 a) 100 000 000 Hz **b)** 3 m **c)** 1500 m

7.13 (page 173)
1 a) 17.8° **b)** 36.9° **2 a)** 30° **b)** greater **3 a)** 124 000 km/s
b) 24.4°

Examination questions (pages 174-175)
4 c) 1.5 **6 c)** 3 **9 a)** green **b)** (i) cyan (ii) magenta (iii) white
10 a) (i) X-rays (ii) infrared **b)** (ii) 3×10^{11} Hz
(iii) microwaves **11 a)** 35° **b)** 42° **12 a)** (i) greater than
(ii) the same as (iii) greater than

8.02 (page 181)
2 1 000 000

8.03 (page 183)
1 a) 0.5 A **b)** 2.5 A **2 a)** 2000 mA **b)** 100 mA **3 c)** 0.5 A
d) A and B **4 a)** 50 C **b)** 10 C

8.04 (page 185)
1 a) volt **b)** volt **c)** coulomb **d)** ampere **e)** joule **2 c)** 8 V
d) 12 J **e)** 4 J **f)** 2 C **g)** 8 J

8.05 (page 187)
1 a) 23 Ω

8.06 (page 189)
1 B **2 a)** 2 Ω **b)** 4 Ω **3** reverse **4 a)** 16 V **b)** 32 V **c)** 0.75 A

8.07 (page 191)
4 a) X: 2 A, Y: 2 A **b)** 6 V

8.08 (page 193)
1 a) 1.5 A **b)** 6 V (both) **2 a)** 3 A **b)** 3 A (both) **c)** 6 A **d)** 2 Ω
3 D (9.9 Ω)

8.10 (page 197)
1 a) 2000 W **b)** 2 kW **2** 920 W **3** 3 A **4 a)** R_1: 4 A, R_2: 2 A
b) R_1: 48 W, R_2: 24 W **c)** 72 W **d)** 288 W

8.11 (page 199)
5 Hairdryer: 13 A, drill: 3 A, iron: 13 A, tablelamp: 3 A

8.13 (page 203)
1 a) 60 J **b)** 3600 J **2 a)** 36 W **b)** 21 600 J **3 a)** 8 kWh
b) 28 800 000 J **4 a)** £4.50 **b)** £0.36 **c)** £0.03 **5** Approx £39

Examination questions (pages 208-209)
4 a) 1 A **b)** 3 A **5 a)** 4.5 J **b)** 4.5 W **6 a)** 6 Ω **b)** 0.2 A
c) 0.2 A **d)** 0.8 V **e)** 0.16 W **7 b)** (i) 2.4 kW (ii) 7.2 Units
(iii) 57.6p **8 a)** 21 A **b)** (i) 2.1 kW **d)** 960 Ω **e)** (i) 50 Hz
9 a) (i) television (ii) kettle **b)** (i) 2 kW (ii) 32p **10 a)** 800 W
b) (ii) 3.5 A (iii) 5 A **c)** 0.95 (95%) **d)** 0.8p

9.01 (page 213)
5 Bars 1 and 3 are permanent magnets, bar 2 is not

9.02 (page 215)
1 b) N pole at right-hand end of magnet **c)** X

9.05 (page 221)
1 b) Upwards

9.06 (page 223)
2 c) Anticlockwise

9.09 (page 229)
3 a) 3 V **b)** 3

9.10 (page 231)
3 a) 10 V **b)** 23 W **c)** 23 W **d)** 2.3 A

9.11 (page 233)
5 2640 MW **6** 0.02 W **7 a)** 2 kW **b)** 0.002 W

9.12 (page 235)
1 Unchanged **2 a)** S-pole **b)** AB

Examination questions (pages 236-237)
2 a) a magnetic material **b)** a magnet **c)** a magnetic material
d) a non-magnetic material **4 a)** F is to the right **6 c)** 32 000
7 c) 115 V **8 a)** 90 C **9 b)** (i) 2 (ii) 4

10.02 (page 243)
2 a) Y **b)** X **c)** Y

10.03 (page 245)
1 c) ON **d)** Bulb OFF **2 a)** 5 mA **b)** 99

10.05 (page 249)
1 AND gate **2** OR gate **3 b)** Both LOW (0)

10.06 (page 251)
1 b) HIGH (1) **2 b)** (i) NOT gate (ii) AND gate

10.08 (page 255)
3 Long wave 0.2 MHz, medium wave 1 MHz, VHF 100 MHz,
UHF 500 MHz, microwave 10 000 MHz

10.09 (page 257)
2 a) 8.0×10^{-17} J **b)** 0.1 C **c)** 6.3×10^{17}

10.10 (page 259)
3 a) 1.5 cm **c)** 15 V **d)** 20 ms **e)** 50 Hz

Examination questions (pages 260-261)
1 b) (i) 0.95 mA (iii) 2400 Ω **3 b)** (i) X = OR, Y = AND
(ii) D **4 a)** (i) A = AND (ii) B = NOT (iii) C = AND

11.01 (page 265)
2 a) 13 **b)** 13 **c)** 14 **4 a)** $^{12}_{6}$C **b)** $^{16}_{8}$O **c)** $^{226}_{88}$Ra **5** X is carbon,
Y is carbon, Z is nitrogen

11.03 (page 269)
4 a) 2 counts per second **b)** 26 counts per second **c)** Gamma

11.04 (page 271)
1 a) Alpha **b)** $A = 228$, $Z = 88$ **c)** Radium **2 a)** 0 **b)** -1
c) Beta particle (electron)

11.05 (page 273)
1 Strontium-90 **2 a)** 400 Bq **b)** 200 Bq **c)** 50 Bq
3 b) 1.5 hours

11.06 (page 275)
a) 391.924×10^{-27} kg **b)** 391.614×10^{-27} kg **c)** 2.8×10^{-11} J

Examination questions (pages 282-283)
2 a) 17 electrons, 17 protons, 18 neutrons **3 a)** (i) 33 (ii) 52
4 b) (ii) 16, 32 **5 b)** (i) 12 hours (ii) $1/16 \times$ original value
6 c) (ii) 8 days **7 b)** (i) 48 counts/minute (ii) 40 hours approx
d) (i) beta (ii) I 22 II 13 **8 c)** (i) 86 (ii) 86 (iii) 136
10 a) 146

12.01 (page 287)
1 a) 1 day **b)** 27 days **c)** 365 days **d)** 27 days

12.04 (page 293)
1 a) B **b)** D **c)** B **d)** D **2 b)** 24 hours

12.05 (page 295)
3 b) 4×10^{13} km **c)** About 100 000 years

12.07 (page 299)
1 a) 5 million **b)** 5 **c)** 15 billion **d)** 15 billion
5 10 000 million (10^{10}) years

Examination questions (pages 302-303)
1 a) (i) A, B (ii) A **b)** 24 hours **2 a)** (ii) 2 – autumn,
3 – winter (iii) summer **3 a)** (i) Earth (ii) Earth; Sun
(iii) Moon; Earth (iv) Moon; Earth (v) Moon; Earth
5 a) (i) D (ii) B **10 b)** 4×10^9 light years

14.03 (page 319)
1 47 °C **2** 36 counts/second **3** 5.4 N **4** 86 kPa **5** 0.79 mV

Multichoice questions (pages 328-329)
1 C **2** D **3** A **4** B **5** B **6** D **7** D **8** D **9** D **10** C **11** C
12 D **13** B **14** B **15** B **16** C **17** B **18** C **19** C **20** A

Index

If a page number is given in **bold**, you should look this up first.